Globalization and Global Citizenship

Globalization and Global Citizenship examines the meaning and realities of global citizenship as a manifestation of recent trends in globalization. In an interdisciplinary approach, the chapters outline and analyse the most significant dimensions of global citizenship, including transnational, historical, and cultural variations in its practice; foreign and domestic policy influences; and its impact on personal identities. The contributions ask and explore questions that are of immediate relevance for today's scholars, including:

- How has globalization diminished, expanded, or complicated notions of citizenship?
- What rights could exist outside the context of state sovereignty?
- How can social accountability be imagined beyond the borders of towns, cities, or states?
- What forms of political representational legitimacy could be productive on the global level?
- When is it useful, possible, or desirable for individuals to identify with global political communities?

Drawing together a broad range of contributors and cutting-edge research, the volume offers chapters that seek to reflect the full spectrum of approaches and topics, providing a valuable resource which highlights the value of an extended and thoughtful study of the idea and practice of global citizenship within a broader consideration of the processes of globalization. It will be of great use to graduates and scholars of international relations, sociology, and global studies/affairs, as well as globalization.

Irene Langran is Associate Professor and Chair, Political Science, at Albright College, USA.

Tammy Birk is Assistant Professor and Director of Women's, Gender, and Sexuality Studies at Otterbein University, USA.

Rethinking Globalizations
Edited by Barry K. Gills, University of Helsinki, Finland and Kevin Gray University of Sussex, UK.

This series is designed to break new ground in the literature on globalization and its academic and popular understanding. Rather than perpetuating or simply reacting to the economic understanding of globalization, this series seeks to capture the term and broaden its meaning to encompass a wide range of issues and disciplines and convey a sense of alternative possibilities for the future.

For a full list of titles in this series, please visit www.routledge.com.

Global Capitalism and Transnational Class Formation
Edited by Jason Struna

Rethinking Border Control for a Globalizing World
A preferred future
Edited by Leanne Weber

Global Governance, Legitimacy and Legitimation
Edited by Magdalena Bexell

Critical Rationalism and Globalisation
Towards the sociology of the Open Global Society
Masoud Mohammadi Alamuti

Globalisation Development and Social Justice
A propositional political approach
Edited by Ann El-Khoury

Globalization
The career of a concept
Edited by Manfred Steger and Paul James

Globalization and Capitalist Geopolitics
Sovereignty and state power in a multipolar world
Daniel Woodley

Dialectics in World Politics
Edited by Shannon Brincat

The Redesign of the Global Financial Architecture
The return of state authority
Stuart P. M. Mackintosh

Markets and Development
Civil society, citizens and the politics of neoliberalism
Edited by Toby Carroll and Darryl S. L. Jarvis

Occupying Subjectivity
Being and becoming radical in the 21st century
Edited by Chris Rossdale

Globalization and Global Citizenship
Interdisciplinary approaches
Edited by Irene Langran and Tammy Birk

Globalization and Global Citizenship

Interdisciplinary approaches

Edited by
Irene Langran and Tammy Birk

LONDON AND NEW YORK

First published 2016
by Routledge
2 Park Square, Milton Park, Abingdon, Oxon OX14 4RN

and by Routledge
711 Third Avenue, New York, NY 10017

Routledge is an imprint of the Taylor & Francis Group, an informa business

© 2016 selection and editorial material, Irene Langran and Tammy Birk; individual chapters, the contributors

The right of Irene Langran and Tammy Birk to be identified as authors of the editorial material, and of the individual authors as authors of their contributions, has been asserted by them in accordance with sections 77 and 78 of the Copyright, Designs and Patents Act 1988.

All rights reserved. No part of this book may be reprinted or reproduced or utilised in any form or by any electronic, mechanical, or other means, now known or hereafter invented, including photocopying and recording, or in any information storage or retrieval system, without permission in writing from the publishers.

Trademark notice: Product or corporate names may be trademarks or registered trademarks, and are used only for identification and explanation without intent to infringe.

British Library Cataloguing in Publication Data
A catalogue record for this book is available from the British Library

Library of Congress Cataloging in Publication Data
Names: Langran, Irene Victoria, editor. | Birk, Tammy, editor.
Title: Globalization and global citizenship : interdisciplinary approaches / edited by Irene Langran and Tammy Birk.
Description: Abingdon, Oxon ; New York, NY : Routledge is an imprint of the Taylor & Francis Group, an Informa Business, [2016] | Series: Rethinking globalizations | Includes bibliographical references and index.
Identifiers: LCCN 2016002229| ISBN 9781315673752 (ebook) | ISBN 9781138941335 (hbk)
Subjects: LCSH: World citizenship. | Globalization–Political aspects. | Globalization–Social aspects.
Classification: LCC JZ1320.4 .G594 2016 | DDC 323.6–dc23
LC record available at http://lccn.loc.gov/2016002229

ISBN: 978-1-138-94133-5 (hbk)
ISBN: 978-1-31567-375-2 (ebk)

Typeset in Times New Roman
by Taylor & Francis Books

 Printed and bound by CPI Group (UK) Ltd, Croydon, CR0 4YY

This book is dedicated to our children
Adam and Delia Langran-Smith
Eva Birk-Petri
who are loved beyond measure.

Contents

List of illustrations x
List of contributors xi
Acknowledgement xvi

Introduction 1
IRENE LANGRAN

PART I
Conceptual and historical contexts 9

Introduction to Part I 11
TAMMY BIRK

1 Historical origins of global citizenship 13
  APRIL CARTER

2 Global citizenship in a post-Westphalian age 25
  IRENE LANGRAN

3 Critical cosmopolitanism as a new paradigm for global learning 38
  TAMMY BIRK

4 Technology's role in global citizenship education 56
  ELIZABETH LANGRAN AND IRENE LANGRAN

5 The global, citizenship, and education as discursive fields: towards disrupting the reproduction of colonial systems of power 69
  KAREN PASHBY

6 Cosmopolitan appropriation or learning? Relation and action in global citizenship education 87
  DAVID JEFFERESS

PART II
Shifting boundaries, the modern state, and new cosmopolitanism 99

Introduction to Part II: shifting boundaries, the modern state, and new cosmopolitanism 101
IRENE LANGRAN

7 International law, citizenship, and changing conceptions of justice 103
DAVID ARMSTRONG

8 Global citizenship as public pedagogy: emotional tourism, feel-good humanitarianism, and the personalization of development 115
AUDREY BRYAN

9 The geopolitics of global citizenship 129
LOWELL GUSTAFSON

10 How "global" can we be? Insights from the environmental field 143
BARTON A. THOMPSON

11 Dismounting the tiger: from empire to global citizenship through pragmatism 156
TERRANCE MACMULLAN

PART III
Identity, belonging, and global citizenship on location 173

Introduction to Part III: identity, belonging, and global citizenship on location 175
TAMMY BIRK

12 Where are the global citizens? 177
PETER A. FURIA

13 Age and global citizenship attitudes 193
BRITTANY H. BRAMLETT

14 Global citizenship in the Middle East: presence and prospects 209
VAUGHN P. SHANNON

15 China and the world: convergence on global governance, divergence on global citizenship? 222
JOHAN LAGERKVIST

16 An assessment of Southeast Asian regional identity 232
SHAUN NARINE

17 The rhetoric of globalization and global citizenship: reconstructing active citizenships in post-cold war sub-Saharan Africa 243
ALI A. ABDI

Index 256

List of illustrations

Figures

4.1	Development stages in global citizenship education	61
13.1	Percentage of civic identity responses by age categories	202

Tables

12.1	World citizenship and UN confidence by country – WVS sixth wave (2010–2014)	182
12.2	Demographic correlates of anti-cosmopolitanism and UN scepticism – WVS sixth wave	186
12.3a	Demographic correlates of anti-cosmopolitanism and UN scepticism – WVS sixth wave	187
12.3b	Additional correlates of UN scepticism – WVS sixth wave	188
13.1	Probit regression on civic identity	203
13.2	Probit regression on world civic identity across waves (years)	204
13.3	Probit regression on alternative indicators of global citizenship	205
14.1	Those who 'see myself as a world citizen' (%)	212
14.2	Responding to which geographic group they belong to first (%)	213
14.3	Responding to 'which is your most important identity'	214

List of contributors

Ali A. Abdi is Professor and Head, Department of Educational Studies, the University of British Columbia. Previously, he taught at the University of Alberta. His areas of research include citizenship and human rights education and anti-colonial philosophies and methodologies of education. His latest edited/co-edited volumes include: *Indigenous Discourses on Development in Africa* (2014); *Decolonizing Philosophies of Education* (2012); *Educating for Democratic Consciousness* (2013).

David Armstrong has held academic positions at Birmingham, Durham, Exeter, and Buckingham universities. He has also worked at various times for the Australian Parliament's research service and the BBC World Service. He is a Fellow of the Royal Historical Society and was Founder/Editor of *Diplomacy and Statecraft* and editor of the *Review of International Studies*. He has many publications, initially on aspects of East Asian international relations and in the last 20 years on international organization and international law. Recent publications include: "Cosmopolitan Justice and International Law", *Review of International Studies* (December 2011); *International Law and International Relations* (2nd edn, 2012, co-authored with Theo Farrell and Hélène Lambert); "The Politics of International Criminal Justice" (with Florencia Montal) in *Routledge Handbook of International Criminal Justice* (co-editors: B. Arrigo and H. Bersot, 2013); "The Crisis in Global Governance after the Iraqi War", in A. Acharya and H. Katsumata (eds), *Beyond Iraq: The Future of World Order* (2011).

Tammy Birk is the Director of the Women's, Gender, and Sexuality Studies programme and Assistant Professor of English at Otterbein University in Westerville, Ohio. Her scholarship has focused on critical cosmopolitan teaching and learning in higher education, and she has presented regular workshops at AAC&U (Association of American Colleges and Universities) meetings on this subject. Recent publications include: "Critical Cosmopolitan Teaching and Learning: A New Answer to the Global Imperative", *Diversity and Democracy* (Spring 2014). She is now working on a monograph, *Becoming Cosmopolitan: Critical Cosmopolitanism as a New Paradigm for Global Teaching and Learning*.

List of contributors

Brittany H. Bramlett holds a Ph.D. in political science from the University of Maryland. Her research focuses on the relationship between a person's local context and their political behaviours. Her recent work has examined the role that age and life experiences play in people's political attitudes and voting behaviour. She currently serves as an honours teaching fellow at the University of Georgia. Recent publications include: *Senior Power or Senior Peril: Aged Communities and American Society in the Twenty-First Century* (2014); "Aged Communities and Political Knowledge", *American Politics Research* (2014).

Audrey Bryan holds a Ph.D. in comparative-international education, with an academic specialization in sociology. She teaches sociology courses on the humanities and education programmes at Dublin City University (St Patrick's Campus). Her published work has focused on racism and anti-racism in education, gender and sexuality, development studies, and citizenship education. She is the co-author (with Melíosa Bracken, 2012) of *Learning to Read the World? Teaching and Learning about Global Citizenship and International Development in Post-Primary Schools.*

April Carter has lectured on politics and political theory at the universities of Lancaster, Oxford, and Queensland. More recently she was an honorary research fellow at the Centre for Peace and Reconciliation Studies, Coventry University and a senior editor on the International Editorial Board for the *Oxford International Encyclopedia of Peace, Conflict and Transformation* (2010). Publications since 2000 include: "Transnational Citizenship and Direct Action", in Wayne Hudson and Steven Slaughter (eds), *Globalization and Citizenship* (2007); "Migration and Cultural Diversity: Implications for National and Global Citizenship", in Sor-hoon Tan (ed.), *Challenging Citizenship: Group Membership and Cultural Identity in a Global Age* (2005); *The Political Theory of Global Citizenship* (2013).

Peter A. Furia directs the Global Studies–Security and Justice programme at the University of Virginia. Much of his research addresses public opinion and comparative foreign policy and utilizes survey data to test claims about group identity and inter-group enmity in international relations. His other interests include mass-elite relations in democracies, the patriotism–cosmopolitanism debate, and the history of international political thought. His articles have appeared in *Global Society, International Interactions, International Studies Quarterly* and *Polity* and he has also published over a dozen book chapters and shorter articles. He is co-editor (with Richard Sobel and Bethany Barratt) of *Public Opinion and International Intervention: Lessons from the Iraq War* (2012).

Lowell Gustafson is Professor of Political Science at Villanova University (since 1986). Publications include: *The Sovereignty Dispute over the Falkland (Malvinas) Islands* (1988); *The Religious Challenge to the State* (co-edited with Matthew Moen, 1992); *Economic Development under*

Democratic Regimes: Neoliberalism in Latin America (1994); *Thucydides' Theory of International Relations: A Lasting Possession* (2000); *Ancient Maya Gender Identity and Relations* (co-edited with Amelia M. Trevelyan, 2002); *Economic Performance under Democratic Regimes in Latin America in the Twenty-First Century* (co-edited with Satya Pattnayak, 2003); *National and Human Security Issues in Latin America: Democracies at Risk* (co-edited with Satya Pattnayak, 2006); "From Particles to Politics", in Grinin *et al.*, *Teaching and Researching Big History: Exploring a New Scholarly Field* (2014, pp. 72–99). He currently serves as Vice-President of the International Big History Association and Editor of its monthly, *Origins*.

David Jefferess lives in the traditional and unceded territory of the Syilx people. He is a non-Indigenous scholar who teaches in the areas of decolonization and global interrelationships at the University of British Columbia's Okanagan campus. His current research focuses on humanitarian discourses, and the particular way in which they imagine social relations of power. Publications include: "Introduction: 'The White Man's Burden' and Post-Racial Humanitarianism", *Critical Race and Whiteness Studies* (2015); "Humanitarian Relations: Emotion and the Limits of Critique", *Critical Literacy: Theories and Practice* (2013); "The 'Me to We' Social Enterprise: Global Education as Lifestyle Brand", in *Critical Literacy: Theories and Practice* (2012); "Unsettling Cosmopolitanism: Global Citizenship and the Cultural Politics of Benevolence", in Andreotti *et al.*, *Postcolonial Perspectives on Global Citizenship Education* (2012).

Johan Lagerkvist is Professor of Chinese Language and Culture at the Department of Asian, Middle Eastern and Turkish Studies, Stockholm University. His main research interests include Chinese state–society relations, global governance, China's political economy and evolving role in "South–South" co-operation. Publications include (monographs): *Tiananmen Redux: The Hard Truth about the Expanded Neoliberal World Order* (2015); *Before Democracy: Competing norms in Chinese Media and Society* (2010); *Sovereignty, Non-interference, and the Challenge of Chinese Authoritarian Capitalism in Africa* (2016); (articles) "The Unknown Terrain of Social Protests in China: 'Exit', 'Voice', 'Loyalty' and – 'Shadow'", *Journal of Civil Society* (2015); "The Ordoliberal Turn? Getting China and Global Economic Governance Right", *Global Affairs* 1(3) (2015); "Principal–Agent Dilemma in China's Social Media Sector? The Party-State and Industry Real-Name Registration Waltz", *International Journal of Communication* 6 (2012).

Elizabeth Langran is Associate Professor of Education at Marymount University in Arlington, VA. Dr Langran started her teaching career in 1992 as a secondary school French teacher. She educated US middle and high school students for six years and taught overseas for five years, including in Morocco as a Peace Corps volunteer. She earned her Ph.D. in Instructional Technology from the University of Virginia with a certificate in

International Leadership in Educational Technology, and then spent five years as assistant professor and director of the Educational Technology programme at Fairfield University. She has travelled for collaborative technology projects and school visits to Nicaragua, India, central Asia, Senegal, South Africa, Botswana, Uganda, Bermuda, and China. Dr Langran is active in the Society for Information Technology in Teacher Education, and co-chaired the Geospatial Technology Special Interest Group before being elected as associate chair to the SITE Teacher Education Council. She has had many conference presentations and publication on geospatial learning and global citizenship.

Irene Langran is Associate Professor, Chair of the Political Science Department, and Director of General Education at Albright College. Dr Langran's research interests include global health, health decentralization, global governance, and global citizenship. Publications include those in: *Journal of Asian and African Studies*; *Asian Studies*; *New Global Studies*; *Canadian Journal of Political Science*; *American Journal of Islamic Social Sciences*; *Journal for Peace and Justice Studies*. Dr Langran received her doctorate from the University of Toronto, specializing in the comparative politics of developing countries; she also received her undergraduate and master's degrees from Villanova University. The field research for her dissertation focused on health sector reform in the southern Philippine region of Mindanao. Before joining Albright's faculty, she worked with NGOs in multiple countries.

Terrance MacMullan is Professor of Philosophy and Honours at Eastern Washington University. His essays on pragmatism, the philosophy of race, and the relationship between public intellectuals and democracy have been published in: *Journal of Speculative Philosophy*; *Philosophy and Social Criticism*; *Transactions of the Charles S. Peirce Society*. His book *The Habits of Whiteness: A Pragmatist Reconstruction* was published in 2009. His work on pop culture and philosophy has been published in *Daily Show and Philosophy* and *Star Wars and History*. He was named Undergraduate Teacher of the Year in 2008, won the President's Award in 2012 and was elected by the faculty to serve as President of the Faculty Organization (2007–2008). He is currently researching a book on the affinities between pragmatism and Latin American philosophy.

Shaun Narine is Associate Professor of International Relations at St Thomas University in Fredericton, New Brunswick, Canada. Dr Narine was a Killam Postdoctoral Fellow at the University of British Columbia (2000–2002) and a Visiting Fellow at the East–West Center (2000). He is author of *Explaining ASEAN: Regionalism in Southeast Asia* (2002). His research focus is on institutions in Southeast Asia and the Asia Pacific. He has published numerous articles on this subject in journals such as: *Asian Survey*; *Pacific Affairs*; *Pacific Review*; *Global Governance*; *Cambridge Review of International Affairs*. He has also published numerous book chapters on Asian institutionalism and is interested in Canadian foreign policy. Dr Narine is currently working on a new book exploring the role of ASEAN in a changing Asia Pacific region.

Karen Pashby currently holds a postdoctoral fellowship at the Centre for Global Citizenship Education and Research at the University of Alberta. Previously, she held a postdoctoral research position at the University of Oulu, Finland where she worked on the project Ethical Internationalization in Higher Education in Times of Global Crises. She completed her Ph.D. at the University of Toronto in a combined philosophy of education and comparative international development education programme. She also taught and coordinated the Global Citizenship and Sustainable Development cohort of the teacher education programme there. Her research probed the assumed mutually beneficial relationship between multiculturalism and global citizenship education. She co-edited *Citizenship Education in the Era of Globalization: Canadian Perspectives* (2008). Her work has been published in such journals as: *Curriculum Inquiry*; *Globalisation, Societies and Education*; *Education Forum*. A former secondary school teacher in Canada and Brazil, her current work involves ongoing research into conceptualizations of global citizenship education in the post-2015 context as well as practical applications of a critical approach. She also facilitates workshops with educators around the world and is part of the coordinating team that facilitated the National (Canadian) and International Youth White Papers on Global Citizenship.

Vaughn P. Shannon is Associate Professor of Political Science at Wright State University. Dr Shannon received his Ph.D. from Ohio State University in 2001. His research interests include international security, Middle East politics, and the interplay of constructivism and political psychology. He is co-author of *Cases in International Relations* (2014); and editor and contributor to *Psychology and Constructivism in International Relations* (2011). His work has appeared in such journals as: *International Organization*; *Security Studies*; *International Studies Quarterly*; *European Journal of International Relations*; *Foreign Policy Analysis*.

Barton A. Thompson holds a Ph.D. in biological anthropology from the University of California, Santa Barbara and an MS in Environmental Engineering from Stanford University. Prior to serving as Associate Professor of Anthropology and Environmental Studies at Albright College, he worked as an environmental engineer for the Environmental Protection Agency. His research has focused on how humans relate to their surrounding environment with a special emphasis on associations to both land and animals. He has conducted research in northern Quebec among the Mistissini Crees, in the mid-Atlantic region of the US, and in the Peruvian Amazon among the Ribereños about which he published "Community Management, Self-interest and Environmental Preservation in the Amazon", *Interdisciplinary Environmental Review* (2011).

Acknowledgement

Both of us are deeply grateful for the dedication and hard work of our contributors as well as the support of the publishing team and reviewers at Routledge, especially Lydia de Cruz, Sabrina Lacey, Nicola Parkin, and Emily Ross. Vanessa de Oliveira Andreotti was an early champion of this collection, and we would like to thank her for her commitment to seeing this conversation through.

Irene Langran thanks her family and friends for their unwavering support of this and other projects: Steve Smith, Adam and Delia Langran-Smith, Bob and Eleanor Langran, Elizabeth Langran, Thomas Langran, and Pam McLean Parker.

Tammy Birk thanks her families of both birth and choice for providing steady and generous love throughout this process (and all else that life requires): Ken Petri, Eva Birk-Petri, Suzanne Ashworth, Barbara Birk, Fred Birk, and Barb Birk.

At Albright College, a sabbatical provided early support for this project. At Otterbein University, a Humanities Advisory Council grant helped to provide support and time for uninterrupted writing. Both of us appreciate the administrative support from our respective institutions: at Albright, Deborah Eckroth and a promising young scholar, Lucas Baun; and at Otterbein, Jenni Hunter.

Introduction

Irene Langran

Globalization and global citizenship represent subjects of continuing interest and controversy among academics, activists, and policymakers at all levels. Scholars from a wide variety of disciplines debate the very meaning of these concepts, academic institutions increasingly require related courses, non-governmental organizations debate their value, and politicians argue about their scope and role. At the heart of this debate are "connectivities" and "disconnectivities" in political, economic, social, and cultural realms that are a part of how we view globalization and its possibilities.

Globalization and *global citizenship* represent concepts that are connected intricately and complexly. In reflecting upon the challenges of developing a common meaning of the former term, Keri E. Iyall Smith (2013, 4) notes that "While some people say 'globalization' and mean 'global capitalism', others say 'globalization' and mean 'Americanization'". Whereas some decry the negative impact of globalization on the environment and communities, others consider it a source for wealth and progress. Global citizenship invites similar debates: some have faith in its ability to solve global problems and view it as the only viable solution to save the world from the war and environmental destruction that threaten our own survival. On the other hand, there are those who see global citizenship as imperialist, a threat to state interests, and a contradiction in terms – if citizenship is defined by states, how it is possible on a global level? This introduction explores definitions of the contested terms of globalization and global citizenship. It concludes with an overview of the book's organization and content.

Globalization: the good, the bad, and the ugly

To James N. Rosenau (1997), globalization is a *process* of "boundary-broadening" that enables "people, goods, information, norms, practices, and institutions to move about" in spite of state boundaries. It can be differentiated from globalism, which involves shared values and a commitment on the part of all people to work together to solve collective problems. Robert Keohane and Joseph Nye (2000) describe globalization as a "shrinking of distance". Keohane and Nye (ibid., 105) view globalization as an increase in "networks of interdependence at multicontinental distances".

Globalization is a process that has received increased attention in the post-cold war era, especially as developments in information technology have revolutionized the cross-border movement of ideas, peoples, and goods. While this technology has certainly increased the *pace* of globalization and the extent to which it is embedded in our lives, it is not "new": globalization has been a part of human history as long as goods (and increasingly services), peoples, and ideas traverse the globe. This movement across borders involves not merely state to state travel, but travel across multiple continents and the emergence of interdependence. With this multicontinental movement, ideas and marketing strategies adapt to local conditions – a trend that has been studied in topics as diverse as the introduction of Shakespeare's works around the world (Bosman 2010) to McDonald's movement into new markets (Watson 2000). Such "glocalization" complicates questions about the extent to which globalization is implicated as a homogenizing, often Westernizing force. Whereas some consider globalization to be a force that is inevitable and impossible to stop, others view it as a reversible process that slows when global economic woes lead to a resurgence of economic nationalism.

Globalization also has meanings that are context- and discipline-specific. For example, *political globalization* can be viewed as a process that connects states, non-state actors, and peoples through international laws, international organizations, and the quest to find shared solutions to common problems. Scholars, politicians, and activists recognize increasingly that twenty-first century challenges are often global in nature – and these global issues require cooperation that extends beyond the confines of states. Global governance is a term that is often used to describe an approach to global problems that incorporates the efforts of a range of state and non-state actors at multiple levels. The increased reliance on non-state actors as well as international laws raises questions about the power of states. Some scholars maintain that states are losing power and influence, while others find that states are still the main actors, establishing the rules by and the environment in which political and economic activities occur. To what extent does globalization contribute, positively or negatively, to problems that are global in nature? What is the impact on states – diminished power or business as usual?

Economic globalization is perhaps the most commonly referenced form of globalization. According to Dani Rodrik (2011, 76), economic globalization refers to "the international integration of markets for goods and capital". Views on economic globalization are also contested. On the one hand, economic globalization can be viewed as a positive force that "lifts all boats" and connects individuals, communities, and states through interdependence as manufacturing and other operations move with ease due to technological changes. It can contribute to a growing global economy in which specialization and retraining ultimately benefit all consumers, workers, and communities.

Economic globalization can also be seen as a negative influence that increases economic disparities and social vulnerabilities. When these operations move, they leave workers and communities behind. In their new settings, they may find less stringent environmental and labour protections. Does economic globalization create winners and losers? If so, who wins? Who loses? Are states losing power to transnational corporations, now able to move jobs and investments with the click of a mouse?

Cultural globalization can be a source of cultural fusion or discord, reflecting the tensions between a cosmopolitan outlook and one that is rooted in local or communitarian interests. Not all cultures view cosmopolitanism or global citizenship in the same manner or with the same enthusiasm, and some scholars contend that there is a strong tendency for this debate to reflect Western views to the exclusion of others. Robert J. Holton (2000) summarizes three ways in which globalization can inform and interact with culture. In the first instance, globalization results in less dominant cultures being subsumed by more dominant cultures – this process is associated frequently with Westernization or Americanization and is referred to as part of the *homogenization* thesis. In the second instance, globalization creates threats and tensions among cultures. Many associate this scenario with Samuel Huntington's "Clash of Civilizations" thesis (1993), which envisions a post-cold war world that is rife with conflict among cultures. Holton refers to this as the *polarization* thesis. In the final instance globalization is considered a force that brings diverse cultures together in a mélange that represents something new; this is referred to as the *hybridization* thesis.

There are many questions raised by the cultural aspects of globalization. For example, is globalization a force that creates new cultures, subsumes them, or places them in confrontation with each other? What social and global imaginaries ground different notions of global citizenship? How do the cultural trends that emanate from globalization influence understandings of citizenship?

Global citizenship and cosmopolitanism

The nature and meaning of "global citizenship" and "cosmopolitanism" have a range of interpretations, even though they are often used interchangeably. This practice tends to obfuscate the real differences between them. Cosmopolitanism is most commonly associated with an ethical stance in which there is an emphasis on a shared global community. As defined by David Held (2010, 25), "Cosmopolitanism is an ethical approach to political life which champions self-determination and freedom from domination and arbitrary power". Global citizenship includes this component but also stresses rights, obligations, and representational legitimacy – in other words, the emphasis is on a more formal or institutionalized context. Today, global citizenship "is the recognition that individuals in the 21st century have rights, duties, identity and the potential for representation on a global scale" (Langran, Langran, and Ozment 2009).

Supporters of global citizenship view it as an essential element of the effort to preserve the earth and even ensure human survival. Critics maintain that the "mirage of global citizenship" hides the persistence of self-interest that drives the disconnected policies of states and, to a lesser degree, other actors. Global citizenship is also challenged by other identities that are based on sub-state forms of belonging. How is the concept of citizenship imagined beyond state borders in this context?

Global citizenship is a popular movement among educational institutions and students in the Global North. At the same time, it is also embedded in structures of power and resource distribution. While it may portend to serve as a force for greater equality in the world, a critical evaluation of global citizenship raises questions about the extent to which it can be self-serving or perpetuate injustice. Several of the chapters in this book assess global citizenship critically.

Regardless of how one views globalization, it influences the way that we see ourselves as "citizens", how states respond to the challenges it presents, and how non-state actors develop new roles as a result. At the same time that globalization challenges the sovereignty and rigidity of state borders, emerging and complex networks of information, people, and goods demand that we teach and learn about the interrelationship of the global and the local in new ways. In response, will the citizens of twenty-first century see the need to imagine themselves as "global citizens" or will they identify primarily as citizens at other levels?

This book will examine the meaning and realities of global citizenship as a manifestation of recent trends in globalization. It will rely on an interdisciplinary approach and examine several of the most significant dimensions of global citizenship, including transnational, historical, and cultural variations in its practice; foreign and domestic policy influences; and its impact on personal identities. As it tracks this ground, the reader will ask and explore questions that are of immediate relevance for today's scholars. How does globalization in its current form present a new set of challenges for states, non-state actors, and individual citizens? How has globalization diminished, expanded, or complicated notions of citizenship? What rights could exist outside the context of state sovereignty? How can social accountability be imagined beyond the borders of towns, cities, or states? What forms of political representational legitimacy could be productive on the global level? When is it useful, possible or desirable for individuals to identify with global political communities?

Interdisciplinary approaches

This book has three main sections. In the first, we explore the foundations – historical, religious, ethical, theoretical, and educational – of cosmopolitanism and global citizenship. April Carter considers global citizenship's ethical, religious, and historical evolution. She pays particular attention to the impact of both Eastern and Western religious traditions as well as the development of a universal moral law that would later lay the groundwork for international codes and courts of law. Irene Langran probes the significance of global citizenship for states with a focus on rights and obligations, identity, and representational legitimacy. She notes that while global citizenship and a cosmopolitan approach hold great promise for addressing some of the most pressing problems facing our world today, they are constrained by self-interest and political realities. Tammy Birk provides a discussion of critical cosmopolitanism as it navigates between the local and global. Elizabeth Langran and Irene Langran consider the ways in which educators can utilize new advances in informational technology to promote goals associated with cosmopolitanism. Continuing the focus on education, Karen Pashby frames *critical global citizenship education* through post/de-colonial perspectives and discourse analysis. Completing this section, David Jefferess examines critically global citizenship education, humanitarianism, and the related use of the southern African idea of *ubuntu* and the statement, "Be the change you wish to see in the world", which is attributed to Mohandas K. Gandhi.

The second section features several chapters that address how leaders, policymakers, states, and intergovernmental organizations respond to the challenges of the twenty-first century, the increasing diminishment of national borders, and practical questions of citizenship in an era of globalization. David Armstrong considers cosmopolitan ideas of justice and the argument that the principles of justice should be applied not only in individual states but in the larger global community. It draws upon international relations theory and models of justice in exploring the complicated questions of international law and cosmopolitanism in today's world. Audrey Bryan follows with a critical interrogation of dominant discourses about international development and global citizenship. Integrating the social and natural sciences, Lowell Gustafson provides a new way of considering geopolitics and the need to rethink loyalty to the state versus loyalty to the world and all people. In the subsequent chapter, Barton A. Thompson argues that the underlying psychology that has hindered the environmental movement is also likely to negatively impact the development of global identities. This section closes with Terrance MacMullan's examination of US foreign policy, especially under President Barack Obama, and the extent to which it reflects pragmatist ideals that may enable it to "dismount the tiger of global empire".

Section three addresses the complex relationship between personal identity, social and geographical location, and the larger goal of global citizenship. Peter Furia draws upon survey data to consider who is a global citizen, challenging popular assumptions. Brittany Bramlett follows with a consideration of the relationship between age and self-identification as a global citizen. Bramlett's work has a particular focus on millennials. Vaughn Shannon considers the prospects for global citizenship in the complicated terrain of the Middle East.

Johan Lagerkvist also considers the question of global citizenship in a specific context – he considers whether global citizenship provides an apt description for China's increasing integration in international society. Shaun Narine examines global citizenship versus competing identities in the context of the Association of Southeast Asian Nations. Lastly, Ali Abdi analyses critically global citizenship as a post-cold war construct from the West that can dilute national citizenship constructions in sub-Saharan Africa and perpetuate socioeconomic harm.

Globalization and Global Citizenship: Interdisciplinary Approaches probes a wide range of questions and its contributors live and work in a variety of disciplines. The biographies of these contributors testify to the extent to which their own backgrounds and interests are interdisciplinary. While many of these authors are engaged and trained in multiple fields, their primary areas include anthropology (Thompson), Chinese (Lagerkvist), cultural studies and/or literature (Birk and Jefferess), education (Abdi, Bryan, E. Langran, and Pashby), philosophy (MacMullan), and political science (Armstrong, Bramlett, Carter, Furia, Gustafson, I. Langran, Narine, and Shannon). Their methods are also diverse, and range from rigorous quantitative analysis to qualitative and case studies.

This work is not only an interdisciplinary reader – it is also a cross-cultural one and, as such, strives to provide multiple and competing perspectives on the subject of global citizenship. Contributors offer often divergent and competing views on the nature and meaning of globalization, global citizenship, and cosmopolitanism in the world today. In this, it guides scholars through larger debates about forms of belonging and community that are emerging in the twenty-first century.

References

Bosman, Anston. 2010. "Shakespeare and Globalization". In Margret de Grazia and Stanley Wells (eds), *New Cambridge Companion to Shakespeare*. Cambridge: Cambridge University Press.

Held, David. 2010. *Cosmopolitanism: Ideals and Realities*. Cambridge and Malden, MA: Polity Press.

Holton, Robert. 2000. "Globalization's Cultural Consequences". *Annals of the American Academy of Political and Social Science* 570 (July): 140–152.

Huntington, Samuel. 1993. "The Clash of Civilizations". *Foreign Affairs* 72(3) (March/April): 22–47.

Iyall Smith, Keri E. (ed.) 2013. *Sociology of Globalization: Cultures, Economics, and Politics*. Boulder, CO: Westview Press.

Keohane, Robert and Joseph Nye Jr. 2000. "Globalization: What's New? What's Not? (and So What?)". *Foreign Policy* 118 (Spring): 104–119.

Langran, Irene, Elizabeth Langran, and Kathy Ozment. 2009. "Transforming Today's Students into Tomorrow's Global Citizens: Challenges for U.S. Educators". *New Global Studies* 3(1).

Rodrik, Dani. 2011. *The Globalization Paradox: Democracy and the Future of the World Economy.* New York and London: Norton.

Rosenau, James. 1997. "The Complexities and Contradictions of Globalization". *Current History* 96(613) (November): 360–364.

Watson, James. 2000. "China's Big Mac Attack". *Foreign Affairs* 79(3) (May/June): 120–134.

Part I
Conceptual and historical contexts

Introduction to Part I

Tammy Birk

The chapters in Part I introduce foundational ideas and central debates about the relationship between global citizenship, globalization, and cosmopolitanism. We know that globalization has been challenging traditional forms of national civic identity and attachment. Whether we praise its promotion of cultural hybridity or criticize its erasure of particularity, globalization is steadily rewriting our relationship to civic belonging. Alternative models of citizenship – global, cosmopolitan, flexible – are emerging at the same time that exclusively national frameworks for civic participation and obligations are becoming less persuasive.

Part I opens with an overview of the historical conversation on global citizenship as well as the complex and changing status of global citizenship in a world shaped by globalization. Later chapters focus their attention on the impact of these new understandings of global citizenship and cosmopolitanism on education. We will examine the benefits of a critical cosmopolitan framework for global learning in higher education; the links between rapidly evolving technology, transnational advocacy, and educational practice; and the gains of a post-colonial perspective when defining the reach of global citizenship education.

April Carter begins Part I by exploring how Western and Eastern religious traditions have claimed and complicated the ethical commitments central to global citizenship. In "Historical Origins of Global Citizenship", Carter also traces how the concept of a universal moral law found expression in codes (and courts) of international law and the Stoic world citizen has shaped international movements against slavery and war.

In "Global Citizenship in a Post-Westphalian Age", Irene Langran examines the varying dimensions of citizenship. The chapter considers the implications of the political shifts of a post-Westphalian age for new conceptions of global citizenship. It also discusses complex aspirations for global governance, the form and feasibility of a global political community, and the role of rights, obligations, and political legitimacy in a world that globalization is redefining.

Tammy Birk defines and explores the central features of critical cosmopolitan teaching and learning in "Critical Cosmopolitanism as a New

Paradigm for Global Learning". As a socially relevant and transformative language for global learning, this chapter argues that critical cosmopolitanism can help refine, deepen, and complicate the shared conversation about global citizenship as well as ask new questions about the complex role that globalization plays in encouraging new forms of belonging.

In "Technology's Role in Global Citizenship Education", Elizabeth Langran and Irene Langran examine the historical and contemporary use of technology in transnational advocacy, with particular attention to the rise of social network participation. While technology can play a key role in supporting global citizenship and civic engagement, they argue that it also has the potential to spread misinformation, division, and inequality.

Both Karen Pashby and David Jefferess ask important and challenging questions about the representation of global citizenship in educational policies and practices that are designed to address injustice and promote humanitarian action. Specifically focused on global citizenship education, both writers interrogate given assumptions of the field and seek to decolonize its premises. Pashby's "The Global, Citizenship, and Education as Discursive Fields: Towards Disrupting the Reproduction of Colonial Systems of Power" considers the risks of ignoring taken-for-granted colonial systems of power and failing to interrogate good intentions in global citizenship education initiatives. David Jefferess's "Cosmopolitan Appropriation or Learning? Relation and Action in Global Citizenship Education" examines the way that specific ideas attributed to the Global South – the injunction to "be the change that you wish to see in the world" and the notion of *ubuntu* – have been appropriated by conventional humanitarian discourse as well as neo-liberal and post-racial discourse on global community.

1 Historical origins of global citizenship

April Carter

The concept of global citizenship seems particularly appropriate to the twenty-first century – a world that experiences globalization through technologies of travel and new methods of communication, and that faces common dangers of environmental damage and disastrous climate change. Belief in universal values and moral obligations can, however, be traced back thousands of years in a variety of both Eastern and Western religious traditions as well as in the evolution of legal and political thought deriving from classical Greece and Rome. This chapter discusses briefly different ways in which global citizenship can be understood and then examines the religious origins and the later (mainly) secular evolution of important strands in the total concept.

Defining global citizenship

Global citizenship as an ideal has a number of characteristic features. Here I identify four:

1. The first is an ethical commitment to respect and treat fairly and humanely all other individuals irrespective of their race, ethnicity, religious beliefs, or social status. This sense of ethical obligation today requires a belief in social and political equality, but this was not generally the case in earlier historical contexts.
2. The second aspect relates to identity: an individual choice to see oneself as a member of a universal human society. Identifying with all human beings suggests recognition of an essential commonality by virtue of being human; but given the major cultural, ethnic, and other diversities that characterize people, it also logically implies a valuing of these diversities. Respect for differences manifested in social life is therefore a necessary value underlying global citizenship.
3. The third strand of global citizenship is linked to a concept of universal moral law, which grants individuals basic rights by virtue of their humanity, and therefore imposes obligations on others to respect those rights. A specific global legal framework of "cosmopolitan law",

embodied in conventions upholding individual human rights and holding individuals responsible for "crimes against humanity" – as opposed to international law constraining states – has mostly evolved since the Second World War. But the concept of a "natural law" applying to all humanity goes back over 2,000 years and has had formal status in Roman law. It was elaborated in the Middle Ages and found a place in the developing theories of international law from about 1600 CE.

4 The fourth strand in the ideal of global citizenship is more specifically political and implied by the word "citizen": a belief in the goal of a world political community and a willingness to support policies or take individual action consistent with this goal. Despite the metaphorical concept of the "cosmopolites" coined by the Stoics around 300 BCE, this political version of world citizenship can be seen as essentially modern: linked to proposals for international confederation and world peace from the seventeenth to the twentieth centuries, and very imperfectly realized in the League of Nations and, after 1945, the United Nations. There is also a more radical version of acting as a world citizen, embraced by movements against slavery and war, and in recent decades by green activists seeking to preserve our common environment. Both the proposals for world political institutions and political activism linked to global citizenship are closely linked to attempts to end violent conflict and create bases for cooperation and greater social and economic well-being around the world.

Religious roots of universal ethical commitment and identification

Religious beliefs and doctrines provide the earliest sources for universal values suggesting an ethical commitment to respect all human beings and also indicate that these values have roots in a great variety of world cultures. However, since religious traditions tend to be very complex, with varying interpretations and allegiances over time and in different geographical and cultural settings, and there are major differences in the degree of sophistication and scholarship between believers, generalization is dangerous. Moreover, religious faith can foster exclusive forms of religious belief and identity. But it is possible to find within many religions an emphasis on compassion towards all human beings (or all living creatures) and a sense of belonging to a wider human society, two facets of a sense of global citizenship. Ways in which this frame of mind can be expressed in the social sphere include acceptance of religious and cultural diversity (within a framework of overarching values) and avoiding violence against others at a personal, and as far as possible, at a social and political level.

Hinduism, the oldest major religion, comprises many strands, and has been tolerant both of divergent spiritual paths within its tradition and (historically) of other religions. This spirit of tolerance was reflected in new forms of religion that arose in India (Buddhism and Jainism) and led to India offering a home over very many centuries to "Jews, Christians, Muslims, Parsees, Sikhs, Bahai and others" (Sen 2006, 16–17). Its philosophy also stresses universal and eternal values.

The ideal of nonviolence can be traced back to ancient Hindu texts, the Vedas. "Ahimsa", strictly "nonharm" but often interpreted now as "nonviolence", was emphasized in an offshoot from Hinduism, Jainism, which became a clearly articulated set of beliefs by the fifth century BCE. Nonviolence is central as well to Buddhism, which was also developed within a Hindu context by Siddhartha Gautama, the Buddha (ca. 563–483), whose transmitted teachings stressed an end to personal suffering through enlightenment and promoted a correct frame of mind and behaviour, which avoids causing suffering to others. Peter Harvey suggests that core values of Buddhism are "loving-kindness" (or benevolence) and compassion related to a spirit of generosity (2000, 103–104). Like most important religions, over time Buddhism evolved into a number of different schools, which gave emphasis to different values. Zen Buddhist techniques were even used by the Japanese military elite as part of their discipline.

Ancient Chinese culture fostered a number of schools promoting theories of the universe and advocating appropriate attitudes and modes of behaviour, associated with sayings of legendary founders. Kongzi (Confucius) is the most widely known, and with the establishment of a unified empire in 221 BCE Confucianism became the dominant religious and political orthodoxy, stressing an ideal of social harmony under a good ruler. Two other early religious traditions can be seen as more radical and more directly relevant to a universalist ethical commitment. Daoism, which looks back to Laozi, reputed to have been a contemporary of Confucius, did not have any written sources until (probably) the fourth century BCE, and only acquired a religious following around 100–200 CE. It is cited as an early inspiration for ideals of peace and harmony and possible advocacy of nonviolence, though the transmitted texts are open to conflicting interpretation (Mayer 1966, 31–35). The school of Mozi, who lived in the latter part of the fifth century BCE, a period of increasing warfare between states within Chinese territory, believed in "universal love" and mutual responsibility; but later followers accepted the necessity of war and a few became noted military experts (Gittings 2012, 66–67). Both Daoism and the school of Mozi, therefore, suggested an original aspiration to peaceful relations between states and an embryonic sense of a universal society.

The core values that can be found in many religions, especially in their early teachings, often contrast with social and political practices which claim validation from that religion. This contrast is strikingly illustrated by the history of Christianity. The teachings of Jesus reached out to people in very varied social and economic circumstances and from diverse cultures, as the early spread of Christianity indicated. A key text from the Gospel of Saint Luke (10: 29–37) is the parable of the Good Samaritan, who stopped to help a man by the roadside who had been robbed and beaten by thieves. Jesus told the parable in response to the question "who is my neighbour?" His answer stressed both that strangers in need should be treated like neighbours, and impressed on his Jewish audience that while two "good" Jews had passed by on the other side, a member of a despised "heretical" group, the Samaritans, had not. (Martin Luther King cited this parable in his very last speech, "I've been to the mountain top", 3 April 1968, and used it to illustrate how compassion crosses racial divides.) Christian teaching has also been influenced by the concept expressed in Saint Paul's Epistle to the Galatians that all people are "children of God", and that "there is neither Jew nor Greek, bond nor free ... male nor female" among those who have faith (3: 26–28). Although Saint Paul links this intrinsic equality to Christian belief, this sentiment is now often extended to non-Christians as well. Christianity was also at first strongly associated with belief in nonviolence and early Christians refused to join the army or fight in wars. Nevertheless, Christianity is associated in many periods with persecution of Jews, and Christian rulers engaged in many wars with Islam, initially over Jerusalem in the crusades, as well as wars between Catholics and Protestants after the Reformation.

In practice, religions have often served to promote political authority resting on repression. In some cases where empires adopt an "other-worldly" religion this may (at least initially) have beneficial effects – as in the adoption of Buddhism by the Emperor Ashoka in India in the third century BCE. Christianity also underwent a major political transformation when the Roman Emperor Constantine made it the imperial religion in the third century CE. In both cases imperial authority helped turn Buddhism and Christianity into major religions with adherents in many parts of the world, but necessarily tended to challenge core original values, such as rejection of violence. But in both there is potential tension between religious precepts and temporal authority, which creates a basis for a sense of universal obligation beyond political boundaries.

Those religious beliefs that transcend political borders and (at least potentially) qualify obligation to political rulers can also provide a sense of self-identification with a moral and social universe that is not limited by the status quo. To count as a sense of "world citizenship" this understanding of identity needs to transcend not only political but exclusive religious affiliation. This is easier in generally tolerant religions like Hinduism and Buddhism that recognize in principle the potential validity of other beliefs than it is in Christianity and Islam. Although Islamic rulers have in the past often shown tolerance for subjects of other faiths (much more so than some of their Christian counterparts), and from the eighth century to the thirteenth centuries often embraced the learning and arts of varied civilizations, Islam can also foster a strong and exclusive political and religious identity, long manifested by the internal division between Sunni and Shia Muslims. Some of the groupings that arose within Islam did, however, absorb very varied religious and intellectual influences (see below).

In the Christian tradition there is an important universalist emphasis in Catholic theology (see below), but it is those Protestant sects which do not demand adherence to a complex theology that tend to reflect most clearly a sense of global citizenship. Unitarianism for example, which evolved out of the Reformation, suggests that no religion holds exclusive truth and stresses the role of rationalism; while the Quakers – founded in the early seventeenth century – look for "that of good in every man". Emphasis on the unity of humanity, core spiritual truths that underlie all religions, and an ideal of peace, distinguish the Baha'i faith, which accepts the revelations of its founders as part of a history of progressive religious revelation. The Baha'i faith arose in Muslim Persia in the nineteenth century, but now has adherents around the world.

Universal moral rules and philosophical debate

Reflection on the moral (and potentially legal) rules that should guide relations not just between individuals, but between social communities and political entities, originally drew on religious sources, but also encourages philosophical debate. The distinction between religion and philosophy is contestable in relation to some traditions, for example in China. But from a contemporary viewpoint it is possible to note the role of intellectual debate within traditional frameworks and to trace various forms of philosophy to religious sages or theoreticians. The ancient Sanskrit Hindu epics, the *Ramayana* and *Mahabharata,* are a collection of stories, but also in Amartya Sen's words are "engagingly full of dialogues, dilemmas and alternative perspectives" (2006, 3). Sen also suggests that the often cited *Bhagavad Gita* (within the *Mahabharata*) contains a still highly relevant moral debate between the god Krishna and the hero Arjuna on the ethic of duty and the ethic of responsibility for consequences of one's actions (ibid., 3–6). Buddhism actively fostered intellectual argument, including organized public debates through "Buddhist councils" that drew together representatives of opposing interests and beliefs to resolve conflicts through reasoned discussion (ibid., 15).

The scholarship within specific religious schools of thought can be illuminated by a policy of tolerance towards varied religions. The successful military advance of Arab Muslim rulers to control the Middle East, North Africa, and Spain created a base for the evolution from the eighth century of an Islamic culture that drew on the existing centres of learning in Iraq, Iran, Syria, and Egypt, as well as on Christian, Jewish, and Zoroastrian scholars and on the heritage of classical and Hellenistic Greek learning. Islamic scholars who embraced, adapted, and developed these traditions often were associated with mystical ideas and practices within Islam (Hourani 2002, 59–79). This Islamic scholarship later reached its peak in the twelfth and thirteenth centuries in Andalus (Spain), where Muslim, Jewish, and Christian thinkers developed philosophy, science, jurisprudence, and other branches of learning, drawing on the legacy of classical Greece.

The attempts to reconcile a rationalist philosophy with divine revelation by figures such as Ibn Rushd (Averroes) and Ibn Sina (Avicena) had an influence on Christian theologians and philosophers like Thomas Aquinas, who were wrestling with the same problem. Aquinas drew on the classical heritage to elaborate on a universal natural law, derived from God but accessible not through faith but reason, that embraced all human beings and provided a basis for right conduct towards everyone (D'Entreves [1951] 1967, 38–42). Natural law, as noted earlier, was a critical concept in the evolution of international and cosmopolitan law. Aquinas's formulation of natural law was revived by later Catholic theorists, in particular Francisco Suarez, whose 1619 work *De Legibus ac Deo Legislatore* argued that individual sovereign states were also part of a universal society derived from the moral unity of humanity. He can be claimed as a forerunner of today's humanitarian law. The Protestant Gentili (a professor of civil law) also argued that the common interests of humanity could override state sovereignty, and that subjects were entitled to protection against sovereigns who broke the laws of nature and inflicted inhuman cruelty.

Renaissance humanism: natural law and cosmopolitanism

The Renaissance, which revived the influence of classical Greece and Rome in many spheres, encouraged greater emphasis on the role of human reason. It also revived the cosmopolitan ideas of the Stoics, the school of philosophy that spanned the period 300 BCE to 200 CE, was developed by Zeno and Chrysippus, and had distinguished exponents in the Roman world, notably Cicero and Seneca. Stoicism created the metaphorical concept of the "cosmopolis" but was also, arguably more importantly, a conduit for the idea of natural law (Schofield 1991, 103). As formulated by Cicero, natural law influenced Roman law and later Christian canon law. Stoicism also stood for sympathy with fellow human beings and opposition to cruelty and tyranny, and therefore in the Renaissance (which was also the period of the Reformation and brutal conflicts between Catholics and Protestants) encouraged humanist attitudes of religious tolerance and a desire to end or prevent bitter wars between Catholics and Protestants. These neo-Stoic attitudes were embraced by thinkers like Montaigne in France and Lipsius in the Netherlands in the sixteenth century (Tuck 1991). The theories of Lipsius had a direct influence on the education of Grotius (1583–1645). Grotius is conventionally regarded as the key thinker in the development of modern international law, but he was also a humanist scholar of the classics and advocate of tolerance between conflicting religious beliefs (Catholic and Protestant), looking for a common underlying Christian ethic.

Commitment to tolerant and cosmopolitan views clearly suggested arguing against cruel and divisive wars. Grotius did not think pacifism realistic. Instead he applied himself to defining just war, and the rules that should constrain combatants, in his major 1625 book, *Law of War and Peace*, published during the Thirty Years War. In this context he drew on (his mature formulation of) the concept of natural law, that has universal validity and could be deduced by reasoning. He distinguished it from "the law of nations" which had evolved historically through "common consent" (*Prolegomena*, 25–26). Although Grotius clearly started from his Christian context, he also gave considerable weight to the classical Greek and Roman legacy of ideas and interestingly drew on examples of practices in the Islamic world and South American cultures to elaborate his argument. He developed the concept of "international society" and his outlook is more cosmopolitan than that of later theorists of international law, who focused on relations between sovereign nation states (Bull *et al.*, 1990). During the twentieth century he became one inspiration for the developing body of humanitarian law, enshrined for example in the Hague and Geneva Conventions, setting moral limits on the conduct of war and protecting the wounded, prisoners, and civilians. Grotius is regularly cited in relation to the development of international courts, both those adjudicating between nation states, such as the International Court of Justice at The Hague, and the recent international tribunals and courts set up to judge individuals accused of war crimes and crimes against humanity. The tenth anniversary of the establishment of the International Criminal Court was celebrated at Grotius's tomb in Delft, the Netherlands, on 4 July 2012.

Political universalism found active expression in the Renaissance and the associated humanist intellectualism. A blending of religious commitment and strong belief in reason as a basis for cooperation and peace between diverse peoples characterized humanist thinkers such as Erasmus of Rotterdam (1467–1536). He was noted for his scholarship, emphasis on the barbarity of war, and role in advising princes, and is now honoured by the European Union as a quintessential European. He also used the phrase "citizen of the world", though his precise meaning has been debated (Augustjin 1991, 183). Erasmus was a Catholic (he trained as a priest) who used Christ's original teachings to criticize Christian rulers, and he was particularly critical of plans to extend Christendom through war against the Ottoman Empire. He was therefore wary of some of the plans for European confederation designed to strengthen Christian states against the Turks, and aspirations to "world empire".

Other humanist thinkers who stressed the bonds of sympathy between all people and the underlying common interests of humanity did, however, look to forms of political confederation. The most universalist of these early federalist proposals was "The New Cyneas", written by the French monk Emeric de Cruce in 1623, who went beyond suggesting a federation of European Christian states to advocate including the Islamic Turks, and also envisaged extending it to Persia, China, Japan, and monarchs in India and Africa (Heater 1996, 65–70). Cruce also stressed religious tolerance and themes that would be taken up in the Enlightenment: free travel and free trade. The Quaker William Penn in his 1693 "Essay Towards the Present and Future Peace of Europe" focused primarily on possible federation of Catholic and Protestant states, though he did envisage the possibility of extending membership to the Turks, and to Orthodox Russia (Penn 1993, 12).

The Enlightenment and cosmopolitanism

The Enlightenment, which drew on and resuscitated the legacy of cosmopolitanism in Greek and Roman thought, is still a key reference point for the idea of global citizenship. It advocated respect for all members of a universal humanity, reviving the Stoic concept of the "cosmopolite" (citizen of the world), who, in the words attributed to Zeno, "should regard all men as our fellow countrymen" (Baldry 1965, 159). Some of the early Stoics, however, interpreted cosmopolitanism primarily as a mode of individual belief and conduct and it could imply a rejection of the political sphere; while some of the later Roman Stoics, for example Seneca or Marcus Aurelius, adapted it to the realities of imperial rule (Griffin 1992). The Enlightenment philosophers gave the Stoic cosmopolitan perspective a stronger social content and promoted the idea of global citizenship as an ideal.

Enlightenment cosmopolitanism was based on rationalism. Although some of its philosophers, notably Voltaire, were extremely aware of the cruelty and intolerance which had often been fostered by organized religion, they did not all repudiate any form of religious belief – this was an age in which a generalized deism appealed to some intellectuals. The philosophers of the Enlightenment stressed the importance of religious tolerance and acceptance of diversity, while condemning "religious bigotry". The "philosophes" were by no means united in all their beliefs and from a contemporary perspective were not always consistent in their own individual arguments. But the general tenor of Enlightenment thought could be seen as an attempt at a genuine universalism, opposing slavery, colonialism, and suppression of indigenous peoples and curiosity about and respect for diverse cultures. While there was an implicit (and sometimes explicit) tendency to assume Western superiority, eighteenth-century ideals were in opposition to nineteenth and early twentieth-century imperialist attitudes towards "inferior" peoples (Said 1994, 290).

As with the cosmopolitanism of the Islamic intellectuals in the Abbisid Empire, the Enlightenment cosmopolitanism – linked as it was to philosophy and scientific learning – had an elitist tendency. Diderot's famous *Encyclopaedia*, launched in 1750, which embodied the ideal of unifying world knowledge, cross-referenced "cosmopolite" with "philosophe". World citizenship was expressed through correspondence between intellectuals across frontiers: through travel, interchange of books and pamphlets, international societies, and journals. It is relatively easy for intellectuals and scholars to find common ground that transcends political divisions, as the proliferation in the later nineteenth century of international societies and conferences drawing on a range of scientific disciplines indicated. But many Enlightenment philosophers were also convinced of the growing reality of common interests between all human beings as a basis for a commitment to a common humanity.

The philosophes consciously adopted the identity of citizens of the world. One of the early Enlightenment theorists, Montesquieu, claimed he should put the interests of humanity above those of his country, and Diderot wrote to

Hume: "You belong to all nations ... I flatter myself that I am, like you, a citizen of the great city of the world" (Gay 1967, 13). Paine, one of the later Enlightenment thinkers and pamphleteers, and the most revolutionary, claimed: "my city is the world and my religion is to do good" (Paine [1791] 1969, 250). The philosophes tended to argue that there was no *necessary* conflict between being a good citizen of one's own country and being a citizen of the world. Indeed, the two commitments tended to coincide, because opposing xenophobic forms of patriotism or aggressive national policies was to promote the true interests of one's country. But as Montesquieu's formulation indicated, there could in practice be a conflict of loyalties, and true world citizenship meant putting cosmopolitan principles first.

Apart from advocating religious tolerance and freedom of thought, and opposing slavery and other forms of systematic cruelty, the philosophes generally looked to free travel and free trade between different parts of the world as a means of fostering common bonds and combating a militaristic culture. Merchants were seen as members of a multinational and cosmopolitan society transcending frontiers (Schlereth 1977, 101). In the eighteenth century a Western policy of the right to travel and free trade could, however, often be associated with imperialist ambitions. Most philosophes opposed overt colonial rule, but Kant was especially aware of potential dangers from travel and trade. He discussed the rights of aboriginal peoples to retain their land and argued that European settlement was only justified by contractual consent. In his *Perpetual Peace* he condemns Western commercial nations that "visit" other parts of the world in order to conquer them, and (as in "East India") bring in foreign troops "under the pretext of merely setting up trading posts" (Reiss 1991, 106). Kant is also well known for developing the most sophisticated (and somewhat ambiguous) proposal for an extending political confederation of states as a means of promoting peace. Although he is sometimes seen as a forerunner of the United Nations, the ideal of the European Union promoting peace within Europe is perhaps closer to embodying his ideas.

Cosmopolitan movements: the nineteenth and early twentieth centuries

Whereas earlier expressions of cosmopolitanism tended to be associated with a small elite, in the more democratic age that developed by the end of the eighteenth century, sections of the common people became actively involved in social movements for cosmopolitan goals. The earliest of these movements was the opposition to the slave trade, and to the whole institution of slavery. This took a "transnational" form (individuals and groups cooperating across borders) and mobilized a wide cross-section of society in Britain (a major slave-trading nation) and the United States, where slavery was central to the cotton industry of the South.

The other cosmopolitan movement that took off from the end of the Napoleonic Wars was the peace movement. Initially fostered in North America and Britain, it soon embraced many countries in Europe. Although peace campaigns have since taken many forms, been divided by debates about just war and wars of national liberation, and had much wider support in some periods than others, genuinely autonomous international peace organizations do uphold cosmopolitan ideals. They have often tried to prevent and end wars and have campaigned for various treaties and conventions to prohibit use of particularly destructive weapons. Individuals and groups now seen as part of a broad peace history have also at various times promoted humanitarian bodies like the Red Cross and humanitarian law, and lobbied during wars for the post-war creation of international organizations, notably for the League of Nations (Carter 2001, 52–56, 61–64).

Other movements, such as the early socialist and feminist movements, have, despite their primary emphasis on promoting the rights and welfare of particular sections of society, been transnational in scope and have often included wider goals of changing conditions for all humanity for the better. Both have also at various points stressed anti-war positions. Although the aspirations of the Second Socialist International to unite workers everywhere to prevent war were shattered by the First World War, and the 1917 Bolshevik Revolution soon divided socialists, the experience of the war prompted new attempts to end the war and promote a more peaceful world.

The sources of the universalist ethical stance adopted by the movements noted above were varied. Christian Protestant groups were very active in the movements against the slave trade and in the early nineteenth-century peace movement. The later peace movement comprised groups within it still strongly motivated by varied Christian beliefs and values, but also extended to embrace a range of explicitly secular and rationalist political ideologies. Other religious traditions have also strongly influenced social movements. A key figure in promoting a worldwide ideal of nonviolence, Mahatma Gandhi (1869–1948), drew on Hindu and Jainist teachings of selflessness and detachment as a basis for conducting social struggle, and interpreted the *Bhagavad Gita*, in which Krishna exhorts Arjuna before battle, as signifying an allegorical "struggle between truth and untruth taking place in the heart of man" (Bondurant 1958, 116). Gandhi was also influenced by Christianity and read widely in other religions, including Islam, believing that all religious faiths were striving towards the same truth.

Conclusion

This chapter has tried to sketch in the diversity of religious and philosophical sources underlying belief in and active commitment to a cosmopolitan ethic, identification with an overarching humanity, and acceptance of universal obligations. While tolerance of competing ideas and beliefs, and an emphasis on reasoned debate, appear to be centrally important to a cosmopolitan outlook, it is overly simple to see increasing secularization as necessarily conducive to achieving an ideal of global citizenship. Adherents of secular political ideology can display as much irrational conviction and intolerance as religious extremists.

The Enlightenment belief in rationally derived universal rules has also been persuasively challenged as a form of Western cultural imperialism, imposing, for example, Western concepts of individual rights upon cultures with differing traditions and priorities. Nevertheless, as Kant argued over two centuries ago, the growing interconnectedness between the peoples of the world does point to the urgent need for common policies based on a sense of a common interest. Appeals to human rights are now also frequently voiced in all parts of the world where groups and individuals suffer repression. Moreover, some recent developments in international law and politics suggest greater readiness to implement ideas associated with global citizenship.

References

Augustjin, Cornelius. 1991. *Erasmus: His Life, Work and Influence*. Translated by J. C. Gower. Toronto: University of Toronto Press.
Baldry, H. C. 1965. *The Unity of Mankind*. Cambridge: Cambridge University Press.
Bondurant, Joan. 1958. *Conquest of Violence: The Gandhian Philosophy of Conflict*. Princeton, NJ: Princeton University Press.
Bull, Hedley, Benedict Kingsbury, and Adam Roberts (eds). 1990. *Hugo Grotius and International Relations*. Oxford: Clarendon Press.
Carter, April. 2001. *The Political Theory of Global Citizenship*. London: Routledge.
D'Entreves, A. P. [1951] 1967. *Natural Law*. London: Hutchinson.
Gay, Peter. 1967. *The Enlightenment: An Interpretation*. London: Weidenfeld & Nicolson.
Gittings, John. 2012. *The Glorious Art of Peace: From the Iliad to Iraq*. Oxford: Oxford University Press.
Griffin, Miriam T. 1992. *Seneca: A Philosopher in Politics*. Revised edn. Oxford: Clarendon Press.
Grotius, Hugo. [1625] 1957. *Prolegomena to the Law of War and Peace*. New York: Liberal Arts Press.
Harvey, Peter. 2000. *An Introduction to Buddhist Ethics: Foundations, Values and Issues*. Cambridge: Cambridge University Press.
Heater, Derek. 1996. *World Citizenship and Government: The History of Cosmopolitan Ideas in Western Political Thought*. Basingstoke: Palgrave Macmillan.
Hourani, Albert. 2002. *A History of the Arab Peoples*. London: Faber and Faber.
Mayer, Peter. (ed.) 1966. *The Pacifist Conscience*. Harmondsworth: Penguin.
Paine, Tom. [1791] 1969. *The Rights of Man*. Harmondsworth: Penguin.
Parekh, Bhiku. 1987. "Hindu Political Thought". In David Miller (ed.), *The Blackwell Encyclopaedia of Political Thought*. Oxford: Blackwell, pp. 205–208.
Penn, William. 1993. *The Peace of Europe, The Fruits of Solitude and Other Writings*. Edited by Edwin B. Bronner. Everyman edn. London: Dent.
Reiss, Hans. (ed.) 1991. *Kant Political Writings*. Translated by H. B. Nisbet. 2nd enlarged edn. Cambridge: Cambridge University Press.
Said, Edward W. 1994. *Culture and Imperialism*. London: Vintage.

Saint-Pierre, Abbe de. [1729] 2008. *An Abridged Version of the Project for Perpetual Peace*. Edited by Roderick Pace, trans. Carmen Depasquale. Valletta: Midsea Books.

Schlereth, Thomas J. 1977. *The Cosmopolitan Ideal in Enlightenment Thought: Its Forms and Functions in the Ideas of Franklin, Hume and Voltaire 1694–1790*. Indiana, IN: Notre Dame University Press.

Schofield, Malcolm. 1991. *The Stoic Idea of the City*. Cambridge: Cambridge University Press.

Sen, Amartya. 2006. *The Argumentative Indian: Writings on Indian Culture, History and Identity*. London: Penguin.

Tuck, Richard. 1991. *Philosophy and Government*. Cambridge: Cambridge University Press.

2 Global citizenship in a post-Westphalian age

Irene Langran

The nature and meaning of global citizenship is contested, elusive, and unsettling. Some activists and academics view global citizenship as a panacea to the world's problems and a cause to celebrate: it elevates universal human rights and our responsibilities to distant others, it unites humanity, and it provides new approaches to global problems. Others view global citizenship as a threat to state sovereignty, an exercise in Western imperialism, and a practical impossibility in a system in which rights, obligations, and political legitimacy exist within the confines of states. There is widespread disagreement not only concerning global citizenship's potential, but its very nature and meaning.

This chapter explores the implications of global citizenship for states and within the context of globalization. It begins with a discussion of how globalization influences contemporary understanding of global citizenship, exploring debates about the purported shift of power from states to other actors – including intergovernmental organizations (IGOs), transnational corporations (TNCs), non-governmental organizations (NGOs), groups engaged in a range of illicit activities, or individuals. It then explores global citizenship in relation to three dimensions of citizenship: the legal dimension, encompassing rights and obligations; the psychological dimension, focusing on membership or exclusion in political communities; and the political dimension of representational legitimacy. Joseph Carens (2000) explores national-level citizenship by focusing on these three dimensions of citizenship. The comparison of citizenship on domestic and global levels is not intended to imply that these types of citizenship are identical in meaning yet merely existing on different levels; rather, the comparison is valuable because it provides a conceptual framework to explore the promise and peril of citizenship on a global scale.[1]

Globalization and global citizenship in the twenty-first century

Ideas about citizenship are fluid and shaped by historical context. Today, globalization and the debate over its impact on state sovereignty is at the heart of the contemporary citizenship debate. Some scholars maintain that the technology that is shaping contemporary globalization is also undermining states. Because of this technology, groups that are engaged in illicit activities have the ability to circumvent state controls and adapt quickly through networks rather than the slow, bureaucratic responses of states. As noted by Moises Naim (2009), states are challenged by globalization's "five wars" – the illicit trade in drugs, arms, intellectual property, money, and people.

Economic globalization fuels the ability of transnational corporations to transfer operations from one state to another with ease, and their power in a world of unequal states results in very different local and regional impacts. States are constrained in the economic realm by the need to adopt certain pro-globalization, neo-liberal policies under pressure from international organizations (such as the International Monetary Fund and World Bank), donor governments, and investors. Thomas Friedman (2012) uses the image of the "Golden Straitjacket" to describe the lack of choice many governments face in adopting economic policies. The activist and scholar Vandana Shiva (2003) decries the impact of globalization on communities in India and around the world, arguing that basic principles of democracy are lost in the face of more powerful corporate interests. Issues of power shifts – to and from states, international organizations, corporations, communities, and individuals – have important implications for citizenship on multiple levels. Derek Heater (2002, 3) warns that globalization "undermines the autonomy of the person, which lies at the heart of the citizenry concept".

In recent decades, new IGOs, NGOs, and international laws have increased in number and expanded their influence in global governance. Whereas some scholars maintain that states remain central actors in the international arena, others claim that this trend portends the shift to a post-Westphalian world. As stated by Richard N. Haass (2005, 54):

> Thirty-five years from now, sovereignty will no longer be sanctuary. Powerful new forces and insidious threats will converge against it. Nation-states will not disappear, but they will share power with a larger number of powerful non-sovereign actors than ever before, including corporations, nongovernmental organizations, terrorist groups, drug cartels, regional and global institutions, and banks and private equity funds. Sovereignty will fall victim to the powerful and accelerating flow of people, ideas, greenhouse gases, goods, dollars, drugs, viruses, e-mails, and weapons within and across borders.

Friedman (2005) writes that the current stage of economic globalization is centred on the individual, now able to take advantage of new forms of technology to advance in spite of circumstance and geography. Whereas some argue that globalization is a "tide that lifts all boats", others maintain that it is a process that creates winners and losers. On the one hand are the privileged; these individuals experience the benefits of globalization and have the resources to travel and work with little regard for state borders. On the other hand, there are those who are disenfranchised, unemployed, or underemployed, and living in extreme poverty. They too may work across borders, but in very different conditions from those more privileged. Saskia Sassen (2005, 84) observes that citizenship on the national level "is affected by the position of different groups". The same observation can be applied to the global level.

Extending citizenship to the global level raises a number of questions. For those who maintain that states remain the central actor in world politics, is this level of citizenship even possible? Have we indeed entered a "post-Westphalian" era when state sovereignty is challenged? Are states losing influence as TNCs, NGOs, and IGOs increase their role on the world stage or do states remain the central actor in world politics? Can a global interest realistically replace the national interest? Can they coincide? In terms of the legal dimension, do rights exist outside the context of state sovereignty? What obligations do individuals have beyond the borders of their own towns, cities, or states? On the psychological level, can individuals identify with global political communities? Finally, to what extent can representational legitimacy exist on the global level? This chapter explores these questions and the implications of new ways of thinking about citizenship in an era where the state-centric character of the modern international system is challenged.

Rights and duties: citizenship's first dimension

At the core of debates over the meaning and nature of citizenship are the concepts of rights and duties, Carens's (2000) "first dimension" of citizenship. The notion that rights are inherent to human beings has existed for centuries. However, it was only after the Second World War and the devastation of the Holocaust that these ideas gained a more widespread acceptance and were codified into international law. Such widespread acceptance – a condition Jack Donnelly (2007, 282) refers to as the "ideologically hegemonic" status of universal human rights – is influenced by the increasing codification of these rights in international (and, subsequently, domestic) laws. Indeed, the post-Second World War era has seen a proliferation of rights-related documents. The 1948 Universal Declaration of Human Rights set the stage for numerous international laws that were passed in subsequent years. These laws addressed a range of topics, including racial discrimination; civil and political rights; economic, social, and cultural rights; discrimination against women; torture; the rights of children; the rights of migrants; and the rights of persons with disabilities.[2] International laws even address the issue of "statelessness" by providing refugees unable to document their status with an international passport (the Nansen passport).

The concept of universal human rights is not unchallenged. Today, many of the challenges that authoritarian regimes use to justify their lack of adherence to these rights have few followers. However, there are other challenges, especially the charge that these rights diminish diversity and reflect Western imperialism. Some of these same arguments challenge our understanding of global citizenship as well. Post-colonial critiques of universal human rights may not in themselves undermine the concept, but they do present unsettling challenges that ask one to acknowledge and situate oneself in a world that is deeply unequal and shaped by legacies of colonialism's injustices, constructions of the Other, and exploitation. A critical analysis of human rights cannot be understood apart from such contextual reality. The challenge of human rights and global citizenship is to reconcile both the universal nature of rights as well as cultural diversity.

Ideas about human rights were, as examined by Donnelly (2007, 286), developed first in the West by such thinkers as John Locke as well as by others during the American and French Revolutions. Donnelly explores further the question of why the West was the first site of these intellectual developments – and his conclusions have relevance for questions of justice in the globalized environment of the twenty-first century. Donnelly notes that the emergence of these concepts in the West was not linked to any particular aspect of Western culture, but rather were a result of particular social and economic conditions and the changes they brought to lives in the seventeenth century to the present time. These changes included the disruption of traditional systems of community support by modern markets and states. As Donnelly observes, "Human rights today remain the only proven effective means to assure human dignity in societies dominated by markets and states" (ibid., 287–288).

There is no disputing that the current economic system is characterized by pervasive globalization. As noted by J. Martin Rochester (2012, 185), at least 20 per cent of the fresh fruits and vegetables that Americans eat are imported. The value of trade in goods and services is further evidence of the increasing globalization of markets: whereas trade as a percentage of world GDP was 42.1 per cent in 1980, it rose to 62.1 per cent in 2007 (IMF 2008). Although recovery from the 2008–9 global recession has been uneven and slowed international trade, in the world economy "a rising proportion of global production of goods and services is being traded across borders rather than sold at home" (UNCTAD 2012).

These economic trends have significant implications for human rights, including economic and social rights, and ideas about citizenship. Globalization in the twenty-first century exists within a particular historical context – one that Barry K. Gills (2008, 10) describes as an attempt "to bring all of humanity into a single ideological and material system" characterized by neo-liberalism. The United Nations Development Programme reports that the number of extreme poor has dropped by 650 million in the past three decades (UNDP 2013). Nevertheless, the notion that globalization is "a tide that lifts all boats" is belied by the more than one billion people are still living in extreme poverty and the reality that global economic inequality is, in the words of Oxfam International, "extreme" (Oxfam 2014). Oxfam notes that 1 per cent of the world's population owns almost half the wealth – which is equivalent to 65 times the "total wealth of the bottom half of the world's population" (ibid.).

Oxfam further states that "The bottom half of the world's population owns the same as the richest 85 people in the world" and "Seven out of ten people live in countries where economic inequality has increased in the last 30 years" (ibid.).

The legal dimension of citizenship involves both rights and responsibilities. When responsibilities are viewed on the state level, they involve obligations towards fellow citizens that work to promote a public, collective good that transcends narrow self-interests. There is a balance between individual rights and the collective good, and as such there are limits to both. Good citizenship involves more than simply doing no harm to fellow citizens – it also entails contributing to the civic life of the polity by being knowledgeable about relevant issues, voting, and participating in its institutions.

What obligations do we have towards other human beings with whom we do not share ties of national citizenship? If we accept that all human beings are equal and are endowed with basic rights, then we must conclude that certain acts are unethical, regardless of where they occur. Dower (2002, 150–51) uses the term "universalisability" to say that it is just as wrong to deceive a foreigner in one's own country as it is to deceive someone in another country (for example, in financial transactions). Although technology has allowed greater information sharing across borders, thus enabling the possibility of a more informed citizenry, we do not personally know the people who may be affected by our actions. This, according to Kwame Anthony Appiah (2006, 153), raises important questions about our "obligations to strangers".

Further global integration and interdependence pose ethical questions to consumers in a global economy. For example, on a daily basis, consumers purchase products that originate in distant locales and are made by individuals they are unlikely to ever meet. Similarly, individual consumption of energy impacts the global environment. These economic trends are not new – indeed, one need only be reminded of the colonial era as an example of their persistence. However, technology has influenced the ease and pace of such interdependence. In many ways, such technological advances can be considered a double-edged sword. These advances bring the potential for exploitation of individuals, groups, communities, and the environment; they can also provide the tools for a greater awareness of these issues and the ability to learn more about the personal lives of the people affected by the actions of others. The positive or negative impact of individual actions on the lives of those they will never meet is, as noted by Appiah (2006), a question of "ethics in a world of strangers". Do we need new ethics for an increasingly interconnected and interdependent world? The questions posed by the realities of the current global economy – its human costs as well as its structural inequities – concern fundamental ideas about justice as well as citizenship. As stated by Gills (2008, 3), the discussion about global justice "will give new meaning and direction to the idea of global society and to the role of global citizenship within it, ideas that in my view are historically ripe for activation and application".

Whereas rights and obligations exist on individual levels, their enforcement lies with states and raises important questions about state sovereignty. As noted by April Carter (2001, 26), as early as the seventeenth century Hugo Grotius called for outside intervention if there were excessive violations of the "laws of nature". Nevertheless, it is only in the post-Second World War era that we have seen a movement away from the non-intervention norm. The 1948 Genocide Convention, which provides states with a *right* to intervene in the internal affairs of states, has now been joined by the *Responsibility* to Protect (R2P) doctrine. The International Criminal Court expanded even further upon the idea of universal human rights by creating a court system to address specific violations of international law (genocide, war crimes, and crimes against humanity – with crimes of aggression yet to be defined). While international norms have changed, their enforcement still resides with states – and as such, implementation remains an uneven and selective process.

The civil war in Syria that began in 2011 provides an apt illustration of the difficulties inherent in enforcing international laws that protect human rights. The conflict itself is fuelled by the illicit trade in arms, antiquities, people, and oil – exemplifying the challenge to states of Naim's (2009) "wars of globalization". The Internet has proven itself a powerful tool in the recruitment of fighters for the Islamic State (ISIS or ISIL), with some reports indicating that half of the 20,000 ISIS fighters are foreigners from an estimated 90 countries (Weaver 2015). These fighters challenge both state and cosmopolitan identities.

The violations of international humanitarian law are numerous and on all sides of the conflict. While a comprehensive list of these violations is beyond the scope of this chapter, consider the following examples:

- use of chemical weapons by the Assad regime;
- torture and illegal detentions by all sides;
- genocide, as committed by ISIS in an attempt to eliminate groups based on religion and through acts that include separation of families, rape, sexual slavery, and murder;
- war crimes, including recruitment of child soldiers by ISIS; and
- crimes against humanity.

There are numerous international laws in existence that address these crimes and several of them fall under the jurisdiction of the recently established International Criminal Court. Nevertheless, the international response is weak and lacks coordination as well as agreement on basic objectives among states. The weak and uneven response to the refugee crisis points to the power of criminal syndicates, which are enjoying a windfall of profits through human smuggling as states fail to observe the basic international laws that are intended to govern the flow of those escaping war and persecution. The ability to work together as a self-identified global community to address such challenges is the topic of the following section.

Citizens of the world, unite! Citizenship's second dimension

The psychological dimension of global citizenship encompasses the extent to which individuals self-identify as members of a political community. Political communities aspire to "extensive self-government" – an aspect of citizenship in the psychological dimension that Carens (2000, 167) notes differentiates political communities from other groups (for example, those based on gender, religious affiliation, or sexual orientation).

One of the most important questions concerning contemporary understandings of citizenship is the extent to which multiple citizenships can be accommodated simultaneously. The debate over global citizenship often focuses on the tensions between patriotism and cosmopolitanism (Nussbaum 1994). Indeed, tensions can arise from a commitment to the equality of all humans and the fear that such commitment will have a negative impact on one's own interests. It is this fear that presents obstacles to collective action on a global level. However, this aspect of the debate tends to dismiss the extent to which individuals accommodate multiple forms of identity.

Surveys yield important information on these aspects of global citizenship. In World Values Surveys, self-identification as a global citizen rises as respondents are asked not to *rank* world identification with other identifications, but to consider the possibility of *multiple* citizenships. Whereas more recent questions asked respondents if they identified as a world citizen, surveys from 1981 to 2004 included the following question: "To which of these geographical groups would you say you belong first of all? And the next? And which do you belong to least of all?" (World Values Survey, 1981–2008) The respondents were asked to rank belonging to their locality, region, country, continent, or world. In these surveys, only 7.5 per cent of respondents replied that they belonged to the world first. This is sizeable in itself but, as noted above, when the question is rephrased to allow for multiple citizenships, more than 70 per cent of respondents identify themselves as global citizens. The idea that multiple levels of citizenship can exist is not a new concept; indeed, Carter (2001, 38) notes that during the Enlightenment, "being a citizen of the world required being a responsible citizen of one's own country".

Contemporary ideas about membership and belonging are shaped by globalization, increased migration, and advances in communication technology. Today, there are more than 200 million international migrants (UNDP 2009, 2). While the increased transborder movement of people and increasing diversity within many states does not preclude multiple citizenships, such citizenships may not automatically result. Indeed, global citizenship competes with national, transnational, religious, and other identities. Several of the chapters in the third section of this work consider this in regional-specific contexts.

Richard Dagger (2000, 30–37) identifies size and mobility as among the "enemies of citizenship". Citing Aristotle, Dagger states that a growing population can be associated with a loss in the quality of citizenship as citizens become less knowledgeable about the issues and their fellow citizens. Dagger notes the negative impact of mobility on citizenship, stating "When the population of a group changes rapidly or frequently, it is difficult for members to learn who the other members are and whether they can be trusted to cooperate" (ibid., 34).

Although Dagger (2000) is critical of the media's ability to contribute to an informed citizenry, advances in information technology can play an important role in overcoming its shortcomings, including size and distance. For example, Richard Falk (2002, 16) notes that the Internet can promote "netizen bonds", creating a sense of community "on the basis of shared interests and affinities among individuals and groups that may be geographically isolated and disparate". Mobility may also be an asset in supporting a sense of global community if it results in a sense of shared existence and empathy. As Stephen Castles (2005, 689) notes, "Technological advances make it possible for migrants to maintain close links with their areas of origin". In turn, these links facilitate the emergence of transnational communities, or "groups with regular and significant activities in two or more countries" (ibid.). Transnational communities can be considered political communities as well, especially when their activities include participation in policy debates or even voting across borders. However, it must be noted that technology and the movement of peoples can also lead to polarization or even antidemocratic and exclusionary movements. The challenge of global citizenship lies in its ability to reconcile both universality and diversity.

The psychological impact of trust and the equal or unequal treatment of citizens is an important factor in assessing the degree to which individuals feel that they are members of political communities. Carens (2000, 167–168) notes that the sense of attachment that comes from being a member of a political community in a state may not always be present. For example, discrimination against a particular group or income inequality can result in a lack of affinity with the state. It is possible that individuals with a similar socio-economic status may have more in common with their counterparts in other countries than individuals from different socio-economic strata within their own countries. Although Peter Furia (2005) found that income was a weak indicator of self-identification as a global citizen, inequality raises important questions about the very nature of citizenship and rights in an unequal world.

When we observe equality on a global scale, we realize that it can also have an impact on self-identification as a global citizen. As noted by Carter (2001, 74), "Globalization in its present form does not, however, necessarily favour global citizenship" and may even be viewed as an example of "ideological imperialism". Carter (ibid., 9) cites a conflict between ideas associated commonly with globalism: a neo-liberal, free trade agenda and a commitment to universal human rights. Neo-liberalism and imperialism can limit the political power of individuals and local communities. Carter (ibid., 41) notes that even Kant, writing in an age of colonization, "explored how a cosmopolitan desire to travel the world could lead to the danger of exploitation".

Representational legitimacy in the post-Westphalian age: citizenship's third dimension

The most challenging argument in favour of global citizenship is arguably in the realm of its third dimension: representational legitimacy. In the absence of a world government, can there be any claim to representational legitimacy on the global level? Are individuals self-identifying as global citizens more accurately part of a larger social movement? Are the answers to these questions different in an age where some argue that states are weaker and often eclipsed by non-state actors?

The modern international system was founded on the idea that states are sovereign – hence, the 1648 Peace of Westphalia, ending the Thirty Years War, provides the basis for this system. Realists would argue that states remain powerful and sovereign, even as globalization leads some to conclude that we are entering a post-Westphalian era. On the other side of the spectrum are those who argue in favour of a gradual diminution of state sovereignty through world federalism. The realists would argue against the possibility of global citizenship, while the world federalist would seek its realization in ways that mirror closely state-level citizenship.

In recent years there has been a movement towards a new conceptual model that differs from those offered by world federalists and realists. This model envisions the political dimension of global citizenship with an emphasis on how we distinguish *government* from *governance*. Whereas governments are associated with the formal institutions of states, governance is associated with an approach to solving problems with the active involvement of both state and non-state actors (including NGOs, IGOs, and transnational corporations). Because there is an increased recognition of the shared nature of global problems that transcend national borders, there is a growing movement towards governance on the global level. As defined by Elke Krahmann (2003, 331), governance consists of "the structures and processes that enable governmental and non-governmental actors to coordinate their interdependent needs and interests through the making and implementation of policies in the absence of a unifying political authority".

The trend towards increased recognition of a shared responsibility towards global issues gained momentum in the 1990s, through the work of the Commission on Global Governance. Today, the trend continues to progress through the formation of new initiatives, including The Lancet-University of Oslo Commission on Global Governance for Health. Technological advances and the strengthening of international institutions bolster this movement. For example, technology enables us to gather more data on global problems, share this information across borders, and use the information to pursue solutions.

An example from the field of global health helps illustrate the governance approach to solving global problems. There are several ways in which globalization affects the health of populations. One such way is the impact of increased travel and trade across borders. As people and goods cross borders, so can diseases – and history is rich with examples, including with the Black Death during the Middle Ages and the 1918 influenza pandemic. These pandemics killed millions and many health experts fear that similar pandemics would kill even more today through increased cross border movements.

The World Health Organization has been engaged in creating protocols and reporting procedures for potential pandemics. The 1951 International Sanitary Regulations relied on states for information on covered diseases (at the time, these diseases were limited to cholera, plague, and yellow fever). These regulations were passed by member states of the World Health Organization (WHO) and were the first health agreements covering communicable diseases that were binding on states. When revised in 2005, the new International Health Regulations recognized NGOs as legitimate sources of information on epidemics (now expanded to include all communicable diseases). This is an example of expanding the actors who are seen as participating in global health governance – and it marks a shift in terms of which of these actors are seen as legitimate in designing and implementing policy. Indonesia's claim of "viral sovereignty" to justify non-cooperation with the WHO in combating avian influenza (Holbrooke and Garrett 2008) is an exception to increasing international cooperation in sharing health information. States are still sovereign, but norms are changing.

Norms concerning representational legitimacy present particular challenges when applied on the global level. Carter (2001, 130) notes that states still control many aspects of citizenship, including the determination of which citizens can vote and restrictions on public service. This begs the question: how can representational legitimacy apply to the global level when there is no global government? The European Union's direct election of representatives to the European Parliament is an exception rather than the rule. Johan Galtung (2000, as cited by Axtmann 2002, 107) envisioned a reformed United Nations in which a People's Assembly represented citizens through direct elections. The People's Assembly would have the "ultimate authority" in the new system, although governments, corporations, and local authorities would have representation in other assemblies.

Even without the creation of Galtung's new assemblies, there are aspects of today's IGOs that lend themselves to claims of representational legitimacy. States are the members of IGOs – and a growing number of these states have varying levels of representational legitimacy in their own national elections. In turn, these elected officials and those they appoint determine policies within the IGOs in which they are members. Within IGOs, some states are more powerful than others – and thus one could argue that some citizens are more powerful than others. Global governance and citizenship would be strengthened through efforts to bolster greater equality among and within states – a considerable challenge to overcome in view of competing visions of state interests.

David Held (2002, 98–100) examines the specific needs for representational legitimacy at the global level. According to Held, the design of the new "cosmopolitan democracies" is to create a means to address global problems. These problems are not addressed effectively at national levels, and as such a new level of governance is created. Global citizenship would not replace other levels of citizenship but, as noted by Held (ibid., 100), "in this system of cosmopolitan governance, people would come to enjoy multiple citizenships". The concept of governance is again distinguishable from government, as it incorporates multiple levels and actors. Held (2002, 99) notes that decisions would be made by at different levels through a "global and divided authority system" according to the nature of the problem; while local democracies would be strengthened, they would serve as a "complement to the public assemblies of the wider global order".

Conclusion

When discussing the EU, Carter (2001, 119) writes that "the overlapping jurisdictions and loyalties created by the EU are indicative of the need to rethink the meaning of citizenship". The growing emphasis on universal human rights, the number of individuals self-identifying as global citizens, and the movement towards global governance are evidence of the need to rethink citizenship as well. Citizenship on global and state levels are not identical – indeed, they differ in enforcement of law, exclusivity versus universality of rights, and the emphasis of government versus governance. However, to the millions of individuals who identify themselves as global citizens, this political community is real and not merely imagined. To those whose rights are protected on the basis of their universality and because of pressure from others, global citizenship takes on a very real and important meaning. An emphasis on solving global problems through governance and not merely by state governments brings new meaning to citizenship in the twenty-first century.

Notes

1 I would like to thank Tammy Birk, Lowell Gustafson, and Vanessa de Oliveira Andreotti for their comments on this chapter.
2 For a full list of core human rights treaties, see Office of the High Commissioner for Human Rights, "The Core International Human Rights Instruments and Their Monitoring Bodies". Available at: www.ohchr.org/EN/ProfessionalInterest/Pages/CoreInstruments.aspx (accessed 10 October 2015).

References

Appiah, Kwame Anthony. 2006. *Cosmopolitanism: Ethics in a World of Strangers*. New York: Norton.
Axtmann, Roland. 2002. "What's Wrong with Cosmopolitan Democracy?". In Nigel Dower and John Williams (eds), *Global Citizenship: A Critical Introduction*. New York: Routledge, pp. 101–113.

Carens, Joseph. 2000. *Culture, Citizenship, and Community: A Conceptual Exploration of Justice as Evenhandedness*. New York: Oxford University Press.
Carter, April. 2001. *The Political Theory of Global Citizenship*. London and New York: Routledge.
Castles, Stephen. 2005. "Hierarchical Citizenship in a World of Unequal Nation-States". *PS: Political Science and Politics* 38(4): 689–692.
Dagger, Richard. 2000. "Metropolis, Memory and Citizenship". In Engin F. Isin (ed.), *Democracy, Citizenship and the Global City*. London and New York: Routledge, pp. 25–47.
Donnelly, Jack. 2007. "The Relative Universality of Human Rights". *Human Rights Quarterly* 29(2): 281–306.
Dower, Nigel. 2002. "Global Ethics and Global Citizenship". In Dower and Williams, pp. 146–157.
Dower, Nigel and John Williams. (eds) 2002. *Global Citizenship: A Critical Introduction*. New York: Routledge.
Falk, Richard. 2002. "An Emergent Matrix of Citizenship: Complex, Uneven, and Fluid". In Dower and Williams, pp. 15–29.
Friedman, Thomas L. 2005. "It's a Flat World, After All". *New York Times Magazine* (3 April): 32–37.
Friedman, Thomas L. 2012. *The Lexus and the Olive Tree: Understanding Globalization*. New York: Picador.
Furia, Peter A. 2005. "Global Citizenship, Anyone? Cosmopolitanism, Privilege and Public Opinion". *Global Society* 19(4): 339–359.
Gills, Barry K. 2008. "The Global Politics of Justice". In Barry K. Gills (ed.), *Globalization and the Global Politics of Justice*. London and New York: Routledge, pp. 1–4.
Haass, Richard N. 2005. "Sovereignty". *Foreign Policy* 150 (September–October): 54.
Heater, Derek. 2002. *World Citizenship: Cosmopolitan Thinking and Its Opponents*. London and New York: Continuum.
Held, David. 2002. "The Transformation of Political Community: Rethinking Democracy in the Context of Globalization". In Dower and Williams, pp. 92–100.
Holbrooke, Richard and Laurie Garrett. 2008. "'Sovereignty' That Risks Global Health". *Washington Post* (10 August).
IMF. 2008. "Globalization: A Brief Overview". Available at: www.imf.org/external/np/exr/ib/2008/053008.htm (accessed 10 October 2015).
Krahmann, Elke. 2003. "National, Regional and Global Governance: One Phenomenon or Many?". *Global Governance* 9(3): 323–346.
Naim, Moises. 2009. "The Five Wars of Globalization". *Foreign Policy* 134: 28–36.
Nussbaum, Martha. 1994. "Patriotism and Cosmopolitanism". *Boston Review* (October–November).
Oxfam. 2014. "Working for the Few: Political Capture and Economic Inequality". Available at: www.oxfam.org/sites/www.oxfam.org/files/bp-working-for-few-political-capture-economic-inequality-200114-summ-en.pdf (accessed 10 October 2015).
Rochester, J. Martin. 2012. *Between Peril and Promise: The Politics of International Law*. 2nd edn. Los Angeles, CA: Sage and CQ Press.
Sassen, Saskia. 2005. "The Repositioning of Citizenship and Alienage: Emergent Subjects and Spaces for Citizenship". *Globalizations* 2(1): 79–94.
Shiva, Vanadana. 2003. "The Myths of Globalization Exposed: Advancing Toward Living Democracy". In James Gustave Speth (ed.), *Worlds Apart: Globalization and the Environment*. Washington, DC, Covelo, CA and London: Island Press, pp. 141–154.

UNCTAD. 2012. "Chapter 1: Globalization and the Shifting Balance in the World Economy". *Development and Globalization: Facts and Figures.* Available at: http://dgff.unctad.org/chapter1/1.1.html (accessed 10 October 2015).

UNDP. 2009. *Human Development Report 2009: Overcoming Barriers: Human Mobility and Development.* New York: UNDP. Available at: http://hdr.undp.org/sites/default/files/reports/269/hdr_2009_en_complete.pdf (accessed 18 October 2015).

UNDP. 2013. "Fast Facts". Available at: www.undp.org/content/dam/undp/library/corporate/fast-facts/english/FF-Poverty-Reduction.pdf (accessed 10 October 2015).

Weaver, Mary Anne. 2015. "Her Majesty's Jihadists". *New York Times Magazine* (14 April). Available at: www.nytimes.com/2015/04/19/magazine/her-majestys-jihadists.html?hp&action=click&pgtype=Homepage&module=photo-spot-region&region=top-news&WT.nav=top-news (accessed 10 October 2015).

World Values Survey. 1981–2008. Official Aggregate v.20090901, 2009. Madrid: World Values Survey Association, Aggregate File Producer: ASEP/JDS. Available at: www.worldvaluessurvey.org (accessed 10 June 2011).

3 Critical cosmopolitanism as a new paradigm for global learning

Tammy Birk

It is increasingly uncontroversial to argue that higher education should teach *for* global learning, awareness, or understanding. Indeed, as Craig Calhoun has observed, "it is hard in Western academic circles to imagine preferring to be known as parochial" (2002, 89). Inward looking and insular, parochialism is identified with a certain narrowing of thought and discomfort with complexity. Global learning, on the other hand, is granted wide conceptual and moral room, as it is generally understood to be expansive, robust, and ecumenical in its sensibility. For this reason, global learning tends to present itself as an antidote to parochialism.

Even so, it can sometimes feel as if we're caught in a closed critical loop: when pressed for specifics, we often insist on the obvious and self-explanatory value of global teaching and learning. It is, we say simply, good to be global. Larger institutional motives and ambitions for a global curriculum are permitted to be vague. Many of us are encouraged to believe that institutional attention to the global – in mission statements, curricular design, and learning goals – announces a college or university's desire to be simultaneously forward and outward looking. It is not necessary to name the philosophical or pedagogical values underlying our investment in global learning; instead, we believe that it is more important to deploy a language of the "global" because it is practically and rhetorically expected. And, as a result, there is a growing sense among academics that "global" has become the new floating – and, regrettably, empty – signifier in higher education discourse.

It appears as if higher education is demanding a wholesale globalizing of its teaching and learning paradigm in advance of a full critical conversation on the motives and mission for global learning. Because of this, I believe that it is important to introduce a more profitable and nuanced set of questions: what is global learning *for*? What ends should global learning serve? And how do our curricular and pedagogical priorities realize or frustrate the goals we aspire to in the name of global learnings? Rather than allow the rhetoric of the "global" to escape scrutiny or specificity, I am interested in defining – and then advocating for – a particular and invested role for the "global" in higher education. As we will see, it is my contention that critical cosmopolitanism offers the most complex, transformational, and socially relevant framework for pedagogical and curricular transformations in global learning.

Global learning: what is it for? Who does it serve?

There are many possible rationales for foregrounding global learning as an institutional, curricular, or pedagogical priority. Those rationales are not always explicit; in fact, I would argue that they are more likely to be assumed than affirmed in our language. If anything, we tend to emphasize a certain *value* or *utility* for global learning – and, because the global is always a self-evident good, all possible rationales are seen as equivalent and, at times, interchangeable.

Broadly speaking, I argue that there are four predominant rationales for global learning. A *neo-mercantilist* emphasis sees global learning as an extended readying for market participation and vocational success, an *intercultural* emphasis enlists global learning for the cultivation of cross-cultural awareness and competencies, and a *liberal–aesthetic* emphasis claims it for the larger goals of self-enrichment and status improvement. Whatever the perceived benefits or challenges of the neo-mercantilist, intercultural, and liberal–aesthetic rationales for global learning, I do want to insist that they share one significant failing: *they do not understand or promote global learning as a critical citizenship project.* What is missing is a recognition of the larger ethical dimension of global learning as well as its link to the larger responsibilities of citizenship.

The assigned priority to personal and civic engagement, an underscoring of responsibility for others (both proximate and distant), and an explicit concern with social justice all distinguish global learning as a critical citizenship project. Broadly allied with the aims of critical global citizenship education, such global learning is decidedly praxis-oriented. It is also driven less by vocational, cultural, or aesthetic values than an ethical investment in human and ecological flourishing and the promotion of transnational forms of justice.

I contend that it is the *cosmopolitan* emphasis that affirms the value of global learning as a critical citizenship project. It is also the cosmopolitan emphasis that deepens and amplifies the ethical and engaged aims of global learning. It acknowledges the need to prepare students for public life and agency, not merely privatized forms of personal and professional enhancement.

Why advocate the significance of cosmopolitanism? A cosmopolitan, quite literally, belongs to both the cosmos (or larger human community and natural world) and the polis (or the community of smaller scale, usually understood as local). Because of this, cosmopolitanism effectively extends our identity and our identifications beyond the bounds of what is familiar or proximate. If we are looking for the most obvious markers of a cosmopolitan emphasis in teaching and learning, we would do well to look for stated commitments to global citizenship because global citizenship is, by definition, a cosmopolitan aspiration. Cosmopolitanism – as a philosophy and a practice – has always been identified with the larger impetus to global citizenship, whether that citizenship has been understood as a moral enterprise or legal status. We will further complicate this identification later in the chapter, but it is fair to say that cosmopolitanism – like global citizenship – seems to be a legible way of naming the desire for forms of belonging that exceed those provided by the nation state.

With the exception of more popular significations of cosmopolitanism that equate it with the performance of bourgeois taste and custom, cosmopolitanism is an ethical perspective.[1] Its core ethic requires us to "think and act with strong concern for all humanity" (Calhoun 2008, 107); at its most robust, the ethic does not allow us to exclude any person from moral concern. Some might argue that such a charge is necessary because most people – as well as liberalism itself – have a tendency to "look after the rights of the local branch of the species" (Appiah 1998, 93). Cosmopolitanism suggests that we have obligations and commitments that are not exclusively territorial, and, as such, it introduces new relational responsibilities, especially between people who do not share the same local group loyalties and identities.

That said, many proponents of global learning privilege competing sources of value: neo-mercantile, intercultural, or liberal–aesthetic rationales. But those rationales bracket the demands of critical citizenship and public engagement. They also ignore or marginalize the complex ethical questions that are raised by global inquiry, and, as a result, higher education forfeits an opportunity to serve the public good and demonstrate its broader social benefits, especially those benefits that exist beyond those that are individual and economic. And, because higher education itself is a public good, I believe that it is particularly well suited and well positioned to affirm cosmopolitan priorities in its mission and curricular work.

Cosmopolitanism modified: critical cosmopolitanism

We need to explain why it is that cosmopolitan teaching and learning best delivers on the promise of global learning, but we also need to explain why it is important that we name that teaching and learning as critically – rather than traditionally or culturally – cosmopolitan. The modifier "critical" is not a trivial one. If we are going to build a model of teaching and learning that avoids the pitfalls of false universalism, the erasure of particularity, and the reduction of cosmopolitanism to a lifestyle option, then we must clarify why our cosmopolitan framework must be a critical one.

Traditional cosmopolitanism, or universal and unmodified cosmopolitanism, is troubled by a number of shortcomings. As suggested by its name, it tends to endorse a false and dangerous universalism that enshrines an abstract idea of humanity. This abstract idea of humanity ignores or minimizes real difference, particularity, and localism. Traditional cosmopolitanism also has a history of collusion with Western and imperial projects that mistake a Euro-American "generic and genderless" citizen as a normative one (Spyra 2006). Finally, traditional cosmopolitanism can become a cover for an unobserved and elitist world-view, largely because traditional cosmopolitan thought is generally generated from above, the Global North, and/or metropolitan centres.

There are a different set of limitations that attach to what is called cultural cosmopolitanism, or the more popular signification of cosmopolitanism. Cultural cosmopolitanism is rooted in an enthusiastic recognition of cultural difference and an appetite for divergent aesthetic and cultural experiences (Hannerz 1992; Urry 1995). Indeed, the ideal cultural cosmopolitan figure is a curious, open, and reflective subject that delights in and desires to consume difference. Unfortunately, the easy face of cultural cosmopolitanism is consumption and travel – and, for the most part, the more exoticized the experience, the better. When cosmopolitism is reduced in this way – as when it is aligned with neo-liberal and late capital agendas – the political and ethical charge of modern citizenship is eviscerated.

A small but growing number of thinkers – among them, Paul Rabinow, Walter Mignolo, Gerard Delanty, and Michael Bérubé – have identified critical cosmopolitanism as the most promising modification of cosmopolitanism, as it sustains the ethical charge of the cosmopolitan project without erasing particularity, difference, and collective forms of local attachment. In fact, Paul Rabinow insists that critical cosmopolitanism is marked by a pronounced ethical orientation, or intense investment in ethical inquiry and action. The critical cosmopolitan foregrounds these investments in a transformative political project – an "alternative to territorial politics and consciousness" (Turner 2002, 46) – but grounds their ethical obligations in what Bruce Robbins calls an "ethics of the everyday" rather than an abstract and falsely universalizing conception of common humanity.

More specifically, I argue that critical cosmopolitanism is an ethic and a practice that challenges binary thinking; thinks the local and the global relationally; resists abstract universal truths about human or global community; insists on a strong and broad ethical concern for the other that does not disregard difference; complicates and decolonizes ways of thinking about social identity and power; and challenges the uncritical commodification of cultural difference. Obviously, these tenets are expansive and complex; each is worthy of extended investigation. Here, I will outline them with attention to both substance and concision.

As noted above, critical cosmopolitanism *challenges the self-evidence of dualistic or binary thinking*, particularly hardened oppositions between the global and the local as well as the self and the other. Andrew Sayer (1991, 285) reminds us of the way in which the powerful "illusion of binary opposition" sees its dualities as fixed and mutually exclusive. In such an "illusion", separation and difference are overemphasized, and the assumption is that the binary terms are inherently contradictory. Some dualities may, in fact, be antonymic, but Sayer suggests that many more seemingly binary oppositions are better understood as continua rather than dichotomies (ibid.). In other words, the terms of a binary are more likely to *presuppose* or *mutually constitute* one another, rather than categorically oppose one another. Thus, if critical cosmopolitanism can help us see binary opposition as inclusive rather than exclusive, we are more likely to represent dualities – like global and local or self and other – as more pliable and less stable than is generally believed.

Because it resists the oversimplification of binary thinking, critical cosmopolitanism *mediates, or reads back and forth, between the global and the local.* Rather than imagine the global and local "as separate objects which impact one another, like billiard balls" (Cox 2005, 181), critical cosmopolitanism sees them as conceptual fields – and socio-spatial categories – that are more inclusive and mutually constituting. Such a reimagining of the relationship between the global and local is one of the key paradigms of critical cosmopolitan teaching and learning, and we will speak of it at greater length in the next section.

Critical cosmopolitanism also resists the tendency to totalize and arrogate universal values for highly particular ends. Rather than assume that what it means to be human is a single, legible, and unchanging thing, critical cosmopolitanism is *self-critical and problematizing in its relationship to universal truths* – whether about humanity or globality. Critical cosmopolitanism debunks ideologies of an inherent human essence, an ahistorical human nature, and a self-determining individual subject.

Paul Rabinow argues that critical cosmopolitanism is "highly attentive to (and respectful of) difference, but is also wary of the tendency to essentialize difference" (1986, 258). Unlike more traditional forms of cosmopolitanism, critical cosmopolitan discourse takes seriously the material and psychic implications of difference. But, rather than anchoring difference in identity distinctions and hierarchies, critical cosmopolitan *thinks difference non-hierarchically* and beyond conventional taxonomies of personhood. In other words, critical cosmopolitanism resists the temptation to fetishize difference, just as it rejects the deployment of difference as a means for sorting the world into hard binary oppositions. Attention to difference – or particularity – need not inspire rigid, dualistic thinking. It also need not preclude a consideration of the ways in which particularity is crossed – and, to a greater or lesser degree, shaped – by its complex encounter with others. Critical cosmopolitanism is suspicious of any ethic that asks us to ignore human particularity and relationality.

Critical cosmopolitanism also asks us to *decolonize the way that we see the world*, the way that we neatly divide into us versus them, here versus there. In fact, learners in the Global North primarily and often encounter "global others" through forms of representation that reinforce colonial legacies (Willinsky 2000). These legacies assume that "global others" constantly need help, rescue, or uplift. As a result, a powerful "helping imperative" typically emerges in educational practice; this "imperative" aligns neatly with institutional calls for students to "make a difference" in the lives of unfortunate others and it is frequently "indebted to the rhetoric and politics of pity and benevolence" (Jefferess 2014, 39). This same "helping imperative" can be fed by what Roger Simon calls the "Too Bad, So Sad" syndrome, a psychology in which learners end up feeling good about feeling bad because the bad feelings "confirm their own humanitarian character" (2013, 133). Critical cosmopolitanism recognizes and challenges how learners in the Global North are still implicated in a way of thinking about the other that presupposes the pathetic subsistence of the other as well as the need for their own benevolent leadership.

Because cosmopolitanism, like identity, is best understood as plural, critical cosmopolitans have also stressed the need to "expand cosmopolitanism beyond its usual association with the West, metropolis, and the intellectual" (Anderson 1998, 273). Unlike traditional cosmopolitanism, which has reified its Western intellectual heritage, critical cosmopolitanism has *sought out alternative histories of cosmopolitan thought and practice*. This has allowed "non-European, non-elitist, and ineligible versions" (Robbins 1999, 156) of cosmopolitanism to circulate more widely and emerge from the peripheries of global centres of power and wealth rather than the metropolitan core.

Perhaps more consistently than any other critic, Walter Mignolo has urged critical cosmopolitanism to "reconceive cosmopolitanism from the perspective of coloniality" (2000, 723). Rather than accede to a cosmopolitan project that is driven by "global design", or the "will to control and homogenize", Mignolo promotes a critical cosmopolitan project that emanates from coloniality, or the exterior of modernity. Identified with "border thinking" and "border epistemologies", such a critical cosmopolitan project decolonizes the imperial idea of humanity that the West has offered as a basis for universality. It also uncouples itself effectively from transcendent global designs – what others might call "cosmopolitanism-from-above" – and insists instead on a critical and dialogic encounter with those who have been "othered" by the discourses of modernity. For this reason, critical cosmopolitanism is an important antidote to traditional cosmopolitan projects that reinforce the global or universal as the experience of the paradigmatic Western subject.

Finally, critical cosmopolitanism is *wary of popular tendencies to frame cosmopolitanism as a "lifestyle option"*. It is deeply sceptical of the ways in which cosmopolitan subjectivity can be repurposed as "the next significant new brand" (Binnie 2004, 129). When cosmopolitan knowledge is chiefly enlisted in the service of self-marketing and self-advancement, cosmopolitan subjectivity becomes little more than social performance. At the same time, critical cosmopolitanism rejects commercial encounters with cultural difference because they work to "largely neutralize" otherness, especially when it "is readily made into an item for sale" (Cheetham 2007, 4). Given that neutralization works to effectively contain the "strange" or "different", it promotes the consumption of the cultural other without complication or engagement.[2]

In sum, critical cosmopolitanism breaks with binaries, challenges hierarchies, acknowledges and complicates difference, and "tries to break with [cosmopolitanism's] history of privilege and recuperate it for more critical uses" (Spyra 2006, 6). Thus, I argue that it is the most productive and promising of cosmopolitan frameworks for global learning. The remainder of this chapter will trace a series of conceptual paradigms and sensibilities that I believe are characteristic of – and central to – a critical cosmopolitan approach to both teaching and learning.

Critical cosmopolitan teaching and learning: key paradigms

As I define it, a paradigm is a critical and theoretical architecture for intellectual work. In other words, these ideas and practices shape what we teach and how we teach it, what we learn, and how we learn it. More fundamentally, these paradigms extend to the learning objectives, modes of inquiry, and organizing questions of an educational practice.

I contend that critical cosmopolitan teaching and learning is marked by three key conceptual paradigms: *a rethinking of the global and local as mutually constitutive and relational, an enlarged and reinvigorated conception of citizenship*, and *a complex engagement with otherness*.

I recognize that these three individual paradigms play an important and highly visible role in many other pedagogical projects, so I am not claiming that they are unique to critical cosmopolitan models of teaching and learning. What I find most compelling about critical cosmopolitan teaching and learning is that it integrates these frameworks – and later, I will argue, a set of sensibilities – into a more progressive model for global learning.

Rethinking the local and global as mutually constitutive and relational

We have already noted that it has become commonplace to set the local and global in opposition to one another. Hopelessly polarized and antagonistic, the two terms are expected to repudiate one another in theory and practice. Moreover, we assume that the superiority of one term subordinates the other. More pointedly, if we prioritize the global, we demote the local. Often enough, the stated worry is that attention to the global will diminish our ability to identify with – and tend to – the concerns of the local. The global, we are told, will both subsume and devalue very immediate, very proximate needs and realities.

While we have noted the way that a more traditional – and unselfconscious – cosmopolitanism can be falsely universalizing and imperial in outlook, critical cosmopolitanism is invested in thinking the local and the global relationally. In other words, it is interested in imagining a more dialogic and dynamic relationship between the local and the global. For this reason, critical cosmopolitan teaching and learning works to complicate – and, ideally, unseat – the binary logic that demands that we rigidly oppose the local and the global.

A call for global learning that does not immediately prioritize its relationship to the global may seem counter-intuitive. Many educators infer that cosmopolitan education must be entirely dedicated to the promotion of global – rather than local or national – forms of inquiry and citizenship practice. Such a reading of cosmopolitanism assumes the clear ascendancy of global categories and frames of reference, whereas a more critical cosmopolitan framework – again, wary of the potential for false universality – stresses that it may be wiser to see "the global [as] decisive without necessarily dominating all the time" (Gunesch 2004, 256). Because critical cosmopolitan teaching and learning insists on seeing the global and the local in relational terms, and because it underscores the ways that the global and the local implicate and inform one another, critical cosmopolitan pedagogy refuses to idealize and romanticize the global. And this, I believe, is a good thing. "A transcendent understanding of the global – common enough in traditional forms of global education and traditional cosmopolitan discourse – is often every bit as fetishistic in its approach to the global as more romantic versions of localism are infatuated with the local" (Birk 2014, 13). Critical cosmopolitanism consistently sees the global and the local as reciprocal and mutually constitutive realities.

I have also previously argued that while many pedagogies attend to the global repercussions of local events – as well as the local effects of global happenings – "it is imperative to move beyond considerations of mutual influences to think about how various scales of place actually *define* and *actuate* one another" (ibid.). This is one of the most significant advantages of a critical cosmopolitan language, especially when we are characterizing a preferred framework for global learning. Critical cosmopolitan discourse refuses to define the "global" as the other of the local. It foregrounds the fact that the local and the global are internally related. It recognizes the intricate interactions between local and global spaces and populations. It destabilizes the matter-of-factness of the binary. Critical cosmopolitan teaching and learning invites students to imagine new identifications, questions, and forms of representation for the space that emerges "in-between" the conventional arenas of the global and the local. And, in so doing, critical cosmopolitan pedagogy challenges the self-evidence of dualistic thinking about place as well as the seemingly "natural" relationship between identity and location.

An enlarged and reinvigorated conception of citizenship

Critical cosmopolitan pedagogy also is marked by an *enlarged and invigorated conception of citizenship*. Rather than define citizenship entirely as a legal status that is conferred on persons who are territorially bound, critical cosmopolitan teaching and learning begins by understanding citizenship as an active practice. This does not negate the legal dimensions of citizenship, but it does acknowledge that a growing number of people who engage in public work across national and cultural differences see that work as critical citizenship practice. More than an occasional and formal exercise in political decision making (e.g. voting), critical cosmopolitan teaching and learning works to expand our understanding of citizenship to include this "direct involvement in public life, not spectatorship" (Cogan 2000, 13).

It is also true that critical cosmopolitan pedagogies call into question orthodox thinking about citizenship practice and work to "problematize the notion of citizenship itself" (Lapayese 2003, 497). Rather than accede to more limited and quiescent understandings of citizenship, critical cosmopolitanism inspires students to visualize new modes of being and doing for twenty-first century civic belonging. In this way, critical cosmopolitan teaching and learning refuses the "passive contemplation of citizenship", just as it challenges the popular notion that citizenship is "a devitalized and static identity" (Birk 2014, 15).

Such pedagogy introduces the possibility that the "good" citizen might be less compliant and docile than is often supposed. In fact, the more effective citizen may be better understood as protesting or dissident. The person who "both critiques and affirms human rights" (Maira 2004, 222) or successfully "contests the prevailing arrangements of power" (Sparks 1997, 83) may enact a more vigorous, robust citizenship. For this reason, critical cosmopolitanism teaching and learning recognizes the necessity of productive antagonisms, counter-discourses (and counter-publics), and the interrogation of notions of citizenship that encourage accommodation rather than deliberation and dissent.

Generally speaking, I believe that higher education is interested in the language of global citizenship for an important reason. This vocabulary connects global learning to an ethical and engaged set of educational aims. When we purposefully prepare students for global citizenship, higher education appears to reject a reductively neo-mercantilist, internationalist, or liberal–aesthetic mission. And when we claim the civic role of higher education, we reinforce the enduring importance of the public interest. While the composition of the global citizen remains open to evolution, the language of global citizenship enables us to identify a desire for attachments and obligations that move beyond the nation state.

At the same time, I want to suggest that we make an even more forceful move: the exploration of a model of citizenship identity and practice that includes a commitment to global citizenship but also affirms other forms of civic belonging. What might be gained by thinking citizenship from a critical cosmopolitan perspective?

In the classroom, critical cosmopolitan citizenship introduces new questions, new subjectivities, and the possibility of new coalitions. It allows for the validity of multiple and overlapping allegiances and attachments as well as sites of political and social responsibility. Unfortunately, when we imagine global citizenship as the "other" to local and more immediate forms of civic belonging, we feed a binary understanding of civic identity and practice that inhibits our ability to maintain these multiple sites of political responsibility. And the truth is that many of us feel increasingly entrenched in various (local, sub-state, national, transnational) communities – both self- and culturally determined. We know that national allegiance no longer monopolizes civic attachment and obligation. We also know that many people – especially young people – affirm scale and allegiance as both flexible and transient, as evidenced by Bramlett's findings in this collection (see Chapter 13).

So how do we express an understanding of citizenship that is more multidimensional, mobile, and evolving? I am not sure that the notion of global citizenship adequately captures the complex and heterogeneous nature of contemporary citizenship, for too often global citizenship is positioned as an alternative or more expansive form of civic identification than local or national ties. Critical cosmopolitanism, in contrast, affirms the multiplicity and changeability of contemporary citizenship. And, because we can acknowledge that "identity is complex and multiple", we must also "allow for multi-placed, multi-scaled and multilayered forms of [civic] identification" (Molz 2005, 520). We must allow for a civic belonging that breaks with traditional and historically rigid boundaries.

Critical cosmopolitan citizenship allows students to own simultaneous and diverse forms of civic belonging and responsibility. It also encourages students to reject any understanding of citizenship that is predicated on a false choice between local, regional, or national identifications and global or transnational commitments. For these reasons, I believe that a critical cosmopolitan – rather than, strictly speaking, "global" or "local" – model of citizenship offers an especially useful and robust model of civic engagement for critical pedagogical work. Because we can recognize the interplay between the global and the local, we are capable of seeing public participation as something that impacts multiple socio-spatial locations.

A complex engagement with otherness

Questions about the constitution of self and other, or the relationship between inclusive and exclusive forms of identity and belonging, drive critical cosmopolitan teaching and learning. We might begin by asking: how do we work through the question of the other? Who is the other to us? And what role does the other play in defining the self? The questions we ask are as important as the answers we discern.

I argue that critical cosmopolitan teaching and learning is complexly engaged with otherness for a number of reasons. But first we must grapple with the many ways that we can define the "other", because the definitions are formative and critically vital. The term "others" can function as a productive shorthand for other people: other people who have lives and bodies that exist independently of our perception of them. An "other", in contrast, may be an ego's phantasmatic fantasy of a person, a projection that does not allow the other to live outside the ego, a projection that has little to do with the other's lived life. The "other" can also be understood in a more sociological sense if we define it as "an abjected effect of a 'power' that works through exclusion, hierarchy, and projection" (Dikecs *et al.* 2009, 7). Otherness, on the hand, is an even larger and conceptually complex matter, because otherness – the fact of radical difference or alterity – constitutes a major challenge to the self and its desire to see the world as an extension of itself.

Embodying that challenge, the stranger stands as an emblematic figure of an unassimilable otherness. Indeed, the stranger personifies otherness. The stranger is the subject that the self cannot recognize. The stranger is the other that the self cannot comprehend with the frameworks that it has been given. The stranger, much like the conceptual frame of the "global", exists elsewhere, in the space where we are not. Yet cosmopolitanism is a "deliberate attempt to make space for the stranger" (Ossewaarde 2007, 384), a stranger that traditionally has been characterized as a figure of civic and moral exclusion. As a result, critical cosmopolitan teaching and learning challenges the reactive boundary-making that shapes both citizenship and identity.

Such teaching and learning might examine the social and psychic processes of exclusion and inclusion that allow us to postulate otherness in the first place. It might also consider what an attentiveness to otherness might mean for critical educational practice. It is fair to ask: should critical cosmopolitan teaching and learning encourage empathic identifications with the stranger?[3] Should it insist on compassion for the suffering other? Or is it more important to acknowledge strangeness within the self as a way of unsettling the self/other binary in the first place?[4] What is at stake when we think together about our relationship to both otherness and responsibility, an intersection that Jacques Derrida has insisted is the site of ethicality itself?

Cultural cosmopolitanism has staked out claims to a more attentive and expansive encounter with otherness, but it neglects the ethical complexity of that encounter. In contrast, critical cosmopolitanism is both aware of and concerned about the tendency to appropriate or recreate the other in the image of the self.[5] Indeed, a full encounter with otherness might not only be estranging, it might also prove "acutely difficult", for there is frequently "real discomfort" in the process of coming to know difference (Heilman 2006, 196). Such discomfort is rarely mentioned in cultural cosmopolitan accounts of culturally diverse encounters, as the constitutional openness of the cosmopolitan is believed to protect her from uneasiness and anxiety. But discomfort and anxiety tend to manifest when we challenge the borders and boundaries that enclose, as well as differentiate, one's identity. Put another way, we only defend against that which makes us anxious. It is a way of managing conflict, a way of managing a disturbance – in this case, the disturbance between what is properly inside and outside. And critical cosmopolitan learning is working to unsettle another old and false binary: the opposition of the self and other.

If educators and students could trouble this self/other binary – a binary that allows for no relationality or learning *from* the other – opportunities for meaningful solidarity might become possible. Not a solidarity based on identicality, but a solidarity based on the shared experience of precarity as well as the "shared feeling for dignity in the face of the inevitable vulnerability of existence" (Edkins 2003, 257). In the process, we see a material, situated, and multidimensional other, and we see our own strangeness, permeability, and impact.

Critical cosmopolitan teaching and learning: key sensibilities

Cosmopolitanism is a paradigm – a way of making meaning – but it is also a sensibility. For my purposes, a sensibility is a disposition, an outlook, and an orientation. Cosmopolitanism reaches into our positioning and perceptions, and this is another reason to recommend it as an approach to global learning: it doesn't just engage a student cognitively, it also invites a student to explore and take seriously the questions that animate subjectivity or personhood.

There are three significant dispositional goals, or sensibilities, that I would argue characterize the work of critical cosmopolitan teaching and learning: *self-reflexivity, a sense of cosmopolitan responsibility,* and *a willingness to challenge cynicism and complacency.*

Self-reflexivity

Perhaps the attribute that is most clearly foundational to a critical cosmopolitan orientation is *self-reflexivity*, or the capacity to critically examine and reflect upon one's habits of thought and feeling. Arguing that cosmopolitanism is a "disposition characterized by a reflexive relation to one's identity [as well as] a refusal to accept the given situations in which one finds oneself" (Delanty 2006, 45), Gerald Delanty explicitly links self-reflexivity to a larger ability to interrogate one's habits and convention. In so doing, Delanty draws attention to one significant requirement of self-reflexive thinking: we must be able sustain some intellectual and emotional distance from the "naturalness and inevitability that surrounds our own practices" (Nussbaum 1997, 55). This is, without doubt, a difficult psychological task, as self-reflexivity not only asks us to observe our habits and values in ways that are defamiliarizing, but also asks us to evaluate the unexamined moral assumptions that guide our thinking and feeling.

Self-reflexivity bears a structural resemblance to perspectval consciousness, an oft-cited perceptual goal for global learning. Perspectival consciousness, like self-reflexivity, relies on the willingness of the individual to self-interrogate and, when necessary, "doubt the unqualified goodness of one's own ways" (Nussbaum 1997, 83). Even so, critical cosmopolitan teaching and learning must be wary of ignoring the role that power and social location play in shaping one's perspectival consciousness (Merryfield 2001, 280). Material or political privilege can deter a deeper understanding of non-dominant or de-colonial world-views. Such privilege can generate powerful – and often unconscious – forms of resistance to critical cosmopolitan learning that challenges the partiality of perspective. There can also be an unacknowledged class dimension to self-reflexivity. The task of critical self-reflection may be differently encouraged and sanctioned for those with more social and cultural capital.

It is also very important to define self-reflexivity in ways that mobilize its progressive potential as well as its ability to catalyze transformative thought and action. Critical pedagogies that appear to be entirely satisfied with the dispositional goal of self-reflexivity – often described as "awareness raising" – can lose an opportunity to harness the hard work of self-interrogation for social change. In other words, while it is crucial to open pedagogical space for self-inquiry and introspection, it is essential that we do not validate learning that externalizes the world as a problem for the self to accept or decline. One does not live outside of culture, history, or social conditions. And critical cosmopolitan teaching and learning insists that it is neither possible nor desirable to examine the self apart from the social and historical conditions of its emergence (Butler 2005, 7).

A sense of cosmopolitan responsibility

Another defining feature of critical cosmopolitan teaching and learning is an enlarged understanding of *cosmopolitan responsibility*. As I see it, critical cosmopolitan pedagogy does not prescribe certain personal or social responsibilities, but it does take seriously the notion that people have them.[5] It also takes seriously the notion that persons might have positive obligations – in other words, a responsibility to respond to others in distress – even if they believe that they have not contributed to the reason for the distress.

Critical cosmopolitan teaching and learning emphasize responsibility as something that people extend to one another because our lives interdepend and are implicated in one another; responsibility is not something that relies on the goodwill of some to recognize the suffering of others. This is too unidirectional, too voluntary, and often too paternalistic in its assumption about the need for rescue rather than care. Doreen Massey, a prominent cultural geographer, explains it this way: "Responsibility in some accounts can be read in terms of a one-way-ness which itself arrogates unto the 'responsible' figure the superiority of a position of power. What is perhaps crucial is the more complex issue of *implication*; it is this which thinking relationally (the mutual constitution of the global and the local) can bring to the fore" (2005, 194; italics added). Here Massey reminds us of the fact that the spatial scales of near and far are constitutively related, mutually implicated, and co-responsible for one another. Thus, the "one-way-ness" that structures many understandings of responsibility – especially when it is coupled with the insistent rhetoric of rescue – works to prop asymmetries of power, as well as prevent people from choosing to act in the name of a relational ethic.

This compels us to resist reading responsibility as a form of humanitarian benevolence "in which our privilege, and the social conditions of that privilege, remain invisible and continue to be reinforced" (Jefferess 2014, 40). Such an understanding of obligation not only reinforces old hierarchies of power and privilege, it also elides substantive material analysis. It ignores the necessity for a complex conversation about the histories and forms of structural inequality that create the endless need – or perception of endless need – in the first place. In fact, if educators are not careful about the way that they rely upon a popular discourse of responsibility, it is possible for global learning to encourage relatively privileged people to "ignore material relations of global power" (ibid, 34) and see themselves as uncomplicated change agents. Urged to get involved, volunteer, make a difference, or "be the change", people of privilege can come to believe that responsibility demands short-term assistance without the need for mutual learning or a deeper understanding of the situation that they feel they must help fix.

As critical cosmopolitan education foregrounds significant questions about a heightened care for the world, it is also crucial that we resist focusing cosmopolitan responsibility on the exclusive care of human persons. In fact, a growing number of cosmopolitan thinkers are eager to extend ethical accountability to the "world" in the most expansive sense of the word. And I would agree that a more robust sense of cosmopolitan responsibility would include concern for non-human animals, the natural environment, and future generations.

A willingness to challenge cynicism and complacency

Finally, I argue that critical cosmopolitan teaching and learning must reckon with the many ways that *cynicism* undercuts the ability of educators and students to entertain cosmopolitan questions and commitments in the first place. Refusing belief in the virtue and efficacy of action, cynicism stands as a powerful obstruction to the praxis-oriented goals of critical cosmopolitan teaching and learning.

One of the best understandings of cynicism affirms that it is, in fact, a "condition of disillusion", or an unspecific "antagonism toward the world" that simultaneously rejects all efforts to improve it (Bewes 1997, 1). Cynicism encourages a person to retreat into solitude and interiority rather than engage with the world. Because this is true, one of the most visible hallmarks of the modern cynic is her or his mistrust of popular efforts to affect meaningful social transformation. Convinced of the inflexibility of dominant political structures and institutions, the modern cynic "doubts the possibility of collective action or social change" (Mazella 2007, 4). However, it is also true that the modern cynic tends to question the viability of political agency more generally. Such scepticism about the ability of individuals or groups to impact the social conditions in which they find themselves justifies a withdrawal of interest in public and political life.

I am not suggesting that ideal critical cosmopolitan teaching and learning is found in the absolute absence of cynicism. Instead, I believe that successful critical cosmopolitan pedagogy will seek to blunt the impact of routine forms of cynicism, and, in so doing, increase the likelihood that students will begin to see themselves as viable historical and political actors. Seeking to eradicate cynicism in the pedagogical situation is excessively directive, especially if we choose to understand cynicism as a complex defensive formation rather than a straightforward exercise in obstructionism. And some of the cynic's disillusion is, indeed, defensive. It is understandable that the self would feel threatened and made anxious by enlarged commitments to the world outside itself. As I see it, cynicism wants to guard us against the difficulties and risk of action.

Modern cynicism represents a sharp challenge to critical cosmopolitan teaching and learning. In so far as it distrusts and disbelieves in the possibilities of political change, it inhibits people from a deeper and more complex understanding of their own agency. In so far as it doubts the feasibility of large-scale social transformations, it disallows higher education from shaping a decisive response to the social needs of the moment. In so far as it encourages the individual to embrace privatized notions of responsibility, it deters her from exploring more collective forms of mutual obligation and solidarity.

Finally and most importantly, I argue that we need to see critical cosmopolitan teaching and learning as open – and not hostile – to the future. The cynic, we are told, is someone who is prematurely disappointed in the future. The cynic shuts down the possibility of future change or future good. Higher education needs to offer learning that protects the right of both students and educators to work for futures that do not inevitably disappoint. We deserve to work for futures that are both meaningful and open-ended. Critical cosmopolitan teaching and learning is – and must be – hopeful about our continued capacity for personal and social transformation as well as global learning that is aspirational and utopian in spirit.

Notes

1 Even more accurately, Martha Nussbaum calls cosmopolitanism an "ethos", as it fundamentally organizes a person's values and outlook.
2 Critical cosmopolitanism also acknowledges that "diversity can be packaged for consumer tastes" and, as a result, "most people claim only the familiar parts of what diversity has on offer" (Calhoun 2002, 104).
3 Dominick LaCapra has suggested that we seek what he calls empathic unsettlement, a willingness to "be responsive to the traumatic experience of others" (2013, 41), at the same time that we insist on an empathy that "resists full identification with, and appropriation of, the experience of the other" (ibid., 79). If we "recognize that another's loss is not identical to [our] own loss", LaCapra believes that we open room for a fuller and more honest encounter with the alterity of the other (ibid.).
4 It is also important for a critical cosmopolitan pedagogical practice to acknowledge the many ways in which we are deeply strange to ourselves (Robbins 1999). For it is not only the other that eludes our understanding, it is also the self.
5 There is the familiar assumption that talk of responsibility compels responsibility, so some educators are hesitant to play any role in generating ethical obligation for others. Of course, there is a measure of legitimate concern here, as a more directive form of social justice pedagogy does "risk becoming a form of rhetoric, a form of persuasion that presumes that those who are subject to it do not already know what they need to act morally" (Todd 2003, 7). This, however, is not representative of a critical cosmopolitan relationship to ethicality or responsibility.

References

Anderson, Amanda. 1998. "Cosmopolitanism, Universalism, and the Divided Legacies of Modernity". In Social Text Collective, Pheng Cheah, and Bruce Robbins (eds), *Cosmopolitics: Thinking and Feeling beyond the Nation*. Minneapolis. MN: University of Minnesota Press, pp. 265–289.

Appiah, Kwame Anthony. 1998. "Cosmopolitan Patriots". In Social Text Collective, Pheng Cheah, and Bruce Robbins (eds), *Cosmopolitics: Thinking and Feeling beyond the Nation*. Minneapolis, MN: University of Minnesota Press, pp. 91–113.

Appiah, Kwame Anthony. 2006. *Cosmopolitanism: Ethics in a World of Strangers*. New York: Norton.

Bewes, Timothy. 1997. *Cynicism and Postmodernity*. New York: Verso.

Binnie, Jon. 2004. *The Globalization of Sexuality*. London: Sage.

Birk, Tammy. 2014. "Critical Cosmopolitan Teaching and Learning: A New Answer to the Global Imperative". *Diversity and Democracy. AACU*: 12–15.

Butler, Judith. 2005. *Giving an Account of Oneself*. New York: Fordham Press.

Calhoun, Craig. 2002. "The Class Consciousness of Frequent Travellers: Towards a Critique of Actually Existing Cosmopolitanism". In Steven Vertovec and Robin Cohen (eds), *Conceiving Cosmopolitanism: Theory, Context, and Practice*. Oxford: Oxford University Press, pp. 86–109.

Calhoun, Craig. 2008. "Cosmopolitanism and the Modern Social Imaginary". *Daedalus* 137(3): 105–114.

Cheetham, Mark. 2007. "Alienated Cosmopolitans". *The Walrus*. Available at: www.walrusmagazine.com/articles/2007.05-cosmopolitanism (accessed 20 July 2015).

Cogan, John and Ray Derricott. 2000. *Citizenship for the 21st Century: An International Perspective on Education*. London: Kogan Page.

Cook, Nancy. 2014. "'I'm Here to Help': Development Workers, the Politics of Benevolence, and Critical Literacy". In Vanessa de Oliveira Andreotti and Lynn Mario T. M. de Souza (eds), *Postcolonial Perspectives on Global Citizenship Education*. London: Routledge, pp. 124–139.

Cox, Kevin. 2005. "Local: Global". In Ron Cloke and Ron Johnston (eds), *Spaces of Geographical Thought: Deconstructing Human Geography's Binaries*. London: Sage, pp. 173–198.

Delanty, Gerard. 2006. "Cosmopolitan Citizenship". In Judith Blau and Keri Iyall Smith (eds), *Public Sociologies Reader*. Lanham, MD: Rowman & Littlefield, pp. 37–50.

Dikecs, Mustafa, Clark, Nigel, and Barnett, Clive. 2009. "Extending Hospitality: Giving Space, Taking Time". *Paragraph* 32(1). Edinburgh: Edinburgh University Press, pp. 1–14.

Edkins, Jenny. 2003. "Humanitarianism, Humanity, Human". *Journal of Human Rights* 2(2): 253–258.

Gunesch, Konrad. 2004. "Education for Cosmopolitanism? Cosmopolitanism as a Personal Cultural Identity Model for and Within International Education". *Journal of Research in International Education* 3(3): 251–257.

Hannerz, Ulf. 1992. "Cosmopolitans and Locals in World Cultures". In Mike Featherstone (ed.), *Global Culture: Nationalism, Globalization, and Modernity*. London: Sage, pp. 237–251.

Heilman, Elizabeth. 2006. "Critical, Liberal, and Poststructural Challenges for Global Education". In Avner Segall, Elizabeth Heilman, and Cleo Cherryholmes (eds),

Social Studies – The Next Generation: Re-searching in the Postmodern. New York: Peter Lang, pp. 189–208.

Jefferess, David. 2014. "Unsettling Cosmopolitanism: Global Citizenship and the Cultural Politics of Benevolence". In Vanessa de Oliveira Andreotti and Lynn Mario T. M. de Souza (eds), *Postcolonial Perspectives on Global Citizenship Education*. London: Routledge, pp. 27–45.

LaCapra, Dominick. 2013. *Writing History, Writing Trauma*. Baltimore, MD: Johns Hopkins University Press.

Lamy, Steven L. 1990. "Global Education: A Conflict of Images". In Kenneth Tye (ed.), *Global Education: From Thought to Action*. Alexandria, VA: Association for Supervision and Curriculum Development, pp. 49–63.

Lapayese, Yvette. 2003. "Toward a Critical Global Citizenship Education". *Comparative Education Review* 47(4): 493–501.

Maira, Sunaina. 2004. "Imperial Feelings: Youth Culture, Citizenship, and Globalization". In Marcelo Suarez-Orozco and Desiree Baolian Qin-Hilliard (eds), *Globalization: Culture and Education in the New Millennium*. Berkeley, CA: University of California Press, pp. 203–234.

Massey, Doreen. 2005. *For Space*. London: Sage Publications.

Mazella, David. 2007. *The Making of Modern Cynicism*. Charlottesville, VA: University of Virginia Press.

Merryfield, Merry. 2001. "Decolonizing the Mind for World-Centered Global Education". In E. Wayne Ross (ed.), *The Social Studies Curriculum: Purposes, Problems, and Possibilities*. Albany, NY: SUNY Press, pp. 277–290.

Mignolo, Walter. 2000. "The Many Faces of Cosmopolis: Border Thinking and Critical Cosmopolitanism". *Public Culture* 12(3): 721–748.

Molz, Jennie Germann. 2005. "Getting a 'Flexible Eye': Round-the-World Travel and Scales of Cosmopolitan Citizenship". *Citizenship Studies* 9(5): 517–531.

Nussbaum, Martha. 1997. *Cultivating Humanity: A Classical Defense of Reform in Liberal Education*. Cambridge, MA: Harvard University Press.

Ossewaarde, Marinus. 2007. "Cosmopolitanism and the Society of Strangers". *Current Sociology* 55(3): 367–388.

Parker, Walter and Katharyne Mitchell. 2005. "I Pledge Allegiance To … Flexible Citizenship and Shifting Scales of Belonging". *Research on Immigration and Integration in the Metropolis: Working Paper Series*. Vancouver: Vancouver Centre.

Rabinow, Paul. 1986. "Representations are Social Facts: Modernity and Post-Modernity in Anthropology". In James Clifford and George Marcus (eds), *Writing Culture: The Poetics and Politics of Ethnography*. Berkeley, CA: University of California Press, pp. 234–261.

Robbins, Bruce. 1998. "Comparative Cosmopolitanisms". In Social Text Collective, Pheng Cheah, and Bruce Robbins (eds), *Cosmopolitics: Thinking and Feeling beyond the Nation*. Minneapolis. MN: University of Minnesota Press, pp. 246–264.

Robbins, Bruce. *Feeling Global: Internationalism in Distress*. 1999. New York: New York University Press.

Sayer, Andrew. 1991. "Behind the Locality Debate: Deconstructing Geography's Dualisms". *Environment and Planning A* 23: 283–308.

Simon, Roger. 2013. "Towards a Hopeful Practice of Worrying: The Problematics of Listening and the Educative Responsibilities of Canada's Truth and Reconciliation Commission". In Jennifer Henderson and Pauline Wakeham (eds), *Reconciling*

Canada: Critical Perspectives on the Culture of Redress. Toronto: University of Toronto Press, pp. 129–142.

Sparks, Holloway. 1997. "Dissident Citizenship: Democratic Theory, Political Courage, and Activist Women". *Hypatia* 12(4): 74–110.

Spyra, Ania. 2006. "Is Cosmopolitanism Not for Women?". *Frontiers* 27(2): 1–26.

Todd, Sharon. 2003. *Learning from the Other: Levinas, Psychoanalysis, and Ethical Possibilities in Education*. Albany, NY: SUNY Press.

Torres, Raymond and Morrow, CarlosAlberto. 2000. "The State, Globalization, and Educational Policy". In Nicholas Burbules and Carlos Alberto Morrow (eds), *Globalization and Education: Critical Perspectives*. New York: Routledge, pp. 27–56.

Turner, Bryan. 2002. "Cosmopolitan Virtue, Globalization, and Patriotism". *Theory, Culture, and Society* 19(1–2): 45–63.

Urry, John. 1995. *Consuming Places*. London: Routledge.

Willinsky, John. 2000. *Learning to Divide the World: Education at Empire's End*. Minneapolis, MN: University of Minnesota Press.

4 Technology's role in global citizenship education

Elizabeth Langran and Irene Langran

The twenty-first century world calls for new approaches to civic education. Indeed, many argue that the very concept of citizenship is changing from one envisioned within the confines of the state to one that acknowledges its existence on a global level. This vision of citizenship is shaped by a growing awareness that technology provides new methods of participating in a global political arena.

These technological changes are transforming how individuals connect with each other and call for a new way of approaching education for citizenship – citizenship that fosters knowledge, empathy, and political participation across borders. While technology can play a central role in supporting these efforts, it can also be used to subvert them by creating misinformation, division, and inequality. This chapter examines these trends and provides a roadmap for global citizenship education in the twenty-first century. It calls upon educators at all levels to guide students in critical reflection of their use of technology and the ways in which that use is shaped by systems of power and influence.

Connectivity in the global classroom

Citizenship education has evolved over several centuries. In the nineteenth century, states began to implement educational policies to impart a sense of loyalty, obedience, and service to the nation. Napoleon Bonaparte recognized the role of education in creating a nation of citizens – not individuals with competing religious, class, ideological, or other identities. Early models of citizenship education tended to adopt a communal and assimilationist approach in attempting to advance the goals of the nation: civic education was used to enforce ideas about enemy states, the glory of the nation, and a unified polity. The model often reinforced the dominance of particular groups. As noted by James A. Banks (2008, 130), the "Anglo-conformity" focus in the United States resulted in the absence of African American, Mexican American, and American Indian history and culture from textbooks.

Ideas about citizenship and its relationship to cosmopolitan ideals have transformed over time, although they remain an area of contention and debate. In the early twentieth century, John Dewey envisioned a cosmopolitan approach to education that integrated a sense of "home", a respect for diversity, and a curiosity about the world. His idea of cosmopolitanism is "framed as a fusion of reflective openness to the world and reflective loyalty to the local" (Hansen 2009, 128). Banks notes that earlier models of citizenship education are "inconsistent with the citizen's role in a global world today" (2008, 132). As Banks explains, citizenship is complicated by the millions of individuals living outside the countries of their birth who may experience "multiple national commitments and live in multiple nation-states" (ibid.). In 2009, the United Nations Development Programme (UNDP 2009, 2) noted that there were 200 million international migrants, a number that continues to increase and pose challenges to the nature and meaning of citizenship.

Global citizenship education draws upon the idea that multiple levels of citizenship can coexist. Adopted by numerous educational institutions in recent years, global citizenship education seeks to foster "those values, knowledge and skills that are based on and instil respect for human rights, social justice, diversity, gender equality and environmental sustainability and that empower learners to be responsible global citizens" (UNESCO 2015). *Critical* global citizenship education challenges the educators and learners to move beyond a prescriptive approach that simplifies issues and positions to one that asks them to analyse critically "complex structures, systems, assumptions, power relations and attitudes that create and maintain exploitation and enforced disempowerment and tend to eliminate difference" (Andreotti 2006).

Global citizenship education has the potential to challenge us to rethink how we envision the world and our own role in it – including the extent to which we participate in activities and power structures that undermine the ideals of universal rights, obligations to others, and an acceptance of cultures and beliefs other than our own. Global citizenship education should force us to rethink how we reconcile our role as citizens on both state and global levels. Educators can play a critical role in preparing students for this role.

Educators today also face the challenge of how to use the constant changes in technology in the classroom as tools for enhanced learning. The question for many educators is not whether students use technology – it is how they use it and the extent to which they reflect upon their use critically. While new information technologies have increased the amount of information that is available, it can be akin to drinking from a firehose. It is necessary to separate the signal from the noise, but there can be a tendency to "filter out news that doesn't connect to our lives and our interests" (Zuckerman 2013, 113).

The use of technology in education is most effective when it corresponds to clearly defined goals. Preparing students for participation as global citizens means preparing them to use the tools to learn and connect, rather than using technology simply as a productivity or content delivery system. The Internet is not only "flattening" the world economically, as Thomas Friedman (2007) notes, but also offering "new hope for educating the citizens of this planet. It is the opening up of education that ultimately makes a flatter or more robust economic world possible" (Bonk 2009, 7–8). As outlined below, the strengths of technology include its ability to enhance knowledge, empathy, and participation.

Knowledge

A cornerstone of civic education at any level is its ability to support an enlightened understanding of rights and issues. While some may dispute the existence of universal human rights, a wide, diverse, and growing set of states and people accept them as legitimate. A key starting point for building student knowledge in this realm is the 1948 Universal Declaration of Human Rights and related laws. Rights on the state level present a key difference with rights on a global level: whereas state governments have the authority to enforce rights within their own borders, universal human rights exist in a world in which states are sovereign. As such, their enforcement is sporadic in a world of unequal and often self-interested states. However, the idea that universal human rights should be enforced has gained growing support and indeed there are increasing instances of such enforcement. Civic education involves an awareness of rights – today's global citizens should be aware of the concept of universal human rights, the Universal Declaration of Human Rights, and how international laws can be used to support these rights. The Universal Declaration of Human Rights, human rights laws, and related documents are widely available online.

Education for global citizenship also requires increased understanding of our world – including the issues that shape our own lives and the lives of people affected by our actions. As noted by J. Michael Adams and Angelo Carfagna (2006, xii), "The future depends on developing a sense of agency, accepting responsibility to address global problems, and acting as world citizens". When teachers ask their students to extend their learning beyond the school campus, the Internet can be an invaluable source to gain further knowledge about the world, whether it is through tools such as Google Earth that allow students to visualize the terrain of geographic areas studied or podcasts that enable them to listen to the voice of someone from a distant land. The ease of finding materials on the Internet and the portability gained by devices such as smartphones and tablets allow learning to take place anytime and anywhere, rather than being restricted to the classroom teacher and textbooks for knowledge. Encouragement of non-traditional and informal learning can develop lifelong learning skills essential to democracy and global citizenship.

Empathy

Building on the knowledge gained of other people, students can take the next step towards developing an empathetic view of others and a sense of belonging to a wider community. The concept of rights, whether on a state or global level, rests on the idea of equality: if all are entitled to equal rights, then rights that belong to one person should not be taken away by another. In other words, we have a duty to observe and protect the rights of others. This aspect of citizenship is especially challenging in a global context, where our actions infringe upon the rights of individuals whose lives are distant – in circumstance and by geography – from our own. As noted by Ethan Zuckerman, globalization increases our dependence on goods and services from locales that may be remote; at the same time, we may be less informed about the sources of those goods and services (Zuckerman 2013, 41). Technology can help us consider the impact of daily activities such as shopping, driving, and even drinking a cup of coffee. Where do the products that we buy originate? How were they made? What impact do these activities have on our environment? We can trace these actions – and learn about the people whose lives they impact – through the Internet.

Communications technology can be central to the effort to create empathy. Again, this is a challenge when notions of citizenship are extended to a global level and personal contact is less likely. As Martha Nussbaum writes, "Each culture – indeed, each student – has blind spots: groups within it or abroad that are especially likely to be treated ignorantly or obtusely. A good arts education will select works specifically to promote criticism of this obtuseness, and a better vision of the unseen" (2006, 69). To Nussbaum, the ability to understand and empathize with the perspective of another is a critical element of citizenship on state and global levels. Not only can students engage in perspective-taking by reading blogs that contain personal stories of people they would likely never meet, but they are also aided in developing an empathetic view of others who live far away by making personal connections with tools that allow them to communicate directly. Text-based conversations can happen via email, online chats, blogs, or posts on social networking sites. Additionally, the multimedia capabilities of the Internet allow for voice and video communication. Web-conferencing tools enable classrooms to connect worldwide without sophisticated equipment. A simple webcam, microphone, and sufficient Internet connection can offer a rich interactive media experience with minimal expense through the online services of Skype or Google hangouts, providing space for personal connections and shared experiences to take place. Several organizations can help primary and secondary classrooms make connections to collaborate on projects, including the International Education and Resource Network (iEARN), Global SchoolNet, and ePals. Higher education institutions have fewer options for these organizations that can assist with the process of pairing college classrooms; groups such as the Erasmus Multilateral Project INTENT, the SUNY COIL Center, and the Soliya Network are connecting higher education students, but generally only for specific groups of colleges and universities. The next step is to move from classes working together to individual students collaborating on a global basis. Thomas Friedman (2007) reminds us that whereas states drove

Globalization 1.0 and companies drove Globalization 2.0, Globalization 3.0 is about the globalization of the individual. Empowered by technology, Friedman envisions Globalization 3.0 as enabling individuals to have greater opportunities to act globally, leading us to participate on a global level.

Critical global citizenship education moves beyond the sharing of experiences to generate a sense of empathy. It involves a critical analysis of systems of power as they shape global relations and impact the ways in which we use technology. Megan Boler (1997, 257) uses the term "passive empathy" to describe "those instances where our concern is directed to a fairly distant other, whom we cannot directly help". Boler (ibid.) further notes that mere empathy is "not a sufficient educational practice". Instead, she calls for educators to help students understand the ways in which they are "implicit" in systems that contribute to these areas of concern.

Participation

Participation is vital to democratic citizenship. Effective participation involves the ability to influence the decisions that impact an individual's life. Students may be knowledgeable about rights and duties, but are they able to act on this knowledge?

Many opportunities for participation are made possible by technology. As the Web has been transformed from a "read-only" format to a space where users are able to create, share, and comment on content, today's learners have become very comfortable with sharing content and interacting socially online. They are already using mobile devices and computers for social networking on sites such as Facebook, uploading and commenting on media on YouTube, and interacting through gaming and in 3-D virtual worlds. Eighty-nine per cent of US teens use a social networking site such as Facebook, Twitter, Instagram, Snapchat, or Tumblr (Lenhart 2015). While they are adept at these types of uses, they do not necessarily know how to use the Web for participation as a modern citizen.

The use of technology for global citizenship education can mark a shift in terms of how students view technology itself. Indeed, students' online activities can shift from those defined by purely social objectives to ones in which participation in a new civic arena is an exciting new possibility. Since 2008, US presidential elections have demonstrated new – and increasingly essential – uses of technology in a democratic context. The Web is capable of supporting citizen journalism and "netizens" who voice dissent, sometimes where free speech is restricted. Cell phones can record video to be uploaded to YouTube; protesters can use Twitter to broadcast from the streets, as they did in Iran in 2009 and in multiple countries throughout the Arab Spring.

The viral spread of images can lead to movements that also go beyond the borders of states. In September 2015, the image of a young child drowned on a beach in Turkey provided momentum to a movement to call world leaders and governments to account for refugees escaping war and violence.

Technology – global citizenship education 61

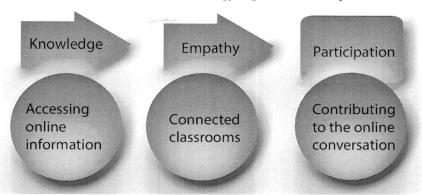

Figure 4.1 Development stages in global citizenship education

Facebook campaigns in Iceland and elsewhere were examples of citizens using technology to try to design solutions to the refugee problem with offers of donations and housing as well as appeals to their government to take in more Syrians. Images are powerful, and their ability to be spread virally can provide momentum for political action that comes from the empathy (or outrage) that they provoke. Educators can seize these moments and work to analyse critically the problem at hand as well as underlying power structures that contribute to these global problems and responses.

Educators can challenge students to use these tools and begin to experiment with this new form of education. They can join online debates, support an issue, or even create web-based material themselves. Classrooms that promote participatory learning environments allow for students to co-construct knowledge and share expertise. Progressing through global citizenship education, students move from consuming web information (knowledge) to classroom-to-classroom communication (empathy) to having conversations with a public audience in social networking environments (participation). These tools can be used to enhance student knowledge about the impact of their actions in a globalized economy, foster a sense of civic duty, and create a sense of belonging to a larger political community.

New technologies create new global citizenship opportunities

Two recent game-changing advances in technologies have impacted how people around the world engage in global citizenship practices: mobile devices and geolocation. Many areas of the world lack the infrastructure – specifically electric and phone lines – to connect to the Internet. The International Telecommunication Union estimates that by the end of 2015, there would be 794 million fixed broadband subscriptions; Africa accounts for just .01 per cent of this type of connectivity (UN Broadband Commission 2015). Even where the infrastructure exists, the affordability of household Internet service is out of reach for many. Once mobile phones became available and reasonably priced throughout the world, they became the most rapidly adopted technology in history, achieving one billion users in five years (ibid.). Mobile devices allow users to participate in the online conversations to organize, share ideas, advocate, record video, and spread their political message here and now – no longer is online participation relegated to those with the means to own a connected computer, and no longer do users need to wait to post messages, photos, and videos until they are able to get to a computer. With nearly half of the world's population under the age of 20 and their willingness to adopt mobile devices, there is great potential for youths' participation in online citizenship activities.

Because most mobile devices are able to record a user's location, the information, photos, and videos become *geolocated*. We can follow not only what is happening, but exactly where it is happening. This allows us to engage in ground-truthing and spatial information analysis (Langran and Beishembaeva 2011). "Ground truth" is a term used in geography for the onsite inspection of a geological feature to determine the accuracy of data collected remotely. We can use mobile devices in the same way, as people who witness events first-hand share this information directly online and bypass traditional as well as government-controlled news agencies. Information, photos, and videos regarding political events can be shared outside a country's borders in order to raise consciousness and put pressure on governments; many people have taken great risks to post these items on social networking sites.

The data shared online, which includes information, photos, and videos, can be mapped online by taking advantage of the metadata that is embedded in what is posted from GPS-enabled phones. For example, photos taken from your smartphone will have geographic information "geotag" about where (and when) the photo was taken. When the photo is uploaded, it can be automatically mapped, creating opportunities to visualize place-based data. Ushahidi is an example of a project that has sought to use geolocated data. Originally created as a way of mapping election violence in Kenya, it is an opensource platform has been used throughout the world to map emergency relief efforts in natural disasters, criminal activity hotspots, community resources, water wells, and more. Users can create a map and then invite others to post information, photos, or videos to a specific location on the online map. Seeing where events occur in relation to resources, epidemics, voting trends, ethnic groupings, and police presence gives students an opportunity to analyse spatial information. Visualizing data and relationships on a map can be much less challenging for learners to interpret and look for patterns than numbers on spreadsheets or dense text-based descriptions. Geospatial literacy thus becomes an important building block for global citizenship.

In addition to asking students to conduct geospatial analysis from mapbased data that has been created in other countries, we can also ask students to generate their own maps using mobile devices by exploring their own communities. Experiential and place-based learning can be structured and supported by using mobile devices (Langran and Dewitt 2015). As students search their local communities for examples of economic, political, ecological, or cultural globalization, the geotagged notes, photos, and videos they collect are mapped as online data that can be shared and analysed. Through such exercises, students gain the ability to reflect upon globalization and its impact on their own environment. For example, they could look at the types of businesses and communities present in their communities; the messages from posters, flyers, and advertisements; or the types of products sold in stores.

Cautionary tales about technology

We have been discussing technology as a classroom tool to engage students in global citizenship development. Technology can play a key role in supporting global citizenship – but it also has the potential to create misinformation, division, and inequality. Despite the promises of open source software, digital books, and mobile devices that put Internet access into the hands of users all over the world, inequities exist, not simply with respect to access but also with essential user skills and the lack of relevant content in users' own language for many. It is important that students become aware of the social implications of the Internet on civic life and political voice, and its ability to redistribute political influence.

A lack of access to new information technologies can limit the civic participation of individuals on several levels. This digital divide refers to the gap between those with access to the Internet and other forms of digital technology and those with no or limited access. It includes inequities both within countries and among countries. While more than 3.1 billion people in the world have access to the Internet, approximately 4.2 billion or 58 per cent of the world's population do not. When these figures are considered by state, those with access to the Internet include approximately 642 million in China, 280 million in the United States, 243 million in India, 109 million in Japan, 108 million in Brazil, and 84 million in Russia (West 2015, 1). Greater Internet access by some states, or groups within those states, means more influence in shaping the online world and participation in the formal economy, only widening existing economic and power gaps. More than half of the world lacks Internet access, and as noted by Darrell M. West, "those individuals are unable to enjoy the social, economic, and civic benefits that derive from digital connectivity" (ibid.).

Bridging the digital divide requires more than putting the digital infrastructure in place. Many of the individuals without Internet access lack the income to support purchasing the necessary device as well as the funds needed for data plans and monthly fees. Other potential users may not use these tools due to a lack of comfort with the technology. Studies demonstrate that the latter is often associated with age and the former may be associated with gender or other indicators of social status. Language is an important consideration as well: while English is the most commonly used language on the Internet, only 7 per cent of the world's population speaks English as their first language (West 2015, 14).

Connectivity is recognized as an important goal for development and the realization of human rights. Individual countries, including the United States, incorporate it through their aid programs. In 2015, the member states of the United Nations adopted the Global Goals, a series of targets to promote sustainable development that include the objective of expanded connectivity. Leaders and organizations, including Mark Zuckerberg, Bill and Melinda Gates, and Bono, support the Connectivity Declaration, urging the implementation of policies that will enable universal Internet access to become a reality by 2020 as envisioned in the Global Goals (One 2015).

Even if obstacles to access are overcome, restrictions on the type of content available to users limit the Internet's potential to level the playing field, broaden the range of ideas discussed, increase the number of citizens participating, and diminish the role of political elites and traditional gatekeepers. While anyone is free to post their thoughts to a blog or website, these postings are only relevant if those ideas are read. Governments may censor and monitor online activity. The infrastructure of the Internet and the rank in search engine results dictate that not all websites are given equal consideration. To visit a new site, one has to first find it, either from a link from a known site or though a search query. Search engines, in fact, guide and limit results, and the Internet's openness is increasingly at risk as commercial interests shape its architecture (Hindman 2008; Lessig 2001). Google, Microsoft Bing, and Yahoo search engines, currently accounting for 99 per cent of search engine queries, rely partially on an algorithm that uses link structure. Sites that receive lots of links from other heavily linked sites are ranked higher in web searches. Thus sites that are heavily linked become prominent in queries, and others are likely to be ignored. Websites for political advocacy and political blogs get only a tiny fraction of the attention that traditional news sources receive. The top 50 political sites receive 50 per cent of political site traffic. Even among blogs, the top five political blogs receive 28 per cent of political blog traffic, and the authors of the top blogs tend to be almost exclusively white, male, highly educated, and from a journalism or corporate elite background (Hindman 2008). Since users generally click on only the top results of a web search, how companies like Google, Microsoft Bing, or Yahoo present the order of search results can have an effect on information (and opinion-forming) about a political candidate (Stewart 2015).

The prevalence of data collection on the Web also results in information that is personalized and targeted. Zuckerman illustrates the outcome of this personalization, noting that:

> Two readers of *The New York Times* may see a very different picture of the world, and that two users of Facebook certainly do, shaped both by our choice of friends and by Facebook's algorithms. Research suggests that these personalized sites may lead us into echo chambers, filter

bubbles, or other forms of ideological isolation that divide us into rival camps that cannot agree on anything, including a set of common facts on which we could build a debate.

(2014)

Educators can help students analyse critically not only what they view online, but the underlying ways in which the Internet is structured.

A Pew Internet and American Life Project study found that the inequalities researchers have seen in offline political activity are similar to those found in online political activity (Smith 2013). Whether online or offline, traditional political activities such as signing a petition, contacting a government official, commenting on a news story, or sending a letter to a newspaper or magazine editor are "most common among the well-educated and financially well-off" (ibid). However, we are seeing less of a gap in social networking sites such as Facebook and Twitter. While users tend to be of higher income and educational levels, political involvement among those who are using social networking sites is identical for those in households earning less than $10,000 per year and those in households earning more than $150,000 per year (ibid.). This tells us that social networking may bring new pathways of political participation across socio-economic groups.

Those who are not politically active will not engage in new civic activities just because more political websites are available; at the same time, those who are politically active are increasingly moving away from news sites with no clear point of view and gravitating towards sites that match their own political viewpoints (Smith 2009). Polarization into insular, homogeneous groups and reposting of unsubstantiated information are made even easier with Twitter and other "narrowcasting" Internet uses and can be picked up by the blogosphere and then mainstream news media (see for example Sarah Palin's Facebook posting about "death panels"). As noted by Ethan Zuckerman, "Information may flow globally, but our attention tends to be highly local and highly tribal; we care more deeply about those with whom we share a group identity and much less about a distant 'other'" (2013, 58).

Facilitating polarization is the increasing diffusion of smartphones and tablets that allow users to "tweet" or post from anywhere and check for updates, enabling postings to go viral quickly as Internet users "pile on" in an effort to take down a person's reputation. Even the source of web information can be suspect: Twitter deleted 33 fake accounts that had been created by Republicans using the names of Democratic state representatives in Connecticut. The fake Twitter accounts were intended to send tweets out under the Democrats' names "mocking the liberal tax-and-spend bastards" (Hladky 2009). Ted Cruz's official 2016 US presidential candidate website is not tedcruz.com – someone had already registered that domain name and it is being used to urge visitors to support President Obama and immigration reform. This underscores the need for our young citizens to develop a literacy that enables them to evaluate the validity of media messages. Take for example how Daesh, also referred to as ISIS or ISIL, has leveraged social media platforms such as Twitter to distribute its messages and "draw in people vulnerable to radicalization" (Berger and Morgan 2015, 2). Spending time in the classroom to develop media literacy skills can help students learn how to use multiple sources and analyse message sources to avoid believing flawed and biased arguments.

Conclusion

The Internet can be a powerful tool for global citizenship education. It can provide knowledge and insights about rights and duties in the twenty-first century. This may in turn lead to greater empathy with others, a sense of a global political community, and the ability to solve more effectively the global problems that challenge our shared future. When people use blogs or social networking sites politically, they are much more likely to be invested in other forms of civic and political activism such as joining a political group, contacting a government official, or expressing their views in the media (Smith *et al.* 2009).

Internet connectivity and the ubiquity of mobile devices such as smartphones and tablets have transformed our ability to connect anytime and anywhere. Alec Ross (2012) points to how these technologies accelerate the growth of social and political movements, with new information networks that disrupt leadership structures and empower individuals. With more than 60 per cent of the world's population under the age of 30, this is the most technologically connected generation yet (Cohen 2010).

However, there are also dangers associated with the use of new technology and its potential to spread misinformation, division, and inequality. A critical approach to global citizenship education requires educators and learners to go beyond a basic understanding of issues and explore the underlying power relations that are embedded in the use of new and emerging technologies. In this light, Zuckerman poses a challenge to educators, students, and all of those who seek to build a better world: "How do we rewire the tools we've built to maximize our impact on an interconnected world?" (Zuckerman 2013, 30). It is by understanding the promise and peril of these tools that we can engage in the complexities and challenges of a new, critical global citizenship education.

References

Adams, J. Michael and Angelo Carfagna. 2006. *Coming of Age in a Globalized World: The Next Generation*. Bloomfield, CT: Kumarian Press.

Andreotti, Vanessa. 2006. "Soft versus Critical Global Citizenship Education". *Global Citizenship* 3: 40–51.

Appiah, Kwame Anthony. 2006. *Cosmopolitanism: Ethics in a World of Strangers*. New York: Norton.

Banks, James A. 2008. "Diversity, Group Identity, and Citizenship Education in a Global Age". *Educational Researcher* 37(3): 129–139.
Berger, J. M. and Jonathon Morgan. 2015. "The ISIS Twitter Census: Defining and Describing the Population of ISIS Supporters on Twitter". *Brookings Project on U.S. Relations with the Islamic World*, 20.
Boler, Megan. 1997. "The Risks of Empathy: Interrogating Multiculturalism's Gaze". *Cultural Studies* 11(2): 253–273.
Bonk, Curtis J. 2009. *The World Is Open: How Web Technology Is Revolutionizing Education*. San Francisco, CA: Jossey-Bass.
Cohen, Jared. 2010. "Children of Jihad". Speech presented at Fairfield University, Fairfield, CT, October.
Cogan, John J. 1999. "Civic Education in the United States: A Brief History". *International Journal of Social Education* 14(1): 52–64.
Friedman, Thomas. 2007. *The World Is Flat 3.0: A Brief History of the Twenty-First Century*. 3rd edn. New York: Farrar, Straus and Giroux.
Hansen, David T. 2009. "Dewey and Cosmopolitanism". *Education & Culture* 25(2): 126–140.
Hindman, Matthew. 2008. *The Myth of Digital Democracy*. Princeton, NJ: Princeton University Press.
Hladky, Gregory B. 2009. "Republicans Overtweet". 20 October. *Fairfield Weekly*. Available at: www.fairfieldweekly.com.
Langran, Elizabeth and Ajara Beishembaeva. 2011. "Teaching for Global Citizenship with Geospatial Technology". In Matthew Koehler and Punya Mishra (eds), *Proceedings of Society for Information Technology & Teacher Education International Conference 2011*. Chesapeake, VA: AACE, pp. 3838–3842.
Langran, Elizabeth and Janine Dewitt. 2015. "Educating Globally, Exploring Locally: Using Mobile Mapping to Explore Cities and Globalization". Paper presented to the International Society for Technology in Education Conference, Philadelphia, PA, 1 July.
Langran, Irene, Elizabeth Langran, and Kathy Ozment. 2009. "Transforming Today's Students into Tomorrow's Global Citizens: Challenges for U.S. Educators". *New Global Studies* 3(1). Available at: www.bepress.com/ngs/vol3/iss1/art4.
Lenhart, Amanda. 2015. "Teens, Social Media & Technology Overview". Pew Research Center. Available at: www.pewinternet.org/2015/04/09/teens-social-media-technology-2015 (accessed 9 October 2015).
Lessig, Lawrence. 2001. *The Future of Ideas: The Fate of the Commons in a Connected World*. New York: Random House.
Nussbaum, Martha. 2006. "Teaching Humanity". *Newsweek International Special Global Education Issue*, 21 August.
One. 2015. "The Connectivity Declaration: Demanding Internet Access for All and Implementation of the Global Goals". Available at: www.one.org/us/2015/09/26/the-connectivity-declaration-demanding-internet-access-for-all-and-implementation-of-the-global-goals (accessed 1 October 2015).
Quigley, Charles N. 1999. "Civic Education: Recent History, Current Status, and the Future". Paper presented at American Bar Association Symposium, Washington, DC. Available at: www.civiced.org/papers/papers_quigley99.html (accessed 1 October 2015).
Ross, Alec. 2012. "How Connective Tech Boosts Political Change". 20 June. Available at: http://articles.cnn.com/2012-06-20/opinion/opinion_opinion-alec-ross-tech-politics_1_mohamed-bouazizi-social-media-sidi-bouzid?_s=PM:OPINION.

Smith, Aaron. 2009. "The Internet's Role in Campaign 2008". *Pew Internet and American Life Project*. Available at: www.pewinternet.org/Reports/2009/6–The-Internets-Role-in-Campaign-2008.aspx (accessed 5 September 2015).

Smith, Aaron. 2013. "Civic Engagement in the Digital Age". *Pew Internet and American Life Project*. Available at: www.pewinternet.org/files/old-media//Files/Reports/2013/PIP_CivicEngagementintheDigitalAge.pdf (accessed 5 September 2015).

Smith, Aaron, Kay Lehman Schlozman, Sidney Verba, and Henry Brady. 2009. "The Internet and Civic Engagement". *Pew Internet and American Life Project*. Available at: www.pewinternet.org/Reports/2009/15–The-Internet-and-Civic-Engagement.aspx (accessed 15 September 2015).

Stewart, Joshua. 2015. "Researchers: Google, Yahoo Could Tip an Election". *San Diego Union-Tribune*, 7 August. Available at: www.sandiegotribune.com.

UN Broadband Commission. 2015. "The State of Broadband 2015: Broadband as a Foundation for Sustainable Development". Available at: www.broadbandcommission.org/Documents/reports/bb-annualreport2015.pdf (accessed 8 October 2015).

UNESCO. 2015. "Global Citizenship Education". Available at: www.unesco.org/new/en/global-citizenship-education (accessed 6 September 2015).

United Nations Development Programme. 2009. *Human Development Report 2009: Overcoming Barriers: Human Mobility and Development*. New York: UNDP. Available at: http://hdr.undp.org/sites/default/files/reports/269/hdr_2009_en_complete.pdf (accessed 18 October 2015).

West, Darrell M. 2015. "Digital Divide: Improving Internet Access in the Developing World Through Affordable Services and Diverse Content". *Center for Technology Innovation at Brookings*. Available at: www.brookings.edu/~/media/research/files/papers/2015/02/13-digital-divide-developing-world-west/west_internet-access.pdf (accessed 5 August 2015).

Zuckerman, Ethan. 2013. *Rewire: Digital Cosmopolitans in the Age of Connection*. New York: Norton.

Zuckerman, Ethan. 2014. "The Internet's Original Sin". *The Atlantic*, 14 August. Available at: www.theatlantic.com/technology/archive/2014/08/advertising-is-the-internets-original-sin/376041 (accessed 6 September 2015).

5 The global, citizenship, and education as discursive fields

Towards disrupting the reproduction of colonial systems of power

Karen Pashby

This chapter considers the growing interest in framing global citizenship education (GCE) using post-/decolonial perspectives and discourse studies. These perspectives alert to the real possibilities that despite good intentions, educating for global citizenship can reinforce unequal colonial systems of power. I draw on Andreotti and Souza's (2011) understanding of post-colonial studies as a set of productive questions. These queries raise for study seemingly neutral frames of references and metanarratives that shape approaches to GCE. In the same way that many scholars call for decolonizing education (e.g. Abdi 2008; Willinsky 2008), Andreotti and Souza conceptualize "the prefix 'post-' in post-colonialism as a constant interrogation, a possibility that is 'not yet' but that may announce the prospect of something new" (2011, 2). This particular movement within the broader field of global education arises from and responds to central tensions inherent in articulating and practicing GCE. Specifically, this chapter examines the ways that GCE emerges from a nexus of interrelated discursive fields, each of them contested as well as marked by particular histories, challenges, and possibilities. It then reviews the main themes of the scholarly literature on GCE and the critiques of the field, highlighting those that call out GCE theory and practice for failing to interrogate or change what are often taken-for-granted colonial systems of power. Finally, it considers the risks of failing to interrogate good intentions behind GCE initiatives in non-formal and formal educational contexts.

One way to begin to examine critiques of global citizenship, particularly as applied in educational policy and practice, is to understand how the words global, citizenship, and education each represent discursive fields. Andreotti (2010c) speaks about the "discursive turn" as a paradigmatic moment when the social sciences moved from a belief in an empirical and objective idea of truth to one that recognized how realties are described and constructed and therefore are not neutral. In this new understanding of reality, social theorists recognize the role of language in relaying worldviews and ideology and governing social relations. The discursive turn coincided with work that is influenced by the post-traditions, including postmodernism, post-structuralism, and post-colonialism (Andreotti 2010a, 2010b). These traditions probe the metanarratives of modern society and expose them as not neutral but constructed out of socio-historic contexts. For example, Anderson (2006) deconstructs the idea of the nation and demonstrates that, although it has significant historical and material impacts on humans, the nation is actually a metanarrative, or imagined human construct. Metanarratives, or legends as Pike (2008a) refers to them, become so taken for granted that they become unquestionable and appear natural and neutral. In this sense, education can help to recognize the legends that construct reality in particular ways and favour certain worldviews which present as universal. In GCE these include a dominant view of helping global others that neither includes the stories of those who are the most marginalized from their own perspective nor accounts for the ongoing reproduction of colonial systems of power. Yet, schooling can also help reconstruct the dominant legend that is currently defining how young people learn about the world.

GCE generally extends the idea of rights and responsibilities beyond the limits of the nation-state. It can be understood in a variety of ways and reflects different ideologies and ideas of what is and ought to be desired of citizens. Specifically, Andreotti argues that it is important to recognize how a term such as global citizenship is: (a) *situated* in one specific culture, era, and/or geopolitical context; (b) *partial* and liable to seen differently by others; (c) *contingent* because its use and understanding depends on the context in which it is used and understood; and (d) *provisional* because its use and understanding can and does change (2010c, 236). In fact, many critiques of global citizenship and GCE have arisen out of such attentiveness to this discursive aspect.

Tully (2008) determines that global citizenship comprises two fields – citizenship and globalization – which are each contested: "When we enquire into global citizenship ... we are already thrown into this remarkably complex inherited field of contested languages, activities, institutions, processes and the environs in which they take place" (2008, 15). Thus, global citizenship as a conjoint field represents the gathering together of "formerly disparate activities" under a new "rubric" wherein global citizenship becomes a topic and problem for research, policy, and theory (ibid.). Similarly, Camicia and Franklin identify GCE as a discursive field in so far as it intersects critical work on globalization, citizenship, and education (2011, 313). Discursive fields occur "when groups construct diagnoses, prognoses, and calls to action, and are partly structured in ongoing processes of hegemony" (Steinberg 1999, 748). Global citizenship discourses are interested in what is going wrong in the world – or what are key global issues – and what should be done about them. In relation to formal education this includes school curriculum, pedagogy, and programming. At the same time, the intersecting discourses are framed by dominant ways of thinking about global relations including who gets to define a global problem and who gets to be a global citizen (Pashby 2011). Mannion *et al.* also argue that GCE is a discursive field in so far as it represents a "floating signifier that different discourses attempt to cover with meaning ...

[and converge] within this new nexus of intentions" (2011, 444). Thus, when understood discursively, global citizenship becomes a complicated idea that is infused with various meanings and can be used and understood in different ways in different contexts including various sites of education.

It is important to understand and map the many ways that critical conversations about globalization converge with conversations about citizenship and educational practice in the contemporary moment. In particular, some key post-colonial critiques have evoked the discursive turn by recognizing the power of particular narratives to construct artificial and colonial divisions between cultures and peoples (Said 1994). Specifically, and relevant to the study of global citizenship, post-colonial critique has questioned and interrogated how constructions of an *us* and a *them* are inherent to conceptualizations of citizenship and schooling (Willinsky 1998). While it is outside the scope of this chapter to offer a full definition of post-colonial critique, Andreotti (2010c) helps to identify key strands or versions of post-colonial theory. One version takes up hyper-self-reflexivity as a strategic way to recognize the complicity of and investment of everyone in "coercive and repressive belief systems" (ibid., 238). This hyper-self-reflexivity is intended to promote a capacity to relate to others that is otherwise from inherited and seemingly neutral sets of relations that are in fact embedded in colonial patterns of thinking and relating. However, it is not prescriptive. Other strands of post-colonial theory focus on bringing to the fore those voices historically marginalized by colonial violence (ibid.). For the purpose of this chapter, I align with Andreotti and Souza who "define postcolonial theories as tools-for-thinking rather than theories-of-truth" (2011, 2).

Unpacking *the global*: globalization and cosmopolitanism as contested fields

Unpacking the *global* referent in the discursive field of global citizenship underscores the centrality of both the idea of contemporary globalization and the notion of a global community. Many of the theoretical contestations have focused on whether globalization creates a global community that is becoming more similar or comprising more difference. Either way, there is a sense of what I have called a global imperative (Pashby 2008) whereby the world seems more global than ever before, global issues take on a particular urgency, and schooling is required to attend to the global. In the global imperative there is a constant pressure to teach students to understand, prepare for, and succeed in a world defined by globalization.

Globalization is as unavoidable today as it is complicated, and social inequalities and conflicts continue and intensify. The political, economic, technological, and cultural processes that characterize globalization are associated with increasing intra-state conflict and increasing inequalities within and between societies (Ibrahim 2005, 177). Many of the processes associated with contemporary globalization seem new: increased mobility, fast access to more and more sources of knowledge via the Internet, and intensifying global marketization, among many others. Yet, movements of peoples and goods are, of course, not at all a new phenomena. There is, however, much concern across academic disciplines and geographical contexts regarding the extent to which there is increasing homogeneity or heterogeneity as a result of today's intensified movements of peoples, resources, and ideas. This puts particular pressures on those seen as needing to save their cultures. Burns warns that "the repetition of this dichotomy [of homogenization or heterogenization] positions globalization in a predatory role, linking the inevitable repercussions of global living with the inability of minoritarian cultures to produce an effective counter-hegemonic polity" (2008, 347). The repetition of such binary narratives – also including globalization from above or from below – is a way of trying to make sense of contradictory transnational conditions but raises new problems. Highlighting the discursive aspect of global citizenship, Burns points out that "rather than seeing globalisation as a finite or linear set of processes [as in both homogeneous and heterogeneous views] it becomes a vast assemblage of competing and contradictory forces that organise and manage populations" (ibid., 348).

Connected to these contradictory understandings of globalization is what Strand refers to as "the cosmopolitan turn" in social and political sciences and in education (2010a, 229). Like globalization, cosmopolitanism is an ambiguous, contested, and conflicting discursive field, and it is a popular way to theorize the complexities inherent to both globalization and belonging to a global community. Cosmopolitanism generally refers to the idea that all humanity belongs to the same community and that this should be cultivated (Strand 2010a). Rizvi underscores the link with globalization when he argues that "the notion of cosmopolitanism has the potential to bring together both the facts and the values associated with complex connectivity" (2009, 259). Drawing on Mignolo's work, Strand (2010b) argues that cosmopolitanism is an ideal still awaiting its realization. There is a central paradox wherein new normative theories reflect an ideal of global connectedness beyond national, religious, and political borders, and, at the same time "long-established ideas and ideals of cosmopolitanism are now being contested by a developing worldwide and extremely complex social reality" (Strand 2010b, 233). Mignolo offers this critique in another way by interrogating the mutually dependent processes of modernization and colonization: "Coloniality ... is the hidden face of modernity and its very condition of possibility" (2000, 722).

The colonization of the Americas in the sixteenth and seventeenth centuries and Africa in the nineteenth and twentieth centuries were global designs representing the consolidation of "an idea of the West: a geopolitical image that exhibits chronological movement" (ibid.). According to Mignolo, it is not impossible to conceive or analyse cosmopolitan projects beyond these parameters. He insists on distinguishing (a) cosmopolitanism from global designs and (b) cosmopolitan projects from critical cosmopolitanism. Global designs are driven by the will to control and homogenize, whereas cosmopolitan projects can either be complementary or dissenting in relation to global designs.

For example, he describes how after World War I, modernizing missions displaced Christian and civilizing missions, and the global market became the final destination of global designs. Mignolo identifies the recent revival of cosmopolitan projects – of which global citizenship education may be one example – as "attentive to the dangers and excesses of global designs" (ibid., 723).

In its current resurgence, a "cosmopolitan outlook" is both "a diagnostic and normative point of view that signifies epistemic ruptures" (Strand 2010b, 233). It is both "a new way of seeing the world and a new and emerging paradigm of social and political analysis" (ibid.). Cosmopolitanism as a new outlook for the twenty-first century is generated by and justified by "the social reality which it examines" (ibid., 234). Mignolo's critique is strongly related to this concomitant recognition of a new reality and new way of understanding and thinking about cosmopolitanism. Critical cosmopolitanism considers how colonialism is reproduced both in the identification of global issues and in the culture of responding to these issues. His work points directly to the normative epistemology at the root of a neutral and decontextualized idea of cosmopolitanism as a universal ideal. Critical cosmopolitanism, on the other hand, attempts to interrogate and negotiate how colonial systems of power and colonial difference continue to be produced, reproduced, and maintained by global designs. Historically, cosmopolitanism has been the imposition of what are constructed as universals but are projections of particular local histories onto other local histories. Thus, critical cosmopolitanism advances critiques that have contested the taken-for-granted assumptions about both globalization and cosmopolitanism.

Citizenship as a contested field: including while excluding

The project of citizenship is another source of contestation in the discursive field of GCE. Citizenship is a modern concept premised on the Enlightenment project of controlling natural forces in order to advance the world and the self in the direction of moral progress. The nation-state has embodied this ideal of control and progress. The structures that are now taken for granted – "formalized constitutions, elected legislatures, and written civil law" – replaced the monarchy as the main focus of loyalty in the seventeenth century: "The people, now become citizens, owed the state their loyalty, while the state, now become the government, owed its citizens protection" (Richardson 2002, 53; see also Delanty 2006). Citizenship in this sense is aligned with universal ideas of cosmopolitanism in that they are situated in modern Western epistemology, ontology and the modern project that produces and reproduces colonial systems of power.

Citizenship is formed through what I have called the "enlightenment dynamic" (Pashby 2013, 46). It promotes a feeling of camaraderie and solidarity that is made possible by emotional ties to the nation and the idea of a shared national belonging (Anderson 2006). At the same time, citizenship is enabled by modern ideas of logic, rationality, and teleological progress institutionalized in the state itself. As Mignolo describes, this development has occurred simultaneously with colonialism. Indeed, national citizenship has always been involved in a paradox of belonging. Even though originally the state was to provide freedom from tyranny, the social inequalities inherited by modernity from feudalism ensured that national citizenship was complicit with perpetuating inequalities and reinforcing who does and does not belong. Goldberg has pointed out that "the rational, hence autonomous and equal subjects of the Enlightenment project turn out, perhaps unsurprisingly, to be exclusively white, male, European, and bourgeois" (1993, 208).

The famous sociologist T. H. Marshall (1950) wrote a historical typology of citizenship in which he argued that, in the mid-twentieth century, citizenship had moved from a strict political definition emphasizing the individual's relationship to the state to a broader conceptualization emphasizing the citizen's relationship to society (Isin and Wood 1999; McCollum 2002). Marshall's work arose from a concern about class segregation in England, and he challenged taken-for-granted ideas of citizenship defined simply by geopolitical territory. He pointed out that the development of citizenship since the eighteenth century had been defined by a series of acquisitions of rights: *civil* (freedom of speech, thought, faith; and development of a judicial system); *political* (decisions and political life and the development of the electoral system); and *social* (economic and social security associated with the development of the welfare state) (Pashby 2008). His typology proposed that citizen rights could be enlarged to allow more classes into the national contract and thereby correct social injustice (Soysal 2011). However, Marshall's work has since been criticized for its exclusive focus on class and for assuming a linear and progressive framework of rights acquisitions without accounting for the various social struggles that have defined the provision of rights to particular groups in certain historical contexts.

Isin and Wood point out that the idea of an inherent conflict between citizenship and class as articulated by Marshall must now be expanded: "The sociological question postmodern societies face today is whether there is a conflict between citizenship and different forms of identity. How does citizenship contribute to or ameliorate sexual, gender, national, ethnic and regional identities?" (1999, 30). And another important question not only problematizes the contested idea of the expansion of rights to citizens, but also the process by which modern citizenship is implicated in reinforcing and managing exclusions and inclusions central to the project of modernity (Said 1994). The colonial legacy of the modern project has continued to be implicated in how citizenship is conceptualized and practiced (Said 1994). On the one hand, contemporary citizenship is central to systems of representative government, international law, the political decolonization of former European colonies, and the formation of supranational regimes and global civil society through such organizations at the UN (Tully 2008, 16). On the other hand, citizenship and its application or denial has also been tied to "the dependent modernization and citizenisation of the non-West through colonisation, the Mandate System, post-decolonisation, nation-building and global governance" (ibid.).

Education as a related and contested discursive field: the paradox of decolonizing

Tully (2008) talks about the intersecting fields of citizenship and globalization, and, as the increasing popularization of the idea of GCE indicates, education proves to be another field of intersection. The philosophical and sociological challenges of deciding how to educate citizens in the contemporary context of globalization inherit the tensions and conceptual ambiguities in both globalization and citizenship.

As the previous sections have outlined, the discursive turn in social sciences has unpacked and interrogated some of the basic terms of social organization, including citizenship. We can recognize that phenomena associated with globalization and with citizenship are: *situated* in certain historical contexts (e.g. states going through political decolonization versus former colonizing states), *partial* in that we cannot recognize all the ways of experiencing the phenomena, *contingent* on the set of analytical tools we employ to make diagnoses and calls for action, and *provisional* because our understandings of them can and do change. As with globalization and citizenship, the discursive turn helps us to understand that schooling, or formal education, is not a neutral social institution but is situated in a Western, modernist project. In this way, schooling is a partial rather than a natural or neutral occurrence. We can also see that normative views of schooling produce and perform particular views of society and nation-building which can be critiqued from various theoretical frames. Schooling in modern Western liberal nation-building projects is contingent on the economic and political climate as well as the settlement processes defining a particular national context. Schooling is also provisional as it changes over time according to the dominant ideology that is framing curricula, content, and pedagogy. Like the nation-state and citizenship, formal education is generally seen as a normative and neutral part of social organization. However, it also is subject to various and specific theoretical critiques that point out how the project of schooling changes and adapts to hegemonic ideologies.

Historically, in Western democracies mass schooling was an extension of state power during the late nineteenth and early twentieth centuries (Osborne 2008). In this sense, it was never neutral. Wrigley *et al.* point out that schooling is situated within – and responds to – a wider set of hegemonic discourses and social and political relations: "School structures and cultures, as well as patterns of classroom language and learning, can either reinforce social inequality or challenge it" (2012, 106). Similarly, Osborne (2008) notes that schooling occupies a particular paradox whereby it is constructed as a solution to perceived "problems" within modern industrialization, and at the same time it produces and reproduces social stratification based on class.

Much like citizenship, schooling is also implicated in the production and reproduction of colonialism. Willinsky points out that education is caught in a double-bind in so far as it is complicit with efforts to define difference by constructing what distinguishes "civilized" from "primitive", "West" from "East", and "first" from "third" worlds: "[w]e are educated in what we take to be the true nature of difference" (1998, 1). However, education has never been simply a straightforward affair of cultural transmission, so "if education can turn a studied distance between people into a fact of nature, education can also help us appreciate how that distance has been constructed to the disadvantage of so many people" (ibid., 1–2). Dominant ideologies are relayed through schooling at the same time that schools are a key institutionalized space for the potential deconstruction of colonial narratives.

Schooling is complicit in the tandem processes of modernization and colonialization, yet it is also a site looked to for the promotion of social justice. Tikly explains that social reality can be discursively challenged and reconstructed through education: "[D]iscourses about the nature of social reality and of human nature itself, including those about education and development provide the bricks and mortar, the final recourse in relation to which hegemony and counter-hegemony are constructed and contested" (2004, 178). This basic tension is unavoidable because if schooling can be the site of discursive struggles, then it can also reinforce discursive domination. Asher and Durand (2012) express this paradox. On the one hand, schooling is a tool for colonization, and teacher and students participate in cultural and political legacies of colonialism as well as continual reproductions of global socio-economic inequities. Yet, "[a]t the same time, [one] recognize[s] the transformative potential of education, precisely because it permits exposing taken-for-granted ideologies, disseminating new and previously silenced ways of knowing, and advancing alternative ways of imagining the future" (Asher and Durand 2012, 2).

Because schooling is a vehicle both for cultivating citizens and reinforcing social inequalities and colonial imaginaries, the global imperative asserts a particular set of pressures on education (Pashby 2008). Schooling must respond to the increasingly diverse and unequal demographics associated with increased mobility at the same time as it responds to the perceived needs of the nation-state in an era of global market competition (Agbaria 2011). Thus, a key area of concern is global education, which is broadly defined as teaching students about global issues and, even more broadly, refers to global trends in education. While global education has a long history, there has been a recent resurgence of interest in bringing global education to classrooms at all levels of schooling. Much scholarship theorizes what best reform in education will fit the demands of globalization, but Agbaria points to a lack of attention regarding how the "global" is being framed and rendered in educational scholarship:

[T]his literature often approaches the "global" as a monolithic concept but not as a discursive formation imbued with competing perspectives. As such, the "global" is regularly employed as detached from the social context, institutional realities, and discursive practices through which it is ratified. Moreover, it is not fully clear as to what kind of globalization educators are urged to prepare their students for. Thus, the little knowledge on how globalization has been represented obscures what has been legitimized about globalization and how to educate about it.

(Ibid., 58)

Therefore, the intersecting discursive fields of global/globalization/cosmopolitanism, citizenship, and education/schooling represent a nexus of inherited and contested discourses and metanarratives contributing to what it means to educate citizens in the twenty-first century.

The nexus of intersecting discursive fields: GCE

The field of GCE has for the most part taken on the challenge posed by Agbaria (2011): give stronger attention to education about globalization and for global community. Davies *et al.* (2005) identified its emergence at the turn of the twenty-first century as a bringing together of global education and citizenship education. Within this bridging of global education and citizenship education, international scholarly literature on GCE encompasses a broad range. Some work draws on liberal humanistic frameworks (e.g., Noddings 2005; Nussbaum 2002) while others employ more critical frameworks to promote GCE (e.g., Andreotti 2006; Andreotti *et al.* 2009; Pike 2008a; Richardson 2008; Shultz 2007). As Andreotti describes, "[t]he different meanings attributed to 'global citizenship education' depend on contextually situated assumptions about globalisation, citizenship and education that prompt questions about boundaries, flows, power relations, belonging, rights, responsibilities, otherness, interdependence, as well as social reproduction and/or contestation" (2011b, 307). In this sense, GCE discourses, for the large part, operate within normative structures and dominant ideologies. Yet, despite differences, there are some overarching themes and rationales in the field of GCE, "especially when placed in Western, liberal–economic country contexts" (Marshall 2011, 415). Based on a review of scholarly literature (Pashby 2013), some of the key themes include:

- an acknowledgement that urgent and troubling issues are global in scope: e.g. poverty, global warming, AIDS, racism, wars (Banks 2004; Ghosh 2008; Noddings 2005; Nussbaum 2002; Richardson 2008);
- a moral imperative for extending a notion of citizenship to those outside of one's national borders (Basile 2005; Noddings 2005);

- a need to promote a sense of agency and action among youth. This ought to go beyond charity to address structural critiques of social issues (Davies 2006; Ladson-Billings 2005; Pike 2008b; Shultz 2007);
- a challenge to and resisting of the overwhelmingly Western–American–Global North-centric nature of most education materials. Educational resources tend to emphasize neo-liberal values of consumerism rather than critical democratic engagement and focus on globalization from above and preparing students to be global workers and consumers (Pike 2008b; Talbert 2005; Kachur 2008);[1]
- a call for global citizenship to become an educational imperative because schools can play a strategic role in promoting a commitment to social justice (Glass 2000; Pike 2008a, 2008b; White 2005) and developing a global sense of community (Abdi and Shultz 2008);
- an imperative to engage with contemporary processes of globalization which problematize homogeneous notions of national citizenship as well as a need to conceptualize schooling as a space for engaging with contemporary complex experiences of citizenship and identity (Banks 2004, 2008; Castles 2004; Davies 2006; Guilherme 2002; McIntosh 2005; Osler and Starkey 2003; Pike 2008b; Scott and Lawson 2002); and
- a focus on pedagogical approaches that are explicit in their inclusion and recognition of different epistemological perspectives and cultural norms. This imperative promotes engaging with "the links between conflict and interpretations of culture" (Davies 2006, 6).

Overall, the GCE scholarship in English both recognizes problematic narratives of globalization and promotes the creation of new "legends" about the relationship between the local and the global (Pike 2008b, 226).

Towards a more critical approach to GCE: post-colonial critiques

Within the wider field of GCE scholarship, a key body of work is promoting a more critical approach. A critical approach would require the explicit treatment of power relations in terms of resource distribution and epistemological privilege (Andreotti 2006). Critical GCE work aims to interrogate and move beyond a benevolent discourse of raising awareness about an identified global problem and helping global others who are worse off. Critical GCE promotes recognition of complicity within geopolitical power relations. This view of GCE does not prioritize helping students to feel good, but rather facilitates a dynamic engagement in recognizing the legacies and processes of the culture and context in which they live and were raised and how this frames their relation to others and to global issues. The intention is to create pedagogical spaces where students can imagine a future that is distinctly different from – rather than that reinforces – current ways of being and relating, and this includes engaging deeply in the idea of what it means to take ethical responsibility for actions and decisions in the complex times in which we live (Andreotti 2006; see also Eidoo *et al.* 2011).

Much of the more critical scholarship within the GCE literature engages post-/decolonial perspectives and critiques. Mignolo defines decolonization as a process of "delinking" from Western macro-narratives (2011, 273). Abdi (2008) also links post-colonial critique to an active attempt to decolonize education. In calling for a decolonization of the imaginary as a precondition for educating for citizenship, he points to "the negative role colonial education (or miseducation) has played in the process of disenfranchisement" and proposes "reeducating people for inclusive citizenship and social development" (Abdi 2008, 66). The work of Andreotti and Souza (2011) aligns with critiques such as those of Mignolo and Abdi that centre on the reproduction of colonial systems of power through modern processes and institutions. They point out that many GCE initiatives "uncritically embrace the normative teleological project of Western/Enlightenment humanism [and] … conceptualizations of humanity/human nature, progress and justice. Such investments structure an epistemic blindness to one's own ontological choices and epistemic categories and thus to radical difference itself" (Andreotti and Souza 2011, 1–2). Critical GCE work rooted in such post-colonial critiques attempts to trouble the paradox of schooling as a site of de- and re-colonization. It attempts to work towards social justice, diversity, equity, and rights without accepting the inherent systemic inequities in a historical and contemporary vision of educating citizens (Pashby 2013). Correspondingly, an approach to GCE focused not just on raising awareness of global issues but also on changing the conditions that create problems in the first place must promote the rights of those historically and currently marginalized. This means not just promoting the rights of recognition and participation as equals, but also enabling a redistribution of power and resources and supporting their right to participation in how issues are named and framed (Fraser 2005).

A post-colonial approach to GCE engages with unequal relations of power rather than solely focusing on the inclusion of those seemingly marginalized into the universally defined good life. In a post-colonial framing, global problems are often rooted in ethnocentrism and hegemonic unequal power relations that result in inequities of distributions of wealth and labour. Andreotti insists that "humanity needs to be faced and its potential for harm recognized" (2011a, 94). The potential for harm includes racism, as it is central to the social order and ideologies of cultural superiority and leads not only to discrimination but also deficit thinking and epistemological violence. The emphasis of GCE in a post-colonial approach goes beyond an awareness of issues that are identified as global problems but are generally understood to be and are framed as problems that are specific to those in so-called "undeveloped" countries (Tikly 2004). It is a GCE for fundamental structural and relational change based on a clear social critique of who controls "knowledge production, power and representation" (Andreotti 2011a, 95). It is an approach to

GCE that also endorses a commitment to reflexivity, "unlearning privilege", and "learning to learn from below" (ibid.).

Unlike Western humanism that tends to avoid or deny conflict and uncertainty and neo-liberalism that seeks to manage it through individual skill development and economic rationalizations, post-colonial versions of GCE see complexity, diversity, uncertainty, conflict, and difference as learning opportunities. However, Andreotti (2011a) notes that a post-colonial approach can also elicit sadness on the part of students when they face of repeated systemic inequalities and can also prompt scepticism towards traditional "making a difference" techniques. This can result in resistance to post-colonial pedagogies and feelings of guilt and paralysis. It is very difficult to work outside of a dominant paradigm seen as benign and neutral, and it is existentially challenging to confront the ways one's well-intended efforts to raise awareness about and campaign against global issues can lead to actions and ideas complicit with inequalities. Working towards a vision of GCE that takes up post-colonial critiques means opening up a new conceptual and ideological space of struggle and relating to others. It can be a dynamic space of possibilities. Andreotti (2011a) suggests that there is a perceived and inevitable choice between uncritical engagement and critical disengagement. This dichotomy reflects a central challenge of not throwing the baby out with the proverbial bathwater. How can we support some key GCE work being done and promote it in certain contexts and at the same time remain critical of and perhaps advocate our opposition to GCE in other contexts (Andreotti 2011a, 211)?

Importantly, there is no one approach to GCE that will be relevant in all contexts. Andreotti explains that "it is important to recognize that 'soft' global citizenship education is appropriate to certain contexts – and can already represent a major step" (2006, 8). However, if educators are unable and unwilling to acknowledge and interrogate the assumptions and implications of approaches to GCE, this lack of reflexivity and contextualized awareness may lead to reproducing the processes and practices that have harmed those members of the global community whom GCE initiatives intend to support. Andreotti and Souza describe the main risk of soft approaches to GCE:

> Despite claims of globality and inclusion, the lack of analyses of power relations and knowledge construction in this area often results in educational practices that unintentionally reproduce ethnocentric, ahistorical, depoliticized, paternalistic, Salvationist and triumphalist approaches that tend to deficit theorize, pathologize or trivialize difference.
>
> (2011, 1)

The concepts of context and complicity are very important, given that GCE is a popular educational discourse in English-speaking, multicultural, Western democracies such as Canada, the UK, Australia, New Zealand, and the USA. There cannot be a one-size-fits-all approach, and GCE must be contextualized as situated and historicized in order to resist reproducing colonial patterns of thought and action.

Andreotti sums up critiques of the concurrent discursive fields of globalization, cosmopolitanism, citizenship, schooling, and the intersecting discursive field of GCE by noting that soft versions of it:

> Have been cognitively shaped by Enlightenment ideals and have an emotional investment in universalism (i.e. the projection of their ideas as what everyone else should believe), stability (i.e. avoidance of conflict and complexity), consensus (i.e. the elimination of difference) and fixed identities organized in hierarchical ways (e.g. us, who knows, versus "them" who don't know).
>
> (2010c, 242–243)

In response to this critique, she promotes a version of GCE that embraces "learning to unlearn" and that makes "connections between social–historical processes and encounters that have shaped our contexts and cultures and the construction of our knowledges and identities" (ibid., 243). In such a case, students would be facilitated to recognize that social groups are internally diverse and experience conflict. Rather than simply celebrating cultural differences in a superficial way (that can unwittingly essentialize), students can understand that "culture is a dynamic and conflictual production of meaning in a specific context" (ibid.). This application of critical GCE is a response to post-colonial critique. And it is a concept that has been taken up quite widely in educational research (e.g. Bryan *et al.* 2011; Edge and Khamsi 2012; Martin 2013).

Synthesis and discussion: towards thinking otherwise

This chapter has reviewed the main rationales for an approach to GCE that aims to interrogate and revise – rather than unintentionally reinforce – colonial systems of power. Applications of the discursive turn in the social studies have facilitated a number of important critiques of key modern ideas that construct and reproduce colonial inequalities through the unquestioned tenets of reason, science, seamless progress, and continued development. Andreotti's (2010c) definition of the discursive turn helps us to understand that key terms and metanarratives such as global citizenship are situated, partial, contingent, and provisional. In fact, GCE represents conjoined and overlapping discursive fields. Each – globalization/the global/cosmopolitanism, citizenship, and education – is contested in terms of both its possibilities to promote justice and equality and also to reinforce the very systems that continue to define difference and inequities.

GCE emerged as a growth area for scholarship and practice at the turn of the twenty-first century. It encompasses a range of approaches, some of which are more critically grounded. Recently, a great deal of work has mobilized around the critical work in the field. Specifically, scholars and educators are looking to push beyond inherited paradigms and to avoid reproducing systems of inequities embedded in taken-for-granted ways of teaching about the world. As studies in Alberta, Canada (Pashby 2013) and in Northern Ireland (Niens and Reilly 2012) demonstrate, there has been important work done to include global citizenship in curricula. However, teachers and students continue to remain constrained by dominant discourses of charity and personal gratitude that, despite good intentions, can reify rather than problematize an idea of an *us* and a *them*.

Global citizenship is now included as a key plank in the UN Secretary-General Ban Ki-moon's Global First Initiative, is a major theme of UNESCO's current work, and, along with sustainability skills, has been named in one of the seven UN post-2015 development targets for education progress. In this sense, it is a mainstream international discourse. And for this reason it is especially important to consider a critical approach informed by post-colonial critiques. It is essential that with this renewed interest we do not repeat the same mistakes and simply inherit approaches from the past repackaged as new. The renewed interest in GCE represents an opportunity for us to interrogate our good intentions and open up spaces for thinking otherwise (Andreotti and Souza 2011). It is possible that such approaches may make new mistakes; however, given the wealth of theoretical work we have to draw on, there is no excuse for failing to do our best to be aware of how our approaches are situated, partial, contingent, and provisional. There will be multiple approaches needed; however, more of the same will certainly not meet the needs of our complex society, nor will it enable us to relate to others differently. For, as Pike asserts, "if our educational institutions cannot be catalysts in constructing the new legend, from where is that impetus likely to come?" (2008b, 236).

Note

1 I have argued elsewhere that the scholarly writing on GCE is itself limited in that it is largely written from within that same geopolitical context of English-speaking liberal democracies of the "Global North" (Pashby 2011).

References

Abdi, Ali. 2008. "De-subjecting Subject Populations: Historico-actual Problems and Educational Possibilities". In *Educating for Human Rights and Global Citizenship*. Albany, NY: State University of New York Press, pp. 65–80.

Abdi, Ali and Lynette Shultz. 2008. "Educating for Human Rights and Global Citizenship: An Introduction". In *Educating for Human Rights and Global Citizenship*. Albany, NY: State University of New York Press, pp. 1–10.

AE (Alberta Education). 2005. *Social Studies: Kindergarten to Grade 12*. Edmonton: Crown in Right of Alberta. Available at: www.education.alberta.ca/media/773701/soc10.pdf.

AE (Alberta Education). 2007. *Social Studies 10–1: Perspectives on Globalization*. Edmonton: Crown in Right of Alberta. Available at: www.education.alberta.ca/media/773701/soc10.pdf.

Agbaria, Ayman K. 2011. "The Social Studies Education Discourse Community on Globalization: Exploring the Agenda of Preparing Citizens for the Global Age". *Journal of Studies in International Education*, 1–17. DOI: 10.1177/1028315309334645.

Anderson, Benedict. 2006. *Imagined Communities: Reflections on the Origin and Spread of Nationalism*. New York: Verso.

Andreotti, Vanessa. 2006. "Soft Versus Critical Global Citizenship Education". *Policy and Practice: A Development Education Review* 3: 40–45.

Andreotti, Vanessa. 2010a. "Engaging the (Geo)political Economy of Knowledge Construction: Towards Decoloniality and Diversality in Global Citizenship Education". Available at: www.ucalgary.ca/peacestudies/files/peacestudies/Engaging%20the%20(geo)political%20economy%20of%20knowledge%20construction.pdf (accessed 31 July 2015).

Andreotti, Vanessa. 2010b. "Global Education in the 21st Century: Two Different Perspectives on the 'Post-' of Postmodernism". *International Journal of Development Education and Global Learning* 2(2): 5–22.

Andreotti, Vanessa. 2010c. "Postcolonial and Post-critical 'Global Citizenship Education'". In *Education and Social Change: Connecting Local and Global Perspectives*. London: Continuum, pp. 238–250.

Andreotti, Vanessa. 2011a. *Actionable Postcolonial Theory in Education*. New York: Palgrave Macmillan.

Andreotti, Vanessa. 2011b. "The Political Economy of Global Citizenship Education". *Globalisation, Societies and Education* 9(3–4): 307–310.

Andreotti, Vanessa, David Jefferess, Karen Pashby, Cash Rowe, Paul Tarc, and Lisa Taylor. 2009. "Difference and Conflict in Global Citizenship in Higher Education in Canada". *International Journal of Development Education and Global Learning* 2(3): 5–24.

Andreotti, Vanessa and Lynn Mario de Souza. 2011. "Introduction: (Towards) Global Citizenship Education 'Otherwise'". In *Postcolonial Perspectives on Global Citizenship Education*. New York: Routledge, pp. 1–6.

Asher, Nina and Durand, E. Sybil. 2012 "Crafting Postcolonial Pedagogies: At the Intersections of Theory and Practice". Paper presented at the American Educational Studies Association Congress, San Diego, CA. April. Available at: http://conference.jctonline.org/index.php/cctcp/2011/paper/downloadSuppFile/655/61 (accessed 31 July 2015).

Banks, James A. 2004. "Introduction: Democratic Citizenship Education in Multicultural Societies". In *Diversity and Citizenship Education: Global Perspectives*. San Francisco, CA: Wiley, pp. 3–15.

Banks, James A. 2008. "Diversity, Group Identity, and Citizenship Education". *Educational Researcher* 37(3): 129–139.

Basile, Carole. 2005. "Jefferson County Open School: Voices of Global Citizenship". In *Democracy at the Crossroads: International Perspectives on Critical Global Citizenship Education*. Lanham, MD: Lexington Books, pp. 347–363.

Bryan, Audrey, Marie Clarke, Sheelagh Drudy, Tony Gallagher, and Lesley McEvoy. 2011. "Social Justice Education in Initial Teacher Education: A Cross Border Perspective". A report to the Standing Conference on Teacher Education North and

South. Available at: http://scotens.org/site/wp-content/uploads/Social-Justice-Education-in-Initial-Teacher-Education-2009.pdf (accessed 24 September 2015).

Burns, K. 2008. "(Re)imagining the Global, Rethinking Gender in Education". *Discourse: Studies in the Cultural Politics of Education* 29(3): 343–357.

Camicia, Steven P. and Barry M. Franklin. 2011. "What Type of Global Community and Citizenship? Tangled Discourses of Neoliberalism and Critical Democracy in Curriculum and Its Reform". *Globalisation, Societies and Education* 9(3–4): 311–322.

Castles, Stephen. 2004. "Migration, Citizenship, and Education". *Diversity and Citizenship Education: Global Perspectives*: 17–48.

Davies, Ian, Mark Evans, and Alan Reid. 2005. "Globalising Citizenship Education? A Critique of 'Global Education' and 'Citizenship Education'". *British Journal of Educational Studies* 53(1): 66–89.

Davies, Lynn. 2006. "Global Citizenship: Abstraction or Framework for Action?". *Educational Review* 58(1): 5–25.

Delanty, Gerard. 2006. "Nationalism and Cosmopolitanism: The Paradox of Modernity". In *The SAGE Handbook of Nations and Nationalism*. London: Sage, pp. 357–368.

Edge, Karen and Khatera Khamsi. 2012. "International School Partnerships as a Vehicle for Global Education: Student Perspectives". *Asia Pacific Journal of Education* 32(4): 455–472.

Eidoo, Sameena, Leigh-Anne Ingram, Angela MacDonald, Maryam Nabavi, Karen Pashby, and Saskia Stille. 2011. "'Through the Kaleidoscope': Intersections between Theoretical Perspectives and Classroom Implications in Critical Global Citizenship Education". *Canadian Journal of Education/Revue canadienne de l'éducation* 34(4): 59–85.

Fraser, Nancy. 2005. "Reframing Global Justice". *New Left Review* 36: 69–88.

Ghosh, Ratna. 2008. "The Short History of Women, Human Rights, and Global Citizenship". In *Educating for Human Rights and Global Citizenship*. Albany, NY: State University of New York Press, pp. 81–95.

Glass, Ronald David. 2000. "Education and the Ethics of Democratic Citizenship". *Studies in Philosophy and Education* 19(3): 275–296.

Goldberg, David Theo. 1993. "Modernity, Race, and Morality". *Cultural Critique*: 193–227.

Guilherme, Manuela. 2002. *Critical Citizens for an Intercultural World: Foreign Language Education as Cultural Politics*. London: Multilingual Matters.

Ibrahim, Tasneem. 2005. "Global Citizenship Education: Mainstreaming the Curriculum?". *Cambridge Journal of Education* 35(2): 177–194.

Isin, Engin F. and Patricia K. Wood. 1999. *Citizenship and Identity*. London: Sage.

Kachur, Jerrold. 2008. "Human Rights Imperialism: Third Way Education as the New Cultural Imperialism". *Educating Citizens for Global Awareness*. New York: Teachers College Press, pp. 177–192.

Ladson-Billings, Gloria. 2005. "Differing Concepts of Citizenship: Schools and Communities as Sites of Civic Development". *Educating Citizens for Global Awareness*. New York: Teachers College Press, pp. 69–80.

McCollum, Ann. 2002. "Citizenship Education and the Challenges of Cultural Diversity". In *Citizenship Education and the Curriculum*. Westport, CT: Ablex, pp. 167–182.

McIntosh, Peggy. 2005. "Gender Perspectives on Educating for Global Citizenship". *Educating Citizens for Global Awareness*. New York: Teachers College Press, pp. 22–39.

Mannion, Greg, Gert Biesta, Mark Priestley, and Hamish Ross. 2011. "The Global Dimension in Education and Education for Global Citizenship: Genealogy and Critique". *Globalisation, Societies and Education* 9(3–4): 443–456.

Marshall, Harriet. 2011. "Instrumentalism, Ideals and Imaginaries: Theorising the Contested Space of Global Citizenship Education in Schools". *Globalisation, Societies and Education* 9(3–4): 411–426.

Marshall, Thomas Humphrey. 1950. *Citizenship and Social Class and Other Essays*. Cambridge: Cambridge University Press.

Martin, Fran. 2013. "Same Old Story: The Problem of Object-based Thinking as a Basis for Teaching Distant Places". *Education 3–13* 41(4): 410–424.

Mignolo, Walter. 2000. "The Many Faces of Cosmo-Polis: Border Thinking and Critical Cosmopolitanism". *Public Culture* 12(3): 721–748.

Mignolo, Walter. 2011. "Geopolitics of Sensing and Knowing: On (De) Coloniality, Border Thinking and Epistemic Disobedience". *Postcolonial Studies* 14(3): 273–283.

Niens, Ulrike and Jacqueline Reilly. 2012. "Education for Global Citizenship in a Divided Society? Young People's Views and Experiences". *Comparative Education* 48(1): 103–118.

Noddings, Nel. (ed.) 2005. *Educating Citizens for Global Awareness*. New York: Teachers College Press.

Nussbaum, Martha. 2002. "Education for Citizenship in an Era of Global Connection". *Studies in Philosophy and Education* 21(4–5): 289–303.

Osborne, Ken. 2008. "Education and Schooling: A Relationship That Can Never Be Taken for Granted". *Yearbook of the National Society for the Study of Education* 107(1): 21–41.

Osler, Audrey and Hugh Starkey. 2003. "Learning for Cosmopolitan Citizenship: Theoretical Debates and Young People's Experiences". *Educational Review* 55(3): 243–254.

Pashby, Karen. 2008. "Demands on and of Citizenship and Schooling: 'Belonging' and 'Diversity' in the Global Imperative". *Brock Education Journal* 17(1): 1–21.

Pashby, Karen. 2011. "Cultivating Global Citizens: Planting New Seeds or Pruning the Perennials? Looking for the Citizen-Subject in Global Citizenship Education Theory". *Globalisation, Societies and Education* 9(3–4): 427–442.

Pashby, Karen. 2013. "Related and Conflated: A Theoretical and Discursive Framing of Multiculturalism and Global Citizenship Education in the Canadian Context". Ph.D. dissertation, OISE/University of Toronto. Available at: http://hdl.handle.net/1807/35921.

Pike, Graham. 2008a. "Citizenship Education in Global Context". *Brock Education* 17(1): 38–49.

Pike, Graham. 2008b. "Reconstructing the Legend: Educating for Global Citizenship". In *Educating for Human Rights and Global Citizenship*. Albany, NY: State University of New York Press, pp. 223–237.

Richardson, George H. 2002. *The Death of the Good Canadian: Teachers, National Identities, and the Social Studies Curriculum*. New York: Peter Lang.

Richardson, George H. 2008. "Conflicting Imaginaries: Global Citizenship Education in Canada as a Site of Contestation". *Citizenship Education in the Era of Globalization: Canadian Perspectives*. Rotterdam: Sense Publishing.

Rizvi, Fazal. 2009. "Towards Cosmopolitan Learning". *Discourse: Studies in the Cultural Politics of Education* 30(3): 253–268.

SACSC [Society for Safe and Caring Schools & Communities]. n.d.a. "Grade 10 Social Studies, English Language Arts: Unit One: Global Issues Awareness: Lesson One: Issues, What Issues?" [Lesson Plan]. Available at: http://sacsc.ca/senior-high-lesson-plans-social-studies (accessed 11 November 2012).

SACSC [Society for Safe and Caring Schools & Communities]. n.d.b. "Grade 10 Social Studies, English Language Arts: Unit One: Global Issues Awareness: Lesson Three: A Lived Experience" [Lesson Plan]. Available at: http://sacsc.ca/senior-high-lesson-plans-social-studies (accessed 11 November 2012).

Said, Edward W. 1994. *Culture and Imperialism*. New York: Knopf.

Scott, David and Helen Lawson. 2002. *Citizenship Education and the Curriculum*. Westport, CT: Ablex, pp. 1–6.

Shultz, Lynette. 2007. "Educating for Global Citizenship: Conflicting Agendas and Understandings". *Alberta Journal of Educational Research* 53(3): 248–258.

Soysal, Yasemin Nuhoğlu. 2011. "Reply to Will Kymlicka: 'Multicultural Citizenship within Multination States'". *Ethnicities* 11(3): 8–312.

Steinberg, Marc W. 1999. "The Talk and Back Talk of Collective Action: A Dialogic Analysis of Repertoires of Discourse Among Nineteenth-Century English Cotton Spinners". *American Journal of Sociology* 105(3): 736–780.

Strand, Torill. 2010a. "Introduction: Cosmopolitanism in the Making". *Studies in Philosophy and Education* 29(2): 103–109.

Strand, Torill. 2010b. "The Making of a New Cosmopolitanism". *Studies in Philosophy and Education* 29(2): 229–242.

Talbert, Tony L. 2005. "Freedom or French Fries: Packaged Democracy for World Consumption". In *Democracy at the Crossroads: International Perspectives on Critical Global Citizenship Education*. Lanham, MD: Lexington Books, pp. 31–54.

Tikly, Leon. 2004. "Education and the New Imperialism". *Comparative Education* 40(2): 173–198.

Tully, James. 2008. "Two Meanings of Global Citizenship: Modern and Diverse". In *Global Citizenship Education: Philosophy, Theory and Pedagogy*. Rotterdam: Sense Publishers, pp. 15–39.

White, Cameron. 2005. "Critical Democratic Education for Social Efficacy". In *Democracy at the Crossroads: International Perspectives on Critical Global Citizenship Education*. Lanham, MD: Lexington Books, pp. 77–104.

Willinsky, John. 1998. *Learning to Divide the World: Education at Empire's End*. Minneapolis, MN: University of Minnesota Press.

Willinsky, John. 2008. "Preface". In *Decolonizing Democratic Education*. Rotterdam: Sense Publishers, pp. vii–x.

Willinsky, John. 2012. "What Was Multiculturalism?". *Precarious International Multicultural Education: Hegemony, Dissent and Rising Alternatives*. Rotterdam: Sense Publishers, pp. 15–39. DOI: 10.1007/978-94-6091-894-0.

Wrigley, Terry, Bob Lingard, and Pat Thomson. 2012. "Pedagogies of Transformation: Keeping Hope Alive in Troubled Times". *Critical Studies in Education* 53(1): 95–108.

6 Cosmopolitan appropriation or learning?
Relation and action in global citizenship education

David Jefferess

Global citizenship education (GCE) initiatives typically are premised upon two related ideas: relation and action. For instance, global citizens learn to recognize that "we live in an *interconnected and interdependent* world in which our lives are shaped by events that take place around the globe" (TVDSB n.d., emphasis original). At the same time, the global citizen is "willing and enabled to take action to make the world a fairer place for ourselves and other living creatures" (University of British Columbia n.d.). In much of global citizenship theory and practice, the *relation* that binds the global citizen with others is understood primarily as the ethical obligation that one has to *act* in the interest of others. As such, global citizenship is often enacted through humanitarianism, such as overseas volunteering, fundraising for development projects, or consciousness-raising about suffering in other places in the world. GCE, at least in its more typical "soft" varieties (Andreotti 2006), invites youth to become "agents of change" who "make a difference". Such uncritical forms of global citizenship reflect the legacy of colonial ideology, in that the global citizen undertakes a "burden" to uplift others. Unlike earlier overtly Euro-centric articulations of humanitarian benevolence, however, today's global citizen aspires to be "post-racial" (Jefferess 2011; 2015); GCE increasingly emphasizes the importance of valuing ideas, philosophies, or ideals attributed to people classified as "non-Western" (Jefferess 2011; 2015).[1] In this chapter, I examine the prominence of two such philosophies or ideals within discourses of global citizenship and/as humanitarianism: the southern African notion of *ubuntu* and the popular statement, "Be the change you wish to see in the world", which is attributed to Mohandas K. Gandhi.

Both of these aspirational ideas have gained wide use in the programming of GCE and development NGOs, and they each affirm one of the two core ideals of global citizenship: relation and action. I contend that *ubuntu* and "Be the Change" have become so prominent within global citizenship discourse because they are so easily incorporated into the familiar registers of humanitarianism. They authenticate global citizenship as cosmopolitan or intercultural, but are also used to affirm dominant Western biases within GCE. While my work has challenged the continuing Western-oriented and humanitarian framework of global citizenship, as a person who is situated as

88 David Jefferess

white, highly educated, and a Canadian citizen, my own aspirations for global justice are not free of the sorts of problems that I outline in this chapter. For instance, while my teaching and research seek to be embedded in a decolonizing – rather than cosmopolitan – project, I have utilized the notion of *ubuntu* in ways that I now recognize as reflecting some of the same limitations that I identify in this chapter (Jefferess 2008, 2012a). To conclude the chapter, I reflect on the larger problem of easy incorporations of "non-Western" or Indigenous knowledge into GCE by engaging with the work of Jeannette Armstrong, whose articulation of Sylix/Okanagan conceptions of relation invite learning and transformation.

Travelling ideas and cosmopolitan appropriation

In the opening to his essay "Travelling Theory", Said argues that the circulation of ideas is an "enabling condition of intellectual activity" (1983, 226). He identifies common stages for how ideas travel, or a process of "deterritorialization", as Appadurai (1990) describes cultural globalization. An idea can be understood in terms of its initial entry into discourse in a particular place and time. From this initial context, the idea might move to another time and/or place in a way that reflects "creative borrowing", "unconscious influence", or "wholesale appropriation" (Said 1983, 226). As Sen (2006) has argued, many of the key tenets of "Western Civilization", including democracy and tolerance, have antecedents outside of Europe, although this lineage is rarely recognized. The travelling idea, Said argues, is transformed by its movement, taking up a "new position" in "a new time and place" (1983, 227).

Within theories of cultural globalization, how we understand this transformation of an idea or cultural practice depends much on where the idea takes its new position. For instance, when so-called Western ideas seem to successfully transfer to places outside the West, such as hip-hop music, fast food, or – ironically – democracy, this transition has been understood either in terms of Western cultural imperialism or glocalization. The cultural imperialism thesis regards such movement of ideas as necessarily an imposition that fosters global cultural homogenization in the image of the West. In the more complicated terms of glocalization, the travelling idea is understood to take on new uses and meanings in the local context; so much more agency is attributed to the receiving culture or locality in this theory. There is recognition that the local culture is altered by the idea, but also revises or manipulates it. In contrast, when ideas that are deemed to be non-Western in origin are taken up in or by the West, the ideas tend more often to be understood as examples of cultural appropriation. Cultural exploitation, as Rogers (2006) defines it, refers to the process by which dominant cultures "mine" elements of subordinated cultures in order to serve their own interests. Appropriation often commodifies ideas, abstracting or universalizing them, which tends to obscure their history and original context. At the same time, though, it is possible to emphasize, at least in superficial ways, the culture of the idea's origin, for instance in New Age appropriations of Indigenous North American culture in health food marketing (Kadish, cited in Rogers 2006).

Appiah emphasizes that "we have much to gain from conversation with one another across our differences" (2007, 2376), and, as such, foregrounds the process of meaning-making through dialogue in contrast to the acquisition of "understanding", as if it were an object. As GCE typically presumes a Western-situated, materially privileged learner, it often foregrounds the importance of intercultural learning, particularly through pedagogies of empathy. For this reason, much GCE programming tends to represent the experiences of others as knowledge for global citizens to gain (e.g. voluntourism), reflecting a long history of exploitation in the guise of cultural understanding (Kapoor 2008). Of course, there are more critical models of GCE. For instance, Andreotti's (2012) work is prominent in this area, drawing upon Spivak to foreground the need for hyper-self-reflexivity, self-implication, and accountable reasoning (21). Yet, as she recognizes, these approaches necessarily understand the world-views and ideas of others outside of their lived contexts, and part of global learning may be to acknowledge the way that our own situated knowledges, or presumptions, provide insurmountable barriers to understanding those contexts (Andreotti 2014). We must contend with the fact that, when we approach the narratives and practices of others marked as different due to culture or marginalized social positions, we "tend to collect information that fits within [our] preconceived narrative frameworks and to overlook elements incongruent with those frameworks" (Stone-Mediatore 2003, 167). Because we cannot be entirely aware of what we overlook, even when we seek to be critically self-reflexive, taking up other's ideas in the interest of intercultural understanding or social justice can be just as exploitative as the commodification with which cultural appropriation is associated. Said notes that an idea can only become established in a new place if the right "conditions" of acceptance exist (1983, 227). In my analysis below, I examine how the conditions of acceptance within GCE and development discourse have shaped the meaning of *ubuntu* and the slogan "Be the Change". Any elements that may not be congruent with a humanitarian ethic are lost in the travel.

The uses of *ubuntu*

The relational notion of *ubuntu*, which is often translated into English as "I am because we are", has gained global currency due to its prominence as a foundational ethic of the South African Truth and Reconciliation Commission (TRC). In my work on post-colonial notions of resistance (2008), I noted that a central trope of the TRC was the restoration of the humanity of the people of South Africa, and this restoration was presented within the terms of *both* a Christian ethic of forgiveness and *ubuntu* (166). In doing so, I reinforced a distinction between modern/European and traditional/African discourses. Such a formulation reifies culture, ignoring South Africa's history of transculturation, to use Rogers's (2006) term.

Praeg (2014) argues that *ubuntu* was reinvented with the new democratic South Africa, and hence should be understood as a "glocal phenomenon" in that its current articulations infuse Christian and human rights discourses (34). It has a particular history of use that is dynamic, emerging as a "philosophy" within anti-colonial narratives of "return" and "recovery", particularly in Zimbabwe and South Africa (Matolino and Kwindingwi 2013; Murove 2014). Nonetheless, *ubuntu* is typically understood both in southern Africa and outside of Africa as an African cosmology.

In my interpretation of Desmond Tutu's writings on *ubuntu,* and in my survey of current scholarship on the idea, I identify three distinct, yet related, ways, in which the term is used: (1) it conceptualizes relation; (2) it signifies the quality of being human; and (3) it represents an ethics of conduct. According to Tutu, "the first law of our being is that we are set in a delicate network of interdependence with our fellow human beings and with the rest of God's creation ... [*Ubuntu*] speaks of the fact that my humanity is caught up and inextricably bound up in yours. I am human because I belong" (Tutu 2004, 26). Understood as a relational philosophy of subjectivity, *ubuntu* is often defined specifically in contrast to the Cartesian rational, autonomous individual (Murove 2014; Sharra 2009, 26; Tutu 2004, 27). There are debates, then, about its applicability today. The original proverb described *ubuntu* as a relation specific to the communal village and the bonds of extended family relationships, and hence in the context of the neo-liberal "global village", *ubuntu* seems only to be a symbolic ideal rather than a description of actually existing relations (Praeg 2014, 51, 106; Matolino and Kwindingwi 2013, 202–203). Yet, it is specifically as a relational cosmology that *ubuntu* has served to inform radical politics in South Africa today. For instance, Abahlali baseMjondolo, a movement advocating for the rights of people living in informal settlements and challenging the state's slum eradication programme, invokes *ubuntu* both to resist and provide an alternative to (neo)liberal presumptions of individualism, private property, and competition (Cina-Sklar 2012; Praeg 2014, 243; "Revolutionary Ubuntu" n.d.).

In the TRC, as well as contemporary South Africa, the violence of the Apartheid era or contemporary xenophobic violence reflects a lack of *ubuntu,* or humanness. Hence, to characterize someone as having *ubuntu,* is, as Tutu (2004, 26) declares, the highest praise, and hence an ideal to which an individual should aspire (Matolino and Kwindingwi 2013, 200; Murove 2014, 37; Sharra 2009). To enact *ubuntu,* then, as an ethics of conduct, means that one should care, share, be hospitable and compassionate (Matolino and Kwindinwi 2013, 199; Murove 2014, 37; Swanson 2009, 9; Tutu 2004, 26). While I want to recognize that my description of *ubuntu* in this atomized way artificially separates its function as an ethical precept from its function as a relational cosmology, I do so in part to highlight the way in which, in practice, it seems increasingly to be understood *only* in terms of individual ethics. For instance, it continues to be used as a means of asserting national identity by the state, but often functions as mere rhetoric, describing what are otherwise (neo)liberal policies of social welfare (Matolino and Kwindingwi 2013; Murove 2014; Praeg 2014), and in many ways has become simply "a shorthand for being nice" (Praeg 2014, 63).

While the relational definition of *ubuntu* – "I am because we are" – is often highlighted in discourses of global citizenship and humanitarianism, such a philosophy of interdependence can seemingly only be understood in the terms of the dominant conceptions of individual ethical conduct. For instance, the Canadian International Development Agency (CIDA) invokes *ubuntu* in the title of a 2004 policy document on its bilateral programme in South Africa. An information box on the title page succinctly explains that in "Southern African culture *ubuntu* is the capacity to express compassion, justice, reciprocity, dignity, harmony and humanity" and that our responsibility to each other flows from the connections we have due to our common humanity (CIDA 2004). There is no further reference to *ubuntu* in the 13-page document, and there seems to be no indication that the development programme is informed by the idea in any way. This sort of symbolic use of the term is prevalent not only in formal development discourse but also in development education, such as the Irish Ubuntu Network that seeks to foster "a world based on human dignity and rights" through development education (Ubuntu Network 2012). In university global citizenship initiatives, *ubuntu* has become a synonym for compassion or the inspiration to be a "change maker".[2] Similarly, the Ubuntu Education Fund, which has offices in South Africa, the United States, and the United Kingdom, describes its model of development as innovative, but ultimately follows a standard development paradigm of providing health and education services as a means to "place children on the pathway out of poverty" (Ubuntu Fund n.d.). Unlike the British Council's Active Citizens toolkit, which invokes *ubuntu* in terms of systems thinking and identifying the importance of undertaking action that is shaped by an understanding of the systems of which we are a part (British Council 2011), the Ubuntu Fund's website does not engage with how people are interdependent but, rather, conceives of interconnection in terms of charitable action.

While each of these examples emphasize the "Africanness" of the concept, presenting it as Africa's "gift to the world" (Praeg 2014, 89), none provide any meaningful engagement with either the history of the idea or the contested way it functions today. Instead, *ubuntu* is believed to reflect an African essence at the same time that it is used purposefully to reaffirm dominant discourses of liberal human rights. As such, it is often characterized as an African humanism (Chaplin n.d.; Praeg 2014; Swanson 2009). Ironically, then, it is the (Western) humanitarian or global citizen who becomes the model of *ubuntu* (see Mungai 2009, 46; Chaplin n.d.). This is particularly evident in *I Am Because We Are* (Rissman 2008), a documentary film that chronicles the pop star Madonna's initiatives to alleviate the suffering of people with HIV/AIDS in Malawi. An unidentified African man explains the Zulu idea of *ubuntu* – rather than the Chichewa term *uMunthu* (Sharra 2009) – early in the documentary, which proceeds to depict Madonna as a saviour figure, performing acts of compassion. This deterritorialization of *ubuntu* is shaped by the conditions of its acceptance into global citizenship discourse; it is incorporated into a "universal" humanitarian ideal, becoming something that the *global citizen* enacts.

Being the change *you* wish to see

The inspirational phrase, "Be the change you wish to see in the world", often shortened to "Be the Change", is a prominent articulation of social justice initiatives, centred on anti-bullying, ecological justice, international development, and volunteerism. The phrase provides the name for NGOs and the title for both business and non-profit projects. Further, it is reproduced on clothing and other products by the transnational social enterprise Me to We and the progressive publisher Syracuse Cultural Workers. Typically, the statement is attributed to Mohandas K. Gandhi. Morton (2011), however, argues that the "gauzy slogan" has been misattributed, as no such quotation can be found in Gandhi's substantial writings, and it "suggests that your responsibilities begin and end with your own behaviour. It's apolitical, and a little smug". Lorrance (n.d.) asserts that it is much more likely that the origin of the phrase is the principle "Be the change you want to see happen instead of trying to change anyone else", first published in her 1978 book, *The Love Project*, which chronicles her work aimed at empowering youth in a Brooklyn, New York high school. While uses of the slogan rarely provide any context for Gandhi's work or critical perspective, the attribution to Gandhi is significant, for it aligns this particular conception of social change with an icon of social justice from the Global South, whose name provides ethical authority.

In workshops at a leadership conference for Canadian high school students, I asked participants to define the slogan in their own words. All of the students had heard the phrase before, identifying primarily citizenship education initiatives as the context, particularly the work of Me to We. On the nearly 80 responses written on notepaper and posted around the room, students provided a range of ideas, from the importance of inspiring or educating others, to serving as a positive influence in one's community, to doing the unexpected, to improving one's self. Nearly one-third of the responses defined the term as some variation of "making a difference". Another 17 emphasized the importance of taking "action", identifying how it is important not to wait for others to act, but to lead, or why it is important to act on one's words and not just talk.

To foster a conversation on what it means to "be the Change" in more concrete terms, I provided participants with the scenario of the Okanagan region in Canada in which residential water use is about twice the national average, despite the fact that the region has less water available per capita than elsewhere in the country (Make Water Work 2012; Okanagan 2011). The students agreed that the region was not using water sustainably. When asked how residents could "Be the Change" on this issue, participants provided a narrow range of suggestions, including using low-flow showerheads, turning off water while brushing teeth, or not watering lawns every day. These articulations of "Be the Change" focus on minor changes to personal behaviour; the suggestion that people might not fill pools, for instance, precipitated laughter, and the students who responded to this suggestion agreed that it would require too great a personal sacrifice.

While it is easy to see how the phrase *could* have been *derived* from the writings of Gandhi (2008), the slogan – as well as the students' responses – disregard the importance of acting in concert with others, and how personal ethics are inextricable from the work of transforming oppressive social structures, two ideas which are at the core of Gandhi's teachings. In Gandhi's writings, there are many other recurrent themes, including the importance of suffering as a part of political action, non-cooperation with unjust laws, or non-possession and material simplicity as an alternative to the exploitation and self-indulgence of capitalist modernity. Yet, the slogan "Civilization consists in the deliberate and voluntary reduction of wants" (Gandhi 2001, 46) or "Renounce and Enjoy" (Gandhi, cited in Dear 2002, 42) are hardly consistent with the practices of development organizations and GCE initiatives like Me to We and Free the Children, which have chosen to foreground "Be the Change" in their marketing. For instance, the We365 cell phone app is designed to "empower" youth to track their volunteer hours and to compile a "social good portfolio" for their resume/CV (Free the Children n.d.). The kinds of action Me to We promotes are limited to fundraising and donating, voluntourism, random acts of kindness, and exuding Me to We "style", emphasizing the happiness one will acquire through being good (Jefferess 2012b).

Me to We's use of the purported Gandhi slogan is indicative of the way it has become largely synonymous with highly personalized acts of goodwill.[3] It does not seem to be used as a tool for a pedagogical practice of critical prefiguration, wherein one investigates a social problem, imagines just relations, seeks to understand a range of perspectives and interests, and then engages with others in order to find ways to achieve such justice. Rather, it foregrounds the will and entitlement of the global citizen to "Be the change *you* wish to see in the world". Not only does it tend to privilege personal behavioural change, but it normalizes the perspective of the global citizen to enact change, as a "model" for – or saviour of – others. The particular phrase is incorporated into a universalized understanding of personal ethics framed by the Golden Rule. Yet, as Appiah (2006) argues, one must not simply do unto others as they would wish done to them, for such a perspective is neither self-conscious nor open to the interests of others; rather it presumes the universality of the self and potentially imposes one's own interests on others. Ultimately, when used in these ways, "Be the Change" ironically requires that the global citizen not entertain how they might be transformed by a recognition of their relation to others; rather, they are taught to only see themselves as an "agent of change".

Conclusion: being change

Of course, *ubuntu* (and similar articulations of relational subjectivity), or the recognition that social change requires personal transformation inform a wide array of social justice movements around the world that are not contained by the conditions of acceptance of GCE and/as humanitarianism. Yet, the highly selective use of these ideals within GCE and development discourse to authorize a politics of helping over other ways of conceiving social justice reflects a form of cosmopolitan appropriation, wherein the "otherness" of the origins of these ideals is used to legitimate and affirm dominant conceptions of human rights and humanitarianism. To conclude, I turn to Jeannette Armstrong's articulations of Sylix/Okanagan understandings of relation, which have been taken up within ecological justice discourses, but do not seem as easily incorporated into GCE, for I think they provide a profoundly different way of thinking about relation and action.

I want to propose that GCE should emphasize *being/change*. By this I mean, if the slogan "Be the Change" often affirms the privileged social position of the "global citizen" by presuming either efforts to model goodness or the responsibility to effect change for/upon others, a more critical approach foregrounds the openness to changing one's own being. By taking up Armstrong's articulation of Syilx/Okanagan understandings of relation, I risk presuming to understand this way of knowing and appropriating it for my own benefit, continuing a long history of Western commodification of Indigenous knowledge. Armstrong challenges non-Indigenous people to "imagine interpreting for us your own people's thinking towards us, instead of interpreting for us, our thinking, our lives and our stories" (Armstrong 1990, 143); yet, she also argues that "our Elders have said that unless we can 'Okanaganize' those people in their thinking, we're all in danger in the Okanagan" (Armstrong 2008, 72). In placing these assertions together, as a non-Indigenous person, I understand this as a call not to "know" and "represent" Indigenous culture but to seek to *learn from* Indigenous – and in this case specifically Syilx – ways of knowing. To do so enacts a practice not of consumption or acquisition but, for me, of being/change. I present this uneasily, for this demand requires an unlearning of much what I have been taught to think I know, and I have difficulty discerning what I understand intellectually and how I might *be* differently because of this.

In Armstrong's essay "Let Us Begin with Courage" (2000) she describes *En'owkin* as an integrative process that seeks to attain ecological sustainability. The schematic she uses to articulate this represents a structure of relations in the form of concentric circles, with the individual at the centre, embedded in the family, embedded in the community, embedded in the land. I use the term embedded, although Armstrong does not, to articulate how she explains that the full human potential of an individual is contingent upon external things – specifically the way that individual is a "single facet of a transgenerational organism known as a FAMILY", how the family functions as the foundation of community, how the community is a living network that exists over centuries and produces collective knowledge, and finally how this community interacts with, is sustained by, and must care for the land (Armstrong 2000, 8–9). Such a schematic represents the "structurally integrative nature" of *En'owkin* principles, "by which they intersect all levels of human experience" (8). Visually, this schematic looks similar to those used to articulate cosmopolitan ethics, but cosmopolitan theories of interrelation often emphasize how the ethical obligations of the global citizen constitute an *act of will*, overcoming distance to care for strangers, and hence transcending *boundaries* between individual, community, nation, and the world (Appiah 2006, 165). In such formulations, it is through acts of humanitarian charity that self and other become constituted as a relation. In contrast, in Armstrong's description of the *En'owkin* process, action is a *function* of relation.

In the student workshop examining the ideal of "Be the Change" I used that slogan as a way to spur approaches to the problem of unsustainable, and deeply damaging, misuse of water in the Okanagan valley. Drawing on the understandings of the ideal that students had derived from their own experiences with GCE we had difficulty as a group approaching the problem beyond or apart from individual acts of conservation. Using the schematic of the *En'owkin* process provides not just a different critical lens, or a different model of prefiguration, to "Be the Change", but the impetus to begin – or continue – the difficult and likely ever incomplete work of understanding our being, in relation, as action.

Notes

1 I use the terms "Western" and "non-Western" rather than other terms such as Global North and Global South in order to identify the European philosophical tradition associated with the geographical metaphor of the civilizational "West".
2 See for instance these two examples from the University of Idaho and Duke University. Available at: http://sites.duke.edu/ubuntu/ and www.uidaho.edu/studentaffairs/Ubuntu.
3 There are, of course, exceptions that utilize this idea outside of the humanitarian frame I am describing. See for instance, Michael Franti's use of #bethechange in promotion for his song, "Same as It Ever Was", which challenges institutionalized racial violence in American law enforcement.

References

Andreotti, Vanessa. 2006. "Soft Versus Critical Global Citizenship Education". *Policy and Practice: A Development Education Review* 3: 40–51.
Andreotti, Vanessa de Oliveira. 2012. "Education, Knowledge, and the Righting of Wrongs". *Other Education: The Journal of Educational Alternatives* 1: 19–31.
Andreotti, Vanessa de Oliveira. 2014. "Critical and Transnational Literacies in International Development and Global Citizenship Education". *Sisyphus* 2(3): 32–50.
Appadurai, Arjun. 1990. "Disjuncture and Difference in the Global Cultural Economy". *Theory Culture Society* 7: 295–310.

Appiah, Kwame Anthony. 2006. *Cosmopolitanism*. New York: Norton.
Appiah, Kwame Anthony. 2007. "Global Citizenship". *Fordham Law Review* 75(5): 2375–2391.
Armstrong, Jeannette. 1990. "The Disempowerment of First North American Native Peoples and Empowerment Through Their Writing". In David Gregoire (ed.), *Gatherings V*. Penticton, BC: Theytus, pp. 141–146.
Armstrong, Jeannette. 2000. "Let Us Begin with Courage". In Z. Barlow and M. Crabtree (eds), *Ecoliteracy: Mapping the Terrain*. Berkeley, CA: Learning in the Real World, pp. 8–12.
Armstrong, Jeannette. 2008. "An Okanagan Worldview of Society". In Melissa K. Nelson (ed.), *Original Instructions: Indigenous Teachings for a Sustainable Future*. Rochester, VT: Bear and Company, pp. 66–74.
British Council. 2011. *Active Citizens: Toolkit*. Vol. 4. Available at: www.britishcouncil.org/sites/britishcouncil.uk2/files/active-citizens-global-toolkit-2014-2015.pdf (accessed 25 June 2015).
Chaplin, Kevin. n.d. "The Ubuntu Spirit in African Communities". *Council of Europe*. Available at: www.coe.int/t/dg4/cultureheritage/culture/Cities/Publication/BookCoE20-Chaplin.pdf (accessed 25 June 2015).
CIDA [Canadian International Development Agency]. 2004. *Ubuntu: Working Together for a Bright Future. CIDA's Programming Framework in South Africa*. Available at: http://publications.gc.ca/site/eng/258775/publication.html (accessed 25 June 2015).
Cina-Sklar, Zoe. 2012. "Q&A: Dara Kell, Filmmaker of 'Dear Mandela'". *Swarthmore College Daily Gazette*. Available at: http://daily.swarthmore.edu/2012/10/26/qa-dara-kell-filmmaker-of-dear-mandela/ (accessed 26 October 2012).
Dear, John. 2002. "Introduction: Mahatma Gandhi, Apostle of Nonviolence". In J. Dear (ed.), *Mohandas Gandhi's Essential Writings*. Maryknoll, NY: Orbis.
Free the Children. n.d. *We365*. Available at: https://itunes.apple.com/ca/app/we365/id722529129?mt=8 (accessed 25 June 2015).
Gandhi, Mohandas. 2001. *Non-Violent Resistance (Satyagraha)*. Mineola, NY: Dover.
Gandhi, Mohandas. 2008. "Accidents: Snake-Bite". *The Collected Works of Mahatma Gandhi Online*. Vol. 13, 241. Available at: www.gandhiserve.org/cwmg/VOL013.PDF (accessed 25 June 2015).
Jefferess, David. 2008. *Postcolonial Resistance: Culture, Liberation, and Transformation*. Toronto: Toronto University Press.
Jefferess, David. 2011. "Benevolence, Global Citizenship, and Post-Racial Politics". *Topia: Canadian Journal of Cultural Studies* 25: 77–95.
Jefferess, David. 2012a. "Unsettling Cosmopolitanism: Global Citizenship and the Cultural Politics of Benevolence". In Vanessa de Oliveira Andreotti and Lynn M. de Suza (eds), *Postcolonial Perspectives on Global Citizenship Education*. New York: Routledge, pp. 27–46.
Jefferess, David. 2012b. "The 'Me to We' Social Enterprise: Global Education as Lifestyle Brand". *Critical Literacy* 6(1): 18–30.
Jefferess, David. 2015. "Introduction: 'The White Man's Burden' and Post-Racial Humanitarianism". *Critical Race and Whiteness Studies* 11(1): 1–11.
Kapoor, Ilan. 2008. *The Postcolonial Politics of Development*. New York: Routledge.
Lorrance, Arleen. n.d. "Who Said 'Be the Change'?". *Consciousness Network*. Available at: www.consciousnesswork.com/who_said_be_the_change.htm (accessed 25 June 2015).

Make Water Work. 2012. Available at: www.makewaterwork.ca (accessed 25 June 2015).
Matolino, Bernard and Wenceslaus Kwindingwi. 2013. "The End of Ubuntu". *South African Journal of Philosophy* 32(2): 197–205.
Morton, Brian. 2011. "Falser Words Were Never Spoken". *New York Times*. 30 August. Available at: www.nytimes.com/2011/08/30/opinion/falser-words-were-never-spoken.html?_r=0 (accessed 25 June 2015).
Mungai, Anne M. 2009. "Ubuntu: From Poverty to Destiny with Love". In Diane Caracciolo and Anne M. Mungai (eds), *In the Spirit Of Ubuntu: Stories of Teaching and Research*. Rotterdam: Sense, pp. 39–50.
Murove, Munyaradzi Felix. 2014. "Ubuntu". *Diogenes* 59(3–4): 36–47.
Okanagan Water Supply and Demand Project. 2011. Available at: www.obwb.ca/wsd/key-findings/water-use (accessed 25 June 2015).
Praeg, Leonhard. 2014. *A Report on Ubuntu*. Scottsville, South Africa: KwaZulu-Natal University Press.
Revolutionary Ubuntu. n.d. *eblackstudies*. Available at: www.eblackstudies.org/ebooks/ubuntu.pdf (accessed 25 June 2015).
Rissman, Nathan (dir.). 2008. *I Am Because We Are*. Semtex films. DVD.
Rogers, Richard A. 2006. "From Cultural Exchange to Transculturation: A Review and Reconceptualization of Cultural Appropriation". *Communication Theory* 16: 474–503.
Said, Edward. 1983. "Travelling Theory". In *The World, the Text, and the Critic*. Cambridge, MA: Harvard University Press, pp. 226–247.
Sen, Amartya. 2006. *Identity and Violence*. New York: Norton.
Sharra, Steve. 2009. "Towards an African Peace Epistemology: Teacher Autobiography and uMunthu in Malawian Education". In Diane Caracciolo and Anne M. Mungai (eds), *In the Spirit Of Ubuntu: Stories of Teaching and Research*. Rotterdam: Sense, pp. 23–38.
Stone-Mediatore, Shari. 2003. *Reading Across Borders: Story-telling and Knowledges of Resistance*. New York: Palgrave MacMillan.
Swanson, D. M. 2009. "Where Have All the Fishes Gone? Living Ubuntu as an Ethics of Research and Pedagogical Engagement". In Diane Caracciolo and Anne M. Mungai (eds), *In the Spirit Of Ubuntu: Stories of Teaching and Research*. Rotterdam: Sense, pp. 3–22.
Tutu, Desmond. 2004. *God Has a Dream: A Vision of Hope for Our Time*. New York: Doubleday.
TVDSB [Thames Valley District School Board]. n.d. "Introduction". *ACT! (Active Citizens Today): Global Citizenship for Local Schools*. Available at: www.tvdsb.on.ca/act/ (accessed 25 June 2015).
Ubuntu Fund. n.d. "Ubuntu Model". Available at: www.ubuntufund.org/approach-impact/the-ubuntu-model.html (accessed 25 June 2015).
Ubuntu Network. 2012. "Vision, Mission, and Values". Available at: www.ubuntu.ie/about/vision.html (accessed 25 June 2015).
University of British Columbia. n.d. "What is Global Citizenship? Road to Global Citizenship: An Educator's Toolbook". Available at: http://gc.ctlt.ubc.ca/toolbook/what-is-global-citizenship (accessed 25 June 2015).

Part II
Shifting boundaries, the modern state, and new cosmopolitanism

Introduction to Part II
Shifting boundaries, the modern state, and new cosmopolitanism

Irene Langran

The debates over globalization and global citizenship are more than mere theoretical exercises that occur within the confines of the academy: such debates frame issues, invoke public debate, and shape policies. These policies encompass a range of issues, including the response to humanitarian crises, international development, foreign aid, and climate change. In this section, we consider how policymakers, transnational advocacy organizations, and intergovernmental organizations respond to the challenges of the twenty-first century, the increasing diminishment of national borders, and the challenges of collective action in an era of globalization.

Part II begins with an exploration of justice and its applicability to the global level. In Chapter 7, David Armstrong utilizes international relations theory to consider the extent to which justice, traditionally confined to the state level, has been transformed throughout history. The questions posed in this chapter have relevance for the post-Second World War era, where we have witnessed a proliferation of international laws, organizations, and courts. In such an environment, ideas of universal justice are transforming, as noted by Armstrong, "an underlying concept of a society of states to a more cosmopolitan structure founded on ideas like human rights and global citizenship".

Audrey Bryan joins Armstrong in a focus on humanitarian concerns. In Chapter 8, Bryan considers global citizenship in terms of how it helps to frame the debate on global poverty and inequality through a transnational education and advocacy project, the Global Poverty Project. Her analysis challenges and complicates this initiative, finding that the lack of a deeper understanding of global poverty can lead to self-serving endeavours that lack political impact.

Perhaps one of the most relevant topics to consider in terms of cosmopolitan's promise is in the area of the environment. Scientists, politicians, academics, and activists have sounded dire warnings about the impact of current human activity on the environment. According to the Intergovernmental Panel on Climate Change (2014), climate change is impacting all continents, countries both rich and poor, and large continents as well as small islands. It threatens food security, economic and social development, and human health (ibid.). While all parts of the world are impacted, low-income populations are especially vulnerable due to their lack of resources with which to respond to such threats. The threat of climate change would appear to be a topic that would demand a cosmopolitan response. However, this response has been slow to arrive.

Both Chapters 9 and 10 and address the challenges of achieving the cosmopolitan approach that may be necessary to confront effectively the challenges of climate change as well as conflict and other global issues. Lowell Gustafson considers the possibilities of cosmopolitanism through the lens of geopolitics. As Gustafson explains, the relationship between citizens and the land has been one that is characterized traditionally by patriotism to one's country – a loyalty that is situated in the land. His analysis, with reference to disciplines that range from history, political science, anthropology, socio-biology, and the natural sciences, calls for a new form of identity – one that is global and which involves defence of the Earth.

Reflecting on extensive public and scholarly experience in the environmental field, Barton A. Thompson considers what lessons the environmental movement has for the development of globalism, an approach that views common problems through the lens of shared responsibilities among all of humanity. Thompson offers a sobering view of globalism's potential, citing psychological impediments that often dissuade individuals from acting collectively and towards shared interests.

Part II closes with Terrance MacMullan's examination of US foreign policy, especially under President Barack Obama, and the extent to which it reflects pragmatist ideals that may enable it to "dismount the tiger of global empire". Through the lens of philosophical pragmatism and considering the implications for realism and idealism, he considers foreign policies under the Obama Administration that include diplomacy in the Middle East and the use of armed drones. This chapter, as well as others in Part II, bring theory to practice in exploring international laws, social and transnational advocacy movements, geopolitics, and foreign policy.

References

Intergovernmental Panel on Climate Change. 2014. "IPCC Press Release: IPCC Report: A Changing Climate Creates Pervasive Risks But Opportunities Exist for Effective Responses". Available at: http://ipcc.ch/pdf/ar5/pr_wg2/140330_pr_wgII_spm_en.pdf (accessed 15 October 2015).

7 International law, citizenship, and changing conceptions of justice[1]

David Armstrong

One classic starting point for any discussion of international law is John Austin's assertion in 1832 that "law properly so-called" is the command of a sovereign backed by coercive sanctions.[2] As international law lacks a higher authority, such as a world government, capable of issuing and enforcing such "commands", it cannot, authentically, be described as "true law". Numerous counter-arguments to Austin's position have appeared since then, but most focus upon the degree to which *states* may, in certain limited circumstances, be regarded as having legal obligations. Here the concern has been to explain how norms and rules may operate in an overall context in which states are seen as *sovereign* and *equal* actors and hence, by definition, subject to no superior authority. Inevitably this apparent conundrum has given rise to a long and complex debate, but one common starting point was the fact that law of any kind was a product of *society* and of what was inevitably required if the members of a society were to enjoy some measure of order, stability, and predictability. So debate about the reality of international law revolved around the degree to which – if at all – global politics took place within some kind of social context.

The idea of a *society of states*, which underpinned international legal thinking from the late seventeenth century, employed a mixture of pragmatic and legalistic reasoning. The highly influential Swiss philosopher and diplomat, Emerich de Vattel (1714–67), began by dismissing the possibility of an authority higher than states. While individual human beings living in society had, inevitably, to surrender some freedom to a superior authority, "nothing of this kind can be conceived or supposed to subsist between nations. Each sovereign state claims, and actually possesses, an absolute independence on all the others". This independence was not something to be deplored but was beneficial because it enabled each state to "govern herself in the manner best suited to her own circumstances" (Vattel 1834, xiv). States were, therefore, akin to individuals living in the complete freedom of a state of nature but, unlike the Hobbesian vision of individuals in such a condition, states could act with "more deliberation and circumspection" and arrive at agreed arrangements to promote order within their own society. As for the nature of rules among sovereign entities, these derived in the first instance from their very sovereignty and the need to underpin this by, in effect, giving it a commonly accepted legal foundation. Hence, the rules applicable to the society of states could be deduced "from the natural liberty of nations, from the attention due to their common safety, from the nature of their mutual correspondence, their reciprocal duties, and the distinctions of their various rights, internal and external, perfect and imperfect". This had two implications in particular: that states needed to *consent* to their obligations as members of this international society and that states were entitled to enjoy their sovereign freedoms without interference from other states in their internal affairs. This principle of non-intervention in a state's internal affairs was repeatedly stressed by Vattel, who gave it a very broad interpretation, encompassing not just a state's freedom to choose its own government and religion but to be free from "manoeuvres" by other states "tending to create disturbance ... to foment discord, to corrupt its citizens, to alienate its allies, to raise enemies against it, to tarnish its glory and to deprive it of its natural advantages" (ibid. 1834, 41). Although, inevitably, countless developments in the last 250 years served to create a much more complex and multifaceted picture, we might, for our purposes, simply note that despite the horrors of the Second World War necessitating some acknowledgement of the need for international protection of human rights, Article 2.7 of the UN Charter states firmly that "Nothing contained in the present Charter shall authorize the United Nations to intervene in matters which are essentially within the domestic jurisdiction of any state". Individuals were citizens of states, not of a world community, with such legal rights and obligations as they possessed deriving from that identity.

It is, however, crucial to note that this understanding of society was far from being the first to emerge in philosophical discussion of international relations and even, to some extent, in the actual conduct of states. Moreover, whereas the Vattelian interpretation focused almost entirely on what was necessary to achieve a modicum of *order* in a world of contending *states*, these earlier formulations were often founded upon a conception of society consisting of people rather than states and the pursuit of *justice* rather than order. As such they may be seen as forerunners of contemporary cosmopolitan thought, including ideas of global citizenship and a world polity.

Forerunners of cosmopolitan thought

Even in the ancient world one may find more nuanced depictions of the key factors operating in international relations than Thucydides' famous Melian dialogue, when the Athenians respond to the Melians' appeal to honour, justice, and the gods with a blunt affirmation of the centrality of power: the goal of all men and the determinant of all outcomes in human interactions. It was certainly the case that power structures, such as monarchies, were coalescing around particular families which were anxious to find ways to consolidate the possession of power in the hands of themselves and their descendants. One means of achieving this was to construct ever-more sophisticated legal systems. However, while one purpose of such legal systems was undeniably to underpin and enforce power, legality alone – then as now – always required some degree of popular acceptance, or, in other words, some measure of *legitimacy*, or moral authority, through claims that the laws embodied universal norms, especially fairness, protection of the weak, truth, honesty, and peace (Versteg 2002, 17–18). For example, one of the earliest known legal codes, that of the Babylonian king, Hammurabi, declared its purpose to be "to make justice appear in the land, to destroy the evil and wicked so that the strong might not oppress the weak" (Greengus 1995, i, 470). As the kings claimed their laws were the enunciation of universally applicable divine commands, their laws could even be seen as embodying a kind of primitive notion of cosmopolitan justice.

The first sophisticated attempts to elaborate an approach to law and justice that went beyond the imposition of rules upon the members of a specific community came with the natural law and Stoic philosophers of Greece and Rome. Their ideas were revived by sixteenth-century thinkers who, in part because of the challenges and opportunities posed by the discovery of the new world, were grappling with issues such as how the occupation and colonization of these territories could be given legal justification and what legal rights were possessed by the existing inhabitants. In the course of their discussions they began to develop the notion that all were part of the "great community of mankind". In the words of the Spanish theologian and philosopher, Francisco Suarez, "The human race, into howsoever many different peoples and kingdoms it may be divided, always preserves a certain unity, not only as a species, but also a moral and practical unity (as it were) enforced by the natural precept of mutual love and mercy: a precept which applies to all, even to strangers of every nation" (Suarez 1994, ii, 351).

In this case Suarez (a Jesuit priest) was drawing upon earlier conceptions of "Christendom" – the underlying unity of all Christians under the authority of the Pope. A similar formulation had emerged in the Islamic world, namely that all Muslims were part of a single community, or *umma*, with both conceptions undercutting – in theory if less often in practice – the idea of sovereignty.

These early attempts to work out how and why norms and rules could have a universal applicability were very far from arguing that nation states had no legal validity. Rather, they were trying to find grounds for arguing that states themselves were bound by rules and it is in that context that their attempts to find a societal basis for their assertions should be seen. In other words, they were not yet willing to move towards the central tenets of the law of a society of sovereign states, in which only states are given rights and obligations and where such laws serve essentially to confirm the sovereignty of states rather than constrain it, except in limited circumstances involving interaction with other states such as diplomacy, treaties and war. The idea at the heart of natural law that it was possible, by the exercise of reason, to work out principles by which all were bound simply by virtue of their shared human identities had the great community principle at its heart but the members of this universal community included states and their rulers, it did not displace them. In Suarez's words:

> although a given sovereign state, commonwealth or kingdom may constitute a perfect kingdom in itself, consisting of its own members, nevertheless, each one of these states is also, in a certain sense, and viewed in relation to the human race, a member of that universal society; for these states, when standing alone, are never so self-sufficient that they do not require some mutual assistance, association and intercourse, at times for their own greater welfare and advantage, but at other times because also of some moral necessity or need.
>
> (1994, ii, 348-9)

Suarez here is using both moral and pragmatic justifications to underpin his arguments in favour of legal and moral obligations applying universally. A later thinker, Grotius, while still employing the underlying idea of a society of men not states, was also careful to distinguish "the law of nations" from natural law and in so doing took one step closer to the society of sovereign states, whose positive consent is necessary for rules to apply: "this Law of Nations is not like Natural Law, which flows in a sure way from certain reasons; but this takes its measure from the will of nations" (1853, I, 1).[3] Later writers continued to struggle with the tensions between the idea of a universal natural law and the consent-based law that was, in reality, what was emerging in the practice of states. Pufendorf, for example, was emphatic in his declaration that "the law of nature and the law of nations are one and the same thing, differing only in their external denomination" (Krieger 1965, 156). Similarly, Christian von Wolff, writing in the eighteenth century, argues that the "great society" and its fundamental laws which existed in a state of nature, remain in being after the formation of states, with natural law having the same binding force upon states that it has upon individuals:

> If we should consider that great society, which nature herself has established among men, to be done away with by the particular societies which men enter when they unite into a state, states would be established contrary to the law of nature, in as much as the universal obligation of all toward all would be terminated; which assuredly is absurd ... individual men do not cease to be members of that great society which is made up of the whole human race, because several have formed together a certain particular society. ... After the human race was divided into nations, that society which before was between individuals continues between nations.
>
> (1934, 12)

Even Wolff, however, could scarcely ignore that such order as did exist in the relations among states was not upheld by natural law but by the balance of power among them, although he added, rather sadly "if nations were to live by such a standard of ethics that they would perform for each other duties which by their nature they owe and if some would not injure others for their advantage, equilibrium among nations would be of no use as there would be no wars to be feared" (1934, 330).

A return to cosmopolitan principles in international law?

The sovereignty-based society of states easily beat off other contenders to a global social identity, with, in the nineteenth century, its most powerful members laying down a "standard of civilisation" which all candidates for membership needed to fulfil (and which, by pure coincidence, happened to suit their commercial and other interests).[4] Although, as indicated earlier, the UN Charter and other post-war agreements acknowledge the importance of human rights, the Cold War and other factors prevented any serious movement towards an international legal structure in which individuals would have legal redress for violations of their human rights – or towards the great community of mankind (rather than the society of states) that the earlier thinkers were promoting.

For some, such as Geoffrey Robertson, QC, this sovereignty-based international order was, fundamentally, the reason why a genuine international legal system that could pursue justice for individuals as well as uphold the rights of states failed to emerge: "The movement for global justice has been a struggle against sovereignty – the doctrine of non-intervention in the internal affairs of nation states asserted by all governments which have refused to subject the treatment they mete out to their citizens to any independent scrutiny" (2002, xxx). However, while Robertson is not alone in pointing to the cynical and self-serving motives he sees as underpinning the insistence of states such as China on sovereignty, there are several counter-arguments that seek to refute the more idealistic assertions that amoral, power-seeking states are all that stand in the way of a global legal system capable of ensuring that those violating human rights can be brought to justice.[5] For example, sovereignty embodies not just the self interest of states but principles such as self determination and the equality of states under international law that in themselves have some clear moral content. If justice is, as Rawls suggests, "the first virtue of social institutions" (1971, 3) can states, taken together, be seen as constituting a particular form of society, but one with the various norms that define justice – reciprocity, fairness, equality – applied to the society of states and deriving from their fundamental rights *as states*? Furthermore, can the basic norms of such a society evolve over time in ways that begin to incorporate individual rights? Could such an evolution be bringing about an even more profound shift in the global social order to a more cosmopolitan framework in which ideas like global citizenship and the world polity are key components? These, in essence, are the questions that I will now consider in the context of international legal developments.

While the post-Second World War international legal order was based firmly and fundamentally on the principle of sovereignty, there were a few developments that may be seen as incorporating early conceptions of global citizenship. The Nuremberg and Tokyo war crimes tribunals referred to "crimes against humanity" (a term also used as the basis for a 1976 UN General Assembly resolution against apartheid). There were seven references to human rights in the UN Charter, and in 1948 the General Assembly adopted the Universal Declaration of Human Rights, although this had no legal force and whose eight abstaining countries included the Soviet bloc, South Africa, and Saudi Arabia. The Cold War also affected the attempts to incorporate human rights into legally binding Covenants, with one Covenant on Civil and Political Rights deriving from Western perspectives and activity, the other, on Social and Economic Rights, reflecting Soviet positions. It should be added that, although all these and similar documents, including the 1950 refugees convention, did embody various principles of justice, the regimes that they established were rather weak and also still firmly statist in their underlying structures.

Even during the Cold War there were a few legal developments that, with hindsight, may be seen as early steps towards a more cosmopolitan outlook. For example there is a clear shift from the conservative approach of the International Court of Justice (ICJ) that prevailed in the 1950s towards a more activist and, arguably, progressive approach. In the 1970 *Barcelona Traction* case, the ICJ introduced the concept of *erga omnes* obligations – ones that apply to the international community as a whole, not just to the individual states involved in ICJ hearings. In its elaboration of what counted as such obligations, it explicitly referred to "the principles and rules concerning the basic rights of the human person" (Jorgensen 2000, 94). Later deliberations at the UN and elsewhere have tried to expand the remit of the *erga omnes* principle to include state obligations relating to climate change, development and international crime (Okawa 2006, 497). However the Court itself was generally cautious in its discussions of more ambitious claims invoking the principle. The same was true of the principle of *jus cogens* – compulsory law – introduced in the 1969 Vienna Convention on the Law of Treaties. This invalidated any treaty that conflicted with a "peremptory norm of international law", which was defined as a "norm accepted and recognized by the international community of states as a whole". In effect this limited the sovereign right of states to agree to anything they wished in a treaty by laying down a countermanding right of the "international community of states".

Both *erga omnes* and *jus cogens* can be interpreted in relatively narrow, statist ways to refer to those basic rules, such as those relating to diplomacy, that are indispensable to the capacity for states to conduct their everyday business in an orderly fashion. Even here there is room for controversy, particularly over the most commonly cited rule bearing a *jus cogens* character: the prohibition of force except in accordance with the UN Charter (Linderfalk 2007, 853–71). Most contemporary interpretations of *jus cogens* give it a clearly cosmopolitan emphasis, with a primary focus on human rights norms (Bianchi 2008, 491–508), although such norms are most often presented in terms of a state's obligations to its own citizens, thus retaining an underlying "society of states" framework. Similarly, several national courts and legislatures have acted as if they accepted *erga omnes* and *jus cogens* as imposing an obligation to apply universal jurisdiction in cases where an individual was accused of serious violations of human rights, most notably when the former Chilean head of state, Augusto Pinochet, was detained in Britain after a Spanish judge had called for his extradition to answer charges of torture, hostage-taking, and other acts deemed crimes under international law (Weller 1999, 599–617; Nolkaeper 2007, 760–99).

The end of the Cold War brought with it an end to the divisions between the superpowers that had effectively prevented the Security Council from implementing and enforcing any major new developments in international law. A more extensive system for monitoring states' observance of their human rights obligations was established, greater publicity was given to serious violations of rights and more effective means of investigating and fact-finding were set up (Forsythe 1991, 55–86). There were also several instances of "humanitarian intervention", where military intervention by the UN or NATO was justified at least in part by reference to the need to prevent extreme suffering following the breakdown of states or other threatening circumstances. These included Somalia (1992), Bosnia (1992), Kosovo (1999), and East Timor (1999). However the Security Council resisted acknowledging in any formal way what some perceived as a clear shift towards a more cosmopolitan approach to international law by ensuring that its resolutions referred to the original purpose of the UN, namely to deal with threats to *international* peace and security and that they indicated that each case was unique.

The ICJ showed greater willingness to appreciate that some more fundamental change might be under way. This was most explicit in its 1996 Advisory Opinion concerning the *Legality of the Threat or Use of Nuclear Weapons*, when it attempted to formulate the changed societal framework within which it saw international law as operating:

> Despite the still modest breakthrough of "supra-nationalism", the progress made in terms of the institutionalization, not to say integration and "globalization" of international society is undeniable. As proof of this, one may cite the multiplication of international organizations, the progressive substitution of an international law of cooperation for the classic international law of coexistence, the emergence of the concept of an "*international community*". ... The resolutely positivist, voluntarist approach of international law still current at the beginning of the century ... has been replaced by an objective conception of international law, a law

more readily seeking to reflect a collective juridical conscience and respond to the social necessities of states organized as a community.

(Simma and Paulus 1998, 227)

Two of the most dramatic developments in recent years that some saw as major steps towards a more cosmopolitan legal order, with individual human beings rather than states being prioritized, were the creation of the International Criminal Court (ICC) from 1998 to 2002 and the enunciation and application of the Responsibility to Protect doctrine (R2P) from 1999 to 2013. The ICC was an attempt to create a permanent and universal version of the various international criminal tribunals that had been established in the 1990s to prosecute political and military leaders accused of crimes against humanity in the conflicts in Rwanda and former Yugoslavia. These had brought to trial individuals, including former leaders such as Slobodan Milošević and Charles Taylor, and the intention was to create a standing court that could issue arrest warrants and bring to trial individuals charged with crimes against humanity, genocide, war crimes, or aggression anywhere in the world. In 2009 the ICC went so far as to issue an arrest warrant against a current, rather than former, leader, the President of Sudan, Omar al-Bashir. The Court is currently considering cases against 18 individuals in eight countries – all in Africa.

In 1999 and 2000 UN Secretary-General Kofi Annan called for humanitarian intervention to be taken a stage further to a point where the international community accepted a legal *obligation* or *responsibility* to intervene in cases which involved "gross and systematic violations of human rights that affect every precept of our common humanity".[6] In response to this the government of Canada and a group of major foundations established the International Commission on Intervention and State Sovereignty, which, in 2001, set out key principles that it saw as involved in the R2P concept. At the heart of these was the assertion that, although states were still sovereign, their sovereignty comprised responsibilities as well as rights, and that "where a population is suffering serious harm, as a result of internal war, insurgency, repression or state failure, and the state in question is unwilling or unable to halt or avert it, the principle of non-intervention yields to the international responsibility to protect" (http://responsibilitytoprotect.org/ICISS%20Report.pdf).

This had no legal force at the time and initially was regarded with suspicion by some African states who believed that the doctrine primarily had them in mind. However, in 2005 a UN General Assembly summit meeting formally adopted these principles, thus bringing them into the category of "soft law" – norms without the binding legal standing that long practice ("custom"), treaties, or Security Council resolutions brought but which embody widely accepted beliefs about how states should behave (Shelton 2011, 68–80). The R2P principle was cited in a Security Council resolution of 2011, authorizing intervention in the armed conflict going on in Libya in the form of establishing a "no fly zone" to prevent Libyan state forces from using air power against civilians. It was also cited in an emergency debate in the British Parliament on 30 August 2013 when Prime Minister David Cameron attempted – unsuccessfully – to secure parliamentary backing for an intervention in the Syrian conflict after an alleged use of chemical weapons by the state forces there.

Globalization and global citizenship

Numerous writers from many different perspectives have pointed to developments such as those outlined briefly here to argue that a fundamental change is under way in which states are no longer the only, or even the principal, determinants of outcomes in world politics. If we restrict ourselves to the narrow international legal context, at one end of the spectrum even some "realist" International Relations scholars have argued that there has been a shift away from the very limited role traditionally allocated to international law in a world dominated by power-seeking sovereign states in permanent competition with each other. For example, a special issue in 2000 of the journal *International Organization* suggested that there had been an – admittedly uneven – shift in state practice towards greater reliance on formal legal obligations in their relations with each other (Goldstein *et al.* 2000). Similarly, some advocates of the "English School", which was founded on a conception of states interacting within an international society, have argued that a shift is under way from a "pluralist" notion of international society, which argues that only minimal cooperation to ensure orderly coexistence is possible between states, to a "solidarist" understanding in which the state members of international society are coming increasingly to act on the basis of a shared and constantly expanding set of values and interests.

Far more radical interpretations flow from the notion of "globalization" and its consequences for the state, including the emergence of a global civil society comprising vast numbers of non-state actors and processes which fundamentally undermines any claims that states alone determine what happens in world politics. In the legal context this view argues, essentially, that we have made a decisive shift towards a cosmopolitan order in which the search for justice for all members of the "great community of mankind" prevails over the far more limited quest for some degree of order among separate sovereign states. We are, slowly but surely, groping our way towards a world in which international law is founded on an underlying conception of global citizenship. In Michael Reisman's words, "it is the people's sovereignty rather than the sovereign's sovereignty" (1990, 866). Apart from the developments outlined here, cosmopolitans might point to the steady expansion of the UN's human rights regime to incorporate specific areas like racial discrimination, women's rights, the rights of the child, minority rights, etc. A related argument is that the increasing consensus about the serious potential damage emanating from climate change has imposed upon states the need to see the world as a community of people rather than states because environmental threats do not observe national boundaries. Furthermore, environmental negotiations have witnessed some measure of "distributive justice". For example the 1997 Kyoto Convention had relatively strong requirements for all to implement their commitments in ways that minimized the social and economic impacts on developing countries and for new technological and other resources to be provided to meet the costs of developing countries. Finally one might note the degree to which some regional organizations, especially the European Union, have gradually displaced or limited in various ways the absolute control by states of their own affairs, with "citizenship" and its rights deriving from the regional rather than national identity.

A degree of scepticism is in order when considering some of the more idealistic cosmopolitan claims. Three reservations in particular need to be noted. First, are the "universal values" invoked by cosmopolitans in reality purely Western values? One leading cosmopolitan thinker, David Held, argues that it is simply the linkages made in many poorer countries between Western culture and their past experience of Western imperialism that makes them resist Western values (Held 2002, 319).[7] While this is certainly a factor, it is also the case that many simply disagree with those values – over gay rights, the rights of women, abortion, capital punishment, for example. Second, power remains of crucial importance in determining the outcome of events in world politics. This is not simply a matter of two permanent members of the UN Security Council, Russia and China, tending to veto moves that they perceive as undermining the sovereign rights of states but also of the strongest power, the USA, ignoring ICJ findings when they conflict with US interests or when the USA refuses to join the ICC or when its responses to the 9/11 attack include measures seen by many as violations of human rights norms in Guantánamo Bay and elsewhere. Finally, an effective global system to implement and enforce human rights standards would cost many billions of dollars to establish.

On the other hand, it would be hard to maintain that the world has not undergone fundamental changes in the last hundred years. Power may still be the ultimate determinant but all players in the many games of global politics – state and non-state alike – are engaged in ongoing and complex interactions and discourses in which processes of argument, learning, and persuasion are always more in evidence than simple assertions of power. The permanent five on the Security Council will retain their veto over judicial intervention in cases where they perceive a vital national interest and there is not the remotest prospect of any of their leaders appearing before an international tribunal, much as some fantasize about that. Yet, while, ultimately, they all remain willing and able to employ their military might even in the face of widespread condemnation, they are also conscious that they are performing on a world stage whose underlying rules and values have radically changed from those of a century ago, when individual justice was considered a purely domestic matter of no concern for the international community and when a state's international reputation was closely related to its prowess on the battlefield rather than its moral standing (Armstrong and Montal 2014, 142).

Notes

1 Parts of this chapter are drawn from Armstrong (2011, 2121–36).
2 I discuss Austin's views and some counter-arguments to them in Armstrong *et al.* (2012, 9–15).
3 I discuss these different conceptions of international society more fully in Armstrong (1993, 12–41).
4 Gong (1984) develops this perspective.
5 I develop these arguments more fully in Armstrong and Montal (2014, 125–46).
6 This paragraph is drawn from my detailed discussion of R2P in Armstrong *et al.* (2012, 144–6), together with a brief consideration of developments relating to the Syrian conflict in August to September 2013.
7 I discuss this in more detail in Little and Williams (2006, 121–40).

References

Armstrong, David. 1993. *Revolution and World Order: The Revolutionary State in International Society.* Oxford: Clarendon Press.
Armstrong, David. 2006. "The Nature of Law in an Anarchical Society". In R. Little and J. Williams (eds), *The Anarchical Society in a Globalized World.* Basingstoke: Palgrave Macmillan.
Armstrong, David. 2011. "Evolving Conceptions of Justice in International Law". *Review of International Studies* 17: 2121–2136.
Armstrong, David, Theo Farrell, and Hélène Lambert. 2012. *International Law and International Relations.* Cambridge: Cambridge University Press.
Armstrong, David and Florencia Montal. 2014. "The Politics of International Criminal Justice". In *The Routledge Handbook of International Crime and Justice Studies.* London and New York: Routledge.
Bianchi, Andrea. 2008. "Human Rights and the Magic of jus cogens". *European Journal of International Law* 19.
Forsythe, D. P. 1991. *The Internationalization of Human Rights.* Lexington, MA: Lexington Books.
Goldstein, J., M. Kahler, R. O. Keohane, and A. Slaughter (eds). 2000. "Legalization and World Politics". *International Organization* 54.
Gong, G. W. 1984. *The Standard of 'Civilization' in International Society.* Oxford: Oxford University Press.
Greengus, S. 1995. "Legal and Social Institutions of Ancient Mesopotamia". In J. M. Sasson (ed.), *Civilizations of Ancient Near East.* Vol. 1. Peabody, MA: Hendrickson.
Grotius, Hugo. 1853. *De Jure Belli et Pacis.* Edited by W. Whewell. Cambridge: Cambridge University Press.
Held, David. 2002. "Cosmopolitanism: Ideas, Realities and Deficits". In D. Held and A. McGrew (eds), *Governing Globalization: Power, Authority and Global Governance.* Cambridge: Polity Press.
International Commission on Intervention and State Sovereignty. Available at: http://responsibilitytoprotect.org/ICISS%20Report.pdf (accessed 5 January 2015).

Jorgensen, Nina H. B. 2000. *The Responsibility of States for International Crimes*. Oxford: Oxford University Press.

Krieger, L. 1965. *The Politics of Discretion: Pufendorf and the Acceptance of Natural Law*. Chicago, IL and London: Chicago University Press.

Linderfalk, Ulf. 2007. "The Effect of jus cogens Norms: Whoever Opened Pandora's Box, Did You Ever Think About the Consequences?". *European Journal of International Law* 18.

Nolkaeper, André. 2007. "Internationally Wrongful Acts in Domestic Courts". *American Journal of International Law* 101.

Okawa, Phoebe. 2006. "Issues of Admissibility and the Law on International Responsibility". In Malcolm D. Evans (ed.), *International Law*. Oxford: Oxford University Press.

Rawls, J. 1971. *A Theory of Justice*. Oxford: Oxford University Press.

Reisman, Michael W. 1990. "Sovereignty and Human Rights in Contemporary International Law". Editorial Comment. *American Journal of International Law* 8: 866.

Robertson, Geoffrey. 2002. *Crimes against Humanity: The Struggle for Global Justice*. 2nd edn. London: Penguin.

Shelton, Dinah. 2011. "Soft Law". In David Armstrong (ed.), *Routledge Handbook of International Law*. London and New York: Routledge.

Simma, Bruce and Andreas L. Paulus. 1998. "The 'International Community': Facing the Challenge of Globalization". *European Journal of International Law* 9.

Suarez, Francisco. 1994. *Selections from Three Works*. Edited by J. B. Scott (2 vols). Oxford: Oxford University Press.

Vattel, Emerich de. 1834. *The Law of Nations or Principles of the Law of Nature Applied to the Conduct and Affairs of Nations and Sovereigns*. Edited by Chitty J. London.

Versteg, Russ. 2002. *Law in the Ancient World*. Durham, NC: Carolina Academic Press.

Weller, Marc. 1999. "On the Hazards of Foreign Travel for Dictators and Other International Criminals". *International Affairs* 75.

von Wolff, Christian. 1934. *Jus Gentium Methodo Scientifica Pentractum*. Translated by J. H. Drake. Oxford: Oxford University Press.

8 Global citizenship as public pedagogy

Emotional tourism, feel-good humanitarianism, and the personalization of development

Audrey Bryan

This chapter offers a critical exploration of global citizenship as a public pedagogy which seeks to transform the way that citizens think about and engage with international development issues. Using a case study approach, it provides a critical exploration of the Global Poverty Project, a transnational education and advocacy project that seeks to engage Northern publics with issues of global poverty and inequality. It argues that, rather than fostering deep understanding of global poverty or promoting meaningful responses to it, the Project enables participants to "feel good about feeling bad" in relation to the suffering of distant others by affirming one's humanitarianism through apolitical and personalized forms of development engagement that reap personal rewards. In this way, "doing good" becomes an individualistic and self-interested endeavour through which one can advance one's sense of moral well-being.

Introduction

This chapter offers a critical exploration of the increasingly prominent discourse of global citizenship as a public pedagogy which seeks to transform the way that citizens think about and engage with global issues.[1] While recognizing the contested nature of the term, public pedagogy – in the present context – refers to "learning and education happening outside of formal schooling systems [that] position informal spaces of learning such as popular culture, the Internet, public spaces such as museums and parks and other civic and commercial spaces, including both old and new social movements, as sites of pedagogy containing possibilities for both reproduction and resistance" (Sandlin *et al.* 2010, 2). These moves to educate the general public about complex global problems are situated within a wider context of recent trends and policy initiatives within international development, especially the interface between global citizenship education and international development policy at a time when new Sustainable Development Goals (SDGs) or Global Goals for Sustainable Development are being rolled out (United Nations 2015).[2] For illustrative purposes, I focus on a large-scale, transnational public pedagogical initiative – the Global Poverty Project – whose stated goal is "to advocate and work towards ending extreme poverty by 2030" and whose campaigns are closely aligned with the SDG agenda (Global Poverty Project 2015a, n.p.). Using the Global Poverty Project as an illustrative case study, the chapter critically explores some of the strategies that are used to engage so-called global citizens with global poverty. Specifically, it asks: what kind of global citizen is being imagined and produced via the Project? How are these global citizens encouraged to express and perform solidarity with distant others? What kinds of understandings of global injustice does it promote and which types of action does it make possible?

Contextual backdrop

The increasing prominence of the discourse of global citizenship as a response to the ecological, economic, and social realities of a globalized world is evident across institutions as diverse as the UN agencies, schools, colleges, and universities (including teacher education programmes), international non-governmental agencies, inter/national media, and philanthropic organizations as well as in the wider public domain. Increasing recognition of the importance of educating people for global citizenship is evident by its inclusion as a priority area under the UN Secretary-General's 2012 Global Education First Initiative (GEFI) and as a named target within the SDGs, which were launched in September of 2015 (Tawil 2013). In other words, while organized efforts to educate for global citizenship have existed for some time, these initiatives are likely to expand considerably over the next 15 years as national governments and international agencies seek to ensure that the 17 SDGs – whose stated goal is to eradicate global poverty by 2030 through international development policy and aid – are met. One of the targets associated with SDG 4, whose focus is education, seeks to ensure that by 2030, all learners will "acquire knowledge and skills needed to promote sustainable development" and directly refers to global citizenship as one of the means through which this can be achieved (UN 2015, n.p.). Learning outcomes associated with global citizenship education are often expressed in terms of values, attitudes, and dispositions, ranging from empathy or care to a willingness to challenge injustice (Tawil 2013).

Despite its increasing popularity, a number of commentators have expressed concern about mainstream efforts to educate for global citizenship, especially in terms of the nature and effects of North–South engagements that occur in formal, non-formal, and informal learning environments. Andreotti's distinction between "soft" and more "critical" versions of global citizenship education has been instrumental as a means of illuminating some of the more problematic aspects of global citizenship as it is enacted across a range of educational settings (Andreotti 2006). Soft versions of global citizenship education include those which fail to acknowledge the role of colonialism in the creation of wealth in the Global North or problematize the power inequalities inherent in North–South relationships. Within this framework, poverty is constructed as a lack of resources, services, markets, and education, while humanitarian engagement is promoted as *the* most appropriate response to global inequality. Critical global citizenship education, on the other hand, is an educational process that engages learners with the ideologies, political–economic systems, and structures that create and maintain exploitation, as well as the ways in which human beings, often through their ordinary actions, are implicated in the suffering of distant others. Critical global citizenship education actively disrupts learners' deeply entrenched, often tacit understanding of how the world works in order to produce alternative ways of "reading" the world.

Research that explores the discursive construction of the "active global citizen" in formal educational settings suggests that soft versions of global citizenship education are far more prevalent than more critical forms of global citizenship education which focus on the historical context and root causes of global inequality and enable learners to interrogate their own positionality with respect to the operations of global capitalism (Andreotti 2006; Bryan 2012). Moreover, research suggests that forms of engagement with global poverty that are based on experiential, affective encounters which seek to enhance participants' understandings of poverty can have the paradoxical effect of promoting reductionist understandings of poverty and simplistic solutions which fail to engage them with the complexities of global poverty and inequality (Bryan and Bracken 2011; Schwittay and Boocock 2015). Andreotti's work points to a tendency for mainstream global citizenship interventions to promote uncomplicated or easy solutions to global problems that do not require systemic change. While ostensibly concerned with enabling young people to come to a deeper understanding of social and global injustice, global citizenship education can, therefore, effectively work to constrain people's imagination about what is possible and how they might engage in struggle for a more equal world (Bryan 2014; Kennelly 2011).

Critically informed research that explores Northern citizens' experiential engagement with development raises further concerns about the *kind* of active global citizen which is being produced through government and non-government-sponsored global citizenship initiatives such as international volunteering programmes or other development tools (Baillie *et al*. 2011; Tiessen 2011). Some scholars maintain that North–South engagements – which are often premised on paternalistic assumptions about benevolent Northerners who are heavily invested in "helping" or "making a difference" – have the effect of reproducing patterns of inequality by treating the "beneficiaries" of their humanitarian efforts as *objects of globalization* rather than *global subjects* themselves (Tiessen 2011). Whether motivated primarily by a desire to "help" or to gain a competitive edge over their peers by accruing (multi)cultural capital, programmes which encourage participants to develop their global citizenry through travel often reproduce existing global power disparities and cause harm to host communities (Jefferess 2012).

This chapter identifies several additional problematic aspects of mainstream global citizenship education by critically interrogating how global citizenship

118 *Audrey Bryan*

is envisioned through the Global Poverty Project (also referred to here as "the Project"). The next section provides a brief overview of the Project, followed by a more detailed, critical analysis of two of its "focus campaigns": the Live Below the Line (LBTL) campaign and the Global Citizen Festival.

Eradicating global poverty by 2030? The Global Poverty Project as public pedagogy

The Global Poverty Project is a large-scale, transnational education and advocacy initiative with an ambitious vision of "a world without extreme poverty by 2030".[3] Established in 2008 by Hugh Evans and Simon Moss, with a grant from the United Nations and AusAid, the Project develops campaigns "with the purpose to increase the number and effectiveness of people taking action to end extreme poverty … within a generation" (Global Poverty Project 2015, n.p.). The Project uses a combination of high-profile events, grassroots organizing, and media campaigning to educate people about global poverty and advocate for tangible commitments from wealthy governments to bring about an end to extreme poverty.

The Project is closely aligned with the UN's development goals agenda. In many respects, it is a continuation of the Make Poverty History campaign, which the Project's founder Hugh Evans had been involved in in Australia (Schwittay and Boocock 2015). Initiated in 2005, Make Poverty History was a global alliance of over 500 NGOs, coordinated by the Global Call to Action against Poverty, intent on putting pressure on the leaders of the richest countries to fulfil commitments they had already made in relation to the Millennium Development Goals (MDGs). As described by Nash (2008), Make Poverty History was a high media profile, celebrity-led campaign which sought to mobilize popular sentiment and promote cosmopolitan solidarity with distant others who were experiencing poverty and injustice. In other words, Make Poverty History – and the media coverage surrounding it – promoted global citizenship as an *identity*, constructing the world as if it were *already* a single space of global citizens.

This same discourse of global citizenship features prominently in the Project's promotional materials and educative efforts. For example, the Project worked in partnership with Plan International to deliver the "I am a Global Citizen" schools programme – an educational initiative for secondary schools based on training and activities focused on poverty reduction. One of Project's most visible programmes is its Global Citizen platform, which seeks to capture the public's imagination and to "grow the number of global citizens through … events, content, partnerships, media and resources" (Global Poverty Project 2015a, n.p.). As part of the Global Citizen initiative, the Project hosts a landmark annual Global Citizen Festival (also referred to here as "the Festival") whose stated purpose is to bring together members of the general public (or "global citizens"), NGOs, companies, and "world leaders", so that people can "learn about global issues, and to take action in support of the organizations campaigning to tackle them" (ibid.). More specifically, the Festival is an awareness-raising tool which seeks to promote the UN's global goals agenda and to spur countries to fulfil their commitments to these goals by 2030. The Festival – which is timed to coincide with the high-level segment of the UN General Assembly – has been described by the UN as "an unofficial side event to the Assembly itself" (UN News Centre 2015, n.p.). Tim Davie, CEO of BBC Worldwide, described it as "one of the biggest musical events of the century". The Festival's popularity is likely to soar in the coming years as Coldplay frontman and activist Chris Martin recently announced that he has agreed to curate the concert until 2030 when the goals are expected to have been achieved (BBC 2015, n.p.). As outlined in more detail below, the Project operates a reward scheme for its participants which provides them with a chance to win tickets for sport and music events if they participate in various "actions" focused on ending global poverty. The Project also relies heavily on social media and the Internet more broadly as a platform through which to cultivate and engage global citizens as well as promote awareness of global themes and issues.

At the same time, the Project coordinates the LBTL campaign, an awareness and fundraising initiative established in 2010 which asks participants to live on the equivalent of the extreme poverty line for five days while raising funds for charity. LBTL aims to enable participants to develop insight into what it is like to have to live below the poverty line through a simulated experience which is designed to engage them experientially and empathetically with issues of extreme poverty (Schwittay and Boocock 2015). Actor Hugh Jackman is a global adviser to the Project and is the public face of the LBTL campaign. In a publicity video for the campaign, Jackman encourages participants to live below the (poverty) line for five days, "so that the world's most vulnerable people can rise above it". According to the campaign's organizers, "Live Below the Line is transforming the way that citizens think about and engage with issues of extreme poverty" (Global Poverty Project 2015b). Some of those who take part in the challenge post online articles, videos, and blogs about their experiences, providing insights into how they interact with and understand global poverty.

Following this brief overview of two of Project's focus campaigns, the next section focuses on the strategies and methods that it uses to engage global citizens with development issues and with global poverty more specifically. Specifically, it asks: how are these global citizens encouraged to enact solidarity with distant others? What function do their actions serve, and for whose benefit?

Living below the line: "Feeling good about feeling bad"

LBTL seeks to provide Western participants with a personalized, embodied, and affective engagement with poverty. Participants gain experiential knowledge of what it means to live below the poverty line by surviving on less than $1.50 or £1 a day for five days. In addition to raising funds for different charities, LBTL seeks to transform how people understand and act in relation to global poverty by enabling them to become more empathetic and insightful about the circumstances of those living with extreme poverty. The assumption is that their experiential knowledge of simulated suffering will increase their capacity for both identification and empathy.

An analysis of New Zealand participants' encounters with LBTL by Schwittay and Boocock (2015) highlights some of the problematic effects of the simulated suffering and imaginative empathy approach of LBTL. While acknowledging the campaign's potential for promoting critical reflection by disrupting the normalcy of participants' lives, Schwittay and Boocock argue that the critical potential of the campaign is muted by its failure to engage participants with the wider structural and political dimensions of poverty or with a consideration of self-implication in the perpetuation of poverty. Based on their interviews with those who took the LBTL challenge, Schwittay and Boocock found that the initiative did not engage participants with the political dimensions or complexities of global inequalities, which resulted in reductionist understandings of poverty and stereotypical, dichotomous "us/them" thinking about North–South inhabitants. Rather than equipping them with a more nuanced appreciation of the dynamics of global poverty and their role within it, the challenge provided participants with "naïve hope" and simplistic solutions that enabled them to move quickly past discomforting emotions that arise from personal privilege in a world marred by profound inequities of power and wealth (ibid.). Arguably, fleeting and simulated encounters with poverty in the LBTL programme benefits privileged inhabitants of the Global North far more than the distant others whose experiences they are simulating. Rather than provide a space to interrogate the myriad advantages that they derive from a structurally unjust political and economic system that benefits inhabitants of the West, LBTL enables privileged participants to offset discomforting, conflicting, or disabling emotions with redemptive, "altruistic", and feel-good actions which remind them how "lucky" they are relative to "less fortunate" others. This reinforces what David Jefferess (2012, 20) refers to as "a dichotomy of the fortunate and the unfortunate" wherein the solution to the problem of global poverty is presented in terms of benevolent obligation: "What can we, the fortunate, do to help the unfortunate?"

Moreover, LBTL's privileging of personal experience and reflection over engagement with the political dimensions of global poverty and injustice helps to ensure that global citizenship as an identity remains at the personal rather than political level (Butcher 2014; 2015). In fact, the discourse of global citizenship is arguably a central mechanism through which personal qualities (such as awareness, care, responsibility) associated with private actions (individual purchases, lifestyle, behaviour) have been extended directly into the political realm (Butcher 2015). Butcher remarks that "the elevation of a discourse of 'responsibility' and 'care' into the realm of the politics of development is indicative of an important trend in politics: that of the diminution of public life and the consequent extension of private concerns and personal qualities into the centre of hitherto political debate" (ibid., 75). Furthermore, as Taylor (2011, 33) remarks:

> The theory of learning underpinning [simulated learning experiences] – that the required knowledge of the suffering of others can be acquired through simulated suffering – clearly ignores that this simulation of suffering is not only a construction that selectively reconstructs certain conditions of that suffering and not others, and that it reproduces conditions only, thereby reductively misrepresenting the lived understandings, the creative resistance and meaning made by its targets (for example, blindfolds can never simulate an experience of blind culture).

In other words, simulated suffering encounters such as LBTL give participants partial and inaccurate insights into the actual lived experiences of those whose lives it seeks to simulate, just as it prevents them from considering suffering others as agents with their own responses to their oppression. In summary then, LBTL is a form of "emotional tourism" (Taylor 2011, 35), which enables participants to "feel good about feeling bad" (Simon 2012, 133), and gloss over the conflictual and disabling emotions that accompany living in a world characterized by asymmetries of injustice, suffering, and responsibility. Rather than promoting deeper understanding of the structural dynamics of global injustice or prompting deeper questions about complicity in relations of transnational harm, it reinforces reductionist and stereotypical thinking about global poverty and promotes fantasies of benevolence and quick-fix solutions that are self-gratifying yet ultimately ineffective as a means of alleviating poverty.

The Global Citizen Festival: five-minute activism and the "fight to end extreme poverty"

This section presents a similarly critical analysis of the Global Citizen Festival, arguably the most significant and public of the Project's campaigns. It locates the analysis within a wider consideration of the SDGs, the Global Citizen Festival's *raison d'être*. The Festival, which comprises a convergence of world leaders, celebrities, corporate sponsors, and members of the public, is a media spectacle that is live-streamed internationally by the event's media partners, which include MSNBC, YouTube, and BBC Worldwide. The 2015 Festival, which was timed to coincide with the UN General Assembly's launch of the SDGS, was described by Hugh Evans, the Project's CEO, as a "critical moment to shed light on the world's agenda for the next 15 years" (MSNBC 2015, n.p.). The event seeks to publicize and realize the SDGs by "channel[ing] the power of hundreds of thousands of global citizens lending their voices to achieve policy and financial commitments that will shape the success of these Goals" (ibid.). Festivalgoers participate in an "action journey" in order to enter a draw to win tickets to the event, and a limited number of VIP tickets are also available for a fee. Richard Curtis, creative director of the 2015 Festival, articulated the rationale for the festival as follows: "We want to give the Global Goals for Sustainable Development the noisiest launch in history in the belief that the more famous they are, the more effective they will be" (ibid.). Like many mainstream global citizenship education programmes, the Project assumes that global citizens, if exposed to the "right" kinds of knowledge and in the "right" ways, will come to deeper understandings of global injustice and will be disposed towards taking action against these injustices (Armaline and Farber 1995). As Schwittay and Boocock (2015, 292) observe:

> [The Global Poverty Project] argues that the main obstacle to poverty eradication is "global apathetic conscience", which prevents political leaders from making crucial policy decisions favourable for the world's poor. Having thus framed the poverty problem as one of an uninformed, uninterested and uninspired Northern public, for [the Project] the solution necessarily becomes to educate Northerners on global issues and provide them with opportunities for action.

The Project addresses this supposedly uninformed, disinterested, and uninspired public with highly inspirational and hopeful messages about the capacity of committed citizens to change the world as well as prescriptive, easily accomplished actions they can take to encourage world leaders to implement SDG-related targets and policies. Festivalgoers, for example, are exposed to positive and feel-good messages from world leaders such as US President Barack Obama and UN Secretary-General Ban Ki-moon. In his video address to the 2014 Festival, for example, President Obama informed his audience that they "are now part of the global fight to end extreme poverty, and this is a fight we can win" (Hampp and Brown 2014, n.p.). Ban Ki-moon delivered a similarly upbeat message on stage at the 2014 Festival in Central Park, telling festivalgoers that they "are the generation that can end extreme poverty by 2030" and that "a better world is around the corner" (UN News Centre 2015, n.p.), while at the 2015 Festival, US Vice President Joe Biden exclaimed that "at no time in history has so much power been available to make such a big difference for so many people" (NPR 2015, n.p.).

Similarly inspirational messages are conveyed by the "celebrity humanitarians" who perform and/or speak at the Festival, and who publicize and mediate the SDGs to their fans. Goodman and Barnes (2011, 71) remark that:

> The development celebrity illuminates something of the contemporary practices of "doing" development today. The celebritisation of development has worked to turn "development" as a wider project into one that is individualised, volunteerised, privatised and, ultimately, "responsibilised" onto audiences, consumers and citizens (mainly of the North) as more celebrities take to their roles as endorsers of campaigns and causes.

Despite a rhetoric that appeals to the collective clout of "people power", the Festival promotes low-cost, individual actions or "five minute activism" (Earl and Kimport 2011, 74), primarily in the form of "clicktivist" or "slacktivist" tactics. These tactics are simple social media and Internet-based measures which are used to show one's support for an issue or cause but which involve little to no effort nor require any real level of commitment and which have been shown to have limited impact on policy (Shulman 2009). As mentioned, those who wished to attend the 2015 Festival could be entered into a lottery for free tickets by participating in an "action journey" based on simple actions which include sending short emails, signing petitions, tweeting world leaders, and leaving voicemail messages for politicians, all of which can be completed from a mobile device. These actions generally require very little effort, and the content of tweets and related messages were often already provided for those who were "taking action", such that they merely had to click a few buttons to complete their "action journey". While "clicktivism" can be potentially useful as a complementary tactic that supports in-depth engagement with development issues, its promotion as the primary means of "taking action" promotes highly obedient forms of activism which foreclose more critical and collective modes of development engagement (Bryan and Bracken 2011).

Chouliaraki (2013) observes a sociopolitical shift in the expression of solidarity among international development agencies and in celebrity-dominated media towards a solidarity that is increasingly based on self-oriented expressions of political engagement. She argues that traditional humanitarian campaigns – which were centred on the plight of the Other – have been replaced by a "post-humanitarian" politics, at the heart of which is a self-oriented morality which is deeply embedded in a public culture of consumption and an ethos of "mutual benefit with minimal effort" (ibid., 178). She contends that the ethic of solidarity characteristic of the present historical moment represents "a shift from the idea that doing good to others without expecting a response is both desirable and possible to the idea that doing good to others is desirable when there is something to gain from the act" (ibid., 179). In other words, global citizenship has become premised upon a form of solidarity that is expressed through "clicktivism", one's lifestyle choices, or consumerist habits, and justified in terms of its capacity to enhance individuals' social conscience or to advance them personally. A "solidarity of conviction", on the other hand, does not require that action be justified or authenticated in terms of something external to itself (ibid., 185).

Another problematic feature of the Global Poverty Project and the Global Citizen Festival more specifically is that, in seeking to generate awareness of and support for the SDGs, they fail to shine a light on the actual structures that maintain, reproduce, and legitimate global inequalities. As Hensby and O'Byrne (2012) observe, awareness-raising campaigns tend to be politically moderate and do not typically call for a radical redistribution of global wealth or the transformation of the global capitalist system that produces such stark inequalities in the first place. Rather, as these authors remark, "the desire to gain popular support among the global public has resulted in a deliberate side-stepping of more complex political and economic debate – debates which according to more radical protest groups would reveal inconvenient truths about who might be culpable in the perpetuation of global inequality" (ibid., 394). Critics have expressed concern about the SDG framework's "business-as-usual" approach to development, such as its emphasis on capitalist growth (as measured by gross domestic product, or GDP) and its concomitant failure to address dangerous levels of corporate extraction and consumption by wealthy countries (Hickel 2015). Klees and Qargha (2013) argue that aid-based initiatives serve a "compensatory legitimation" function for wealthy, capitalist countries. In other words, development aid and related frameworks are not designed to bring about major improvement in the conditions of the world's poor, but rather work to restore legitimacy in the face of widespread poverty and inequality by ameliorating some of the oppressive conditions produced by a system that is structurally unjust. As Klees and Qargha state: "The world system must look like something is being done to improve the situation even if it is not" (ibid., 20). The Global Citizen Festival is arguably the perfect platform to promote the illusory impression that something is being done to redress global injustice while the structures that maintain reproduce inequality remain intact. The audience's sense of individual moral well-being is enhanced as they enjoy their favourite bands for free while simultaneously being exposed to "feel-good" messages about how they can end global poverty through low-cost actions which fail to address structural inequality in any meaningful way. Couched in a post-humanitarian rhetoric, global citizens are constructed as citizens who deserve to have it all. Their sense of morality is bolstered by "doing their bit" for humanity while they reap rewards and take part in challenges which serve to remind them how lucky they are not to be those distant others whose suffering they simulate.

Conclusion

The discourse of global citizenship and its accompanying educative component are central mechanisms through which personal qualities such as awareness, empathy, and responsibility have been extended directly into the realm of development politics in recent years (Butcher, 2015). In other words, the construct of global citizenship – which is likely to become even more prevalent in international development policy as a result of its inclusion as a specific target in the SDGs – functions as part of a wider apparatus within which development politics is individualized and privatized and questions of structural inequality are reduced to questions of individual morality (Butcher 2015; Hickel 2013; Mostafanezhad 2014). Reflecting this wider trend towards the personalization of development politics, the global citizen who is imagined and produced by the Project's campaigns is someone who possesses a generalized cosmopolitan empathy as opposed to a strong political consciousness (ibid.).

Advocates of a critical approach to global citizenship education maintain that one of its goals is to historicize global poverty and to address its root causes. Another goal is to enable learners to see how they are implicated in historical and contemporary relations of harm so that the world can be imagined and created "otherwise" (Andreotti 2014). The public pedagogy that the Global Poverty Project affords, however, is utterly lacking in criticality and political sensibility. In fact, despite its purpose as an awareness-raising platform to aid in the elimination of extreme poverty by 2030, the Project is devoid of substantive political critique and fails to engage participants with a consideration of the actual causes of poverty, such as international political–economic arrangements and loan conditionalities imposed by the World Bank and International Monetary Fund (IMF), debt peonage, Western corporate tax evasion and corporate corruption, unfair trading processes and practices, land grabs, and unfair labour laws (Hickel 2013). The Global Poverty Project as a public pedagogical project provides Northern publics with experiential, emotionally touristic encounters with global poverty and injustice as well as personal rewards for being "good" global citizens. These learning experiences promote simplistic responses to poverty which enable participants to gloss over discomforting emotions rather than engaging them with their own implication in complex relations of global inequality (Andreotti 2014; Schwittay and Boocock 2015; Taylor 2011). In other words, they enable participants to "feel good about feeling bad" about global poverty by affirming their humanitarianism through apolitical, personalized forms of development engagement that reap personal reward or dividends, such that "doing good" becomes an individualistic, self-interested endeavour through which one can simultaneously advance and empower oneself (Chouliaraki 2013; Kennelly 2011).

Notes

1 Organized efforts to educate members of the general public about global or international development-related issues have been in existence since the 1950s under the guise of development education. As globalization intensified in the 1990s, the term "global citizenship education" entered the pedagogical lexicon as a response to the emergence of new global trends and processes and a perceived need for more cosmopolitan conceptions citizenship as a result of increased global interdependence and interconnectedness (Tawil 2013). Although the concept of global citizenship is contested and takes many different forms, pedagogically speaking, educating for global citizenship refers to efforts to raise awareness and promote action in relation to matters of global concern – including issues pertaining to the environment, human rights, economic and social justice, and interculturalism – within a context of intensified globalization (ibid.).
2 The post-2015 development framework is referred to interchangeably as the Global Goals for Sustainable Development or the Sustainable Development Goals.
3 The Global Poverty Project operates in several countries including Australia, the US, the UK, New Zealand, Canada, and the Netherlands.

References

Andreotti, Vanessa. 2006. "Soft Versus Critical Global Citizenship Education". *Policy and Practice: A Development Education Review* 3: 83–98.

Andreotti, Vanessa. 2014. "Critical Literacy: Theories and Practices in Development Education". *Policy & Practice: A Development Education Review* 19: 12–32.
Armaline, William D. and Kathleen S. Farber. 1995. "Developing Social and Cultural Foundations from a Multicultural Perspective". In Christine Sleeter and Joseph Larkin (eds), *Developing Multicultural Teacher Education Curricula*. Albany, NY: State University of New York Press, pp. 45–63.
Baillie Smith, Matt and Nina Laurie. 2011. "International Volunteering and Development: Global Citizenship and Neoliberal Professionalisation Today". *Transactions of the Institute of British Geographers* 36: 545–559.
BBC. 2015. "BBC Worldwide to Oversee International TV Rights for Global Citizen Festival 2015". *BBC.Co.UK*. Available at: www.bbc.co.uk/corporate2/mediacentre/worldwide/2015/global-citizen-festival (accessed 30 September 2015).
Bennett, W. Lance. 2012. "The Personalization of Politics: Political Identity, Social Media, and Changing Patterns of Participation". *The Annals of the American Academy of Political and Social Science* 644(1): 20–39.
Bryan, Audrey M. 2012. "Using International Development-Themed Film to Promote a Pedagogy of Discomfort". In Mags Liddy and Marie Parker-Jenkin (eds), *Education that Matters: Critical Pedagogy and Development Education at Local and Global Levels*. Oxford: Peter Lang, pp. 75–103.
Bryan, Audrey M. 2014. "Learning to Read the World? Educating for 'Active (Global) Citizenship' in the Formal Curriculum". In Stephen McCloskey (ed.), *Development Education in Policy and Practice*. New York: Palgrave Macmillan, pp. 32–46.
Bryan, Audrey and Meliosa Bracken. 2011. *Learning to Read the World? Teaching and Learning about Global Citizenship and International Development in Post-Primary Schools*. Dublin: Irish Aid.
Butcher, Jim. 2014. "Moralizing Tourism: Personal Qualities, Political Issues". In Kevin Hannam and Mary Mostafanezhad (eds), *Moral Encounters in Tourism: Current Developments in the Geographies of Leisure and Tourism*. Burlington, VT: Ashgate, pp. 17–30.
Butcher, Jim. 2015. "Ethical Tourism and Development: The Personal and the Political". *Tourism Recreation Research* 40(1): 71–80.
Chouliaraki, Lilie. 2013. *The Ironic Spectator: Solidarity in the Age of Post-Humanitarianism*. Cambridge: Polity Press.
Earl, Jennifer and Katrina Kimport. 2011. *Digitally Enabled Social Change: Activism in the Internet Age*. Cambridge, MA: MIT Press.
Global Poverty Project. 2015a. Available at: www.globalpovertyproject.com/about-us (accessed 15 August 2015).
Global Poverty Project. 2015b. "Live Below the Line Campaign". Available at: www.globalpovertyproject.com/live-below-the-line (accessed 15 August 2015).
Goodman, Mike and Christine Barnes. 2011. "Star/Poverty Space: The Making of the 'Development Celebrity'". *Celebrity Studies* 2(1): 69–85.
Hampp, Andrew and Harley Brown. 2014. "Global Citizen Festival 2014: Beyoncé Duets with Jay Z, Sting Joins No Doubt and Eight More Highlights". *billboard.com*. Available at: www.billboard.com/articles/list/6266558/global-citizens-festival-2014-beyonce-jay-z-sting-no-doubt-carrie-underwood-alicia-keys (accessed 28 September 2015).
Hensby, Alexander and Darren O'Byrne. 2012. "Global Civil Society and the Cosmopolitan Ideal". In Gerard Delanty (ed.), *Routledge Handbook of Cosmopolitanism Studies*. London: Routledge, pp. 387–399.

Hickel, Jason. 2013. "The 'Real Experience' Industry: Student Development Projects and the Depoliticisation of Poverty". *Learning and Teaching* 6(2): 11–32.

Hickel, Jason. 2015. "The Problem with Saving the World: The UN's New Sustainable Development Goals Aim to Save the World Without Transforming It". 8 August. Available at: www.jacobinmag.com/2015/08/global-poverty-climate-change-sdgs (accessed 25 September 2015).

Hickel, Jason and Arsalan Khan. 2012. "The Culture of Capitalism and the Crisis of Critique". *Anthropological Quarterly* 85(1): 203–227.

Jefferess, David. 2008. "Global Citizenship and the Cultural Politics of Benevolence". *Critical Literacy: Theories and Practices* 2(1): 27–36.

Jefferess, David. 2012. "The 'Me to We' Social Enterprise: Global Education as Lifestyle Brand". *Critical Literacy: Theories and Practices* 6(1): 18–30.

Kennelly, Jacqueline. 2011. *Citizen Youth: Culture, Activism and Agency in a Neoliberal Era*, New York: Palgrave Macmillan.

Klees, Steven and Omar Qargha. 2013. "The Economics of Aid: Implications for Education and Development". In Suzanne Majhanovich and Geo-JaJa Macleans (eds), *Economics, Aid and Education: Implications for Development*. Rotterdam: Sense Publishers, pp. 15–28.

Mostafanezhad, Mary. 2014. *Volunteer Tourism: Popular Humanitarianism in Neoliberal Times*. Burlington, VT: Ashgate.

MSNBC.com. 2015. "Pearl Jam, Beyoncé, Ed Sheeran, Coldplay to headline Global Citizen Festival". 7 July. Available at: www.msnbc.com/msnbc/pearl-jam-beyonce-ed-sheeran-coldplay-headline-global-citizen-festival (accessed 28 September 2015).

Nash, Kate. 2008. "Global Citizenship as Show Business: The Cultural Politics of Make Poverty History". *Media, Culture and Society* 30(2): 167–181.

NPR. 2015. "At Global Citizen Festival, a Unifying Message from Pop Stars and Policymakers". 27 September. Available at: www.npr.org/sections/goatsandsoda/2015/09/27/443921473/at-global-citizen-festival-a-unifying-message-from-pop-stars-and-policymakers (accessed 25 September 2015).

Sandlin, Jennifer, Brian Schultz, and Jake Burdick, 2010. "Understanding, Mapping, and Exploring the Terrain of Public Pedagogy". In Sandlin *et al.* (eds), *Handbook of Public Pedagogy: Education and Learning Beyond Schooling*. New York: Routledge, pp. 1–6.

Schwittay, Anke and Kate Boocock. 2015. "Experiential and Empathetic Engagements with Global Poverty: 'Live Below the Line So That Others Can Rise Above It'". *Third World Quarterly* 36(2): 291–305.

Shulman, Stuart W. 2009. "The Case against Mass E-mails: Perverse Incentives and Low Quality Public Participation in U.S. Federal Rulemaking". *Policy & Internet* 1(1): 23–53.

Simon, Roger I. 2012. "Towards a Hopeful Practice of Worrying: The Problematics of Listening and the Educative Responsibilities of Canada's Truth and Reconciliation Commission". In Pauline Wakeman and Jennifer Henderson (eds), *Reconciling Canada: Critical Perspectives on the Culture of Redress*. Toronto: University of Toronto Press, pp. 129–142.

Tawil, Sobhi. 2013. *Education for "Global Citizenship": A Framework for Discussion*. UNESCO Education Research and Foresight, Paris. [ERF Working Papers Series, No. 7.]

Taylor, Lisa. 2011. "Feeling in Crisis: Vicissitudes of Response in Experiments with Global Justice Education". *Journal of the Canadian Association for Curriculum Studies* 9(1): 6–65.

Tiessen, Rebecca. 2011. "Global Subjects or Objects of Globalization? The Promotion of Global Citizenship in Organisations Offering Sport for Development and/or Peace Programmes". *Third World Quarterly* 32(3): 571–587.

United Nations. 2015. *Sustainable Development Goals.* Available at: www.un.org/sustainabledevelopment/sustainable-development-goals (accessed 2 October 2015).

UN News Centre. 2015. "At Global Citizen Festival, Ban Tells Crowd 'A Better World is Around the Corner'". Available at: www.un.org/apps/news/story.asp?NewsID=48927#.VfqsOcJRFlA (accessed 15 August 2015).

9 The geopolitics of global citizenship

Lowell Gustafson

A new global geopolitics is supporting the development of global citizenship.[1] Changing experiences of the relationship among land, water, climate, history, and politics have led to changes in key components of global citizenship, such as political identity, security, and globalization. A citizen feels part of a homeland, often has been born and raised there, seeks to protect it, and is committed to its future. Now homeland is no longer restricted to a nation, but encompasses the entire globe. The "land of my birth" is no longer only a nation, but also the Earth. Threats to the homeland are no longer restricted to foreign armies or terrorist groups, but include exhaust pipes and smokestacks that endanger both the atmosphere and the security of humanity.

Geopolitics has traditionally analysed the relationship between geography and human political conflict among nations and other political actors in their struggle for access to land, strategic position, and resources. World political maps outline the fixed borders that need to be defended by the citizens of each nation. Between 1648 and 1989, according to Kalevi Holsti (1991), the single most important issue over which wars were fought was territory. A security dilemma often emerged when a nation felt insecure due to the capabilities of neighbours who may have been planning a surprise attack. This insecurity often led to aggression in the alleged service of pre-emptive defence. The motivation to defend one's own territory has led to attacking that of others.

Global geopolitics analyses geography and its relationship to politics in a broader context that includes factors for the cooperation among global citizens necessary to protect the Earth, from which all life, including human life, originated and is sustained. A narrative drawn from the results of scientific research of Earth's past places Earth in the context of the cosmos. The history of the Earth includes the emergence and sustenance of life – and eventually of humanity. Defending territory at this point in the history of the Earth entails a global geopolitics in which humans protect the Earth from the ill effects of the Anthropocene. The term Anthropocene was introduced by Crutzen and Stoermer (2000). Geological periods are given various names, such as the Quaternary (Pleistocene/Holocene) 2.588 million years ago (mya) – until now; the Neogene (Miocene/Pliocene) 23.03–2.588 mya; the Paleogene (Paleocene/

130 Lowell Gustafson

Eocene/Oligocene) 66.0–23.03 mya; the Cretaceous 145.5–66.0 mya; and, famously, the Jurassic 201.3–145.0 mya. The Anthropocene is sometimes used to name the current geological age, viewed as the period during which human activity has been the dominant influence on climate and the environment (Hamilton et al. 2015; Schwägerl et al. 2015; Vince 2014). Global citizenship requires a sense of global identity. In this chapter, I will look at the anthropological and sociobiological aspects of territorial defence, discuss traditional national and imperial geopolitics, and conclude with a discussion of how global geopolitics contributes to global citizenship.

Land of my birth

The anthropology of land

Political anthropology often observes that cultures understand themselves to have originated from their land. The land gives birth to them, sustains and nurtures them, and demands obligations of care and reverence in return. In a Yoruban myth, the divine being Orisha Nla created humans from earth. Olorun, the supreme being, gave them life. In the *Popol Vuh*, the Maya account of creation, the hero-twins' father was resurrected from the underworld, sprouted through the land, and became the Corn God. Ixmucane, the semi-divine Grandmother, fashioned the kernels of corn that were produced into the meal from which the Maya were created. Every time the Maya ate a meal of corn meal, beans, and squash, they were eating the God who was given birth from their land and from whose fruit they were created and nurtured. Books Four and Five of the *Popol Vuh* are concerned with the origins of a particular group of Maya, not all humans. The Genesis account (1:24) states that, "And God said, 'Let the land produce living creatures according to their kinds: the livestock, the creatures that move along the ground, and the wild animals, each according to its kind.'" The account later states that the first human being was named Adam, perhaps arising from the Hebrew word *adama*, meaning earth, soil, light brown or red. A literally translated name for Adam into English might be Earthling or Humus-being (human). The Tanakh is concerned with the origin and development of the Hebrew people as well as their special relationship with a defined, holy portion of land (sometimes called Canaan, Palestine, Eretz HaQodesh, or Israel).

In other words, a great number of cultural and sacred myths emphasize how life and a people originate from the land. The land itself gives birth to a nation or a people. It is sacred land. The soil itself is the stuff of which we are made. Humus is the clay from which humanity is moulded. My people are human, others are foreigners or something else altogether. My territory is nurturing and sustaining. The land is fertile; it has soil from which sustenance-giving plants emerge. The Earth itself may be seen as a living female. Earth goddesses are common, such as Coatlicue in Aztec mythology, Pachamama for the Inca, Ki in Sumerian, Mahimata or Great Mother in the *Rigveda* (1.164.33), Mut in ancient Egypt, and Gaia for the ancient Greeks. For all of these reasons, the land of one's birth deserves filial loyalty and protection. Land, ancestry, and kinship go together.

Social science and defending the nest

Edward O. Wilson has long argued that human nature is deeply rooted in and connected to the natural world. In his 1975 book *Sociobiology: The New Synthesis*, he first investigated how society is rooted in biology. Almost four decades later, he continues to develop his argument. Wilson contends in *The Social Conquest of the Earth* that humanity's social nature has contributed to our ability to conquer the Earth. Our ability to organise ourselves is our most powerful skill. We may lack fangs, claws, shells, wings, or cheetah-like speed, but we can work together. We are not the only social beings and not the only ones who have done well in surviving and thriving through social organization. Ant colonies and bee hives are highly organized, with specialists in various functions. And they defend their nests to the death, as Wilson argues (Wilson 2012). The survival of the group depends on the defence of where the young are born and raised, and where food is found or kept. Birds sometimes sing to warn others of their kind to stay away from territory with limited supplies of preferred foods. The desire of members of a group to survive and reproduce often leads to in-group cooperation and conflict with others of the same or other species who might compete for resources. If citizenship includes a sense of belonging, membership in a group that works together to protect the nest, it has an origin deep in the past. Social creatures – including humans – cannot survive without maintaining access to the land that gives them birth and sustains them.

Because land or the nest appears to be permanent to its human residents, it necessitates a kind of special protection. Building one's nation on permanent land is as wise as building one's house upon solid rock. If it can be secured, the land will stay under our possession for generations to come, and my group's ties to this land will be as permanent as the land itself. In short, protection of the land is not just for the present, but also for our children and our children's children. Each of us experiences our own aging, but the mountains seem to remain.

Motherland/fatherland

Land is a powerful source of political identity, especially when it is linked to family. Political identity as formed by a group's relationship to a defined geographic location has often been an important factor in politics. We are loyal to where we were born and raised, we root for the home team of our city or state or country, we fight for the motherland or fatherland, and we see land as our origin. Nationalists have often referred to their motherland or fatherland. It is closely linked to kinship; it is where we make our nests and raise our families.

Kinship was likely one of our species' oldest sources of identity. The need to care for young *Homo sapiens* for an extended period of time is one of the driving forces of human culture. Our ability to work together in societies is made possible by our complex and relatively large brains. It may well be that the growth in hominins' brain size and complexity over the past seven million years was in a positive feedback loop with our sociability. Each of our approximately 100 billion neurons with a trillion synapses makes our brains the most complexly structured matter of which we know. Our ancestors' brains and sociability turned out to be more powerful than those fangs and claws on the African savannahs where our ancestors and their competitors evolved.

But large brains came at a cost. They made childbirth for bipedal hominins dangerous and lengthened the period of childhood dependence while the brain developed after birth. It took a number of adults a long time to bring children to sexual maturity. Prolonged relationships among child caretakers, who had to figure out how to work together for many years, led to intensely strong relationships within a kinship group. Memories of one's own former caretakers and a sense of ongoing obligation to them led to hominin burial rituals that are more elaborate than how other species, such as elephants, mourn their dead. Ancestor worship may be one of the origins of religion. The nurturance and sustenance of caretakers within kinship groups, not only mothers but also fathers and other relatives, often become linked to "the land of my birth". The hills behind the mother in William-Adolphe Bouguereau's painting are part of the message, not just a backdrop (Bouguereau 1883). The land is my parent and I am fiercely loyal to it, in this association.

There are seemingly endless cultural expressions about the motherland and fatherland. One might point to classics like *Rigveda*, part of Hindu sacred writings, which says that:

> One should respect his motherland, his culture and his mother tongue because they are givers of happiness. ... A person who is respectful towards his land, civilization and language, attains greatness and he acquires all the happiness of life. His deeds should be such that makes the motherland, the culture and language proud.
>
> (First Mandal, 13/9, *Rigveda*)

One might also point, in a very different cultural setting, to the evocative painting by Jacek Malczewski entitled *Motherland* (Malczewski 1903).

A fully developed discussion about the different gendered views of the motherland and fatherland would be important, but beyond our purpose here. Still, it is virtually obligatory to include a quote from Adolf Hitler, who said: "There is a road to freedom. Its milestones are Obedience, Endeavor, Honesty, Order, Cleanliness, Sobriety, Truthfulness, Sacrifice, and love of the Fatherland" (*Life* 1939). But suffice it to say that not all art devoted to the fatherland is aggressive. There is *Má vlas*, a set of six symphonic poems composed in the nineteenth century by the Czech composer Bedřich Smetana.

The second poem is *Vltava, Mein Vaterland* (My fatherland). There is the moving *Finlandia* by Jean Sibelius. These are expressions of the great significance attached to land as an ancestor from which we have been born and that deserves our protection or veneration.

Many famous expressions of American attachment to the land easily come to mind. Irving Berlin's "God Bless America", Woodie Guthrie's "This Land Is Your Land", and "America the Beautiful" by Katharine Lee Bates are iconic American songs that celebrate the land.

Not to be outdone, the Brazilian national anthem praises the "beloved, idolized homeland". The *Lied der Deutschen*, written by Hoffmann von Fallersleben, from which the German national anthem was taken, praises the "German fatherland". A famous English poem by William Blake, whose words are still sung at some English sporting events, celebrates "England's mountains green" (BBC Sport 2005). One might also recall Elton John's tribute to Princess Diana at her funeral, which closely follows Blake's line with "England's greenest hills". These are but a few of the many expressions of reverence for the motherland or fatherland, the land which is an ancestor, the hills where the ancestors still walk. Nations have a powerful relationship with defined portions of land. Nationalists often seek to protect their nest, mourn the loss of their nation and the losses it has suffered. Sometimes they call for pre-emptive aggression against imminent or possibly future attacks.

National geopolitics, history, and identity

Ownership and access to land is one way that nations have traditionally affirmed their power. The relationship between political identity and defined pieces of the Earth's territory has been of great importance in the national era since 1648. Political maps of national boundaries are routinely used in many settings. In the United States, the America-centric world map in the Mercator projection is commonly shown. America is placed top and centre, with South America below and the rest of the world split in half and placed on either side of America. The message is clear. The United States is at the top of the world and at the pivotal centre of world affairs. American identity as the greatest nation in the world is confirmed by the Mercator projection (*Chicago Daily Tribune* 1942).

National geopolitics is often linked to national histories and identity. The teaching of history often relies on a national origin story in order to facilitate the larger political objective of identity formation. When my daughter came home from her first day of public school kindergarten, she had a colour-in-the-lines picture of George Washington. The process of state-sponsored identity formation began right off the bat. Her first day away from her immediate family at school began with a story about the father of her country. The issue was not to teach how to make personal decisions about which type of leader she admired; she did not come home with group of pictures of the Father of Our Country, a British king, a German dictator, a Chinese emperor, a Germanic hero (e.g. Bandel 1840), and many other leaders.

American political identity is bound up with a full awareness of the history of the American experience. The academic field of history has often been associated with promoting national identities. When the American Historical Association (AHA) was founded in 1884, "history had only recently emerged as a distinct academic discipline. The first few professors in the field of history had only been appointed at major universities in the 1870s" (AHA n.d.). The country had survived its Civil War and the last spike of the transcontinental railroad had been driven in 1869. The nation had achieved its Manifest Destiny of integrating territory from sea to shining sea (see Gast 1872). It was ready to tell its story. And the state was ready to sponsor it in public schooling as a way of fostering nationalism and civic pride. To become a citizen of the United States requires passing a test in part about American history, with questions about the wars in which the nation has fought (US Citizenship and Immigration Services n.d.). Apparently, it is important for citizenship to know what is required to defend the nation.

A key part of American identity was to be part of – and know about – the great stories of migration from the Pilgrims' landing at Plymouth Rock to Manifest Destiny and the Oregon Trail. American identity incorporates a rock on a seashore and ruts from covered wagons in the Great Plains.

The study of political science, like history, was associated with being American and even participating in American public life. Shortly after the AHA was founded, the American Political Science Association was established in 1903. After American history, the other most prominent questions on the naturalization test are about American politics. College courses on American political science are often about the three branches of government. Knowing about and understanding the events leading to – and the text of – the Declaration of Independence, Constitution, Gettysburg Address, the Letter from a Birmingham Jail, and much else became part of being a good American citizen. All of this just barely begins the topic of how nationalism is instilled through the teaching of history and politics (see Anderson 1991; Díaz-Andreu 2007; Ferro 2003; Geary 2002; Gellner 1983; Hobsbawm 1992; Kohl 1996; Smith 1988). National citizens identified with the nation.

New identities from older histories

Ironically, new histories push the narrative of the past further back in time. Human histories foster human identity, perhaps a prerequisite for human citizenship. The human past did not begin with the American Declaration of Independence in 1776, the European International System in 1648, the Golden Age of Athens in 500 BCE, or with writing in Sumer in 2,700 BCE. It began with the beginning of *Homo sapiens* about 200,000 years ago in Africa.

The Father of Humanity was not George Washington, Julius Caesar, or Gilgamesh.

A fuller story of humans begins with the evolution of hominins not long after our common ancestors with chimpanzees lived about seven million years ago. The political lesson drawn from this story was made on his state visit to Ethiopia by President Barack Obama in 2015. The US President viewed and touched the 3.2-million-year-old fossilized bones of "Lucy" and "Ardi", whose bones are even a million years older. Obama referred to Lucy in his toast at the state dinner and again the next day in a speech at the African Union. "I had the privilege to view Lucy", he told the audience at the African Union. "You may know Lucy; she's our ancestor, more than 3 million years old. In this tree of humanity, with all our branches and diversity, we all go back to the same root. We're all one family; we're all one tribe. And yet", he added, "so much of the suffering in our world stems from our failure to remember that – to not recognize ourselves in each other" (quoted in Baker 2015).

The common ancestors of all living humans today did not live in Mesopotamia about 6,000 years ago, but in East Africa many millennia before (Baker 2015). The story of migration did not begin a few centuries ago at Plymouth Rock, but some 70,000 years ago from East Africa as *Homo sapiens* first left their homeland where they had evolved. They reached Australia by about 50,000 years ago after having travelled along the coasts of South Asia. Eventually, they learned how to survive the trip across Siberia and made it across Beringia, the land bridge connecting Russia and Alaska during the last ice age. Some may have sailed across the Pacific to South America. By about 20,000 years ago, they had settled the Americas. This is a human migration story that is a heroic one. Without maps or previous knowledge of the routes they would take, our ancestors made their way across the globe. Human history did not begin with writing five millennia ago. It began with humans 200 millennia ago, with roots in earlier ancestors that push our common narrative back much further than that.

Envisioning global geopolitics

Along with a new migration story, we have been seeing new ideas about the relationship between land and politics. In the emerging global geopolitics, there is a key role for the Earth's story – rather than only nations' stories – and that of the origins and sustenance of life on Earth in the context of the cosmos. As a result of this shifting perspective, there is a growing desire to defend the nest at the global level. The Earth as a whole is seen as the nest that produces and sustains the lives of humans throughout the globe, so it becomes increasingly important for humans to act in ways that defend our common global nest. There are changing public attitudes about the relationship between people and the Earth's geography. With the growing environmental movement, there is an increasing perception of the interconnectedness of the Earth's conditions and human well-being. Changing understandings of the relationship of humans and Earth in space may be reshaping political identity and producing a global geopolitics (see Anders 1968).

One of the most reproduced and evocative pictures of the past half-century is that of the Earthrise from the moon, taken by astronaut William Anders during the Apollo 8 mission in 1968. The Blue Marble was another famous photograph of the Earth, taken in 1972, by the crew of the Apollo 17 spacecraft (NASA 1972). The picture showed the entire, white cloud covered blue earth in an empty, very black space. In 1990, the Voyager 1 spacecraft took a picture of the Earth from 3.7 billion miles away, showing our home planet as a small speck in an enormously large and forbidding space (NASA 1990; see also Sagan 2014). The famous "Blue Marble" picture was retaken in 2012 (NASA 2012).

At its current impressive speed of about 37,000 miles per hour, it would take Voyager about 50,000 years to get to Alpha Centauri, the nearest star outside our solar system. For all practical purposes, we are alone. And there is nowhere else to go, until and if we ever have the technology to get to other habitable planets. We either make it together on our one habitable planet or we slide towards oblivion. There have been five great extinction events in Earth history, with a sixth self-inflicted one now in progress. Over 99 per cent of all species that have ever existed are now extinct. There is no assurance about our species escaping the same fate others have experienced. Postponing that inevitable occurrence will take concerted action. Earth security and human security are perhaps our most pressing public policy concerns. Defending the nest now means defending the Earth, not exclusively or even primarily the nation. Global geopolitics is a crucial component of global citizens ensuring basic well-being and even survival.

Earth is humanity's homeland. It is a one-of-a-kind planet in our solar system. Our ability to get to another inhabitable planet is, at least now, not within our reach. It is our Earth with all of its Goldilocks conditions that keeps us alive. Earth is just the right distance from the sun, keeping water in the liquid form that is necessary for life as we know it. It has just the right oxygen content in the atmosphere. It has a magnetic shield that protects us from solar winds. And we are made from the same stuff of which it is made.

Globalization and global identity

As we have discussed, national identity has often seen land as ancestor. The land and kinship have often been tied together. The land as father and mother has been a commonly held idea throughout much of history. Current histories of the origins of life support the emergence of global identities. Global identity is formed not only through increased international trade or transnational corporations and investments, but also through scientific accounts of the emergence of life on earth.

The story of globalization of humans begins much further back than the migration of our kind from Africa. It begins with the elements and molecules that make us up right now. It is generally thought now that a complex process of chemical evolution combined metabolism, membranes from lipids, and reproduction in response to the environment in the first life forms almost four billion years ago. The knowledge of the exact process remains elusive, but LUCA, or the Last Universal Common Ancestor from about that time, seems likely to be the ancestor of all life on Earth, including one of its most recent forms: us (Deamer 2011; Hazen 2005; Pross 2012). The common cultural motif of the Earth mother remains evocative.

The new attitudes towards the Earth and human relations are being reinforced by innovative curricula, in which history is not taught within national frameworks, but as the history of the entire past from the Big Bang to the present. The Earth and its inhabitants are placed within a cosmic framework that has spanned billions of years. The Big History Project is a new curriculum supported by Bill Gates which was piloted in 2011 and 2012, and now being adopted by schools in Australia, the Netherlands, the United States, and elsewhere. Gates initiated the project after listening to a video course offered by David Christian, who is the author of *Maps of Time: An Introduction to Big History*. In the book and the course, Christian discusses what he sees as the major periods of time since the Big Bang, each distinguished by one of a number of major thresholds. In Christian's account, history is not framed by national histories, but by the 13.82-billion-year-long history of the cosmos, Earth, life, and humanity (Brown 2007; Chaisson 2004; 2006; Christian *et al.* 2014; Spier 2015).

As we saw, the test for US citizenship requires a knowledge of basic events in American history and the constitutional structure of government. Global citizenship is formed by a knowledge of basic events in cosmic, Earth, and life history, as well as in the basic laws that govern their development. The beginning of big history is not in 1776 or 1787 with the Declaration of Independence or the US Constitution. It begins with a singularity, a point of infinite heat and density without space or mass, from which energy, matter, space, and time emerged into a rapidly expanding universe. Immediately after the "Big Bang", up and down quarks formed relationships through the strong force within protons and neutrons. Three hundred thousand years later, the universe had expanded and cooled enough to permit the electromagnetic force to form relationships between protons and electrons within hydrogen and helium atoms. Gravity drew some of these asymmetrically spread-out atoms tightly together enough to start fusion, and stars within galaxies were born. The result was heavier atoms, all the way up to iron in some stars. The largest stars then exploded in a supernova that produced all elements heavier than iron. These mixed with still pre-existing clouds of hydrogen and helium to form second-generation stars, like our own sun. Since we are made of the elements fused in long-dead stars, Carl Sagan made the famous observation that we are made of stardust. If we left it there, we could talk about a story making us universal or galactic citizens. However, for our purposes here, we need to continue the progression of events.

While over 99 per cent of our solar system's matter was drawn into the sun, there was just enough cosmic dust to form the terrestrial planets like Earth 4.5672 billion years ago. The elements that had been fused in stars and the molecules like water that had formed in space were drawn together by gravity to form what was then a molten planet with no oxygen in the atmosphere. Chemical evolution increased the complexity of the relationship of matter and eventually produced life. As Walter Alvarez (2014) says to develop Sagan's famous phrase, "We are stardust ... concentrated by Earth!" It took almost two billion years before prokaryote cells became eukaryote cells, and then a half-billion years to get from the explosion of complex life in the Cambrian period to hominins and then finally humans. The Big History curriculum teaches how embedded the natural past of the cosmos and the Earth is in each of us. The Earth is made of stardust, and we are made of Earth mud.

The Big History curriculum is part of a growing consciousness of the Earth as the changing, rather fragile home for all of humanity. The Earth is a nest that has given birth to all life on Earth. It has sustained life for a long time, but by no means every species. The requirements for sustained human life are complex and by no means assured. There was virtually no oxygen in Earth's atmosphere when it was first formed through accretion of particles left over from an earlier supernova. Over two billion years, cyanobacteria and other prokaryote cells which developed photosynthesis excrete oxygen, which gradually built up in the atmosphere. One effect of this was that the ozone layer of O_3 absorbed much of the sun's harmful radiation. With human-made chemicals breaking down that ozone layer, human security is being endangered.

Human use of fossil fuels emits carbon dioxide, which traps heat and is causing global warming. Levels of carbon dioxide have steadily risen since the beginning of the industrial revolution, but especially over the past 50 years, from just under 320 parts per million in 1960 to over 400 now (Tans and Keeling n.d.). For a half-century now, these levels are higher than they have been for 400,000 years. NASA concludes that, as a result, "scientific evidence for warming of the climate system is unequivocal" (NASA n.d. (a), NASA n.d. (b)). The effects on weather patterns, global warming, rising sea levels, and the melting glaciers and polar caps are accepted by virtually all scientists who study the issue.

A story of the cosmos and Earth's place in it has been developed over the past couple of centuries, transforming our understanding of geopolitics. In recent years, world opinion leaders have also developed a vision of global geopolitics and enjoyed some success in raising it on the world's political agenda. At the 2015 meeting of world political, economic, and cultural leaders in Davos, Al Gore introduced the headlining presenter, David Christian, who presented the history of the universe, earth, life, and humanity in one lecture (Christian 2015). Since leaving office, the former vice-president made the environmental film, *An Inconvenient Truth,* and wrote *The Future: Six Drivers of Global Change* (Gore 2015). At the Davos meeting, he wanted world leaders to be aware of cosmic, earth, life, and all of human history as they together worked to fashion a more global age.

Even if one is sceptical about the intent of elites at Davos, there are many more common, citizen-led global movements. One of these is the cogent statement of the new vision in the Earth Charter:

> The Earth Charter is a product of a decade-long, worldwide, cross-cultural dialogue on common goals and shared values. The Earth Charter project began as a United Nations initiative, but it was carried forward and completed by a global civil society initiative. The Earth Charter was finalized and then launched as a people's charter on 29 June, 2000 by the Earth Charter Commission, an independent international entity, in a ceremony at the Peace Palace, in The Hague.
> (Earth Charter International n.d.)

The Charter notes that we are at a critical moment in Earth's history and humanity's place in a vast evolving universe. Earth, it affirms, is our common home and is alive with a community of life. "The forces of nature make existence a demanding and uncertain adventure, but Earth has provided the conditions essential to life's evolution ... The protection of Earth's vitality, diversity, and beauty is a sacred trust" (Earth Charter International n.d.) Pando Populus is another platform for people who care about the Earth and creating an ecological civilization (Pando Populus n.d.). There are by now hundreds of other such efforts (350.org n.d.).

Concluding questions

Many segments of humanity are still protecting their own territorial nests, even if this is at the expense of the sustenance of life on earth, including but not limited to humans. Many national governments remain motivated by national geopolitics to gain advantage in a zero-sum game in which the relative power of nations is a hierarchy that matters even more than human well-being and survival. Non-state actors battle states for control of territory. The use of fossil fuels is melting glaciers and polar ice caps, resulting in rising sea levels that are threatening many coastal communities.

Can state policy follow the lead of Big Historians, the educators, and others who produce such work as the Earth Charter and realize the limits set at major environmental conferences? Can transnational corporations be motivated by profits in protecting the Earth that protects us or do they need to be regulated to do so? Can we expect to see a transition to global geopolitics after centuries of national geopolitics that is sufficiently robust to change behaviour before we follow the lead of other extinct species? Can global citizens with a global identity, concerned for global security, and aware of human kinship emerge in sufficient numbers to affect public policy? The need is clear. The outcome is not.

Note

1 I appreciate the comments and suggestions of Tammy Birk, Cynthia Brown, Irene Langran, and Robert Moore on earlier versions of this chapter. Of course any remaining issues with it are my responsibility.

References

350.org. n.d. "Friends and Allies". Available at: http://350.org/about/allies (accessed 25 September 2015).

Alvarez, Walter. 2014. "We Are Stardust ... Concentrated by Earth!". *Expositions: Interdisciplinary Studies in the Humanities* 8(1). Available at: http://expositions.journals.villanova.edu/issue/view/130.

American Historical Association. n.d. "Brief History of the AHA". Available at: www.historians.org/about-aha-and-membership/aha-history-and-archives/brief-history-of-the-aha (accessed 20 February 2015).

Anders, William. 1968. "Earthrise". Available at: www.nasa.gov/images/content/331786main_as16-120-19187_full.tif (accessed 21 December 2015).

Anderson, Benedict R. O'G. 2006. *Imagined Communities: Reflections on the Origin and Spread of Nationalism*. London, New York: Verso.

Baker, Peter. 2015. "Traveling with the President, and Meeting Lucy, in Africa". *New York Times*, 31 July. Available at: www.nytimes.com/times-insider/2015/07/31/traveling-with-the-president-and-meeting-lucy-in-africa (accessed 5 August 2015).

Bandel, Ernst von. "Hermann Memorial Near Detmold, Germany". Available at: https://en.wikipedia.org/wiki/Hermannsdenkmal#/media/File:Arminius1.tif (accessed 21 December 2015).

BBC Sport. 2005. "Sing Jerusalem for England!". 6 September. Available at: http://news.bbc.co.uk/sport2/hi/cricket/england/4217144.stm#jerusalem (accessed 14 September 2015).

Bouguereau, William-Adolphe. 1883. "The Motherland". Available at: http://commons.wikimedia.org/wiki/File:William-Adolphe_Bouguereau(1825-1905)_-_The_Motherland_(1883).tif (accessed 21 December 2015).

Brown, Cynthia Stokes. 2007. *Big History: From the Big Bang to the Present*. New York: New Press. [Distributed by Norton.]

Chaisson, Eric. 2006. *Epic of Evolution: Seven Ages of the Cosmos*. New York: Columbia University Press.

Chicago Daily Tribune. 1942. "America – the Real Center of the World Today". Printed map. Geography and Map Division, Library of Congress (157). Available at: www.loc.gov/exhibits/churchill/images/wc0157s.tif (accessed 21 December 2015).

Christian, David. 2004. *Maps of Time: An Introduction to Big History*. Berkeley, CA: University of California Press.

Christian, David. 2010. "Big History: From the Big Bang to Us and the Future". Lecture at Villanova University, 18 October. Available at: www.youtube.com/watch?v=yeRjqNiFZPk.

Christian, David. 2011. "The History of Our World in 18 Minutes". TED talk March. Available at: www.ted.com/talks/david_christian_big_history.
Christian, David. 2015. "How Did We Get Here? Big History 101". Introduced by Al Gore, World Economic Forum Annual Meeting, Davos-Klosters, Switzerland, 21 January. Available at: www.weforum.org/sessions/summary/how-did-we-get-her e-big-history-101 (accessed 20 February 2015).
Christian, David, Cynthia Stokes Brown, and Craig Benjamin. 2014. *Big History: Between Nothing and Everything*. New York: McGraw-Hill Education.
Christian, David and Teaching Company. 2008. *Big History the Big Bang, Life on Earth, and the Rise of Humanity*. Chantilly, VA: Teaching Co., 8050 Teaching Co.
Crutzen, Paul J. and Eugene F. Stoermer. 2000. "The 'Anthropocene'". *Global Change Newsletter* 41 (May).
Dalbotten, Diana, Patrick Hamilton, and Gillian Roehrig. 2014. *Future Earth: Advancing Civic Understanding of the Anthropocene*. Hoboken, NJ: American Geophysical/Wiley.
Deamer, D. W. 2011. *First Life: Discovering the Connections between Stars, Cells, and How Life Began*. Berkeley, CA: University of California Press.
Díaz-Andreu García, Margarita. 2007. *A World History of Nineteenth-Century Archaeology: Nationalism, Colonialism, and the Past*. Oxford: Oxford University Press.
Earth Charter International. n.d. "The Earth Charter". Available at: www.earthcha rterinaction.org/content/pages/read-the-charter.html.
Ferro, Marc. 2003. *The Use and Abuse of History, or, How the Past is Taught to Children*. London, New York: Routledge.
Gast, John. 1872. "American Progress". Available at: https://en.wikipedia.org/wiki/Ma nifest_destiny#/media/File:American_progress.tif (accessed 21 December 2015).
Geary, Patrick J. 2002. *The Myth of Nations: The Medieval Origins of Europe*. Princeton, NJ: Princeton University Press.
Gellner, Ernest. 1983. *Nations and Nationalism*. Ithaca, NY: Cornell University Press.
Gore, Albert. 2015. *The Future: Six Drivers of Global Change*. New York: Random House.
Hamilton, Clive, Christophe Bonneuil, and François Gemenne. 2015. *The Anthropocene and the Global Environmental Crisis*. Abingdon: Routledge.
Hazen, Robert M. 2005. *Genesis: The Scientific Quest for Life's Origin*. Washington, DC: Joseph Henry Press.
Hobsbawm, E. J. 2012. *Nations and Nationalism since 1780: Programme, Myth, Reality*. 2nd edn. Cambridge: Cambridge University Press.
Hobsbawm, E. J. and T. O. Ranger. 2012. *The Invention of Tradition*. Cambridge: Cambridge University Press.
Holsti, K. J. 1991. *Peace and War: Armed Conflicts and International Order, 1648–1989*. Cambridge and New York: Cambridge University Press.
Kohl, Philip L. and Clare P. Fawcett. 1995. *Nationalism, Politics, and the Practice of Archaeology*. Cambridge and New York: Cambridge University Press.
Life. 21 August 1939. Available at: www2.muw.edu/~tvelek/HitlerFascism.html (accessed 14 June 2015).
Malczewski, Jacek. 1903. "Country". Available at: https://commons.wikimedia.org/ wiki/File:Malczewski_Jacek_Ojczyzna.tif#/media/File:Malczewski_Jacek_Ojczyzna. tif (accessed 21 December 2015).

NASA [National Aeronautics and Space Administration]. n.d. (a). "The Relentless Rise of Carbon dioxide". Available at: http://climate.nasa.gov/climate_resources/24 (accessed 21 December 2015).

NASA. n.d. (b). "Climate Change: How Do We Know?" Available at: http://climate.nasa.gov/evidence (accessed 21 December 2015).

NASA. 1972. "Blue Marble – Image of the Earth from Apollo 17". Available at: www.nasa.gov/content/blue-marble-image-of-the-earth-from-apollo-17 (accessed 21 December 2015).

NASA. 1990. *"Pale Blue Dot", Taken by Voyager 1, 4 Billion Miles from Earth*. Available at: http://photojournal.jpl.nasa.gov/jpegMod/PIA00452_modest.tif (accessed 21 December 2015).

NASA. 2012. *"Blue Marble". Taken from the VIIRS Instrument Aboard NASA's Most Recently Launched Earth-Observing Satellite – Suomi NPP. This Composite Image Uses a Number of Swaths of the Earth's Surface Taken on 4 January*. Available at: www.nasa.gov/images/content/618486main_earth_full.tif (accessed 21 December 2015); see also www.nasa.gov/multimedia/imagegallery/image_feature_2159.html.

Oppenheimer, Stephen. 2003. *The Real Eve: Modern Man's Journey out of Africa*. New York: Carroll & Graf.

Pando Populus. n.d. Available at: www.pandopopulus.com (accessed 25 September 2015).

Pross, Addy. 2012. *What Is Life? How Chemistry Becomes Biology*. Oxford: Oxford University Press.

Renner Jones, Lucy. 2015. *The Anthropocene: The Human Era and How It Shapes the Planet*. Santa Fe, NM: Synergetic Press.

Rigveda, First Mandal, 13/9. n.d. Available at: www.neelkanthdhaam.org/rigveda1.html (accessed 14 June 2015).

Sagan, Carl. 2014. *"The Pale Blue Dot". Speech, Reproduced in "Cosmos: A Space Time Odyssey" – Episode 13 "Unafraid of the Dark"*. Available at: www.youtube.com/watch?v=XH7ZRF6zNoc (accessed 21 December 2015).

Schwägerl, Christian. 2014. *The Anthropocene: The Human Era and How It Shapes Our Planet*. Santa Fe, NM: Synergetic Press.

Smith, Anthony D. 1987. *The Ethnic Origins of Nations*. Oxford and New York: Blackwell.

Spier, Fred. 2015. *Big History and the Future of Humanity*. Chichester: Wiley.

Tans, Pieter. n.d. NOAA/ESRL (www.esrl.noaa.gov/gmd/ccgg/trends) and Ralph Keeling, Scripps Institution of Oceanography (scrippsco2.ucsd.edu). Global Monitoring Division, Earth System Research Laboratory, National Oceanic & Atmospheric Administration, US Department of Commerce, "Trends in Atmospheric Carbon Dioxide".

US Citizenship and Immigration Services. n.d. "100 Civics Questions and Answers". Available at: www.uscis.gov/citizenship/teachers/educational-products/100-civics-questions-and-answers-mp3-audio-english-version (accessed 15 June 2015).

Vince, Gaia. 2014. *Adventures in the Anthropocene: A Journey to the Heart of the Planet We Made*. Minneapolis, MN: Milkweed Editions.

Wilson, Edward O. 1975. *Sociobiology: The New Synthesis*. Cambridge, MA: Belknap Press.

Wilson, Edward O. 2012. *The Social Conquest of Earth*. New York: Liveright.

World Economic Forum. 2015. David Christian Introduced by Al Gore, "How Did We Get Here? Big History 101". World Economic Forum Annual Meeting, Davos-Klosters, Switzerland, 21 January.

10 How "global" can we be?
Insights from the environmental field

Barton A. Thompson

Globalism refers to the expansion of an individual's identity to include the concerns that transcend national borders and incorporate global interests, rights, and duties. It shares the same challenges that proponents of environmentalism have wrestled with for years, and which Irene Langran discussed in Chapter 2 of this book. The issue is whether humans are psychologically equipped to adopt the worldly perspectives and expanded ethics which are needed to truly engage in a global state of mind. This chapter will examine the underlying psychology that has hindered the environmental movement and which is also likely to negatively impact the development of global identities. Specifically, the focus will be on the American political response to various environmental issues. However, because the belief is that many of these reactions are based on universal psychological attributes, it will apply to humans around the world. It is hoped that some of the difficulties which are still challenging environmentalists can be avoided by those who are promoting global agendas.

When working as an environmental engineer for the Environmental Protection Agency (EPA) in the mid-1980s, I came to the realization that we had many of the technical solutions to our environmental problems, but we did not have the will to carry them out. Granted, the EPA was constrained by the anti-environmental policies of then President Ronald Reagan and Secretary of the Interior James Watt, but it seemed like the problem was far more complex than the wayward thinking of some of our administrators. I returned to academia in part to search for an answer to this conundrum, and I recall teaching environmental studies courses to undergraduates and becoming even more perplexed about environmental resistance. From a rational perspective it seemed obvious that we needed to restrict our behaviour in a variety of ways so that we did not damage our environment. Sure, it would take sacrifices from everyone, but it was also serving everyone by preserving the very basis of our shared survival. So, why did it always seem as though environmentalists were fighting against the social mainstream? After all, environmentalists were not pushing for policies that served their individual interests in the way that corporations were, but instead were promoting the overall group interest. Why was it an uphill battle? Was it politics, economics, or cultural traditions? The answer is that it is a bit of all of them – and more. Human nature (Pinker 2002), or in more contemporary terms our evolved psychology, has had a tremendous impact. Environmentalists rarely employ the psychological dimension to explain our environmental problems, and, as a result, they have been blind to one of their essential adversaries. Pogo was quite prophetic when he stated, "We have met the enemy, and he is us!" (Kelly 1972), and it is surely time to heed him in the environmental movement.

In attempting to understand the behavioural problems that plague environmentalism, one must look carefully at the tragedy of the commons, which was described by Garrett Hardin in 1968. A common resource can take a wide variety of forms including forests, fisheries, and water as well as capacities, such as an ability to store waste or the capacity of the earth to sustain human population growth. Hardin pointed out that when dealing with a common unregulated resource, humans acting to enhance their own interests will be likely to overuse the commons unless regulations are put in place. His solution, which entails regulation of the commons seems simple, but it is actually quite difficult because our socio-political–economic system tends to cater to those with more economic resources. They, in turn, are the ones who tend to resist regulations on their activities most vehemently and effectively due to their economic interests and compliant political connections.

However, it is not as simple as one group having more interest in preserving their favourable economic realities. That does not explain the irrational behaviour that is exhibited on the group level. From the point of view of a self-interested individual, it may seem rational to pursue the most immediate benefits because, if an individual voluntarily restricts his or her harvest, he or she only compromises his or her own benefits and leaves more for the competition to take. On the other hand, in terms of the overall consequences, they are likely to overuse the common resource and ultimately destroy it, which is irrational at the group level and ultimately at the individual level. Why do humans seem to struggle with this level of analysis? Below the surface of the tragedy of the commons lurks a complex multitude of mental processes, which help to account for why humans often lack the will to effectively deal with problems that also require them to transcend their psychologically imposed perspectives of what is in their interest. Both environmental and global issues fall squarely into this realm.

The psychology

Aristotle exhorted humans to extend beyond their natural tendencies to ally with their close family members and reach their destiny as humans through the formation of a larger political entity, the state, which is a polity formed through the coalition of proximal villages. Aristotle was delving into one of the core aspects of humanity – the interplay between our individual and group interests. A number of researchers have hypothesized that the reason our brain has evolved the way it has was to enhance our social adeptness (Baron-Humphrey 1976; Cohen 1995; Whiten and Byrne 1997). Humans represent

How "global" can we be? 145

an astonishing dynamic between individual and group interests (Wilson 2012), and much cognitive complexity is devoted to weaving this tightrope between group and individual interests. We work to maintain our group affiliation while simultaneously maintaining our individual interests within them. We are even able to jump to another group, like the proverbial rats from the sinking ship, when our own coalition becomes relatively weak or no longer serves our individual interests as well as another.

Why did we become this amalgamation of conflicting group and individual desires? When we observe hunter-gatherers today, we find that they all live in flexible groups that have the potential to ebb and flow with the ecological conditions. They depend on each other for subsistence, reproduction, defence, and many other basic needs. Without their social networks, individual foragers living on their own would not be likely to survive, and so our tendency to develop a coalitional identity became indispensable at some point in our evolutionary past. However, we did not evolve like the social insects and develop strictly defined social castes. Rather, we maintained our individual interests and developed cognitive abilities to work within and between groups to advance them (Wilson 2012).

What this means is that humans have evolved complex and sophisticated forms of coalitional psychology (Barkow *et al.* 1992) in order to maintain and negotiate those social networks on which they depend. This coalitional psychology allows us to judge the costs and benefits of alternative activities, such as engaging in different types of altruism with various individuals (Hamilton 1964; Trivers 1971). So humans are able to uphold two sometimes seemingly conflicting interests: group and individual. Simultaneously, we also developed tendencies to avoid, look down on, and even abhor members of out-groups who represented threats to our group and individual interests (De Waal 1996; Sober and Wilson 1998; Wilson 2012).

To further complicate matters, there are a multitude of possible coalitions that humans can form, and again, we can turn to hunter-gatherers to gain some insights about the types of groups that our coalitional psychology typically produces. Human foragers tend to consistently acknowledge at least two representative social units above the level of the nuclear family (Kelly 1995; Binford 2001; Marlowe 2010). The first is what anthropologists label as the band and consists of the residential-foraging group, in which members live and work together on a daily basis to gain their subsistence needs. This band is usually composed of related and familiar individuals who are tied together through long-term reciprocal relations as well as kinship. The second common coalition, the tribe, consists of the conglomeration of proximate and somewhat familiar and related bands. Mating partners are obtained from this larger alliance and it is instrumental in the defence of the group from outside humans who are neither well known nor trusted. Humans usually look at others who are beyond their tribal barriers as threatening, untrustworthy, and even sub-human.

In modern society, there are a multitude of possible coalitions with whom one could identify and some of them seem broadly analogous to the hunter-gatherer units. For instance, the band has been replaced by an array of possibilities, including one's social network of extended family and friends, which may be defined by one's community, school, religion, or work. The nation may have conceptually replaced the tribe, but for many individuals, their identification is stronger to a sub-group within the nation such as their ethnic group or a region of the country (like the "south" in the United States). Although our sense of loyalty can flare up for our larger coalitions, such as occurred after 9/11 when Americans embraced against the common enemy of "terrorism", our loyalty is usually stronger for the closer coalitions.

Another influential psychological process that plays a role in our environmental decisions is discounting. A number of researchers have pointed out that humans tend to value the present far more than the future (Rogers 1991; Henderson and Sutherland 1996; Wilson *et al.* 1996). This made sense as hunter-gatherers needed to live for the present and did not have the knowledge or the ability to predict the future as well as we do today. As a result, they evolved to value the present more than the future.

Finally, our moral sentiments also play a role in this process. Kohlberg (1969) argued that our ethical system operates through rational judgement, but new evidence (Haidt 2001) demonstrates that our seemingly objective ethics are actually far more intuitive than we originally imagined. It is through a combination of genetics and life experiences that we develop the basis for our moral judgements. Those judgements can be biased to support our own personal and group values (Mahoney 1977; Lord *et al.* 1979; Kerr *et al.* 1996; Smolin 2006). Overall, this process operates as a governor on our conscious thought in order to prevent us from rationalizing against our short-term individual and coalitional interests. It is interesting to note that poets and philosophers, observing these traits in humans from what might be labelled as a phenomenological perspective, also note this tendency of the human mind to ally our moral sentiments with existing perspectives. Melville eloquently proposed this process operating in his fictional character, Claggart, as he strove to justify his desire to destroy Billy Budd:

> Claggart's conscience, being but the lawyer to his will, made ogres of trifles, probably arguing that the motive imputed to Billy in spilling the soup just when he did, together with the epithets alleged, these, if nothing more, made a strong case against him; nay, justified animosity into a sort of retributive righteousness.
>
> (2006, 55)

The consequence of these psychological tendencies is that we tend to choose actions that support our short-term individual and close coalitional interests. Environmental causes, which call for sacrifices for the good of the larger group in the long term, are hard for many humans to swallow. What's worse is that our moral sentiments are designed to step in and bolster choices that benefit our interests.

The impact of our coalitional psychology on our response to current environmental problems is perhaps most evident in the American political response to global warming. The consequences of global warming are significant and have been well researched by successive reports every five years since 1990 from the Intergovernmental Panel on Climate Change (IPCC). Based on this robust body of evidence, the prudent, rational, and responsible course would be to mitigate the expected detrimental consequences by taking action as soon as possible. This represents a classic example of what archaeologist Joseph Tainter (Diamond 2005) labelled as a case where a rational actor noting an environmental problem would determine to prevent or solve the problem. Yet, so far, the US federal government has either resisted worldwide efforts to prevent global warming or it has taken half-hearted, ineffective actions that are more for show than actually making headway against this problem. Why aren't our federal representatives acting in a rational manner to prevent or at least minimize the effects of global warming as Tainter predicted they would? It is at least in part because of the complex mix of their individual, group, ethical, and discounting psychology.

Individual self-interest is working on several levels for US elected representatives who oppose climate change action. Mitigating regulations are likely to result in increases in energy costs, which extend to nearly all facets of economic production. These higher costs could potentially have a ripple effect whereby they could cause a major economic recession, which in turn would result in a variety of forms of economic hardship – including unemployment and declines in income, buying power, profits, and opportunities to develop enterprises. All of these changes could potentially decrease the economic prosperity of the representatives themselves, but also their constituents, who represent their more valued coalition. In addition, the representatives are dependent on the donations of many of the companies and agencies that would suffer economically from efforts to mitigate climate change. By supporting regulations to prevent global warming, they might be cutting off their own lifeline to re-election by losing the financial support of their sponsors.

Many of our political representatives are also embroiled in a coalitional demarcation which identifies them with a particular political party. Their allegiance is more firmly allied to the ideals of their political party than those of the world or even the nation at times. However, by serving their party interests, they rationalize that in the long run they are serving the needs of their nation. This creates another coalitional barrier. The vast majority of our delegates also perceive themselves as representing a particular region of the United States. At times they may rise to support the concerns of the nation as a whole, but usually the focus is on more parochial interests. This is in part due to the limits of their job descriptions, but it is no coincidence that it also supports the constraints of their underlying coalitional psychology.

One might argue: what about the greater hardship that climate change presents to a far higher number of people from around the world, such as the millions of farmers in the lowlands of Bangladesh who are likely to be flooded out by the rising seawaters? From a utilitarian perspective (Bentham 2007), it makes sense to ask this question, but our psychology often does not emotionally tie us to this larger group of humans (nor to the larger group of nonhuman beings that environmental causes seek to support) and therefore, we don't tend to be swayed by their worse plight as much by our own less severe economic hardship. The tighter connections that we form to the smaller more familiar coalitions, which are more likely to serve our interests, are driving this dynamic.

Unfortunately, that is not the end of psychological forces that operate to promote these narrowly defined interests. If it were, we might break through this psychological barrier a bit more easily. There is an additional and powerful ethical component that shapes our response and justifies our resistance to change. Like Claggart in *Billy Budd, Sailor*, we tend to create moral justifications for our intuitively based perspectives. Many of our conservative representatives have developed a righteous justification of their cause against a supposed conspiracy of the government or some unknown coalition of scientists who have infiltrated the IPCC and are trying to spin the truth to make it seem as though human-influenced global warming is occurring when, in fact, it is not. This fabulously tall tale has little basis for support (Pachauri and Meyer 2014), but is imagined as a situation of good versus evil where they are obviously on the right side. Essentially, they have unconsciously created a coalitional opponent in order to ethically validate their denial of reality so that they can support policies that are consistent with their political world-views. It has enabled them to justify their ignorance of the scientifically based findings that indicate that global warming is occurring due to human actions (Mooney 2012). It is this bias in our moral reasoning that enables us to righteously support our smaller coalitional interests even when empirical reality is weighing heavily against it.

It should also be pointed out that the discounting factor is working in the legislator's favour because, by and large, it seems that the most dire global warming consequences are further in the future. It is no coincidence that many conservatives have consistently denied any possible connection between the devastation of Hurricane Sandy and global warming. Otherwise they would be opening up this discounting factor to count against them – both in their own minds and those of others.

So, we have individual interests, allying with a relatively narrow set of coalitional interests that are reinforced with an ethical bias that enables our representatives to ignore the dire consequences of global warming. Oh, how wrong Joseph Tainter was! Why? Because he made the monumental mistake of assuming that humans were rational decision-makers, when in fact they frequently are not. This same cocktail of individual, coalitional, and ethical psychology influences decision-making in many other environmental scenarios and prevents us from making globally sustainable decisions.

Solutions

In essence, we need to consider how we can work with a psychology that is designed to act in the manner described above in order to create the results that we desire. In terms of globalism and environmentalism, we need to find a way to get humans to extend beyond the usual "ICE" (individual/coalitional/ethical) shield. This section explores the conditions, which might lead to this result.

In general, humans tend to transcend their more narrow interests when they need the larger coalition to offset a threat from another hostile coalition. This is evident in warfare when smaller coalitions band together in order to thwart hostile coalitions. Recent work on our alliance detection psychology indicates that a common foe which is threatening humanity, such as hostile space aliens, would raise one's coalitional circle to the humankind and maybe even to all species of the planet (Sherif *et al.* 1961; Kurzban *et al.* 2001; Pietraszewski *et al.* 2014). Environmentalists have labelled a similar phenomenon as "butt conservation", and it is well known that if one wants support, it is necessary to argue for utilitarian strategies that are based on our shared interests rather than selfless altruism based on ideas of intrinsic rights (Næss 1973).

The limited tendency of humans to expand moral concern to animals also provides insights into the psychological obstacles that inhibit action. In 1975, Peter Singer (1990) asked people to extend their ethical concerns beyond humankind to include non-human species. He was presenting his thesis from a philosophical – and more specifically utilitarian – viewpoint and was not focusing on the psychology involved. If he had realized that humans work within these common psychological limitations, he may have been more careful to dictate precisely how we were going to expand our circle of concern. Today most animal rights groups still simply proclaim that humans need to extend morals to animals. As I have attempted to explain, it is a lot easier said than done. However, it is interesting to note that about 15 to 20 per cent of humans do seem to adopt strong ethics for animals (Kellert 1983; Kellert and Berry 1981; Wuensch *et al.* 2002). It provides hope that at least some people may be more naturally predisposed to expanding their circle beyond what the other 80-plus per cent will be likely to do. Kolberg's (1969) research confirms this, and Haidt (2012) and Pinker (2002) have added evidence that, in addition to intellectual development, other personality differences can powerfully influence one's ability to rise above coalitional psychology. Other conditions that might mitigate our psychological obstacles arise when certain social and political situations create opportunities whereby our normal coalitional boundaries are stretched and/or the ethical support for doing so is primed.

Environmental historians have identified various surges of environmentalism in America (Nash 2001; Shabecoff 1993) when a relatively high quantum of environmental legislation was passed. The first occurred around the turn of the nineteenth century and was focused on forestry resources. The second arose in the 1930s and focused on soil conservation, and the third erupted in the 1960s over industrial pollution, such as pesticides (Carson 1962) and wastes (industrial, municipal, and hazardous). What is most obvious is that all of these major changes were accompanied by pre-existing social movements. The first surge was complemented by the expanding ethics of the Progressive Movement, which was calling for more equality and opportunity in America. Trust busting and decreasing the power of the robber barons so that all Americans could benefit from America's riches was the mantra of the day, and the forestry preservation actions aligned well with this movement as they worked to make the forests resources more available to all citizens for a longer period of time (Nash 1989). The second stage was complemented by Roosevelt's New Deal and larger efforts to combat the deplorable economic conditions wrought by the Great Depression. The third stage of environmentalism occurred at the end of the 1960s and beginning of the 1970s. It too was accompanied by counter-cultural social movements and large-scale events (e.g. the Vietnam War and Civil Rights initiatives) which fought ethical inertia and pushed people beyond their usual psychological limitations. These larger social movements were already calling for people to expand their usual ranges of coalitional concern to all Americans who were suffering from injustices wrought on them by more powerful segments of society. It opened the door for similar extensions to be applied for the environment.

Another reason for significant governmental action in all of these cases is that environmental threat seemed imminent. Timbering had devastated our forestry reserves such that they had been reduced by more than 90 per cent in the eastern half of the country during the nineteenth century (Nash 1989). The threat of topsoil loss became apparent with the onslaught of the Dust Bowl, where due to drought and unregulated ploughing of the western prairie, significant amounts of topsoil had blown away and dust storms raged across the US. Finally, the threat of industrial pollution was made clear in a number of ways, but most prominently by the publication of *Silent Spring*, a text in which Rachel Carson (1962) clearly and robustly demonstrated the looming dangers of the petrochemical industry. These warning signs clarified the need to take action and made it apparent that most Americans were threatened in one way or another.

Key leadership was a feature of the first two surges of the environmental movement, but not the third one. Both Presidents Teddy Roosevelt and Franklin Roosevelt were strong and charismatic leaders, able to persuade Americans to step beyond their coalitional ranges and act for the good of the larger group. This is an instance where another psychological tendency – the interest in following a charismatic leader – can overwhelm the usual narrow confines of our coalitional psychology. It is interesting to note that the third environmental movement did not include a strong charismatic president, as it was directed from the grass roots and gained its momentum on the coat-tails of the anti-war movement, which ratcheted upwards into the counter-culture movement and called for dramatic changes in many areas of American life, including our response to environmental crises. So, while strong political leadership can help to expand our range of concern, it is not a necessary element.

If we move beyond the national level, a global example of the expansion of environmental concern was sparked by fear of the growing ozone hole that arose in the 1970s and 1980s. Ultimately, this fear prompted the Montreal Protocol to be signed in 1987. In 1974, Molina and Rowland published a paper explaining the chemistry of ozone depletion due to rising halogenated compounds such as chlorofluorocarbons (CFCs) in the atmosphere. DuPont and other chemical companies strongly resisted efforts to reduce the production of CFCs because it was in their personal and corporate interest to do so. Why was a binding treaty signed relatively quickly to limit the threat of ozone depletion? And how was the threat of such depletion so different from the current threat of global warming? The conditions, which allowed for what Kofi Annan labelled as the most successful international environmental treaty in history, were not that the ozone loss was well documented, nor that it was the honourable action to take to save the planet.

In retrospect, there were a number of salient conditions that led to the passage of the Montreal Protocol. First, the threat of ozone depletion was perceived more personally and directly by individuals around the world, and this was a situation where it was difficult for any nation or privileged segment of society to insulate themselves from the potential consequences. People were afraid that they and their loved ones would become exposed to far higher rates of UV-B radiation due to depleted ozone. These fears became exaggerated by the finding of an "ozone hole" over the Antarctica in 1985 (Farman *et al.* 1985). In some ways this situation was not unlike that of an alien threat, and it worked impressively to pull us together to act as a global coalition to subdue the harmful rays from outer space. Not only did all human beings feel equally threatened, but the deleterious effects of ozone depletion seemed imminent, so there was little discounting resistance. Perhaps as important, the cost for amelioration was relatively minor for most people and would not require massive changes and effects on the economy, which would in turn, affect our livelihoods.

The primary lesson from the environmental movement is that occasionally we are capable of rising beyond psychological obstacles when a number of factors align and encourage us to extend our concerns beyond the usual limits of our individual, coalitional, and ethical tendencies. These factors include social movements that prime us for extended considerations; strong and charismatic leaders who persuade us to extend beyond our usual limits; and imminent threats, which impel us to acknowledge the need for action. Unfortunately this adjustment in our perspective is usually short-lived, as many humans can only momentarily stretch the limits of their normal ranges of concern.

It is noteworthy that each of these surges of environmental activism was followed by back steps which seemed to revert us to our older and more base perspectives, and environmental priorities were once more on the backburner and actually attacked (Dowie 1996). This is an example of how the war is never won – battles rage and are sometimes won, but like entropy working on order, so our human psychology continually challenges our need to enlarge our coalitional range.

Conclusion

The lessons from the environmental movement can be instructive for the present movement to affirm global priorities because both movements require humans to extend their interests beyond their personal and coalitional concerns to a more expansive arena, which is difficult for humans to achieve. Our psychological impediments will provide recurrent obstacles. Like engineers building on the permafrost, we must be aware of the inadequacies of underpinning conditions and the need for continual repairs and massive troubleshooting as climatic conditions continue to ebb and flow. The road to globalism, like the road to environmentalism, is a frequent uphill battle where we often will find ourselves running against psychological tendencies that propel us to serve our personal and coalitional interests with rational-like reinforcement from our ethics against imminent threats. Once we understand that adopting global perspectives will be an ongoing struggle and that we will always have to work against eroding psychological forces, then we will have won, perhaps, the hardest aspect of the battle. We will know better how to persuade, resist, cajole, or even manipulate our psychology so that we can adopt global principles.

In this chapter, I have utilized lessons from the environmental movement to help to illuminate similar psychological obstacles to globalism. The challenges involve the promotion of individual self-interest, limited coalitional interests, ethical biases, and discounting capacities. I have demonstrated how such problems have impacted the environmental movement and pointed out that many of the same dynamics will challenge efforts to expand a sense of globalism. Finally, I have pointed out that there are ways to confront and even overcome these psychological obstacles, through leadership, collaboration with social movements, and acknowledgement of threats to the larger coalitions, and they should be utilized as we try to find ways to encourage globalism.

At no point was the assumption made that there are no other issues to consider. These psychological tendencies do not operate in a vacuum, but are responses to the political, economic, and social conditions that create the context in which they operate. Other chapters in this edition have done a far more complete job of investigating these other factors. It is hoped that the reader will be able to merge these many different factors together to gain a more holistic understanding of all of the complexities and challenges of global citizenship.

References

Barkow, J., L. Cosmides, and J. Tooby. (eds) 1992. *The Adapted Mind: Evolutionary Psychology and the Generation of Culture.* New York: Oxford University Press.

Baron-Cohen, S. 1995. *Mindblindness: An Essay on Autism and Theory of Mind.* London: MIT Press.
Bentham, Jeremy. [1789] 2007. *An Introduction to the Principles of Morals and Legislation.* Mineola, NY: Dover.
Binford, L. 2001. *Constructing Frames of Reference.* Berkeley, CA: University of California Press.
Byrne, Richard and Andrew Whiten. (eds) 1988. *Machiavellian Intelligence: Social Expertise and the Evolution of Intelligence in Monkeys, Apes and Humans.* Oxford: Clarendon Press.
Carson, Rachel. 1962. *Silent Spring.* Boston, MA: Houghton Mifflin.
De Waal, Frans. 1996. *Good Natured: The Origins of Right and Wrong in Humans and Other Animals.* Cambridge, MA: Harvard University Press.
Diamond, J. 2005. *Collapse: How Societies Choose to Fail or Succeed.* New York: Penguin.
Dowie, Mark. 1996. *Losing Ground: American Environmentalism at the Turn of the Twentieth Century.* Boston, MA: MIT Press.
Farman, J. C., B. G. Gardiner, and J. D. Shanklin. 1985. "Large Losses of Total Ozone in Antarctica Reveal Seasonal ClO3/NO3 Interaction". *Nature* 315(6016): 207.
Haidt, J. 2001. "The Emotional Dog and Its Rational Tail: A Social Intuitionist Approach to Moral Judgment". *Psychological Review* 108: 814–834.
Haidt, J. 2012. *The Righteous Mind.* New York: Vintage.
Hamilton, W. D. 1964. "The Genetical Evolution of Social Behaviour I and II". *Journal of Theoretical Biology* 7: 1–16 and 17–52.
Hardin, Garret. 1968. "The Tragedy of the Commons". *Science* 162(3859): 1243–1248.
Hauser, M. 2006. *Moral Minds: How Nature Designed Our Universal Sense of Right and Wrong.* New York: Harper Collins.
Henderson, N. and W. Sutherland. 1996. "Two Truths About Discounting and Their Environmental Consequences". *Trends in Ecology and Evolution* 11: 527–528.
Humphrey, Nicholas. 1976. "The Social Function of the Intellect". In P. P. G. Bateson and R. A. Hinde (eds), *Growing Points in Ethology.* Cambridge: Cambridge University Press, pp. 303–317.
Joyce, Richard. 2006. *The Evolution of Morality.* Boston, MA: MIT Press.
Kellert, Stephen. 1983. "Affective, Evaluative and Cognitive Perceptions of Animals". In I. Altman and J. F. Wolhwill (eds), *Behavior and the Natural Environment.* New York: Plenum, pp. 241–267.
Kellert, Stephen and J. Berry. 1981. "Knowledge, Affection and Basic Attitudes toward Animals in American Society". Washington, DC: US. Govt. Print. Off., Supt. of Doc. [024-010-00-625-1].
Kelly, Robert L. 1995. *The Foraging Spectrum: Diversity in Hunter-Gatherer Lifeways.* Washington, DC: Smithsonian Institution Press.
Kelly, Walt. 1972. *Pogo – We Have Met the Enemy and He is Us.* 2nd edn. Delran, NJ: Simon & Schuster.
Kerr, N. L., R. J. Maccoun, and G. P. Kramer. 1996. "Bias in Judgment: Comparing Individuals and Groups". *Psychological Review* 103: 687–719.
Kohlberg, L. 1969. "Stage and Sequence: The Cognitive–Developmental Approach to Socialization". In D. A. Goslin (ed.), *Handbook of Socialization Theory and Research.* Chicago, IL: Rand McNally, pp. 347–480.

Kurzban, R., J. Tooby, and L. Cosmides. 2001. "Can Race Be Erased? Coalitional Computation and Social Categorization". *Proceedings of the National Academy of Sciences USA* 98: 15387–15392.

Lord, C. G., L. Ross, and M. R. Lepper. 1979. "Biased Assimilation and Attitude Polarization: The Effects of Prior Theories on Subsequently Considered Evidence". *Journal of Personality and Social Psychology* 37: 2098–2109.

Mahoney, M. 1977. "Publication Prejudice: An Experimental Study of Confirmatory Bias in the Peer Review System". *Cognitive Therapy and Research* 1: 161–175.

Marlowe, Frank. 2010. *The Hadza: Hunter-Gatherers of Tanzania*. Berkeley, CA: University of California Press.

Melville, H. [1924] 2006. *Billy Budd, Sailor*. New York: Pocket Books.

Molina, M. J. and F. S. Rowland. 1974. "Stratospheric Sink for Chlorofluoromethanes: Chlorine Atom-Catalysed Destruction of Ozone". *Nature* 249(5460): 810.

Mooney, Chris. 2012. *The Republican Brain*. Nashville, TN: Turner Publishing.

Næss, Arne. 1973. "The Shallow and the Deep, Long-Range Ecology Movement". *Inquiry* 16: 95–100.

Nash, R. 1989. *American Environmentalism: Readings in Conservation History*. 3rd edn. New York: McGraw-Hill.

Nash, R. 2001. *Wilderness and the American Mind*. 4th edn. New Haven, CT: Yale University Press.

Pachauri, R. K. and L. A. Meyer. (eds) 2014. *IPCC, 2014: Climate Change 2014: Synthesis Report. Contribution of Working Groups I, II and III to the Fifth Assessment Report of the Intergovernmental Panel on Climate Change*. Geneva: IPPC.

Pietraszewski, D., L. Cosmides, and J. Tooby. 2014. "The Content of Our Cooperation, Not the Color of Our Skin: An Alliance Detection System Regulates Categorization by Coalition and Race, But Not Sex". *PLoS ONE* 9(2): e88534. DOI: 10.1371.

Pinker, Steven. 2002. *The Blank Slate: The Modern Denial of Human Nature*. New York: Viking Press.

Rogers, Alan. 1991. "Conserving Resources for Children". *Human Nature* 2(1): 73–82.

Shabecoff, Philip. 1993. *A Fierce Green Fire*. New York: Hill & Wang.

Sherif, M., O. J. Harvey, B. J. White, W. Hood, and C. W. Sherif. 1961. *Intergroup Conflict and Cooperation: The Robbers Cave Experiment*. Norman, OK: University Book Exchange, pp. 155–184.

Singer, Peter. 1990. *Animal Liberation*. 2nd edn. New York: Random House.

Smolin, L. 2006. *The Trouble with Physics: The Rise of String Theory, the Fall of a Science, and What Comes Next*. London: Allen Lane.

Sober, E. and D. S. Wilson, 1998. *Unto Others: The Evolution and Psychology of Unselfish Behavior*. Cambridge, MA: Harvard University Press.

Trivers, Robert L. 1971. "The Evolution of Reciprocal Altruism". *Quarterly Review of Biology* 46: 35–35.

Welborn, J. E. C. 1890. "The Politics: Book I by Aristotle". In C. Warren Hollister (ed.), *Landmarks of the Western Heritage, Volume 1, The Ancient Near East to 1789*. 2nd edn. New York: Wiley, pp. 105–111.

Whiten, Andrew and Richard W. Byrne. (eds) 1997. *Machiavellian Intelligence II: Extensions and Evaluations*. Cambridge: Cambridge University Press.

Wilson, David Sloan. 2002. *Darwin's Cathedral*. Chicago, IL: University of Chicago Press.

Wilson, E. O. 2012. *The Social Conquest of the World*. New York: Liveright Publishing.
Wilson, M., M. Daly, S. Gordon, and A. Pratt, 1996. "Sex Differences in Valuations of the Environment". *Population and Environmental: A Journal of Interdisciplinary Studies* 18(2): 143–159.
Wuensch, K. L., K. W. Jenkins, and G. M. Poteat. 2002. "Misanthropy, Idealism, and Attitudes Towards Animals". *Anthrozoös* 15: 139–149.

11 Dismounting the tiger

From empire to global citizenship through pragmatism

Terrance MacMullan

He who rides a tiger is afraid to dismount.

Chinese proverb

This chapter examines the problems and opportunities associated with global citizenship and globalization from the perspective of philosophical pragmatism, the only major school of philosophy to emerge from the United States.[1] It also assesses the policies of President Obama on issues such as diplomatic engagement in the Middle East and the increasing reliance on drone strikes as they are timely examples that illustrate what a pragmatist approach to foreign policy might look like. Finally, it argues that US foreign policy directed by a commitment to a pragmatist conception of global citizenship would not only satisfy the realist's demands for security as well as the idealist's insistence to preserve guiding moral values but would also offer a way to dismount the tiger of empire.

As you know from the other chapters in this volume, advancing the ideals of global citizenship poses a challenge within the complex and evolving realities of globalization. While global citizenship is a politically and philosophically complex idea, this chapter will only focus on the facet of global citizenship that is more or less synonymous with cosmopolitanism: the idea that we should all think of ourselves, in the words of Diogenes of Sinope, as citizens of the world. Cosmopolitanism does not necessarily reject our commitments to smaller groups, institutions, and identities associated with nations, ethnic groups, or regions, nor is it necessarily anathema to patriotism. It is a political philosophy with ancient roots in many different cultures that adapts well to a globalized context. It calls on all people to realize that our actions potentially affect the lives of people around the world who might have less power or privilege, but who are no more or less worthy than ourselves.

The Ghanaian-American philosopher Kwame Anthony Appiah argues in *Cosmopolitanism: Ethics in a World of Strangers* that to be a global citizen, or a cosmopolitan, is to accept two basic ideas:

> One is the idea that we have obligations to others, obligations that stretch beyond those to whom we are related by the ties of kith and kind, or even

the more formal ties of citizenship. The other is that we take seriously the value not just of human life but of particular human lives.

(Appiah 2006, xv)

Appiah's conceptual framework for cosmopolitanism steers us away from the common misconception that global citizenship is just a feel-good invocation of universal brotherhood. Quite the contrary, living a life where one extends the boundaries of one's moral community to include *all people – possibly even all living creatures* – is in fact the ultimate moral challenge. It can be profoundly unsettling to realize that choices that might at first seem morally frictionless, for example buying the latest hand-held device, are in fact freighted with moral weight when seen through the lens of globalization. Such actions might make us complicit in working conditions that we would not want for ourselves or tolerate in our own community. We might even find the conditions unlivable, as did a young 17-year-old girl named Tian Yu who, after a month of assembling parts for smart phones under brutal conditions at Foxconn's Longhua facility, attempted to commit suicide by throwing herself from a fourth-floor window (Chakrabortty 2013). Philosophers such as Peter Singer appeal to the idea of global citizenship when they argue that it is unethical to spend money on luxuries that could be used to save thousands of lives in impoverished parts of the world where children and others die from preventable diseases (Singer 2009). To ask of every person in the world – whether they be impoverished, beset by chronic violence or ecological disaster – "what would I ask of them were our situations reversed?" is to peer through a veil of self-regard and moral isolation that, once seen through, cannot be ignored.

The question of how to transition from a declining superpower to a community of global citizens contributing to a humane and fair globalized world is particularly important for citizens of the United States. The United States has been in a state of internal moral struggle since its inception, between heeding the call to be global citizens and succumbing to the temptation to be just another self-serving empire. Its founding documents speak of self-evident and *universal* human equality and concomitant rights shared by all people. We could not find a more eloquent call to global citizenship than the famous line penned by Thomas Paine who said "my country is the world, and my religion is to do good" (Paine 1984, 228). However, just as soon as this republic expressed these grand ideals, it failed – grotesquely – to live them, opting instead to extend these rights to a small, privileged minority of white men while subjecting women to patriarchy, committing genocide against Native peoples, and enslaving African-descended peoples. This infamous hypocrisy testifies to the fact that selfishness, greed, and ignorance can snuff out cosmopolitan ideals even in the hearts of those who ardently proclaim them.

While the struggle between greater ideals of justice and more local structures of oppression has taken different forms over the years, our (by which I mean mine and that of my fellow US citizens) behaviour still falls far short of our ideals, both domestically and globally. Speaking for a moment from my position as a US citizen, I am ashamed that, rather than treating our membership within a powerful and (still just barely) prosperous nation as a *calling to do good* as Paine once said, those of us with the privilege to do so too often abuse our power to take, use, and consume more than our share.[2] Of course, citizens of other powerful and prosperous nations also fail to live up to the calling to use their power and influence for good. Rather than seeing ourselves as individuals fortunate enough to be born into a prosperous and powerful country, many of us imagine ourselves to be superior to others. As a 2003 Global Attitude survey by the Pew Research Center found, "Americans stand out for their sense of cultural superiority" noting that six in 10 Americans polled believed that "our culture is superior to others" (Pew Research Center 2003, 93). This sense of superiority has a lot to do with the fact that, since the end of the nineteenth century, our role on the world stage has been less a cosmopolitan city on a hill than the world's most recent and largest empire. The American philosopher Richard Rorty spoke to this very danger when he warned that our nation is "a republic that is always in danger, thanks to its ever increasing wealth and power, of becoming an empire" (2009, 210). Rorty did not fear that we would adopt an imperial political structure headed by an emperor: he meant that powerful republics are always in danger of losing their soul by eschewing their commitment to discourse in favour of defining relationships inside the nation and with their neighbours according to power. Being a good global citizen is largely just being a good neighbour in a global neighbourhood. Unfortunately, empires make for dreadful neighbours!

Embracing global citizenship – both individually and collectively as a nation – would be the morally right thing to do and the consistent thing to do if we are to view our founding principles as anything other than lip-service. Furthermore, if you take the long view of history, moving away from *de facto* imperialism towards global citizenship would also be the practical thing to do. One reason for that is the proverbial advice at the start of this chapter. Running an empire is like riding a tiger: it's all well and good ... until it's time to get off. Ex-empires tend not to be happy places filled with prosperous people. Americans are just *beginning* to pay the huge, possibly ruinous, financial costs of two, unfunded wars: some analysts estimate the cost to be as much as $6 trillion (Foster 2013). Such actions on the world stage have badly damaged America's global reputation (Pew Research Center 2012, 11). And no one can calculate the cost of the lives lost to war as well as the lives that could have been saved had the United States waged war on global poverty, disease, and hunger with the sort of zeal that was shown in Iraq and Afghanistan. Would-be global citizens need to figure out how to dismount the tiger of empire without getting eaten. Would-be global citizens need to figure out how to change from being an empire to being a nation guided by cosmopolitan ideals. Thankfully, for citizens of the United States, their legacy includes more than just their rise to superpower status: it also includes a vibrant philosophical tradition that might help guide everyone towards a more sustainable and ethical future.

A pragmatist perspective on global citizenship

A discussion of pragmatism fits hand in glove within the topic of global citizenship and globalization generally, as pragmatism is just a recent example of the many world philosophies centred on the moral vision of cosmopolitanism. The campaign to end war conducted by American pragmatists like William James, John Dewey, and Jane Addams (Beisner 1968), the pluralistic vision of world citizenship espoused by Alain Locke (1989), and the arguments against racism and imperialism made by W. E. B. Du Bois (1968) fulfil the cosmopolitan call to transcend insular and limiting identities rooted in nation, tribe, and creed to live in the light of the truth that we are all citizens of the same world.

Pragmatism defies easy categorization and has endured a disproportionate amount of straw-manning and misunderstanding since its inception. Before we summarize what it is, it is important to clarify what it is *not*. When we speak of pragmatism as a philosophical school (sometimes called "principled pragmatism") it is important to separate it from the conventional notion of pragmatism-as-pure-expediency. Pragmatist philosophers will often distinguish the different versions of *philosophical* pragmatism (which might include Classical or Paleo-Pragmatism as well as Neo-Pragmatism and Rortian Pragmatism) from *generic* (Eldridge 2009) or *vulgar* (Ralston 2010) pragmatism which is the idea that principles can be sacrificed for outcomes and that the ends justify the means. We are all familiar with vulgar pragmatism: we have all heard someone say that they were justified to lie or cheat in order to achieve a goal with a minimum of effort. A philosophical pragmatism focuses on human experience and outcomes but does not abandon ideals: instead, it argues that beliefs, values, means, and ideals *all* need to be tested within experience through inquiry.

Most historians trace the dawn of philosophical pragmatism to the 1870s with the works of C. S. Peirce and William James, although contemporary scholarship traces its roots much further back to the encounter between Europeans and Native Americans.[3] Peirce coined the term from the Greek word for action, *pragma*, to underline his distinctive views on the nature of belief. James described Peirce's argument this way:

> [B]eliefs are really rules for action, [and that] to develop a thought's meaning, we need only determine what conduct it is fitted to produce: that conduct is for us its sole significance. ... To attain perfect clearness in our thoughts of an object, then, we need only consider what conceivable effects of a practical kind the object may involve.
> (1975, 29)

While pragmatism evolved greatly over the next 140 years, it never moved far from the idea that *beliefs* are best understood as precursors to *actions*. They don't *copy* the world: they are *part* of the world and they that interact with other parts of the world within experience. Beliefs are not mirrors of the world but are instead *tools that we use* as we act and live in the world. The importance of this belief about beliefs is that it leads us to not judge beliefs by how well they hang together (which philosophers call a coherence account of knowledge) or by how well they supposedly match facts in the world (which they call a correspondence account), but by the effectiveness of the actions they generate (which is sometimes called a transactional or instrumentalist account). This transactional view of belief led pragmatists to argue that what was most promising about pragmatism was its *method* for judging the suitability of our beliefs about the world.

The *pragmatist method* is essentially an open method for determining which ideas work in experience. While it holds no commitment to any *particular* belief ahead of experience, it argues that certain beliefs have proved their effectiveness over time and for so many people that we ought to work from them *provisionally*, that is to say, until and unless a better belief comes along. James famously explained how this method of belief places an essential openness at the heart of pragmatism with a metaphor that he borrowed from the Italian pragmatist Giovanni Papini:

> As the young Italian pragmatist Papini has well said, [pragmatism] lies in the midst of our theories like a corridor in a hotel. Innumerable chambers open out of it. In one you may find a man writing an atheistic volume; in the next someone on his knees praying for faith and strength; in a third a chemist investigating a body's properties. In a fourth a system of idealistic metaphysics is being excogitated; in a fifth the impossibility of metaphysics is being shown. But they all own the corridor, and all must pass through it if they want a practicable way of getting into or out of their respective rooms.
>
> (1975, 32)

This metaphor gives us a particularly nice window into pragmatism's usefulness within the subject of global citizenship. First, while pragmatism is often criticized as an insular North American phenomenon, it was, at its outset a global movement. In the essay quoted above, James mentions the Italian philosopher Papini, the German philosopher Schiller, and the German chemist Ostwald not so much to show that they agree with him, but to demonstrate that this is a method that is being used to great effect by people all over the world. Larry Hickman draws an even clearer connection between the metaphor of the "James Hotel" and the issue of global citizenship when he argues that:

> What James was suggesting, therefore, was that cultural differences, as well as differences that are intellectual and political, can in many cases be negotiated under the umbrella of the pragmatic method. If his view is correct, therefore, we would expect to find in it a tool for fostering global citizenship and its corollary, the formation of global publics.
>
> (2004, 69)

One reason that the pragmatist method is particularly apt for addressing the issue of global citizenship is its *methodological pluralism*: experience is so varied and dynamic, that we should include a plurality of perspectives and approaches when solving problems. Shane Ralston argues that one of the lessons that pragmatism offers for problems of international relations is that "effective problem-solving begs for a plurality of theoretical approaches, whether the scope of the problem is local or global, moral or prudential, domestic or international" (2011b, 82).

Pragmatism's focus on problem solving brings up its *meliorism*, which Colin Koopman describes as "the thesis that we are capable of creating better worlds and selves" (2006, 107). As a middle ground between pessimism and optimism, pragmatist meliorism entails both an acceptance of *contingency*, or the idea that there are no guarantees and that sometimes all we can do is our best, as well as a rejection of one-size-fits-all cures driven by ideological rigidity. The pragmatist focus on contingency makes it *especially* well suited for any discussion of international relations as global politics involve so many variables it is important to accept that no one can ever guarantee the success of even the best-laid plans.

A pragmatist approach to global citizenship would focus on addressing the pressing problems that we share through an experimental method that maximizes broad input, incorporates a wide range of insights and theories and is directed at improving concrete situations as much as possible. Such an approach, Ralston argues:

> Would bring the rigorous methods of inquiry and experimentation to a panoply of international problems, from the unfair wages and factory conditions offered by multinational corporations, to child soldiering and human trafficking, to illicit exchanges in arms and drugs and, perhaps most importantly, to situations where military force is exercised unilaterally, whether by state or non-state actors, and for the sake of achieving narrow goals (e.g. increase geo-political power or exclusive control of scarce resources).
>
> (2011b, 83)

Pragmatism offers a flexible guide for addressing these, and other, global problems. More importantly, pragmatism helps us envision a path from our current, fragmented world towards one where the ideal of global citizenship is realized. Pragmatism calls on us to be mindful of the fact that there are no guarantees and that our beliefs might well turn out to be wrong. This mindfulness of contingency is valuable as it reminds us to be humble and cautious. It reminds us that it is easy to break something through well-intentioned zeal, but difficult or impossible to put it back together. However, it also calls on us to have faith in each other and to act collectively and, it is hoped, with an eye on changing the world for the better.

With this brief summary of pragmatism in mind we can see why Barack Obama is sometimes referred to as a pragmatist president. He was swept into the White House on a promise of meliorism: he gave voters hope that the United States and the world might change for the better. The next section will examine his policies and actions in office through the lens of the pragmatist perspective on global citizenship to see whether he is indeed leading the world towards the ideals of cosmopolitanism or just digging deeper the trenches of the American global empire.

Obama as pragmatist in chief

Barack Obama was twice voted into the US presidency by millions of American who hoped – along with others around the globe – that he represented a new kind of politician who was less partisan and more global: less concerned with projecting American supremacy abroad and more committed to leading the world towards peaceful coexistence. Many authors framed his uniqueness in terms of his commitment to pragmatism (Sunstein 2008; MacMullan 2010; Kloppenberg 2011; Ralston 2011a; Cormier 2012; Romano 2012). Carlin Romano argues in his work *America the Philosophical* that "[c]ritics mock him as 'professorial,' but they've got the wrong *p* word" (Romano 2012, 22). Romano makes a persuasive case that, at least up to the year 2012, Obama was something of a pragmatist philosopher-king:

> In his commitment to multiple points of view, his pragmatist insistence on data and flexible thinking, his outreach to opponents, his stern refusal to be lured into the gutter of ad hominem denunciations, his acknowledgement of errors, he brings to fruition forces of American philosophical maturity that remain uncredited by almost all scholars and observers of this country.
>
> (2012, 22)

Romano warrants his view of Obama as pragmatist by pointing to Obama's methodological pluralism, intellectual flexibility, and reliance on empirical evidence when making decisions. In so doing Romano echoes an earlier assessment by Cass Sunstein in his 2008 essay "The Empiricist Strikes Back: Obama's Pragmatism Explained". Sunstein argues that Obama will not be Bush's opposite: a doctrinaire liberal who will push the left's agenda with the same blind zeal that Bush showed for the right. Instead, "his empiricism, his curiosity, his insistence on nuance, and his lack of dogmatism [shows he] is indeed a sort of anti-Bush" (Sunstein 2008, 10). Drawing a direct line from William James to Obama, Sunstein explains that "Obama's form of pragmatism is heavily empirical; he wants to know what will work" (Sunstein 2008, 10).

We see a valence to Obama's pragmatism that more specifically relates to issues of global citizenship and globalization when we compare him to Alain Locke. As MacMullan points out in his 2010 "Global Citizenship through Reciprocity", Obama shares Locke's pragmatist commitment to achieving peace through broadening a global community based on mutual respect:

Neither Locke then nor Obama now are ideological purists whose future actions could be easily deduced by ideals voiced in the past: both men shared a careful and fallibilist approach that strived to unify as many people as possible upon shared respect for values, both common and different.

(2010, 214)

Here we see how Obama's pragmatism and his cosmopolitanism are two sides of the same coin. As a fallibilist (someone who accepts that any belief might prove wrong and therefore every experience needs to be approached with openness and humility) and a meliorist, Obama is also a cosmopolitan: he strives to foster cooperation whenever possible so that we might learn from each other through dialogue and also address our shared problems as best we can.

One of the most useful studies of Obama's pragmatism that relates to global citizenship is Shane Ralston's "Obama's Pragmatism in International Affairs". Ralston demonstrates that:

Obama's approach to international affairs is oddly Deweyan, acknowledging that some problems (such as imperialism) are multi-causal and systemic (not mono-causal and isolable to one or more aggressors) and that exercises of soft power will more often serve American interests than exercises of hard power.

(2011a, 88)

Further, he shows that Obama's decisions in the field of international relations are hard to anticipate because he relies on a thoroughly pragmatist approach to international relations (IR). Just as Obama does not fit nicely into a preconceived political category:

Pragmatism does not fit nicely into any one of the three traditional International Relations ... theoretic frameworks (realism, liberalism and constructivism), [and] I argue that it represents a flexible policymaking approach that floats freely between multiple theories, tailoring them to the conditions of the international situation and helping practitioners craft tools to resolve or ameliorate particular global problems.

(Ralston 2011a, 82)

Ralston draws our attention to the fact that pragmatism is so difficult to categorize because of the fact that it is based not so much on a fixed set of beliefs about the world or ideological values, but on a method for addressing problems.

Obama's international conduct seems to warrant Ralston's assessment. If Ralston is right to say that a pragmatist president would treat theories as intellectual tools instead of constraints, then Obama seems to walk a pragmatist path when it comes to international affairs. He is an occasional constructivist, as when he frames global problems as human-made and solvable, not inevitable or intractable clashes of civilizations. We see this constructivism on display with his frequent calls for cooperation within the Middle East as well as his willingness to dialogue with antagonists like North Korea, Iran, and the Taliban. He most often fits the mould of the IR liberal with his frequent appeals to ideals of autonomy and self-determination. For example, on the issue of Israel he says that his administration is "committed to a comprehensive, just, and lasting peace in the Middle East, including two states for two peoples – Israel as a Jewish state and the homeland for the Jewish people and the State of Palestine as the homeland for the Palestinian people – each enjoying self-determination, mutual recognition, and peace" (White House 2013). At the same time, Obama has been willing to set aside a liberal's emphasis on respecting political autonomy in order to adhere to the realist's emphasis on the importance of using power to protect state interests when it is called for in the situation. His willingness to be an IR realist was no more evident than when he gave the order to send US Special Forces into Pakistan to kill Osama bin Laden, even though it violated Pakistan's sovereignty. Obama's penchant for placing meliorism above ideological purity, his preference for dialogue, his willingness to use force when necessary, and his hope that Americans can peacefully resolve their problems through cooperation seem to mark him as a pragmatist president who is at the same time a self-conscious global citizen. This gave many people hope that he might be the rare sort of leader who would help Americans dismount the tiger of imperialism without getting eaten.

However, despite these factors that warrant the claim that Obama is a pragmatist in chief, others problematize this assessment. Harvey Cormier summarizes some of the reasons we might question either Obama's pragmatism or the efficacy of pragmatism itself.

> Obama the pragmatist has failed to achieve a big-enough economic stimulus package, the public option, strong re-regulation of the banks, the closing of the prison at Guantánamo Bay, a quick end to two wars, and so on. Should we take this as evidence that pragmatism saps faith and damps down activity? Does it make us unable to make and stick to hard choices? Is that the bug in Obama's programming?
>
> (2012)

Obama's difficulty in solving many of these pressing problems illustrates one of the primary risks in being a pragmatist or anyone else committed to the foundational ideas of global citizenship. If you commit to solving problems through cooperation and associated living, then you are committing to trusting others: you need to have *faith* in other people's willingness to cooperate with you. Having faith in others can look unrealistically optimistic. In July of 2015 President Obama was criticized harshly, not just by opposition Republicans, but by members of his own party over his support for a nuclear accord with Iran. As

Peter Baker framed this criticism, it came down to a conflict between "Mr. Obama's faith in diplomacy as the most rational way to resolve differences and his critics' deep skepticism over the wisdom of negotiating with what they see as an adversary that cannot be trusted" (2015). While Obama has accomplished a great deal of his stated goals, many of the times that he failed to fulfil his agenda he lacked necessary domestic or international partners willing to cooperate with him. To use the language of the American pragmatist philosopher John Dewey, pragmatism's ineffectiveness can be traced to the fact that humanity is losing faith in itself and many intransigent problems persist because we've lost, or never really had, a true democratic global community.

Dewey did not see democracy as primarily as system of government: it is much more a way of life based on a kind of faith in associated living that, when shared by enough people, is the best – though still imperfect – way for making our way through life:

> Regarded as an idea, democracy is not an alternative to other principles of associated life. It is the idea of community life itself. It is an ideal in the only intelligible sense of an ideal: namely, the tendency and movement of something which exists carried to its final limit, viewed as completed, perfected ... The clear consciousness of a communal life, in all its implications, constitutes the idea of democracy.
>
> (LW 2, 328)[4]

Dewey later called democracy "a way of life ... controlled by personal faith in personal day-by-day working together with others" (LW 14, 228). Unfortunately, if enough people lack this faith or simply refuse to work with others, there is little that a pragmatist (or anyone else for that matter) can do beyond using education and dialogue to encourage others to see the value of associated living.

The persistence of many of the most pressing problems around the world, especially in the Arab world and the Middle East, can also be traced to a lack of democratic faith. The collapse of autocratic regimes across the Arab world in the few years (like those in Iraq, Libya, Egypt, and Afghanistan) might appear to be an unalloyed victory of cosmopolitan ideals and presage hope of a Deweyan democratic future. If pragmatism and global citizenship call for dialogue and a reliance on experience to settle disputes, then it would seem that it is always the right thing to try to uproot dictatorships. Indeed, Larry Hickman explains that the only perspective that can't book a room in the James Hotel is one that denies or silences other perspectives, saying:

> The pragmatic hotel cannot accommodate the democrat *and* the dictator. The method of the former is experimental, whereas the method of the later is not: in dictatorial situations many voices, many sources of relevant information, are occluded or extinguished.
>
> (2004, 79)

However, the fall of dictatorial regimes has not ushered in a spirit of global cosmopolitanism in the region.

For just one example of many, when Muhammad Morsi became the first legitimately elected president in Egypt's history in June of 2012, it seemed to bode well for the possibility that the Arab world might finally enjoy a relatively peaceful transition from dictatorship. Many hoped that the Arab Spring of 2012 might replicate the successes of the Velvet Revolution of 1989 in what was then Czechoslovakia. Unfortunately, this hope did not bear fruit as Morsi seemed more intent on governing Egypt for his supporters in the Muslim Brotherhood rather than for all Egyptians. When his administration was rocked by the same sorts of massive protests that drove Mubarak from power, the military leaders of Egypt detained him and removed him from power. In May of 2015 Morsi was sentenced to death for the crime of fleeing prison in 2011 in a trial that lacked minimal standards of fairness and due process (Malsin 2015).

This highlights the fact that while dictatorships *are* horrible and completely contrary to the ideals of global citizenship, their collapse does not lead inevitably to a functioning democracy. Democracy – true democracy in the pragmatist sense – is a game that people have to want to play well and fairly. It is less about ballots and inky fingers than it is about a community of people who share a certain level of trust in each other. Sadly, trust is an unaffordable luxury among people who've had to survive under a dictatorship. Morsi's supporters simply did not have a high regard for secular Egyptians and their lack of regard was repaid a year later with the mass protests that paralyzed the nation and ousted their standard-bearer.

Dewey would not have been surprised that a vibrant democracy did not fill the void after a tyrant was removed by external force. He explained decades ago that it is folly to think that one can create a democratic public within a country that had been crushed by tyranny for generations just by giving them ballot boxes. Enemies of democracy – military coups, theocracies, and plutocratic oligarchies – can't be shocked or awed or spied or locked away. Instead:

> Enemies of democracy can be successfully met only by the creation of personal attitudes in individual human beings; that we must get over our tendency to think that its defense can be found in any external means, whether military or civil, if they are separated from individual attitudes so deep-seated as to constitute personal character.
>
> (LW 14, 226)

We cannot spread the ideal of global citizenship unless we actually address the issue of people's attitudes and habits. We have to work through education and association: the slow, mutual process of adjusting our ideas, attitudes, and habits to a broader range of operating conditions. Fostering a democratic public is one of the best ways to help people currently or recently living under autocracies or when trying to solve intractable international problems. Ralston explains that while this might seem hopelessly naive to the IR realist, it is the only way forward towards a world where global citizenship might be a living, shared ideal:

> More importantly, genuine – and one might add, pragmatic – engagement requires less ideological confrontation, more empathy and hope, more cooperative problem solving and a greater commitment to overcoming deep differences – instrumentalities that often appear naïve to the IR realist, yet perfectly suited to an IR pragmatist.
>
> (2011a, 86)

This helps us to see that Obama's famous early international speeches (in Berlin in 2008 and Cairo, Prague, and Oslo in 2009) were hardly the "apology tour" derided by his critics. They were instead empathic attempts to change people's attitudes and foster cooperation.

Of course, Obama's speeches aren't the only things that are affecting global opinion of the United States. While he cannot be reasonably blamed for that fact that many populations and leaders do not yet share his pragmatist faith in cooperation and dialogue, he is accountable for the fact that some of his policies corrode the already weakened state of international cooperation that is one of the few bulwarks from even more armed conflict. As such, these policies not only jeopardize our security in the long run, but are also at odds with the principled pragmatism he supposedly champions.

A 2012 report by the Pew Research Center Global Attitudes Project found that "[g]lobal approval of President Barack Obama's policies has declined significantly since he first took office" (Pew Research Center 2012, 5). The report goes on to attribute this decline in large part to the fact that "in nearly all countries, there is considerable opposition to a major component of the Obama administration's anti-terrorism policy: drone strikes" (Pew Research Center 2012, 6).

The Obama administration has greatly increased its reliance on drone strikes because they are supposedly effective: drone strikes keep the American public and its security interests safe by killing enemies without risking our troops. They are, in many ways, the quintessential realist's tool of international relations as well as a perfect example of vulgar pragmatism: it is odious to think of technicians sitting in ergonomic chairs in Denver or Florida controlling silent, all-seeing death-bots half a world away that have the power to annihilate any target they see, but they get the job done.

A pragmatist would argue against the use of drones in all but the rarest circumstances because, while drones offer a probability of unparalleled tactical advantages, these short-term returns come at the cost of loss of security and respect in the long term. First, just like every other supposedly "surgical strike" capacity in military history, evidence shows that drone strikes are in fact a horrendously blunt scalpel. A 2012 report by CNN found that only 2 per cent of the total victims of these strikes are the actual high-value and intended targets (Bergen and Braun 2012). However, as low as this percentage might be, some analysts argue that drones are more precise than their closest alternative, which is strategic bombing (Kaag and Kreps 2014, 203). Yet, even when these strikes were effective in killing militants who intend to harm Americans, in the long run they generate such extreme (and reasonable) hatred towards the US that they sow far more future enemies than they reap (International Human Rights and Conflict Resolution Clinic 2012, 132).

Second, drones are a tool whose use undermines the only legitimate way that deadly force can be used within a democracy. For a nation to be a democracy in anything more than name, it must work through dialogue, debate, and consensus. Its public must consent to the use of force, and in order to consent, they must fully understand what is at stake. As Peter Singer explains in "Do Drones Undermine Democracy?", drones pose a novel and serious threat to the ability to deliberate on war. He writes that "[f]or the first 200 years of American democracy, engaging in combat and bearing risk – both personal and political – went hand in hand. In the age of drones, that is no longer the case" (2012). Now that drones enable us to kill around the world without facing any human cost at home, governments could wage war with little to no discussion or political consequence. Indeed, President Obama argued in 2013 that since drones do not involve boots on the ground in countries like Yemen and Pakistan, he does not need to consult Congress before launching drone attacks (Lichtblau 2013).

Finally, the ideals of global citizenship and cosmopolitanism would call on the American government to either stop, or at least drastically reduce the use of, the military drone programme because we are subjecting other people to conditions Americans would not tolerate for themselves. When the US public was polled about the idea of allowing their own government to use drones for internal policing, the public vociferously protested against the idea (Koebler 2013). Armed drones are fundamentally terrifying and few people would consent to them flying over their house while they slept. If Americans won't countenance drones watching over them, they can't fairly condone their military use among people they are supposedly trying to save. Remember that Appiah argues that a cosmopolitan person does not respect the value of human life *abstractly, but individually and concretely.* The innocent victims of these strikes – including children, wedding guests, pilgrims, and even rescue workers – are not abstract humans or collateral damage, but individual people whose lives have been snuffed out in the name of security. A pragmatist always remains open to the lessons of new experiences, but at this point evidence seems to show that a government who authorizes drone strikes among civilians doesn't fit in the James Hotel any better than the tyrant.

Conclusion: global citizenship is hard

The question of how the US could be a better global citizen in the pragmatist sense boils down to a very simple question: is the United States an empire or a democracy? It is difficult to maintain, let alone create, a democratic public. They are fostered only through honest and thoughtful dialogue among people who *want* such a way of life. Imperialism, on the other hand, is not hard, as John Dewey points out in the title of his 1927 essay "Imperialism Is Easy" (LW 3, 158). Imperialism is *so* easy that powerful nations often become empires without even knowing it! While in this essay he discusses the way that the US appropriated industries and land in Mexico, it just as well fits American incursions around the globe in the twenty-first century:

> Imperialism is a result, not a purpose or plan. It can be prevented only by regulating the conditions out of which it proceeds. And one of the things which most stands in the way of taking regulatory measures is precisely the consciousness on the part of the public that it is innocent of imperialistic desires. It feels aggrieved when it is accused of any such purpose, then resentful, and is confusedly hurried into dangerous antagonisms, before it perceives what is happening. The charge of imperialistic desires sounds strange even to the group of men who have created the situation in which they appeal to their home country for intervention. All they want, as they indignantly assert, is protection of life and property. If their own government cannot afford that protection, what is it good for anyway?
>
> (LW 3, 159)

Dewey points out here, as he does frequently in his moral philosophy, that problems like imperialism and racism are not primarily matters of bad desires or intentions, but bad habits. The fact that the American public – then as now – harbours no imperialist *designs* is beside the point if it continues to *act* unintelligently abroad in search of security. In 1927 American businessmen said that the only way to protect our interests and the lives of American workers in Mexico was to use legal and physical force to expand our *imperium* into Mexico. In 2003 we invaded Iraq and Afghanistan for the expressed purposes of preventing future 9/11 terrorists attacks and to spread democracy. In 2015 Americans use drones attacks across the Arab world for the expressed purpose of preventing future terrorist attacks. Dewey would conclude that it is not enough for Americans to say, even honestly, that they are acting in good faith and with as much care as possible to prevent the loss of innocent lives. It is not enough because while they might not have imperial desires, they are nonetheless acting through imperial habits. Though America might not want to be, it is still riding the tiger.

The only remedy is difficult, imperfect, and without promises. First, Americans must become aware of these habits that have caused them to spend more money on defence than any other nation in history and to be the only one in the history of the world to garrison armed troops on every inhabited continent. Americans must come to terms with their propensity for sacrificing the ideals that are the best they have to offer the world for material gains and temporary security. Most importantly, they must reconstruct these imperial habits into new democratic ones that allow these ideals to live through their actions and not just their words. Only then can they participate with others of good will around the world to foster a global faith in cooperation, dialogue, and a pluralistic democratic spirit.

Notes

1 I would like to thank Kevin Decker, Daniel Fryer, and Jereny Mendoza for their assistance in drafting this chapter and advice on relevant literature on the subject.
2 While Americans continue to consume far more than their proportional global share of water, fuel, and food it is also the case that the United States leads the world in charitable giving (Charities Aid Foundation 2011, p. 11).
3 For excellent sources on a traditional history of pragmatism in America, see Menand (2001) and Misak (2013). For a more pluralistic account, see West (1989), Pratt (2002), and McKenna and Pratt (2015).
4 Citations for John Dewey will follow the conventional method where LW stands for volumes of his Later Works, MW for Middle Works, and EW for Early Works.

References

Allen, Charles. 2012. *Ashoka: The Search for India's Lost Emperor*. New York: Overlook Press.
Appiah, Kwame Anthony. 2006. *Cosmopolitanism: Ethics in a World of Strangers*. New York: Norton.
Baker, Peter. 2015. "Obama's Iran Deal Pits His Faith in Diplomacy against Skepticism". *New York Times*. 15 July. Available at: www.nytimes.com/2015/07/16/world/middleeast/obama-diplomacy-iran-nuclear-deal.html (accessed 3 August 2015).
Beisner, Robert L. 1968. *Twelve against Empire: The Anti-Imperialists, 1898–1900*. New York: McGraw-Hill.
Bergen, Peter and Megan Braun. 2012. "Drone is Obama's Weapon of Choice". *CNN*. 6 September. Available at: www.cnn.com/2012/09/05/opinion/bergen-obama-drone (accessed 1 August 2013).
Chakrabortty, Aditya. 2013. "The Woman Who Nearly Died Making Your iPad". *The Guardian*. 5 August. Available at: www.theguardian.com/commentisfree/2013/aug/05/woman-nearly-died-making-ipad (accessed 10 June 2015).
Charities Aid Foundation. 2011. *World Giving Index 2011*. Available at: www.cafonline.org/pdf/World_Giving_Index_2011_191211.pdf (accessed 22 September 2015).
CNN Wire Staff. 2012. "Drone Strikes Kill, Maim and Traumatize Too Many Civilians, U.S. Study". *CNN.com*. 25 September. Available at: www.cnn.com/2012/09/25/world/asia/pakistan-us-drone-strikes (accessed 1 August 2013).
Cormier, Harvey. 2012. "Reconsidering Obama the Pragmatist". *New York Times*. 14 October. Available at: http://opinionator.blogs.nytimes.com/2012/10/14/reconsidering-obama-the-pragmatist (accessed 22 September 2015).
Dewey, John, Folio Corporation, and InteLexCorporation. 1997. *The Collected Works of John Dewey, 1882–1953 the Electronic Edition*. Windows Version. Charlottesville, VA: InteLex.
Du Bois, W. E. B. 1968. *Dusk of Dawn: An Essay Toward an Autobiography of a Race Concept*. New York: Schocken.

Eldridge, Michael. 2009. "Adjectival and Generic Pragmatism: Problems and Possibilities". *Human Affairs* 19: 10–18.
Foster, Peter. 2013. "Cost to US of Iraq and Afghan Wars Could Hit $6 Trillion". *The Telegraph*. 29 March. Available at: www.telegraph.co.uk/news/worldnews/ northamerica/usa/9961877/Cost-to-US-of-Iraq-and-Afghan-wars-could-hit-6-trillion .html (accessed 10 June 2015).
Guardian Staff. 2006. "Doctors Demand End to Guantanamo Force-Feeding". *The Guardian*. 10 March. Available at: www.theguardian.com/world/2006/mar/10/guanta namo.usa (accessed 4 June 2015).
Hickman, Larry A. 2004. "Pragmatism, Postmodernism, and Global Citizenship". *Metaphilosophy* 35(1/2) 65–81.
International Human Rights and Conflict Resolution Clinic at Stanford Law Schooland Global Justice Clinic at NYU School of Law. 2012. *Living under Drones: Death, Injury and Trauma to Civilians from US Drone Practices in Pakistan*. Stanford Law School. Available at: https://law.stanford.edu/publications/ living-under-drones-death-injury-and-trauma-to-civilians-from-us-drone-practices-in -pakistan (accessed 1 August 2013).
James, William. [1907] 1975. *Pragmatism*. Cambridge, MA: Harvard University Press.
James, William. [1891] 1979. "The Moral Philosopher and the Moral Life". In *James (1975–88). Vol. vi: The Will to Believe and Other Essays in Popular Philosophy*, pp. 141–162.
Kaag, J. and Sarah Kreps. 2012. "Pragmatism's Contributions to International Relations". *Cambridge Review of International Affairs* 25(2): 191–208.
Kaag, J. and Sarah Kreps. 2014. *Drone Warfare*. London: Polity Press.
Kloppenberg, James T. 2011. *Reading Obama: Dreams, Hope, and the American Political Tradition*. Princeton, NJ: Princeton University Press.
Koebler, Jason. 2013. "Activists Organize Nationwide Series of Drone Surveillance Protests". *US NEWS*. 29 March. Available at: www.usnews.com/news/articles/2013/ 03/29/activists-organize-nationwide-series-of-drone-surveillance-protests (accessed 1 August 2013).
Koopman, Colin. 2006. "Pragmatism as a Philosophy of Hope: Emerson, James, Dewey and Rorty". *Journal of Speculative Philosophy* 20(2): 106–116.
Levy, Daniel, Max Pensky, and John Torpey. 2005. *Old Europe, New Europe, Core Europe: Transatlantic Relations after the Iraq War*. London: Verso.
Lichtblau, Eric. 2013. "In Secret, Court Vastly Broadens Powers of the NSA". *New York Times*, 6 July. Available at: www.nytimes.com/2013/07/07/us/in-secret-court-va stly-broadens-powers-of-nsa.html (accessed 11 June 2015).
Locke, Alain. 1989. *The Philosophy of Alain Locke: Harlem Renaissance and Beyond*. Edited by Leonard Harris. Philadelphia, PA: Temple University Press.
Locke, Alain. 2010. "Moral Imperatives for World Order". In J. A. Carter and L. Harris (eds), *Philosophic Values and World Citizenship: Locke to Obama and Beyond*. Lanham, MA: Lexington Books, pp. 1–2.
Malsin, Jared. 2015. "Egyptian Court Sentences Ousted President Morsi to Death". *New York Times*. 16 May. Available at: www.nytimes.com/2015/05/17/world/middleea st/egyptian-court-sentences-ousted-president-morsi-to-death.html (accessed 28 May 2015).
McCumber, John. 2001. *Time in the Ditch: American Philosophy and the McCarthy Era*. Evanston, IL: Northwestern University Press.

MacMullan, Terrance. 2010. "Global Citizenship Through Reciprocity: Alain Locke and Barack Obama's Pragmatist Politics". In J. A. Carter and L. Harris (eds), *Philosophic Values and World Citizenship: Locke to Obama and Beyond*. Lanham, MA: Lexington Books, pp. 203–216.
McKenna, Eric and Scott Pratt. 2015. *American Philosophy: From Wounded Knee to the Present*. New York: Bloomsbury.
Menand, Louis. 2001. *The Metaphysical Club: A Story of Ideas in America*. New York: Farrar, Straus and Giroux.
Misak, Cheryl. 2013. *The American Pragmatists*. Oxford: Oxford University Press.
Paine, Thomas. 1984. *Rights of Man*. Middlesex: Penguin.
Pew Research Center for People and the Press. 2003. *Views of a Changing World: How Global Publics View War in Iraq, Democracy, Islam and Governance, Globalization*. Pew Research Center. Available at: http://people-press.org/reports (accessed 22 September 2015).
Pew Research Center Global Attitudes Project. 2012. *Global Opinion of Obama Slips, International Policies Faulted*. Pew Research Center. Available at: www.pewglobal.org/2012/06/13/global-opinion-of-obama-slips-international-policies-faulted (accessed 22 September 2015).
Pratt, Scott. 2002. *Native Pragmatism*. Bloomington, IN: Indiana University Press.
Ralston, Shane. 2010. "Pragmatism and Compromise". In Richard Couto (ed.), *Civic and Political Leadership: A Research Handbook*. Newbury Park, CA: Sage, pp. 734–741.
Ralston, Shane. 2011a. "Obama's Pragmatism in International Affairs". *Contemporary Pragmatism* 8(2): 81–98.
Ralston, Shane. 2011b "Pragmatism in International Relations Theory and Research". *Eidos* 14: 72–105.
Romano, Carlin. 2012. *America the Philosophical*. New York: Alfred Knopf.
Rorty, Richard. 2009. "The Unpredictable American Empire". In Chad Kautzer and Eduardo Mendieta (eds), *Pragmatism, Nation and Race: Community in the Age of Empire*. Bloomington, IN: Indiana University Press.
Rosenthal, Andrew. 2013. "Taking Note: Odious Provision in the Defense Bill". *New York Times*. 3 January. Available at: http://takingnote.blogs.nytimes.com/2013/01/03/odious-provisions-in-the-defense-bill (accessed 31 July 2013).
Russell, Bertrand. 1910. *Philosophical Essays*. London: Routledge.
Singer, Peter. 2009. *The Life You Can Save*. New York: Random House.
Singer, Peter. 2012. "Do Drones Undermine Democracy?". *New York Times*. 21 January. Available at: www.nytimes.com/2012/01/22/opinion/sunday/do-drones-undermine-democracy.html?src=xps (accessed 4 August 2013).
Sunstein, Cass. 2008. "The Empiricist Strikes Back: Obama's Pragmatism Explained". *New Republic*, 10 September, pp. 9–10.
West, Cornel. 1989. *The American Evasion of Philosophy: A Genealogy of Pragmatism*. Madison, WI: University of Wisconsin Press.
White House. 2013. "Foreign Policy: Promoting Peace and Security in Israel and the Middle East". Available at: www.whitehouse.gov/issues/foreign-policy (accessed 30 July 2013).
Wike, Richard. 2012. "Wait, You Still Don't Like Us?". *ForeignPolicy.com*. 19 September. Available at: http://foreignpolicy.com/2012/09/19/wait-you-still-dont-like-us/ (accessed 28 June 2013).

Part III
Identity, belonging, and global citizenship on location

Introduction to Part III
Identity, belonging, and global citizenship on location

Tammy Birk

In this final part, we will address the complex relationship between personal identity, social and geographical location, and the larger goal of global citizenship.

Part III opens with two chapters that rely on quantitative data – more specifically, results from the World Values Survey – in order to examine who is inclined to affirm global citizenship attitudes. Peter Furia's "Where Are the Global Citizens?" tries to discern whether members of certain economic, social, and cultural groups are systematically likely to identify themselves as global citizens. Expanding on Furia's earlier scholarship on the World Values Survey, this chapter argues against a widely held view that global citizenship is primarily appealing to privileged persons in the Global North. In "Age and Global Citizenship Attitudes", Bramlett also uses the data from the World Values Survey to explore whether a youthful society promotes nationalism or globalism. Finding that young adults are more likely to identify as global citizens by most measures, this chapter considers what changing age demographics worldwide might portend for global citizenship attitudes in the future.

The next four chapters approach global citizenship and cosmopolitan identifications from a variety of culturally specific locations, each with its own history and complex contemporary context. Johan Lagerkvist begins by examining contemporary China's dynamic relationship to the global economy, international society, and world media in "China and the World: Convergence on Global Governance, Divergence on Global Citizenship?" Noting that there is a growing convergence on politic–economic issues between China and the West, Lagerkvist argues that there is a concomitant divergence on the question of global citizenship and issues of human rights.

Vaughn Shannon's "Global Citizenship in the Middle East: Presence and Prospects" goes on to analyse the presence and potential prospects of global citizenship identity in the Middle East. This chapter contends that the relative absence of interest in cosmopolitanism is the result of the multiplicity of local, historically prior identities that compete for loyalty in a region that already sustains a measure of distrust for Western ideologies. Prospects for cosmopolitanism in the Middle East are tied to psychological measures of trust-building, and Shannon argues that they must include a more complex model of what global citizenship means for those seeking to maintain both local and global identities.

Similarly, Shaun Narine's "An Assessment of Southeast Asian Regional Identity" discusses the many ways that traditional ethnic and religious identities and economic nationalism continue to divide the Association of Southeast Asian Nations, pose insurmountable barriers to the creation of a strong regional identity, and complicate a Southeast Asian response to cosmopolitan ideals and practice.

Finally, Ali A. Abdi's "The Rhetoric of Globalization and Global Citizenship: Reconstructing Active Citizenships in Post-Cold War sub-Saharan Africa" examines the problematic nature of the rhetoric of global citizenship, especially as it has been theoretically constructed in the West and exported to sub-Saharan Africa with little or no formal input from the African public. Unidirectional and often neo-colonial, global citizenship expectations have ignored national citizenship concepts in Africa as well as the necessity of indigenous content. In this chapter, Abdi considers what tangible results and practical considerations might be required in order for global citizenship to work in and for the African situation.

12 Where are the global citizens?

Peter A. Furia

Political philosophers have long debated whether global citizenship – a term I here use interchangeably with cosmopolitanism – is a practicable social ideal. Perhaps because its best-known early advocates were Diogenes and Kant, the doctrine has long been associated with an arid, artificial, and solipsistic perfectionism. Beginning with Kant's own former student, J. G. Herder (2004), and continuing through the contemporary commentary of authors such as Benjamin Barber (1994), metaphors about solitary cosmopolitan intellectuals stranded on mountaintops have become ubiquitous. But is cosmopolitanism really an ideal that only a hopelessly cerebral philosopher would embrace?

It is of course difficult to know, but contemporary researchers do have options unavailable in the time of Herder and Kant. Today, those of us genuinely interested in the attitudes of the non-philosopher global *Volk* can study these attitudes by examining responses to the World Values Survey (WVS). The recent genesis and expansion of this survey is itself indicative of globalization. First carried out in ten countries between 1981 and 1984, it now canvasses respondents from "almost one hundred countries which include almost ninety percent of the world's population" (World Values Survey 1981–2014).[1] Based on evidence from the most recent wave of the WVS, carried out between 2010 and 2014, I here argue that cosmopolitanism is a more popular or *völkisch* sentiment than its critics allege, that its prevalence is increasing, and that, if ever it seemed to appeal disproportionately to stoic misanthropes, it is now similar to localism and patriotism in that it appeals disproportionately to happy, civic-minded, sociable "joiners".

How prevalent is global citizenship?

Consider, first of all, the most recent WVS question that asks explicitly about global citizenship. When asked whether they agree or disagree with the statement, "I see myself as a world citizen", an impressive 71 per cent of respondents worldwide say that they agree. Thus one very provisional answer to the question, "where are the global citizens?" is "pretty much everywhere". To be sure, a democratic theorist might immediately ask whether the billions of people represented by these respondents have done anything at all in the way of global citizen action, and, if they have, whether it's been exclusively virtual participation in much-criticized global campaigns like "KONY 2012" and "#bringbackourgirls". But note that we are already beginning to describe a world almost diametrically opposed to the one imagined by Herder and Barber, i.e., one in which at least a thin cosmopolitanism is the popular global norm and in which it is perfectionist non-cosmopolitan theorists who are questioning the wisdom of the multitude. Let us now look much more closely at the empirical status of cosmopolitanism worldwide.[2]

Beginning with the fifth wave of the WVS – carried out between 2005 and 2009 – and continuing through the most recent sixth wave, respondents have, as noted above, been asked quite explicitly about global citizenship (World Values Survey 1981–2014).[3] The full text of the relevant question, as well as that of the related questions with which it is grouped, is as follows:

> People have different views about themselves and how they relate to the world. Using this card, would you tell me how strongly you agree or disagree with each of the following statements about how you see yourself?
> V212: I see myself as a world citizen
> V213: I see myself as part of my local community
> V214 I see myself as part of the [country] nation
> V215 I see myself as a citizen [or part] of a specific regional supranational, often continental community, e.g., the European Union

We might first begin to contextualize the finding that 71 per cent of respondents to the most recent WVS see themselves as "world citizens". By comparison, 93 per cent of respondents see themselves as part of their national community, 83 per cent see themselves as part of their local community, and 63 per cent see themselves as citizens of a specific regional supra-national (often continental) community such as the European Union (EU). In other words, global citizenship attitudes lag behind patriotic and localistic attitudes, but they are more prevalent than "regionalist" attitudes.[4] No less interesting than the ordinal ranking of these four levels of citizenship, however, is the fact that all four are embraced by a majority of respondents. At least implicitly then, it appears that many respondents would agree with the view that academic claims about tensions between these various citizenship commitments have been overdrawn.[5]

As we turn to the WVS evidence on "political cosmopolitanism", however, we find the global public in an apparently sourer mood. Consider the following question on confidence in the United Nations (once again in context):

> I am going to name a number of organizations. For each one, could you tell me how much confidence you have in them: is it a great deal of confidence, quite a lot of confidence, not very much confidence, or none at all?
> V115 The government (in your nation's capital) ...

V125 Regional organizations (e.g., the EU) ...
V126 The United Nations

Specifically, only 42 per cent of respondents express at least "quite a lot" of confidence in the United Nations. By comparison, only 46 per cent of respondents express confidence in their national governments and only 39 per cent of respondents express confidence in regional organizations. (The WVS neglects to ask about confidence in local governments.) So if the global public is fairly consistent in its positive feelings about belonging to a variety of human communities – i.e., in that it doesn't much discriminate between communities on the basis of size – it is even more consistent in its rather negative feelings about the various institutions by which these human communities are governed.[6]

Although the WVS contains various other more substantive questions with relevance to global citizenship, the world citizenship question and the confidence in the United Nations question stand out as two in regard to which references to a genuinely global opinion are less problematic than, say, questions about international economic aid.[7] I will discuss societal and individual differences with regard to cosmopolitanism momentarily, but before so doing, I want to maintain focus on these two core questions in order to assess overall global trends in cosmopolitanism and other allegiances.

Is global citizenship on the rise?

Analysing trends in global citizenship is trickier than taking a snapshot of cosmopolitan attitudes in the present day. For one thing, the WVS questionnaire changes from wave to wave. The "Confidence in the UN" question was only added to the WVS with the third wave survey, and, for the first four waves of the survey – running from 1981 to 2004 – respondents were asked not about global citizenship in its own right, but rather "to which of these geographical groups [locality, province, country, continent, world] would you say you belong *first of all* ... ?" Another complication arises because the countries participating in the WVS vary considerably from wave to wave.[8]

But this does not render an analysis of trends in regard to global citizenship impossible. When it comes to the generic global citizenship question measuring what we might also call general cosmopolitan "sensibilities", we can first examine trends within the eight countries that participated in each of the first four waves of the WVS (Argentina, Finland, Japan, Mexico, South Africa, South Korea, Sweden, and the United States). Over the approximately 20-year period covered by these first four survey waves, the percentage of respondents expressing a *primary* allegiance to the world as a whole increased from about 5 per cent in the first wave to about 8 per cent in the fourth wave. Though modest in absolute terms, this increase is more impressive when one considers that localism, patriotism, and regionalism were all flat to negative over the same 20-year period.[9]

Although just five years have passed between the two more recent waves of the WVS (in which the questionnaire has asked respondents to "rate" rather than "rank" their various allegiances) looking at the trend between these two waves nonetheless seems helpful in that it involves a much more populous and diverse sample of countries than participated in the earlier waves.[10] And trends in regard to cosmopolitanism continue to be positive. Among the 30 countries participating in both of the two most recent waves, agreement with the statement "I see myself as a world citizen" has increased from 71.2 per cent in the fifth wave to 73.6 per cent in the sixth wave. By comparison, both localism and patriotism have continued their fractional declines through the most recent waves (from 88.6 to 87.8 per cent and 94.0 to 93.1 per cent, respectively).[11]

When it comes to the WVS question on confidence in the United Nations, however – a question we might think of as measuring "political" cosmopolitanism – the trend is modestly negative. Among the 30 countries participating in both the first and last surveys that included a question about the UN, the percentage expressing at least "quite a lot" of confidence in the UN dropped from 49.1 per cent (for 1994–1998) to 45.4 per cent (for 2010–2014). Within this same subsample of countries, confidence in national governments starts from a lower base (39.6 per cent for 1994–1998) but it also drops less over the same period (to 38.5 per cent for 2010–2014).[12] So the relatively strong growth in general cosmopolitan sensibilities over the past 35 years is not matched by trends in regard to political cosmopolitanism.

As is always the case, these findings are open to interpretation. Although it is trending down faster than is confidence in national governments, confidence in the UN remains the higher of the two. Confidence in the UN is lowest of all in the fifth wave WVS survey, carried out between 2005 and 2009, perhaps suggesting that the UN's inability to prevent the Iraq War may have hurt its worldwide reputation. And it would obviously be inappropriate to impugn the cosmopolitanism of advocates of alternatives to the UN based on attitudes toward an institution that these advocates wish to reform, replace or transcend.[13] Even so, one presumes that most WVS respondents have a fairly vague sense of the UN as "the closest thing to a world government that the world has", and, as such, the fact that many have less confidence in it than they did 15 to 20 years ago may give cosmopolitans pause. Other cross-national surveys suggest that publics worldwide want the UN take a larger role in resolving international problems, but as publics have long said they want the UN to do more, they do not fully offset recent concerns about declining confidence in the UN to actually do so.[14]

In summary, generic global citizenship has slowly and steadily risen throughout the 35-year period of the WVS, even as patriotism and localism have decreased. On the other hand, confidence in the United Nations is lower today than it was when it was first asked about 20 years ago, and this confidence has eroded more rapidly than has confidence in political institutions at other levels. The available data do not permit us to say whether publics worldwide want different cosmopolitan political institutions, or, alternatively, whether they are simply less enthusiastic about cosmopolitanism in the political than in the general or ethical sphere.

Do societal differences impact global citizenship?

Although early critiques of cosmopolitanism often linked it to Western imperialism and societal privilege (Barber 1994; Marx 1994; Scarry 1994; Huntington 1996; Pagden 2000), there is now a vast qualitative literature on subaltern and post-colonial cosmopolitanism (e.g., Appadurai 1996; Rao 2007; Go 2013; Webb 2014). Quantitative analyses of how cosmopolitan attitudes vary across societies are less common, but most analyses conclude that it is at least as common in the Global South as it is in the Global North (e.g., Furia 2005; Davidson et al. 2009). Table 12.1 clarifies that this remains very much so as of the 2010–2014 WVS.

The first two columns of Table 12.1 list countries according to the percentage of respondents that agree that they are world citizens, and perhaps the first thing that one notices about the table is that none of the top 10 countries (Malaysia, Ghana, the Philippines, Ecuador, Thailand, Mexico, Nigeria, Qatar, Rwanda, and Colombia) are included in Samuel Huntington's (1996) list of "Western" societies. On the other hand, the same could be said of the 10 countries in which cosmopolitan sensibilities are weakest (Morocco, Egypt, Azerbaijan, Russia, Georgia, Belarus, Lebanon, Tunisia, Iraq, and Algeria). Correlational analysis confirms that there is no statistically significant relationship between cosmopolitan sensibilities and Western status, or, for that matter, between cosmopolitanism and national wealth.[15] Cosmopolitan sensibilities are, however, systematically less common in Arab countries ($r = -0.45$, $p = .00$) and Former Soviet Union (FSU) countries ($r = -0.39$, $p = .00$).[16]

The next two columns of Table 12.1 list countries in descending order according to their confidence in the United Nations. Here again, wealthy Western countries are largely absent from both the top and bottom of the list, and, here again, neither national wealth nor Western status is systematically predictive of cosmopolitanism.[17] One prominent difference in terms of the societal prevalence of self-described world citizenship and confidence in the United Nations is that three of the five countries most confident in the UN are FSU countries, namely, Uzbekistan, Kazakhstan, and Kyrgyzstan. More generally, even though Russia itself ranks in the bottom third of countries in UN confidence (as do its fellow P-5 members China and the United States) FSU membership more generally is a systematic positive predictor of confidence in the UN ($r = .31$, $p = .02$). By far the strongest pattern in terms of societal variation in support for the UN is the systematic lack of confidence in the UN expressed by Arab publics ($r = -0.67$, $p = .00$). A closer look at country-specific trend data suggests that the reasons for this are complex. Neither events pertaining to the Iraq War, nor to the Arab Spring, nor to the Israeli–Palestinian conflict seem a decisive driver of

Table 12.1 World citizenship and UN confidence by country – WVS sixth wave (2010–2014)

Country	% World citizens	Country	% Confident in UN
Malaysia	97	Uzbekistan	73
Ghana	96	Kazakhstan	69
Philippines	96	South Korea	68
Ecuador	93	Philippines	67
Thailand	93	Kyrgyzstan	66
Mexico	92	Ghana	65
Nigeria	91	Sweden	64
Qatar	91	Singapore	63
Rwanda	91	Malaysia	62
Colombia	90	India	59
Pakistan	88	Zimbabwe	59
Turkey	86	Estonia	57
South Africa	83	Hong Kong	57
India	82	Belarus	56
South Korea	82	Nigeria	55
Armenia	81	Australia	54
Kyrgyzstan	81	Mexico	49
Peru	81	Ukraine	49
Spain	81	Thailand	48
Brazil	80	Bahrain	47
Sweden	79	Georgia	47
Poland	78	Germany	46
Trinidad and Tobago	78	Rwanda	45
Zimbabwe	78	Spain	45
Australia	77	New Zealand	45
Hong Kong	77	Taiwan	44
Singapore	76	Chile	43
Taiwan	76	Colombia	43
Argentina	74	Peru	43
Slovenia	74	Romania	43
Uruguay	74	South Africa	43
Bahrain	73	Armenia	42

Where are the global citizens? 183

Country	% World citizens	Country	% Confident in UN
Japan	71	Japan	42
Cyprus	69	Netherlands	42
Chile	68	Poland	40
Kuwait	68	Uruguay	40
Netherlands	67	Cyprus	39
United States	67	Ecuador	39
Kazakhstan	64	Trinidad and Tobago	39
Uzbekistan	64	Turkey	38
Estonia	62	Brazil	37
Jordan	62	United States	36
Romania	61	Kuwait	35
Germany	60	Azerbaijan	34
Ukraine	60	Russian Federation	34
Libya	57	China	32
Yemen	57	Lebanon	30
China	56	Argentina	27
Algeria	54	Qatar	26
Iraq	54	Slovenia	24
Tunisia	53	Pakistan	23
Lebanon	52	Libya	20
Belarus	49	Morocco	19
Georgia	48	Iraq	17
Russian Federation	46	Jordan	17
Azerbaijan	42	Tunisia	12
Egypt	41	Algeria	9
Morocco	32	Egypt	8
		Yemen	8

Note: Only the question about UN confidence was asked in New Zealand, hence the extra row for this question.
Source: World Values Survey (1981–2014).

opinion throughout the region. Nor does it seem that the weakness of global citizenship attitudes in Arab countries is part of a broader weakness in citizenship commitments more generally. Clearly, the absence of cosmopolitanism in the region is associated with an absence of peace, and deeper analysis of the causal direction of this relationship is an interesting topic for future research.

Although our global view of cosmopolitanism should not be unduly influenced by its lack of appeal in a region with only 5 per cent of the world's population, cosmopolitans equally interested in human beings wherever one finds them may be especially interested in the status of cosmopolitanism in more populous countries, as a finding that the median country or society is cosmopolitan does not directly address the cosmopolitanism of the median human being.[18] If, for example, China and India were to stand out as countries in which cosmopolitanism was especially weak, this would cast doubt on the above analyses in which, in effect, respondents from more and less populous societies are weighted equally. Yet as Table 12.1 suggests, and as a correlation analysis confirms, the size of a country's population is not significantly related to cosmopolitanism (whether measured by generic global citizenship sensibilities or by confidence in the United Nations).[19]

The fact that cosmopolitanism among Indian respondents is "above average" whereas cosmopolitanism among Chinese respondents is "below average" does suggest we should look further into a possible relationship between cosmopolitanism and (societal) liberalism and democracy. If we provisionally measure national liberalism and democracy according to a country's status on Freedom House's tripartite "free", "partly free", "not free" metric, we find that respondents from more liberal countries are a bit more likely to have general cosmopolitan sensibilities ($r = 0.33$, $p = .01$), and that they are modestly, but not significantly, more likely to express confidence in the UN ($r = 0.20$, $p = .14$). Although much has been written about cosmopolitan democracy, and although cosmopolitanism's critics (e.g., Barber 1994; Marx 1994; Miller 2000) have often asserted that it is in tension with democracy at the level of the nation state, I know of few scholars who have expressly argued that cosmopolitanism and national democracy are mutually reinforcing.

Kwame Anthony Appiah (1994, 2010) is among these few. To generalize Appiah's argument a bit, it is one thing to live in a country, such as the United States or the United Kingdom, in which national public opinion runs against global public opinion on a host of economic and security issues, but quite another to live in a country in which such tensions are much less prominent. (Consider, for example, how a global redistributive tax would affect the US demos on the one hand and the Ghanaian demos on the other.) And this brings us back to a point that we have already touched on above. People worldwide tend to see less tension between that which is good for their country and that which is good for the world than do Anglo-American participants in the patriotism–cosmopolitanism debate.

Where are the global citizens? 185

Do individual differences impact global citizenship?

A final gripe about cosmopolitanism is that, as Craig Calhoun (2002) has memorably put it, it is the "class consciousness of frequent travellers". Particularly in the economic realm, it is sometimes argued that the cosmopolitanism of a US tech billionaire (or even a US college student majoring in global studies) works against the interests of her worse-off compatriots, and similar worries may or may not apply to the cosmopolitanism of better-off persons in the Global South. Happily, the WVS also allows us to explore the extent to which high socio-economic status and other socio-demographic traits are associated with cosmopolitanism.

Whereas, in the previous section, our analysis was limited by the fact that we had a relatively small sample size of 59 countries, our sample is now the 85,000 or so individuals who actually responded to the most recent WVS survey. A sample size this large is a mixed blessing, in that it uncovers numerous statistically significant yet substantively miniscule relationships. Provided we keep this in mind, however, a large sample does make it much easier to consider a given predictor of cosmopolitanism while controlling for multiple others.

Based in part on an analysis of fourth-wave WVS data, I have elsewhere suggested (Furia 2005) that the putative relationship between high income and cosmopolitanism is at best exaggerated, and, more generally, that there is not really any demographic trait that is particularly strongly associated with cosmopolitanism. I now want to re-examine that previous conclusion by consulting more recent evidence on cosmopolitanism's association with income, education, access to the Internet, sex, political orientation, and age.[20]

The first three columns of Table 12.2 present Pearson *r* correlation coefficients and *p* values for each of the above demographic variables and the WVS world citizenship variable, taking each variable in exactly the form that it appears in the WVS.[21] Because low values of the world citizenship variable correspond to "agreement" with the statement, "I see myself as a world citizen", the table should be read as associating demographic characteristics with *anti-cosmopolitanism*. The last three columns of Table 12.2 present parallel analyses for the WVS UN confidence variable, and, for similar reasons, the table should be read as associating demographics with UN *scepticism*.

Due to our enormous sample size, all but two of the empirical relationships in Table 12.2 are considered statistically significant. In terms of magnitude, however, even the strongest of the 10 significant relationships in Table 12.2 – the positive relationship between age and anti-cosmopolitan sensibilities – explains just over one-third of 1 per cent of the variation in such sensibilities worldwide. Even when we examine all of the demographic predictors of each of our two indicators of cosmopolitanism together, they jointly explain only about 0.6 per cent of the variation in cosmopolitan sensibilities and only about 1.2 per cent of the variation in confidence in the UN.[22] Moreover, some of these variables change sign depending on the indicator of cosmopolitanism in question – older individuals, for example, are minimally *more* likely to express confidence in the UN than are younger individuals. The only consistent statistically significant relationship across both indicators is that, as per Craig Calhoun's contention, respondents higher in income relative to their compatriots are at once more likely to describe themselves as world citizens and more likely to express confidence in the United Nations.[23] This is stronger support for Calhoun's hypothesis than was found when respondents to earlier waves of the WVS were asked about a *primary* allegiance to the world as a whole (Furia 2005). It indicates that respondents to the world citizenship question in the three lowest deciles of their national income distribution rate their "agreement" with the statement "I see myself as a world citizen" as about a 3.0 on a 1–4 scale, whereas respondents in the three highest deciles rate their agreement as about a 3.2. However, this is still a far cry from suggesting that global citizenship is a straightforward mark-up on economic privilege. Rather, individual income relative to national norms explains at most one-quarter of 1 per cent of global variation in our two indicators of cosmopolitanism.[24]

In short, there is no easily recognizable profile of a global citizen. The majority of members of every major socio-demographic group express cosmopolitan sensibilities, and demographic traits are even less fruitful in distinguishing levels of confidence in the United Nations. Put another way, global citizenship is embraced not only by people in all societies, but by people in all types of life situations within those societies.

Of course, to assert that global citizenship is embraced by a majority of the world's people is not to assert that the majority of the world's people are

Table 12.2 Demographic correlates of anti-cosmopolitanism and UN scepticism – WVS sixth wave

Correlate	Anti-cosmopolitanism Pearson r	Anti-cosmopolitanism P value	UN scepticism Pearson r	UN scepticism P value
(High) Age	.06	.00	−.01	.00
(High) Income	−.05	.00	−.05	.00
(High) Education	.02	.00	−.05	.00
(Low) Internet Usage	.00	.73	.04	.00
(Right) Political Orientation	−.03	.00	−.01	.25
(Female) Sex	.01	.00	−.03	.00

Source: World Values Survey (1981–2014).

effective global citizens. Although privilege has little impact on people's sensibilities, it clearly does affect people's capabilities for cosmopolitan – and other – forms of citizenship. Even so, to concede that, say, a typical teenager in the Global South is a less impactful global citizen than Bill Gates is not to say that the teenager has no impact whatsoever. And whatever an individual teenager's impact, the fact that approximately 80 per cent of the teenagers of the Global South self-identify as global citizens is itself pertinent to debate about whether cosmopolitanism's appeal is limited to wealthy Western solipsists.

Finally, we might expand our analysis of the correlates of cosmopolitanism beyond socio-demographic traits. Here again, we see evidence that global publics perceive fewer trade-offs between cosmopolitanism and other things than do Anglo-American commentators on cosmopolitanism. Again, this is not to deny that citizens of wealthy countries, and, in particular, citizens of wealthy countries in which majority opinion is at odds with world opinion, face trade-offs between cosmopolitanism and, in particular, patriotism. But the WVS reminds us that the majority of the world's people live in non-rich, non-great power countries, and, in turn, that they are less likely to face such trade-offs. Specifically, as indicated in Tables 12.3a and 12.3b, the variables most strongly associated with cosmopolitanism – often an order of magnitude greater in their association than the demographic variables reviewed in Table 12.2 – are numerous generic "civicness" and "social capital" variables and, in fact, several variables that directly measure patriotism and/or localism. For

Table 12.3a Demographic correlates of anti-cosmopolitanism and UN scepticism – WVS sixth wave

Correlate	Anti-cosmopolitanism Pearson r	Anti-cosmopolitanism P value	UN scepticism Pearson r	UN scepticism P value
(High) Age	.06	.00	−.01	.00
(High) Income	−.05	.00	−.05	.00
(High) Education	.02	.00	−.05	.00
(Low) Internet Usage	.00	.73	.04	.00
(Right) Political Orientation	−.03	.00	−.01	.25
(Female) Sex	.01	.00	−.03	.00

Source: World Values Survey (1981–2014)

Table 12.3b Additional correlates of UN scepticism – WVS sixth wave

Correlate	UN scepticism Pearson r
(Low) Confidence in women's organizations	.428
(Low) Confidence in environmental organizations	.421
(Low) Confidence in charitable or humanitarian organizations	.401
(Low) Confidence in parliament	.385
(Low) Confidence in political parties	.374
(Low) Confidence in the civil service	.364
(Low) Confidence in major companies	.361
(Low) Confidence in labor unions	.349
(Low) Confidence in universities	.339
(Low) Confidence in banks	.335
(Low) Confidence in the national government	.332
(Low) Confidence in the press	.318
(Low) Confidence in the courts	.300
(Low) Confidence in television	.292
(Low) Confidence in the police	.251
(Low) Confidence in the armed forces	.242
(Low) How democratically is this country being governed?	.171
(Low) Trust people of another religion	.168
(Low) How much respect is there for individual human rights nowadays?	.163
(Low) Trust people of another nationality	.162
(High) Whenever science and religion conflict, religion is always right	.139
(Low) I see myself as a world citizen	.130
(Low) Confidence in the churches	.129
(Low) Information source: printed magazines	.127

Source: World Values Survey (1981–2014).

most of the world's people, in other words, the question of *where* they will exercise citizenship seems secondary to *how much* citizenship they will exercise.

Conclusion

Critics of cosmopolitanism often speculate that ordinary persons worldwide lack cosmopolitan sensibilities. Ordinary persons worldwide tend to say otherwise. A strong majority of persons worldwide describe themselves as world citizens, and the tendency to embrace this description has increased gradually over time. Although global citizenship commitments do not yet rival those of patriotism and localism, these other modes of allegiance seem to be in gradual decline. Relatively low confidence in the United Nations already rivals or surpasses similarly low confidence in national governments, but public confidence in the UN has recently declined more than has public confidence in other institutions. Cosmopolitanism is not strongly associated with geographic and demographic variables, but it is positively associated with citizenship commitments at the local and national levels. In sum, cosmopolitanism appears less limited by sensibilities than it does by capabilities and institutions.

Acknowledgement

I thank Lauren Stapleton, Ted Wieland, and Sebra Yen for their helpful research assistance.

Notes

1 In any given wave of the WVS, the figure is likely to be no more than 70 countries examined.
2 Although I and others (Norris 2000; Furia 2005; Jung 2008; Davidson et al. 2009) have already begun some of this work in earlier publications, the newest available WVS data is nonetheless helpful in refining previous conclusions.
3 I discuss the different formulation of cosmopolitanism questions in the earlier waves of the WVS below.
4 This remains true both for European respondents, approximately 64 per cent of whom feel a part of the relatively institutionalized EU and, for example, North American respondents, about 66 per cent of whom feel part of a much less institutionalized North America. The strongest regional identifications are among Caribbean respondents identifying with the Caribbean (91 per cent), African respondents identifying with the African Union (77 per cent) and ASEAN-country respondents identifying with the ASEAN region (73 per cent). The weakest regional identifications (35 per cent) were those expressed by Japanese respondents asked about APEC.
5 For related arguments, see Appiah (1994) and Beitz (1994). Note that the fact that a majority of respondents "agree" that they are citizens of each community elides differences between those who merely "agree" and those who "strongly agree", but zeroing in on strong agreement does little to change the comparative picture. Specifically, about 54 per cent of respondents strongly identify as patriots, 38 per cent strongly identify as localists, 30 per cent strongly identify as globalists, and 24 per cent of respondents strongly identify as (supranational) regionalists.
6 Consistent with the literature on the decline of traditional politics, non-governmental organizations fare a bit better. Fifty-seven per cent of respondents express confidence in charitable or humanitarian organizations and 54 per cent express confidence in environmental organizations. It might be argued that the relatively strong performance of humanitarian and environmental organizations bodes well for cosmopolitanism (in that humanitarianism and environmentalism are cosmopolitan virtues) but it might also be that these organizations are lauded for "acting locally".
7 This is because people everywhere inhabit "the world" and societies everywhere have UN membership. By contrast, even if most all societies participate in "foreign aid", we tend to make a fundamental distinction between societies that are mainly

190 Peter A. Furia

donors and societies that are mainly recipients. Hence, references to trends in "world opinion" that failed to take that distinction into account would seem problematic.
8 The sixth wave of the WVS, for example, has greater participation from both Arab and Former Soviet Union (FSU) countries than the fifth wave, and this is pertinent to an analysis of trends because cosmopolitanism is less common in both of these types of societies.
9 The first four waves of the survey also included a question about primary allegiance to "province", and, like localism, provincialism increased fractionally (both were up about 0.4 per cent) between the 1981–1984 and 1999–2004 waves. Both patriotism (−0.5 per cent) and regionalism (−0.6 per cent) declined over the same period, as did "No Answer"/"Don't Know" responses (−2.3 per cent). Clearly, all of these changes over time are quite small, and none of the ordinal rankings of the four modes of allegiance shifted over the period. Throughout the first four surveys, local communities were always the most popular form of allegiance, followed by patriotism, provincialism, cosmopolitanism, and, finally, regionalism.
10 The countries are Argentina, Australia, Brazil, Chile, China, Columbia, Cyprus, Georgia, Germany, Ghana, India, Japan, Jordan, Malaysia, Mexico, Morocco, Poland, Romania, Rwanda, Slovenia, South Africa, South Korea, Spain, Sweden, Thailand, Trinidad and Tobago, Turkey, Ukraine, United States, and Uruguay.
11 Some of the 11 regional identifications asked about in the sixth-wave survey were not asked about at all or not asked about in particular countries in the fifth-wave survey, and comparisons across the different regions are tricky, but perceived regional citizenship was up in 14 of the 24 instances it is asked about and the increases are generally greater in magnitude than the decreases. (The largest increase that we observe is a 30 per cent increase in identification with Asia in Australia, as compared to a 10 per cent decrease in identification with APEC in Japan.)
12 Only 11 societies are asked about confidence in the same regional organization in both the third- and sixth-wave surveys, but among these, confidence actually increases a bit from 41.3 per cent to 42.0 per cent.
13 See Chapter 1 in this volume.
14 Other cross-national surveys on international institutions are compiled at Council on Foreign Relations (2015) and World Public Opinion-Program on International Policy Attitudes (2015).
15 The respective Pearson r correlation coefficients and p values are $r = .00$, $p = .99$ for Western status and $r = .09$ and $p = .52$ for per capita gross national income.
16 The figure for non-Arab majority Muslim countries is $r = -.09$, $p = .51$.
17 The respective Pearson r correlation coefficients and p values are $r = .09$, $p = .50$ for Western status and $r = .02$ and $p = .84$ for per capita gross national income.
18 The idea that global governance institutions like the UN might be more popular in weak countries than in strong ones goes back at least to Sigmund Freud (Einstein and Freud (1933)).
19 The respective Pearson r correlation coefficients and p values are $r = .00$, $p = .98$ for world citizenship and $r = .02$, $p = .91$ for UN confidence.
20 See Chapter 13 for a more detailed analysis of age and cohort effects in regard to cosmopolitanism.
21 Although non-parametric correlations are ideal for analysis of the 4–10 point ordinal scales on which both the WVS demographic traits and the WVS global citizenship variables are measured, the calculation of non-parametric correlations on an 85,000 case dataset requires more computing power than I have. I therefore utilize Pearson-r correlations and have confirm their (extreme) similarity to non-parametric correlations in a separate analysis of 2,500 randomly selected cases that is available from the author upon request.

22 For bivariate relationships, we obtain an R-squared value by squaring Pearson-r, hence .06*.06 = .0036 = "just over one-third of 1 per cent". For multivariate analysis, R-squared is calculated via a simple OLS regression. More sophisticated regression techniques seem unnecessary given the (profound) weakness of the bivariate relationships in question.

23 The WVS measures income on multiple national scales rather than on a single global scale. Thus, when we refer to high income respondents we mean respondents who are richer than their fellow national citizens.

24 This percentage of variance explained weakens to about one-tenth of 1 per cent in a multivariate analysis of confidence in the UN, but remains around one-quarter of 1 per cent in a multivariate analysis of world citizenship. Recall that there is no statistically significant relationship between societal level wealth and cosmopolitanism, but the sample size of our analysis is a large driver of statistical significance. Though we can't be at all confident about substantively tiny relationships observed in small samples, and although in the case of confidence in the UN societal wealth really appears to have nothing to do with cosmopolitanism, Calhoun et al. might reasonably add that, despite the lack of statistical significance, our findings suggest that societal wealth may explain about four-fifths of 1 per cent of the societal variation in self-described world citizenship.

References

Appadurai, A. 1996. *Modernity at Large: Cultural Dimensions of Globalization*. Vol. 1. Minneapolis, MN: University of Minnesota Press.

Appiah, Kwame A. 1994. "Cosmopolitan Patriots". In Martha Nussbaum et al., "Patriotism and Cosmopolitanism", *Boston Review* 19(5).

Appiah, Kwame A. 2007. *Cosmopolitanism: Ethics in a World of Strangers (Issues of Our Time)*. New York: Norton.

Barber, Benjamin. 1994. "Constitutional Faith". In Martha Nussbaum et al., "Patriotism and Cosmopolitanism", *Boston Review* 19(5).

Beitz, Charles. 1994. "Patriotism for Cosmopolitans". In Martha Nussbaum et al., "Patriotism and Cosmopolitanism", *Boston Review* 19(5).

Calhoun, Craig J. 2002. "The Class Consciousness of Frequent Travellers: Toward A Critique of Actually Existing Cosmopolitanism". *South Atlantic Quarterly* 10(4): 869–897.

Council on Foreign Relations. 2015. "Public Opinion on Global Issues". Available at: www.cfr.org/thinktank/iigg/pop.

Dahl, Robert A. 2000. "Can International Organizations Be Democratic? A Sceptic's View". In Ian Shapiro and Casiano Hacker-Cordon (eds), *Democracy's Edges*. Cambridge: Cambridge University Press, pp. 19–36.

Davidson, Roei, Nathaniel Poor, and Ann Williams. 2009. "Stratification and Global Elite Theory: A Cross-cultural and Longitudinal Analysis of Public Opinion". *International Journal of Public Opinion Research* 21(2): 165–186.

Freud, S. 1933. "Why War?". *The Standard Edition of the Complete Psychological Works of Sigmund Freud (vol. XXII) (1932–1936): New Introductory Lectures on Psycho-Analysis and Other Works*. London: Peace Pledge Union, pp. 195–216.

Furia, Peter A. 2005. "Global Citizenship, Anyone? Cosmopolitanism, Privilege and Public Opinion". *Global Society* 19(4): 331–359.

Go, Julian. 2013. "Fanon's Postcolonial Cosmopolitanism". *European Journal of Social Theory* 16(2): 208–225.

Herder, Johann G. [1774] 2004. *Another Philosophy of History and Selected Political Writings*. Edited by Ioannis D. Evrigenis and Daniel Pellerin. Indianapolis, IN: Hackett.

Huntington, Samuel P. 1996. "The West: Unique, Not Universal". *Foreign Affairs* 75(6): 28–46.

Huntington, Samuel P. 1996. *The Clash of Civilizations and the Remaking of World Order*. London: Penguin.

Jung, Jai Kwan. 2008. "Growing Supranational Identities in a Globalising World? A Multilevel Analysis of the World Values Surveys". *European Journal of Political Research* 47(5): 578–609.

Marx, Leo. 1994. "Neglecting History". In Martha Nussbaum *et al.*, "Patriotism and Cosmopolitanism", *Boston Review* 19(5).

Miller, David. 2000. *Citizenship and National Identity*. Paris: OECD.

Norris, Pippa. 2000. "Global Governance and Cosmopolitan Citizens". In Joseph S. Nye and John D. Donahue (eds), *Governance in a Globalizing World*. Washington, DC: Brookings Institution Press.

Pagden, Anthony. 2000. "Stoicism, Cosmopolitanism, and the Legacy of European Imperialism". *Constellations* 7(1): 2–3.

Rao, Rahul. 2007. "Postcolonial Cosmopolitanism: Between Home and the World". Doctoral dissertation, University of Oxford.

Scarry, Elaine. 1994. "The Difficulty of Imagining Other People". In Martha Nussbaum *et al.*, "Patriotism and Cosmopolitanism", *Boston Review* 19(5).

Webb, Adam K. 2014. "The Rise of the Cosmopolitan Traditionalists: From the Arab Spring to a Global Countermovement?". *International Political Science Review* 36(4): 425–440.

World Public Opinion-Program on International Policy Attitudes [PIPA]. 2015. Available at: www.WorldPublicOpinion.org.

World Values Survey. 1981–2014. Longitudinal Aggregate v.20150418. World Values Survey Association. Aggregate File Producer. Madrid: JDSystems. Available at: www.worldvaluessurvey.org.

13 Age and global citizenship attitudes

Brittany H. Bramlett

Youthfulness is often associated with idealism, vitality, and openness to new ideas. This openness can encourage a young person to seek new experiences as well as entertain and examine differing viewpoints, adopting some and rejecting others. This is part of the process of political socialization, one that involves political learning and the acquisition of political attitudes (Greenstein 1970), including those that shape how we see the world and our position in it. Such questions of identity and citizenship have become increasingly complex when we consider the expanding possibilities for globalization and its concomitant integration of economic and social practices across the globe. How do young adults think about global identity and their place in the world in the contemporary context of globalization?

Providing an answer to this question requires an understanding of how individuals conceptualize citizenship. Citizenship is a fluid and disputed concept, often meaning different things at different times to different people (Kratochwil 1996; Shorter 1993; Turner 1993). Broadly conceived, citizenship has legal, political, economic, and cultural implications (Turner 1993). This chapter focuses on the way that the social and psychological dynamics of citizenship are crucial to our understanding of how people consider themselves in a modern world where traditional national boundaries face challenges from globalization (Kratochwil 1996; Turner 1993). Given the extent to which globalization's pace has been influenced by recent technological advances and knowing that the meaning of citizenship varies over time, should we not expect generations of people to also vary in how they identify themselves within the world?

In this chapter, I argue that young adults, age 18 to 25,[1] are more likely to think of themselves as citizens of the world. This is especially true of young adults coming of age in recent decades, during the context of globalization. Using data from the World Value Surveys, I explore this psychological identification with world citizenship over time.

Citizenship theory and globalization

Citizenship means many things, but this chapter focuses on the concept's social–psychological underpinnings. Global citizenship is not a legal identity, so we must focus on feelings and/or behaviours tied to global citizenship to measure and understand it. What does it feel and look like to identify with a global community first and foremost?

Some citizenship theorists concentrate on these psychological aspects of citizenship to understand who we are in the midst of various social trends like globalization. Both Shorter (1993) and Kratochwil (1996) discuss citizenship as a feeling of belonging (or not belonging) and what it means for how people feel about and act towards themselves and others. Kratochwil stresses the importance of knowing whether national citizenship still provides a "meaningful experience of identity and allegiance" given globalization and "the increasing diversity among the 'members' of a society" (1996, 181). In this chapter, I provide quantitative analysis addressing whether recent generations of young people are more likely to first identify as a citizen of their country or of the world.

Ideally, global identity is more than a psychological attachment. Proponents of global citizenship education would like to think it involves favourable attitudes or beneficial actions towards others in the global community. In the introduction to the edited volume *Citizenship and Social Theory*, Bryan S. Turner highlights this social component, defining citizenship as "That set of practices (juridical, political, economic, and cultural) which define a person as a competent member of society, and which as a consequence shape the flow of the resources to persons and social groups" (1993, 2). Turner (1993) points to the social dimensions of citizenship as distinct from the legal and/or political ones. He goes on to elaborate on these social dynamics by theorizing that citizenship involves the content and form of social rights in addition to the social forces and arrangements that produce such practices and distribute benefits to the rest of society (Turner 1993, 3). An analysis of global citizenship attitudes should not only ask about identity but also about responsibilities towards others within the global community.

This link between global citizenship and social responsibilities may not always be clear because of differing conceptions of globalization. The present analysis mostly concerns citizenship attitudes deriving from forces associated with globalization-from-below. *Globalization-from-below* is marked by a variety of "transnational social forces animated by environmental concerns, human rights, hostility to patriarchy, and a vision of human community based on the unity of diverse cultures seeking an end to poverty, oppression, humiliation, and collective violence" (Falk 1993, 39). This conception of globalization differs from the official collaboration of governments, a top-down approach, which is certainly related to the social forces described above, but a distinct concept for the present analysis (Falk 1993).[2]

In sum, this chapter focuses on the modern view of citizenship and related responsibilities towards global society as discussed by Kratochwil (1996) and Turner (1993). If views of citizenship (and where people feel they belong) have changed or differ among generations, we should expect implications for how we think about borders and immigration policy as well as international problem solving (Kratochwil 1996). This chapter takes an empirical approach to answering these questions and considers survey data, asking whether young people: (1) identify first as a citizen of their country of origin or as a citizen of the world; and (2) view immigration policy and global problem solving through the lens of globalization.

Age and global citizenship

Recent globalization has enhanced the exchange of ideas via new technologies, connecting nations of the world, their cultures and economies, as never before. Given these developments, it is possible and highly likely that *global citizenship* – consideration of oneself as something larger than oneself, as a citizen of the world – has become an identifiable movement among people all over the globe. This may be especially true for younger people.

While many write about global citizenship and especially global citizenship education, there is little systematic analysis of global citizenship attitudes. This is particularly true for analysis of the relationship between age and global citizenship, which is missing from related scholarship. Many of the past studies lay important theoretical groundwork on the topic, but the authors draw conclusions without the benefit of quantitative research – empirical and systematic research based on numeric data, and in our case, coded answers from large-scale surveys with relevant questions. Perhaps scholars and journalists alike take for granted that young people are more likely to identify as global citizens than middle or older adults.

The significance of the global citizenship movement is noted throughout this text, but this chapter stresses the importance of the concept and subsequent action related to one specific age group: young people, or those on the verge of or beginning adulthood. The common assumption is that young people think about the world and their place in it differently from their parents' and grandparents' generations.

There are a number of reasons to focus on young adults' attitudes towards global citizenship. First, the early years of adulthood constitute a time in life when political orientations take root, solidifying by the third decade of life (Jennings 1989). If people are not exposed to ideas about global citizenship in the early years, it seems very unlikely that older adults will develop global awareness later in life. This period of emerging adulthood – 18 to 25 years old, neither adolescent nor adult – is an especially critical one for exploring beliefs, values, and questioning world-views (Arnett 2000). However, this period of emerging adulthood is often limited to young people of industrialized nations in the Global North who are more likely to experience an extended period of time without adult roles (Arnett 2000).[3]

Second, there is reason to think that the most recent generation of young people in particular will have distinct attitudes regarding global citizenship. Some argue that contemporary young adults are the most worldly and cosmopolitan generation to come of age. More recent generations of young people are more connected than ever (Sanders 2012; Watkins 2010) and thus, may feel more similar to people and experiences which seem quite foreign to their elders. In addition, young people who consider themselves global citizens often refer to their diverse upbringings, which lead them to think about their lives "as extending well beyond the borders of their native countries" (Schattle 2008, 8). Relatedly, educators have taught global awareness in the classroom with global citizenship-themed curriculum for the past few decades (Hicks 2003). Recent young adults, in contrast with those of the past, have lived and learned global citizenship during their formative years, which are ripe with socializing opportunities (Finlay *et al.* 2010).

In the case of the United States, young people have broadening views of the world and are shedding nation-centred, American forms of attachment. Famed pollster John Zogby identifies this trend in his report, *The Way We'll Be: The Zogby Report on the Transformation of the American Dream* (2008). In it, he describes the many ways that young Americans are changing what it means to be an American citizen in the twenty-first century. These young people, the *First Globals*, were born between the years of 1979 and 1994 and are also known as Millennials or belonging to Generation Y (Zogby 2008; Zogby and Kuhl 2013).

This chapter sets out to test the expectation that young adults, especially more recent generations, identify as global citizens and with the global community, using data from people across time, cultures, and nationalities. Data collected from 1981 to 2008 as part of the World Values Surveys (WVS) include responses to a series of questions related to global citizenship from tens of thousands of people across the world (World Values Survey Association 2009). This collection of surveys also notes the age of respondents, making the data extremely useful for analysing whether young adults during this time period differ from older generations in their attitudes about citizenship. Before analysing this data, the most relevant global citizenship studies are considered. How have social scientists with an interest in youth and/or education answered related research questions? Reviewing related studies help to both inform and lay the foundation for the present analysis.

Related research on age and global attitudes

Scholarship supporting the relationship between biological age (or generation) and global citizenship identification and attitudes is surprisingly lacking, given the amount of attention paid to global citizenship curricula. Educators teach global citizenship to young people and trust they will adopt a global perspective. However, there has not been a comprehensive and systematic study of what young people think about global citizenship – especially compared with previous generations.

Many have speculated that youth are more inclined to embrace global citizenship, and it is true that some country-specific data suggest a trend towards increasing global citizenship among young people (Zogby 2008; Zogby and Kuhl 2013), but is this consistent for all young people across the world and over time? One past study focuses on the effect of age and views on justice by asking young people about the role that government and individuals should play in the well-being of others (Flanagan et al. 2003).

The Flanagan et al. (2003) study does not address the extent to which age shapes global citizenship attitudes, but its findings are instructive for the present study. The authors find that the responses of the teens surveyed depended on the type of society – security versus opportunity – they lived in as well as their individual socio-economic status (Flanagan et al. 2003). Working class teens in the security societies, those where the state traditionally provided for people's basic needs, were more supportive of a social safety net while the middle class were more in favour of the state promoting self-sufficiency and competition. Working-class teens in the opportunity societies, those with market economies and where the state plays less of a role in regulating social services, were more likely to make a connection between accomplishments and personal merit than these nations' middle-class teens. Young people's attitudes about their relationship with and responsibility for other members of society seem to be predicated on their individual socio-economic status as well as their nation's economic system. A proper examination of global citizenship should also consider these factors.

Another recent study examines a comparable association, looking at young people and their motivation for public engagement. Haste and Hogan's (2006) civic engagement study of British youth found evidence for a moral component to youth engagement and what it means to be a citizen. The study found that young people feel motivated to act when they become agitated or concerned by news stories that challenge their personal values or beliefs. Young people's attitudes are malleable and they may be particularly concerned with making things right and thus motivated to civic action (Haste and Hogan 2006). This study provides additional evidence for young adulthood as the prime time for considering their developing citizenship and then taking action on those newly formed attitudes.

Although these studies are helpful and relate to our question of interest, it is odd that academic communities have not focused more on the empirical relationship between age and global citizenship. Again, observations have been made but few of these have been based on empirical studies, providing solid evidence for or against a relationship between age and global citizenship attitudes. One exception is John Myers's "'To Benefit the World by Whatever Means Possible': Adolescents' Constructed Meanings for Global Citizenship" (2010). Myers's research design sets an excellent example for future research on the topic. The study included interviews with 77 students who were involved in an international studies programme in the United States, and it sought an answer to the question: how do young people understand global citizenship, individually and more generally? Myers found that the students considered global citizenship a moral commitment, a finding similar to the civic engagement study by Haste and Hogan (2006) discussed above.

The young adults of the new millennium, who have been the focus of the comparative studies discussed in this section, seem aware of global issues, become concerned with the detrimental outcomes faced by people across the globe, and ultimately feel some moral responsibility for others outside of themselves, their families, and their nation. However, we need further research that focuses on global citizenship attitudes to verify what others have only suggested. The Myers study (2010), while laying important groundwork, closely examines students from a single educational programme. In this chapter, I aim to balance and build on the focused, qualitative approach by the Myers study with an equally important and overdue quantitative approach. My research design includes analysis of global citizenship data collected for tens of thousands of individuals across many years and many cultural and political contexts.

Using quantitative methods

Both qualitative and quantitative methods are important for the study of global citizenship and social science research more broadly. Studies like Myers's (2010) have the advantage of precision but lack in generalizability for other contexts. The quantitative analysis in this chapter considers the relationship between age and global citizenship identity and attitudes across many cultural contexts by using a large sample of respondents from the WVS. A large sample of individuals allows the researcher to statistically control for other confounding factors, other individual traits or attitudes which may be related to global citizenship. By considering confounding factors in this chapter, I can focus in on the relationship of interest, age, and global citizenship, and ensure that other factors are not driving the results.

Here is an example of how this works: suppose that young people are more likely to identify as citizens of the world than older people. Suppose also that liberal political ideology is associated with greater levels of world citizenship. And, suppose that young people are more likely to identify with a liberal ideology. In this scenario, if we are not controlling for the potentially confounding factor of political ideology, we have less confidence in our results. It is possible that youthfulness has nothing to do with global identity, but because more young people claim liberal ideology, it only appears that way. Instead, liberal ideology may be the driving force behind global identity, and young people just happen to be more liberal.

In sum, to confound is to confuse. Political ideology is considered a possible confounding factor because it may confuse the observed relationships if not accounted for in the analysis. Consideration of confounding factors in the statistical models estimated for this chapter will raise our confidence in the results. We will have greater confidence that the relationships observed between age and global citizenship attitudes are real and not just a product of other associations.

While quantitative analysis is lacking for global citizenship research, it is not entirely absent. The current volume certainly makes use of relevant quantitative research where appropriate. Quantitative data is especially valuable when addressing public opinion or attitudes. For example, Peter Furia examines opinions on cosmopolitanism, or global citizenship, using data from the WVS in earlier work (2005) and in Chapter 12 of this volume. He empirically tests the hypotheses that cosmopolitanism and global citizenship are related to elitism. Contrary to popular wisdom, he finds that cosmopolitan attitudes and global identity are not necessarily linked with or correlated with the elite members of society. Furia's work provides evidence, based on quantitative data, that global citizenship is a teachable and practicable ideal for all people, regardless of socio-economic status.

Over 20 years ago, Turner (1993), Shorter (1993), and Kratochwil (1996) discussed increasing global developments in the 1990s as relevant for ideas about citizenship, and now we have the data to test how people of different ages understand global citizenship over time. Given the theory and literature review discussed in the opening part of the chapter, I propose two hypotheses:

1 Young people will be more likely than older people to identify as global citizens.
2 Young people coming of age since the 1990s will be more likely to identify as global citizens than younger adults of past generations.

Measuring global citizenship: dependent variables

Measurement of concepts is critical for quantitative data analysis. When analysing attitudes related to global citizenship, we want to know: what does global citizenship mean? The complexity of the concept has already been noted, with many authors citing the disputed nature of the global citizenship definition (Dower and Williams 2002; Haste and Hogan 2006; Kratochwil 1996; Lister *et al*. 2003; Shorter 1993; Turner 1993).

The present analysis mostly defines global citizenship as a person's identification as a citizen of the world. I measure this conceptualization with a question from the WVS that asks: which geographical boundary defines the respondent's primary citizenship identification? People were asked which geographical group they belonged to first: locality, region, country, continent, or the world. The analyses used in this chapter consider respondents who either chose identification with country or with the world, compared with all other respondents. Although the aspects of global citizenship have been disputed, many agree that global citizenship may refer to a sense of belonging to a community "beyond the nation-state or other political community of which we are normally thought to be citizens" or with all of humanity (Dower and Williams 2002, 1).

My research will consider attitudes for issues that traditionally have been discussed at the national level. However, many of these issues – economic, environmental (Jelin 2000), and job-related – are increasingly understood as problems necessitating global solutions. This "interdependence among countries, cultures, economies, ecosystems, and all life on the planet" fosters a growing tendency towards global responsibility (Schattle 2008, 32, 44). The WVS includes a series of questions about global responsibility. These questions assess whether respondents believe a country cannot solve environmental, crime, or employment problems by itself. In other words, do people ascribe to this depiction of interdependence and/or feel responsibility towards other nations?

There are a few final considerations that round out the analysis. I consider responses from a couple of survey questions that ask after people's immigration policy stances as well as people's answers to whether they have heard about the Millennium Development Goals. Attitudes about immigration tap into global identity because these views are often "formative experiences in the lives of many self-identifying global citizens" (Schattle 2008, 10). Exploring respondents' openness to immigration within their own country will also require controlling for whether the individual grew up in an immigrant family or community. These socializing experiences may influence policy attitudes and be related to global citizenship. It will be important to sort out the relationships with statistical controls.

The last variable records whether people have heard of the Millennium Development Goals, eight goals constructed by 189 countries and several international organizations in 2000, ranging from "halving extreme poverty rates to halting the spread of HIV/AIDS and providing universal primary education" by the year 2015 (United Nations 2013). Knowledge of these goals will indicate an interest in global concerns and, relatedly, a global identity and some moral responsibility for taking on these global challenges.

Measuring age and confounding factors: independent variables

For this chapter, we are interested in whether age – young adulthood, especially – predicts global citizenship identity and attitudes. The expectation is that young people will be more likely to claim global citizenship and to hold beliefs that correspond with a global perspective, compared with other generations. In the analyses, age is measured with three categories: *young adult age* (18 to 25), *older–middle adult age* (50 to 64), and *older adult age* (65 and above).[4] These age groupings are similar to those used for a wide range of social science research, although one could certainly argue for different groupings. Our purpose here is to achieve a basic understanding of how each broadly defined age group comprehends global citizenship, compared with the others.

The upcoming results section explores *multivariate regression analyses*, which allow researchers to control for potentially confounding variables. Remember that these are factors which might also influence the dependent variables (measures of global citizenship) and, therefore, confuse the relationship of interest. The quantitative analysis performed by Flanagan *et al.* (2003) considers social class and gender to be important when predicting attitudes about justice. The present models build from this framework, controlling for *gender, education,* and *income levels* – common factors to account for when considering social and political questions. I also account for *levels of religiosity* and *political interest*, as well as *political ideology*. Social scientists know that these factors tend to influence attitudes with political aspects, such as opinions on global citizenship. Again, we statistically control for these factors in order to isolate and understand the primary relationship of concern: age and global citizenship.

Finally, to test whether rates of global identity among young adults have increased over time, I analyse data over different years, or survey waves. The WVS consists of several waves, and I make use of questioning from five waves: 1981 to 1984, 1989 to 1993, 1994 to 1999, 1999 to 2004, and 2005 to 2007 (World Values Survey Association 2009).[5] The WVS includes nationally representative samples from nearly 100 nations all over the globe.[6]

The age effects for global citizenship attitudes

Let's first consider the range of responses to the WVS question that asks people which geographical group they belonged to first: locality, region, country, continent, or the world. I look at these responses across the age categories mentioned above to get an idea of the relationship between age and global identity without controlling for other factors. Figure 13.1 presents the bivariate analysis. Remember that this first examination includes a sample of people from all over the world and from different points in time. We can see that most people either identify primarily with their locality or their nation. Overall, fewer people identify primarily as a citizen of the world. However, the combined sample includes over 100,000 participants, so these smaller percentages still represent thousands of people. Taking a closer look, we see that young adults make up a higher percentage of the global identifiers, compared with the older age categories. This data supports hypothesis 1, that younger people would be more likely to identify as citizens of the world, but there is more to do.

Table 13.1 shows the results for the quantitative analysis using Probit regression to predict civic identity while controlling for many factors that are often associated with political attitudes, or more specifically, global citizenship attitudes. *Probit regression* is a method of analysis used when the dependent variable comprises only two values. Each of the measures of global citizenship has been coded this way, so probit regression is used throughout the chapter's analysis.

Table 13.1 shows results for factors predicting primary identity with country and primary identity with the world. We can interpret results by looking at the coefficients and the stars beside them. For instance, religiosity is positively related to identification with nation but not with the world. If the coefficient has one star next to it in the table, that indicates a statistically significant relationship. Two stars indicate an even stronger and robust relationship. The absence of stars means that we cannot be sure whether the relationship, positive or negative, is significant or merely due to chance.

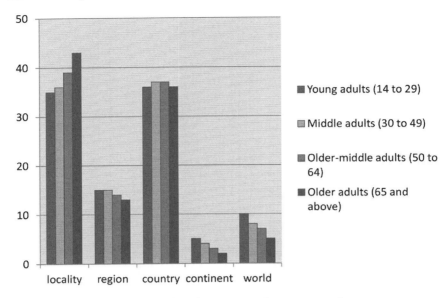

Figure 13.1 Percentage of civic identity responses by age categories
Source: World Values Survey (1981–2008).

Leftist political ideology is significantly associated with global identity but negatively associated with national identity. The results for the relationship with income level are mixed and less clear. Income may not have as much to do with global attitudes as expected, which corroborates with Furia's (2005) findings.

We pay attention to the results for the confounding factors for a couple reasons. First, by noting the statistical significance of a relationship, we can be assured of the appropriateness of including the variable in the model. In the present case, political interest, political stance, and socio-economic status clearly play a part in predicting global citizenship attitudes, so it is wise to control for the effects of these characteristics. From here on, I will mostly focus on the results of primary interest: the relationship between the young adult age group and global citizenship attitudes. In Table 13.1, we see that young adulthood is associated with less likelihood of primarily identifying with nation but more with global identity. The older age groups are negatively associated with initially identifying with the world. These relationships hold, even controlling for all of the other relevant factors.

The above analysis certainly seems to support the first hypothesis, that young adults are more likely to identify first as a citizen of the world compared with other age groups and controlling for relevant factors. However, does this relationship hold up over time? Does it get stronger or disappear when considering young adults of the past with more recent cohorts of young adults? Table 13.2 provides the same analysis but broken down into the

Table 13.1 Probit regression on civic identity

	Primary ID country	Primary ID world
	Coef (std dev)	Coef (std dev)
Independent variables – age		
14 to 29	−0.046** (0.011)	0.118** (0.015)
50 to 64	0.017 (0.012)	−0.092** (0.017)
65 and above	0.057** (0.016)	−0.201** (0.026)
Control variables		
Religion importance	0.038** (0.009)	−0.009 (0.012)
Political interest	0.042* (0.013)	0.068** (0.017)
Leftist political identification	−0.051** (0.011)	0.114** (0.015)
Female	−0.034** (0.009)	−0.001 (0.012)
Low level education	−0.038** (0.011)	−0.167** (0.016)
High level education	0.021 (0.011)	0.152** (0.014)
Low level income	−0.015 (0.013)	0.043* (0.014)
High level income	0.024 (0.013)	0.106** (0.017)
Constant	−0.323** (0.010)	−1.426** (0.015)
Pseudo R2	0.001	0.015
N =	90,015	90,015

Source: World Values Survey (1981–2008).

WVS's waves of questioning. Wave 1 is not included because the first wave of respondents was not asked the civic identity question.

Results in Table 13.2 show the factors that predict primary identification with the world (global citizenship) across waves 2, 3, 4 and 5, covering a timespan of nearly 30 years (1981 to 2007). Again, we can see that many of the variables have a statistically significant relationship with feelings of global citizenship. We see that young adulthood is a statistically significant predictor of primary identification with the world for every wave except the earlier second wave. Given the introduction to this chapter, it makes sense that we would see the relationship emerge over time. Global identity may be a relatively new civic identity. Conversely, the oldest adults in every wave are negatively associated with a primary global identity.

The final analysis examines alternative indicators of global identity/ citizenship. Do younger and older adults vary in their attitudes across these related measures? Table 13.3 presents these results. For all five measures, age (a continuous measure here) has a statistically significant negative association, controlling for other relevant factors.

The older the respondent was, the less likely they supported open immigration, had knowledge of the Millennium Development Goals, and understood

Table 13.2 Probit regression on world civic identity across waves (years)

	Wave 2 (1989–1993) Coef (std dev)	Wave 3 (1994–1999) Coef (std dev)	Wave 4 (1999–2004) Coef (std dev)	Wave 5 (2005–2007) Coef (std dev)
Independent variables – age				
14 to 29	0.080 (0.046)	0.123** (0.021)	0.120** (0.026)	0.232* (0.086)
50 to 64	−0.095 (0.060)	−0.082** (0.023)	−0.112** (0.032)	−0.254* (0.102)
65 and above	−0.211* (0.105)	−0.232** (0.034)	−0.129* (0.046)	−0.376* (0.153)
Control variables				
Religion importance	−0.062 (0.040)	0.046* (0.017)	−0.021 (0.022)	0.184* (0.077)
Political interest	0.101* (0.048)	0.083* (0.024)	0.037 (0.030)	0.152 (0.121)
Leftist political identification	0.201** (0.047)	0.144** (0.021)	0.046 (0.027)	0.176 (0.099)
Female	0.016 (0.039)	−0.008 (0.016)	0.004 (0.021)	−0.119 (0.070)
Low level education	−0.583 (0.050)	−0.223** (0.022)	−0.080* (0.027)	−0.177 (0.101)
High level education	0.003 (0.048)	0.139** (0.019)	0.225** (0.025)	0.157 (0.083)
Low level income	0.108* (0.043)	0.027 (0.018)	−0.016 (0.025)	0.132 (0.085)
High level income	0.145* (0.063)	0.075* (0.023)	0.142** (0.031)	−0.042 (0.108)
Constant	−1.452** (0.051)	−1.362** (0.020)	−1.528** (0.027)	−1.464** (0.083)
Pseudo R2	0.011	0.018	0.016	0.041
N =	8,463	46,321	32,489	2,742

Source: World Values Survey (1981–2008).

the environment, employment, and crime as international problems in need of global solutions. On the other hand, younger respondents were more likely to say that they supported open immigration, had knowledge of the Millennium Development Goals, and understood the environment, employment, and crime as international problems in need of global solutions.

These final measures of global citizenship are hardly perfect. The samples of respondents for each WVS question come from different countries over different years. For example, the sample for the Millennium Development Goals question is somewhat smaller than for the immigration question and not asked of earlier respondents, because the goals were developed in 2000. Also, respondents in only 11 nations and over two waves had the opportunity to answer the three remaining questions/measures. Even with these limitations, using various measures that tap into ideas about global identity furthers our understanding of what it means to be a global citizen. Most importantly, this final set of analyses provides additional support for the relationship between age and global citizenship and identity.

Global citizenship in the new millennium

The results from the analysis indicate that young adulthood in the new millennium consistently relates to a range of global identity measures. These relationships hold even after considering other factors that may also predict global citizenship attitudes. By analysing many facets of global citizenship, we can be more confident that young people are more likely to claim global citizenship and hold attitudes consistent with that identification, compared

Table 13.3 Probit regression on alternative indicators of global citizenship

	Immigration policy open	Millennium Goals	Environment problems	Employment problems	Crime problems
	Coef (std dev)	Coef (std dev)	Coef (std dev)	Coef (std dev)	Coef (std dev)
Age	−0.008** (0.0003)	−0.004** (0.0004)	−0.005** (0.001)	−0.004** (0.001)	−0.003* (0.001)
Religion importance	0.008 (0.010)	0.137** (0.014)	0.260** (0.030)	0.184** (0.030)	0.168** (0.031)
Political interest	0.238** (0.013)	0.508** (0.018)	0.121* (0.045)	0.029 (0.045)	−0.010 (0.046)
Leftist political identification	0.118** (0.012)	−0.009 (0.018)	0.126* (0.039)	0.071 (0.039)	0.095* (0.040)
Female	−0.040** (0.010)	−0.144** (0.014)	−0.059* (0.030)	−0.040 (0.030)	−0.051 (0.030)
Low level education	0.178** (0.011)	−0.036* (0.016)	0.026 (0.036)	0.116* (0.036)	0.085* (0.036)
High level education	0.000 (0.012)	0.236** (0.017)	0.013 (0.038)	−0.054 (0.039)	−0.090* (0.039)
Low level income	−0.006 (0.011)	−0.256** (0.016)	0.219** (0.048)	0.109* (0.033)	0.038 (0.033)
High level income	−0.014 (0.015)	0.009 (0.021)	−0.070 (0.048)	−0.219** (0.049)	−0.220** (0.049)
Constant	−0.927** (0.016)	−0.621** (0.023)	−0.506** (0.050)	−0.449** (0.050)	−0.529** (0.051)
Pseudo R2	0.015	0.040	0.019	0.014	0.011
N =	118,368	42,069	7,977	7,969	7,991

Source: World Values Survey (1981–2008).

with older people. We also see these effects more clearly in recent decades, as expected. This chapter provides evidence that more recent generations of young adults are more likely to identify as global citizens than with past generations.

The evidence provided by this analysis is quite important for global citizenship scholarship. We know a lot about the best practices for teaching global citizenship, and a few scholars have considered global citizenship and related attitudes on a small scale – but this is one of the first studies to analyse quantitative data on age and global citizenship attitudes with large-scale questionnaires like the WVS. We now have evidence for what many have been assuming all along: the young people of recent decades are more globally aware than older generations. This is exciting news for those who teach global citizenship and for those looking to employ First Globals in the twenty-first century. With many young people gaining a solid foundation in knowledge of global concerns and global citizenship, it is likely that this generation of Millennials will likely enjoy increased opportunities to work with and understand diverse groups of people and continue to connect with people from all over the world throughout their lives.

The contribution of this chapter is an important first step for empirical work that uses quantitative research to answer global citizenship questions. Studies like this complement the qualitative work asking similar questions as with the Myers (2010) study. Yet, it is important to note this chapter's limitations. This chapter does not adequately account for the very different social and cultural contexts that shape each respondent's views. Comparativists will have better ideas about how to compare respondents within various government systems and cultural settings. Also, definitions of citizenship will often differ based on the type of government and/or culture that one experiences (Haste and Hogan 2006; Kennedy et al. 2008). The current analysis provides a solid foundation for further research in this area, but scholars interested in global citizenship can add to this exploratory work and address these remaining concerns.

In conclusion, the findings discussed in this chapter provide good news for people who care deeply about the practice of global citizenship. A persistent theme taken from the Zogby polling results, discussed earlier in this chapter, is the role of sacrifice involved with global citizenship (Sanders 2012). First Globals do not only identify as global citizens or know about global issues, they are also engaged and active. Practising global citizenship ultimately includes participation in those issues and with those people in far-off places (Schattle 2008). First Globals, with their increasing global identity and awareness, may well have the potential to socialize a second and maybe a third generation of globals with unparalleled interconnectivity.

Notes

1 There are many ways social scientists define young adulthood. Age 18 is often used as the lower boundary because it marks legal adulthood across many different

nations. The upper bound usually falls between 24 or 29. I use the cut-off of 25 as a more exclusive, and thus, conservative measure of young adulthood.
2 Various features of this conception of global citizenship and its measurement are discussed in further detail in the measurement section of the chapter.
3 But not limited to only those who attend college (Arnett 1997, 2000).
4 When using categorical measurements, it is necessary to omit one category from the analysis and designate it as the comparison group. This is what I do here, leaving out the middle-aged adults, ranging from age 26 to 49.
5 This chapter does not include data from the most recent WVS wave in order to keep question wording for my main dependent variable consistent. The most recent wave uses updated question wording. I briefly discuss the updated measure in the discussion section for this chapter, but other chapters in this volume discuss it at length.
6 However, not every nation is represented in every wave of questioning.

References

Arnett, Jeffrey Jensen. 1997. "Young People's Conceptions of the Transition to Adulthood". *Youth & Society* 29(1): 3–23.
Arnett, Jeffrey Jensen. 2000. "Emerging Adulthood: A Theory of Development from the Late Teens Through the Twenties". *American Psychologist* 55(5): 469–480. Doi: 10.1037/0003–066X.55.5.469.
Dower, Nigel and John Williams. 2002. *Global Citizenship: A Critical Introduction*. New York: Routledge.
Falk, Richard. 1993. "The Making of Global Citizenship". In *Global Visions: Beyond the New World Order*. Boston, MA: South End Press, pp. 39–50.
Finlay, Andrea, Laura Wray-Lake, and Constance A. Flanagan. 2010. "Civic Engagement During the Transition to Adulthood: Developmental Opportunities and Social Policies at a Critical Juncture". In *Handbook of Research on Civic Engagement in Youth*. Hoboken, NJ: Wiley, pp. 277–305.
Flanagan, Constance A., Bernadette Campbell, Luba Botcheva, Jennifer Bowes, Beno Csapo, Petr Macek, and Elena Sheblanova. 2003. "Social Class and Adolescents' Beliefs About Justice in Different Social Orders". *Journal of Social Issues* 59(4): 711–732.
Furia, Peter A. 2005. "Global Citizenship, Anyone? Cosmopolitanism, Privilege and Public Opinion". *Global Society* 19(4): 331–359.
Greenstein, Fred I. 1970. "A Note on the Ambiguity of 'Political Socialization': Definitions, Criticisms, and Strategies of Inquiry". *Journal of Politics* 32(4): 969–978.
Haste, Helen and Amy Hogan. 2006. "Beyond Conventional Civic Participation, Beyond the Moral-Political Divide: Young People and Contemporary Debates About Citizenship". *Journal of Moral Education* 35(4): 473–493.
Hicks, David. 2003. "Thirty Years of Global Education: A Reminder of Key Principles and Precedents". *Educational Review* 55(3): 265–275.
Jelin, Elizabeth. 2000. "Towards a Global Environmental Citizenship?". *Citizenship Studies* 4(1): 47–63.
Jennings, M. Kent. 1989. "The Crystallization of Orientations". In *Continuities in Political Action: A Longitudinal Study of Political Orientations in Three Western Democracies*. Boston, MA: Walter de Gruyter Studies on North America, pp. 313–348.

Kennedy, Kerry J., Carole L. Hahn, and Wing-on Lee. 2008. "Constructing Citizenship: Comparing the Views of Students in Australia, Hong Kong, and the United States". *Comparative Education Review* 52(1): 53–91.

Kratochwil, Friedrich. 1996. "Citizenship: On the Border of Order". In *The Return of Culture and Identity in IR Theory*. Boulder, CO: Lynne Rienner, pp. 181–197.

Lister, Ruth, Noel Smith, Sue Middleton, and Lynne Cox. 2003. "Young People Talk About Citizenship: Empirical Perspectives on Theoretical and Political Debates". *Citizenship Studies* 7(2): 235–253.

Myers, John P. 2010. "'To Benefit the World by Whatever Means Possible': Adolescents' Constructed Meanings for Global Citizenship". *British Educational Research Journal* 36(3): 483–502.

Sanders, Sam. 2012. "'Globals' Generation Focuses on Experience". *NPR.org*. 10 July. Available at: www.npr.org/2012/07/10/156463825/globals-generation-focuses-on-experience.

Schattle, Hans. 2008. *The Practices of Global Citizenship*. Lanham, MD: Rowman & Littlefield.

Shorter, John. 1993. "Psychology and Citizenship: Identity and Belonging". In *Citizenship and Social Theory*. London: Sage, pp. 115–138.

Turner, Bryan S. 1993. "Contemporary Problems in the Theory of Citizenship". In *Citizenship and Social Theory*. London: Sage, pp. 1–18.

United Nations. 2013. "United Nations Millennium Development Goals". 28 June. Available at: www.un.org/millenniumgoals.

Watkins, S. Craig. 2010. *The Young and the Digital: What the Migration to Social Network Sites, Games, and Anytime, Anywhere Media Means for Our Future*. Boston, MA: Beacon Press.

World Values Survey Association. 2009. *World Values Survey 1981–2008 Official Aggregate v.20090901*. Available at: www.worldvaluessurvey.org; www.wvsevsdb.com/wvs/WVSData.jsp?Idioma=I.

Zogby, John. 2008. *The Way We'll Be: The Zogby Report on the Transformation of the American Dream*. New York: Random House Digital.

Zogby, John and Joan Snyder Kuhl. 2013. *First Globals Understanding, Managing, & Unleashing the Potential of Our Millennial Generation*. John Zogby & Joan Snyder Kuhl.

14 Global citizenship in the Middle East
Presence and prospects

Vaughn P. Shannon

Any consideration of global citizenship necessitates assessing its prospects in different parts of the world. Globalization and cosmopolitanism, forces emanating substantially from the West, need to be considered in terms of how they are perceived and received in non-Western parts of the world. For this reason, this volume includes chapters focused on the regional impact of globalization and global citizenship, including this one that addresses the problem of identity and prospects of global citizenship in the Middle East.

This chapter shows empirically that cosmopolitanism is not a widespread feature of the Middle East's cultural terrain. I argue this is the case for two chief reasons: (1) the multiplicity of competing identities in the region vying for loyalty; and (2) the perceived Western nature of cosmopolitanism, fraught with the legacy of Western intervention in the region. Not unique to the Middle East, all regions have a menu and multiplicity of identities: ethnic, religious, and national, among others. In the Middle East, ethnic identities – Arab, Persian, Turk, and Kurd – as well as religious identifications – Sunni Muslim, Shi'a Muslim, Druze, Alawite, and Coptic Christian, among others – define many people's sense of Self. Some of these identities have transnational variants, so that one may count as their in-group "all Arabs" (pan-Arabism) or "all Muslims" (pan-Islam). Add to the mix national identities that are not based on ethnicity or religion, such as "Egypt First". Add still the subnational, patrilineal loyalties of family and kinship, and it seems the stage is crowded with loci for loyalty and political mobilization.

To the extent that global citizenship exists in that crowded cultural terrain, it can coexist with or challenge these other, local identities. One can possess multiple identities and still accommodate a pluralist, multicultural sense of belonging. Global citizenship is not inherently incompatible with local identities. So the second matter is really the more important one: how is global, cosmopolitan identity perceived in the Middle East? If it is seen as yet another form of Western penetration and cultural imperialism, an "imported" ideology threatening local identity, it may not be a popular choice and may even be seen as a symbolic threat.

My analysis presents secondary data of public opinion from the World Values Survey (WVS) and Zogby International surveys in various countries of the Middle East. The data show what has been found elsewhere (see Chapter 12 in this volume), that the Middle East is seemingly not as cosmopolitan as other parts of the world. This chapter seeks to appraise why this may be the case. It will review Middle East and broader non-Western perspectives on cosmopolitanism, as well as provide an assessment of competing Middle East identities. The focus on identity, from a subjectivist viewpoint, necessitates a discussion of psychological aspects of us/them dynamics and the prospects for changing boundaries of us/them in Middle East identity politics.

Globalization, cosmopolitanism, and identity

As discussed in previous chapters, globalization is a set of economic, technological, and cultural forces removing barriers across traditional borders. Its link to cosmopolitanism is a theme of this book and is tied to the question of identity: does the technology and interconnectedness of the world change how people view themselves and others? Globalization brings people together and exposes us to them, but whether this definitively challenges the Westphalian state in terms of identity is questionable, as is whether this increasing contact has the capacity to promote a positive "we" identity.

Both cosmopolitanism and global citizenship introduce new and complex questions about identity. Scholarly approaches to identity tend in one of two directions: they are either essentialist, fixed, and assigned, or subjectivist and thus open to situational and temporal fluidity of various degrees. Hanley (2008, 1360) argues that Middle Eastern identities are usually treated as fixed and absolute in the literature, and there is evidence of that. Lewis (1998, 6–7), for example, argues that primary identities in the Middle East are "those acquired at birth" – referring to the "involuntary identity" of blood and religion or the "compulsory identity of the state".[1] Most famously, Huntington (1996) declared a "clash of civilizations" emerging between the "West" and an "Islamic civilization" that he argues rejects "Western culture".

Despite the presence of naturalized and homogenized treatments of identity in some works, the broad scholarly consensus is that identity is to a large degree socially constructed. By taking a subjectivist approach, in which "imagined communities" are ultimately potentially mutable, we can conclude that cosmopolitanism is an identity that can vary in adherents, as well as an identity that can be perceived positively or negatively in different circumstances. To say that cosmopolitan identity can exist in the Middle East does not mean it is inevitable. Its arguments and arguers must have legitimacy and resonate with the region's inhabitants and in competition with other existing narratives of ethnic, religious, nationalist, and kinship affiliation. Whether one participates in a given identity is one question; what priority they give to one over another is an important second consideration. Views of loyalty and in-group identity, as well as views of out-group Others, are shaped by circumstances, history, and the framing and persuasion of elites and media channels.

One question to consider is which elites and which ideas about cosmopolitanism are persuasive and under what circumstances. Broadly, we can distinguish cosmopolitan optimists and pessimists. Yunker (2000, 204) disputes the conventional wisdom that world government is impossible given "too many nations, ideologies, religions, languages". He (ibid., 28–29) envisions "a convergence within global human society" involving the need for changes in "psychological attitudes" towards "supranational patriotism". He acknowledges "inertial forces" to such change by existing political leaders as well as the "general public" (ibid., 214–216), which begs the question of how to overcome political forces against supranational identities. It also indicates the relevance and virtue of paying attention to public opinion about identities and perceptions of cosmopolitanism in the Middle East, which we will do below.

Other optimists for Middle East cosmopolitanism include Holton (2009, 43), who notes cosmopolitan predispositions and practices are not inherently Western nor do they require supranational identity but include the ability to appreciate aspects of "the Other". While his analysis suggests that Cairo "depended for their cosmopolitanism solely on the impact of Western socio-cultural institutions", he warns against treating the cosmopolitanism of nineteenth- and twentieth-century Middle East cities "during the epoch of colonization and western power" as "simple cultural imperialism" (ibid., 46). Schattle (2008, 28–47) also advocates that, rather than displace other identities and traditions, the hope is for "cosmopolitan citizens ... capable of mediating between national traditions, communities of fate and alternative styles of life".

Overcoming communal discord can be a daunting task not just because of state sovereignty but also because of the menu of identities defining contemporary relations and the histories of jealousy and pain behind many of them. Critics focus on the "cultural invasion" of the West as a threat to various traditions and identities while advocates hope to allow the Arab world "flourish" under a "universal culture in which Arabs may come under its umbrella as equals" (Moussalli 2003; Kinnvall and Nesbitt-Larking 2011, 1). Jabri (2011, 640–641) concludes that "liberal cosmopolitan discourses and practices constitute modes of dispossession ... of history, territory, the right of access to the international and political subjectivity itself". Hanley (2008, 1351–1357), for example, refers to the "contrived nostalgia of cosmopolitanism as a European, Eurocentric, elitist, racist, essentially exclusionary, quasi-colonial form that nurtures a myth of open tolerance in contrast to rabid nationalism". Western analyses like Benjamin Barber's 1996 *Jihad vs. McWorld* and Franklin Foer's (2004, 198) *How Soccer Explains the World: An Unlikely Theory of Globalization*, exemplify cases of backlash of traditionalism and a resurgent defence of identity, leaving cosmopolitanism an "illusion".

Nevertheless, as Furia (2005) and the optimists point out, cosmopolitanism is not merely the bastion of Western intellectuals but has broader – if sparse – roots globally. The issue is how many people share some version of cosmopolitan identity, however defined or realized, and compared to what? In this chapter, we present and discuss the empirical, subjective perceptions of people's identities in the Middle East. Specifically, I will explore to what degree people in the Middle East have a cosmopolitan identity and whether they are more likely to prioritize particular local, national, ethnic, or religious identities. I then analyse the results and give attention to psychological theories about how to change the identity conundrum of Middle East cosmopolitanism.

Cosmopolitanism and identity in the Middle East

The following section presents descriptive statistics of survey data collected from the WVS and from Zogby International (Telhami 2008). Together they show cross-national and longitudinal views of important aspects of Middle East identity, including the relative presence or absence of a cosmopolitan identity. Beyond self-reported identity, they reveal which identities matter more in terms of rank.

So what can we say about the presence and prospects of true cosmopolitanism in the Middle East? The WVS asks two different items at different times germane to our topic: "I consider myself a citizen of the world" and "To which of these geographical groups would you say you belong first of all? And the next? And which do you belong to least of all?"

In the 2005–2009 the WVS of certain Middle East countries (Jordan, Morocco, and Egypt), 55.1 per cent of Middle East respondents agreed with the statement "I see myself as a world citizen" (see Table 14.1). Jordanians were higher on the agreement (67.3 per cent), Egyptians next (56.2 per cent), and Moroccans lowest (39.8 per cent). While many respondents agreed with the statement of global citizenship, the number is far below the overall global survey, which as reported elsewhere (see Chapter 12 in this volume) averaged 78 per cent from 1999 to 2002.

Given the multiplicity of identities that we have discussed, prospects of cosmopolitanism are more realistically appraised by the WVS question that asks to which geographical group do you belong *first*. In the results of the 2000–2004 survey, sampling Middle East countries – Algeria, Iran, Iraq,

Table 14.1 Those who 'see myself as a world citizen' (%)

	Total	Jordan	Morocco	Egypt
Strongly agree	26.3	34.1	14.0	28.0
Agree	28.8	33.2	25.8	28.2
Disagree	22.2	13.9	26.3	23.9
Strongly disagree	17.6	12.9	19.9	18.5
N	5,451	1,200	1,200	3,051

Source: World Values Survey 2005–2009.

Global citizenship in the Middle East 213

Jordan, Saudi Arabia, and Egypt – the percentages who answered "the world" were 3.6 per cent (Algeria), 5.3 per cent (Iran), 0.7 per cent (Iraq), 5.0 per cent (Saudi Arabia), and .9 per cent (Egypt). This compares to a positive response rate of 19.1 per cent of US respondents in the same survey, and 7.5 per cent in the overall 1981–2004 analysis of all countries reported in Chapter 2 of this volume (quite the outlier, and worth exploring, was Jordan's 45.3 per cent response).

Outside of Jordan, the identities that respondents felt were "first" and most prevalent were those of country and locality (see Table 14.2). Majorities of Algerians and Iraqis put country first, and it was the number one category for Iran, Egypt, and Saudi Arabia, speaking to the surprising power of nationalism in the Middle East.

A related line of questioning about priority identity comes from a Zogby International poll (Telhami 2008) conducted 2003–07 in Egypt, Jordan, Lebanon, Morocco, the Kingdom of Saudi Arabia (KSA), and United Arab Emirates (UAE). Respondents were also asked "When you think about yourself, which of the following is your most important and second most important identity: As a citizen of your country, as an Arab, as a Muslim (or Christian), or as a citizen of the world (cosmopolitan)"? As shown in Table 14.3, 44 per cent of respondents cited country citizenship as their most important identity, 31 per cent cited religion, just under 20 per cent claimed Arab identity as most important, and only 4.8 per cent cited the primary importance of being a "citizen of the world". Less than 9 per cent of respondents cited "citizen of the world" as even their second most important identity, far behind Arab identity (49 per cent), religion (24.7 per cent), and citizenship (16.5 per cent).

These results show clearly that global citizenship is taking a back seat in most Middle East respondents' self-definitions, which is evidence of the lack of cosmopolitanism in the region. But just because identities have been ranked does not mean one could not support policies that support world, not just local, priorities. The Zogby surveys allow an investigation into the percentage of respondents' wishes for government priorities in policymaking.

Table 14.2 Responding to which geographic group they belong to first (%)

	Algeria	*Iran*	*Iraq*	*Jordan*	*Saudi Arabia*	*Egypt*
Locality	27.7	32.0	21.4	9.5	21.4	35.4
Region	5.9	6.8	12.7	18.1	15.4	10.6
Country	55.1	49.5	58.8	4.1	48.3	44.8
Continent	6.2	1.1	4.9	21.7	8.3	8.1
The world	3.6	5.3	0.7	45.3	5.0	0.9
Don't know	1.1	1.5	2.5	0.6	1.3	0.6
N	1,282	2,532	2,325	1,223	1,502	3,000

Source: World Values Survey 2000–2004.

Table 14.3 Responding to "which is your most important identity"

	Most important		Second most important	
	N	%	N	%
Citizen of your country	1791	44.3	669	16.5
As an Arab	789	19.5	1993	49.3
Religion	1261	31.2	1001	24.7
Citizen of the world	196	4.8	361	8.9

Source: Zogby International, "Annual Arab Public Opinion Poll" 2008.

Asked "When your government makes decisions, do you think it should base its decisions mostly on what is best for your country, for Arabs, for Muslims, or for the world as a whole?", the results are revealing. Just under 42 per cent of respondents answered that governments should base decisions on what is best for "your country", compared to only 8.9 per cent answering "for the world as a whole". The response that government should base decisions on what is "best for Arabs" was the second-highest response rate, at 26.7 per cent, followed by what is "best for Muslims" (21.7 per cent).

Analysis

Why does cosmopolitanism fare poorly relative to family, state, Arabism, and Islam as a locus of identity? First, we can acknowledge the limits of the survey questions themselves, which do not permit respondents to select multiple identities but are forced to rank. But to the extent that these forced choices relegate global identity to lower priorities, the first broad reason for the dearth of cosmopolitanism in the Middle East is the vast array of competing identities crowding the cultural terrain, with much longer histories, indigenous roots, and local legitimacy. Given that all regions have multiple identities, and such diversities do not inherently pose competition and conflict, the second reason for cosmopolitanism's shallow roots relates to the legacy of globalization, modernization, and cosmopolitanism in the era of Western political and military dominance after the First World War. We address each factor in turn below.

A multiplicity of identities

Short of cosmopolitanism, the identity levels vary in degrees of inclusion: from family to clan or tribe, to ethnic and religious identity groups, national state identity, regional identity, and transnational collectivities such as the "Non-Aligned", defined in opposition to Western/imperial domination and Cold War politics.

The kinship level, some argue, is perhaps the oldest and most fundamental. Khoury and Kostiner (1991, 5, 8–9), defining tribes as "a localized group in which kinship is the dominant idiom of organization, and whose members consider themselves culturally distinct", point to the longstanding institutions of chiefdoms as the traditional source of both moral authority and the "continuous flow" of goods and services to tribal members bound together by "a common identity based on kinship". Gellner (1991, 109–110) elaborates on the institutions of the "Middle Eastern tribal quasi-state" as a source for resolving feuds and providing order and leadership through mostly patrilineal lines.

The nation state, on the other hand, was "not only new but also foreign to the civilizational area known as the Muslim world" (Tibi 1991, 127). The development of territorial states based on "citizenship" rather than kinship has been seen to be problematic in the Middle East, particularly given the colonial roots of many states and borders in the Sykes–Picot tradition that emerged from the First World War. Nonetheless, nation states represent another source of loyalty and allegiance, and some states have evolved independently over the past several centuries fostering national identity, such as Egypt and Iran.

Religious identity constitutes another locus of identity and loyalty. The Middle East as the "cradle of monotheism" hosts the origins of Islam, Christianity, and Judaism. Christian Orthodox, Coptic, Maronite, and Assyrian Christians form pockets in various countries. Sunni Islam represents some 85 per cent of the region, while Shi'a Islam makes up another 10 to 15 per cent. Beyond the three major religions, there are other minority religions, such as Zoroastrians in Iran. In any religion, there are also degrees of "fundamentalism" from conservative to liberal to secular, so that religious identity may or may not alone speak to the possibility of cosmopolitanism.

Contrary to Lewis's (1998, 30) claim that "for most of the recorded history of most of the Muslim world, the primary and basic definition of identity ... is religion", Eickelman (1989, 11) reminds us, "most people in the Middle East are Muslim, but this fact alone has not always provided a basis for common sentiment and identity". Ethno-nationalism, the idea of providing an independent state to a particularly ethno-linguistic group, represents another level of identity. Ethnicity in the Middle East includes Turkic, Semitic (Arabic and Hebrew), Persian, and Kurdish. Lawson (2006) points to nationalist movements pre-dating European "exports" during the First World War, when the British sought to foster an "Arab revolt" against the Ottoman Turks. Jewish nationalism from Europe fostered the Zionist migration to Ottoman Palestine, where Palestinian and Arab nationalism lay waiting as well.

While many define their in-group narrowly in terms of family, clan, nation, ethnicity, or religious affiliation, or possess multiple identities with differing affinity and salience, what about those who transcend particularism? Two other regional identity trends that embrace a universalizing identity on their own terms are pan-Arabism and pan-Islam. Uniting the region or world under a singular vision with Arabism or Islam at the centre, these two movements leave open questions of the status of minorities under such a framework.

The notion of the Islamic *umma* or "community of believers" as a transnational community of Islam is one such identity (Ezzat 2011). Alavi (2015) points to the 1857 mutiny rebellion in British India as the source of the spread of Islamic cosmopolitan thinkers, who envision pan-Islamic civilization in transnational terms. With the rise of European dominance, Lawrence (2009, 158) posits that the ideology of empire and colonization shaped "Islamicate" civilization, putting the Muslim world on the defensive as the "Other" on the receiving end of the "Civilizing mission". Roy (2004, ix) analyses those whose response to globalization and westernization is to "distance from a given culture and stress belonging to a universal *umma*".

The tendency in civilizational analysis can trend towards essentialism and stress the conflict between Islam and the West (see, for example, Huntington 1996). Kinnvall and Nesbitt-Larking (2011, 2) warn that civilizational discourses essentializing identity in oppositions such as the "West against the rest", have increased Western ethnocentrism towards minority Muslim populations. Salvatore (2007) advocates the Islamic *umma* as an identity to replace the secular and Western version of cosmopolitanism, pointing to the view that Islam can be a transnational, tolerant organizing principle. Yunker (2000, 15) notes that Christians and Muslims have warred in the past, but argues that "at this point ... the vast majority of people ... proclaim in favor of religious toleration", though conceding that "within every major religion today there still exists a minority of extremists who are ready, willing, able ... to strike down infidels".

Yet again, we come back to the fundamental point that the diversity of religions, and identity in general, is not inherently competitive and conflictual. Coexistence and toleration of "Other" is a possibility, and the vision inherent in "emergent cosmopolitanism", which creates 'space for localisms'" rather than "wishing away national and local solidarities" (Mirsepassi and Fernee 2014, 204). The ultimate questions, then, are whether: (1) local identities perceive Out-group Others as threats or not; and (2) whether cosmopolitanism is pluralist and inclusive, or imposed and exclusivist. These are no doubt dialectically related questions to some degree.

Inclusive identities and forms of cosmopolitanism

Regarding local identities, key questions include who politicizes religion, or religious identity, and towards what end? Religion can be tied to political agendas in various ways. Gellner (1991, 117–119) points to the ability of tribal formations to fuse religion into what he calls "faith-linked chiefaincy", by which tribal leaders legitimate rule with "hereditary saints" and religious advisers, which – if successful – allows religion to "endow one leader with sufficient legitimacy" to overcome tribalism in order to set up the makings of a state. Armstrong (2000, xiii) identifies Christian, Jewish, and Muslim fundamentalisms (for lack of a better term, she concedes) as the "embattled forms of spirituality" who feel threatened by globalization, modernization, and secularization, as they seek to "resacralize" their worlds. Mirsepassi and Fernee (2014, 206) lament fringe groups like Al Qaeda, whose apocalyptic ideology and violent practices threaten democratic and cosmopolitan hopes "for Muslims and non-Muslims".

Just as the so-called Islamic State or 9/11 can set back cosmopolitanism, so too can cosmopolitanism be advanced in more or less healthy ways. Mirsepassi and Fernee (ibid.) note that cosmopolitanism "stands between two ideals": global human understanding with peaceful transcultural coexistence, and a "West-centrist mission" they say is found in US military practice behind the "messianic" and "neoconservative, ideological revolution". More broadly, the modernist impulse to bring the "third world" into "modern times" often meant adopting Western modes of secular rationalism, counting on "localisms" to "yield" to this definition of "progress" (ibid., 204). Such a call for the passing of traditional society fed cultural backlashes in some quarters, especially as the globalizing trends of modernization coincided with Western political and military intrusion into the post-Ottoman Middle East.

Conclusion

How, then, can cosmopolitanism succeed in the Middle East? For those seeking to promote cosmopolitan identity, particularly in areas like the Middle East with a light footprint and substantial ideational obstacles, the question for the future may be: "can ... the creation of a superordinate identity overcome powerful ethnic and racial categorizations on more than a temporary basis?" (Gaertner and Dovidio 2000, 68). Studies show that some forms of identity are more difficult to change than others (McCauley 2014, 804).

But Gaertner and Dovidio (2000, 40–48) remind us that reducing intergroup bias is possible without requiring "each group to forsake its less inclusive group identity completely". That is, the multiple, local identities need not give way to supranational identity, only that toleration of the Other be promoted and accepted. Tilly (2002, 207, 209) notes, "identity claims and their attendant stories constitute serious political business", requiring political entrepreneurs to "create we–they boundaries and manoeuvre to suppress competing models". Tilly (2002, 10–12) argues that the boundary construction of "us and them" is a crucial and social aspect of identity, depending on the adoption and modification of shared stories about the boundary – as when "leaders of two ethnic factions compete for recognition as valid interlocutors for their ethnic category". While this usefully focuses us on the role of political entrepreneurs and on the malleability of identity, it downplays the psychological-level variables affecting identity and does not help us understand which stories or narratives will be persuasive.

Psychological studies long have shown people possess multiple identities and that one or another can be situationally activated by events or prompting. The salience of a social identity can promote a shared group interest, related to greater cooperation with in-group members (Katzarska-Miller *et al.*

2012, 167). Gaertner and Dovidio (2000, 36–37) note that when social identity is activated, "people perceive themselves as interchangeable exemplars of a social category" whose collective needs, goals, and standards are primary. But *apropos* of cosmopolitanism, Allport (1954, 43–44) declared "The clash between the idea of race and of One World ... is shaping into an issue that may well be the most decisive in human history". When people are categorized into different groups, those differences "become exaggerated for members of a different social category" (Gaertner and Dovidio 2000, 34).

Activating one's in-group identification results in a heightened tendency to become protective of the group's culture and values and any perceived threat to the group's symbolic resources may result in prejudice towards out-groups (Bloom *et al.* 2015, 204). Ben-Nun Bloom et al. (2015) found that a sample of Catholics, Muslims, and Jews in the West opposed immigration by those seen as religiously different, while showing positive feelings and compassion towards immigrants perceived as being similar to group members' religions.

Fostering cosmopolitanism, then, requires overcoming histories of distrust and power inequalities and either build a new sense of "in-group" in a world of multiple identities, or build tolerance and empathy towards "out-groups". Erskine (2008) argues persuasively for the need and duty to treat the "strangers" and even "enemies" with respect and rights. As the so-called Islamic State has shown since 2014, not all groups share this view of treatment of the "Other". How can positive, tolerant relations be built among out-groups, to facilitate cosmopolitanism?

Norris and Inglehart (2009, 31) suggest that the persuasiveness of outside messages, such as Western appeals for cosmopolitanism, would be a function of media freedom and access to mass communications resources, but also differing moral codes and mistrust of outsiders. Messages about cosmopolitanism from the West may face cultural obstacles but also issues of trust. If "we-group" feelings and message credibility requires trust and empathy, the mechanisms for trust and empathy are several, including: "ideally, equality of power structures"; time for people to prove their trustworthiness; reciprocity; not passing judgment in initial encounters; perspective-taking ("imaginative placement of oneself in the shoes of the other"); and meeting expectations established by the normative order (Weber and Carter 2003, 22–52). The violation of such expectations constitutes a ripe cause for distrust, requiring efforts at apology and reconciliation. Given this inventory, in the context of the Middle East, trust and identity change may come slowly and with conscious effort from both sides.

The answer, to some, is reciprocal, democratic, cross-cultural dialogue in building a world together. Hazenberg's (2015, 296) position, derived from Kant, is that for moral cosmopolitan principles to be integrated into the world, "structural conditions must become similar for all persons in the world, so that each can come to recognize that the moral–political obligations each has to each other are equal and reciprocal". In terms of Middle East receptivity to cosmo politanism, Mirsepassi and Fernee (2014, 4) argue for pluralist, democratic ideals to promote "a multisided conception of universality", rejecting "a homogeneous and tacitly Eurocentric world historical temporality". Kinnvall and Nesbitt-Larking (2011, 92) advocate "engagement across communities that resist fundamentalisms and securitizing ideologies of race, faith, nation, and gender". To counter negative images and narratives of real or imaginary others, Kinnvall and Nesbitt-Larking (2011) further advocate narratives, voice, and agency to express identity in dialogue with others in a multicultural context. Whether that context can be nurtured in the Middle East and in Western societies, in an age of a "War on Terror" and violent extremists from Al Qaeda to ISIS, remains to be seen.

Note

1 These, he contrasts, with the "influence of the West" in bringing the option of "freely chosen cohesion and loyalty of voluntary associations" (Lewis 1998, 7).

References

Alavi, Seema. 2015. *Muslim Cosmopolitanism in the Age of Empire*. Cambridge, MA: Harvard University Press.
Allport, Gordon. 1954. *The Nature of Prejudice*. Reading, MA: Addison-Wesley.
Armstrong, Karen. 2000. *The Battle for God*. New York: Ballantine Books.
Barber, Benjamin. 1996. *Jihad v. McWorld: Terrorism's Challenge to Democracy*. New York: Ballantine Books.
Ben-Nun Bloom, Pazit, Gizem Arikan, and Marie Courtemanche. 2015. "Religious Social Identity, Religious Belief, and Anti-Immigration Sentiment". *American Political Science Review* 109(2): 203–221.
Eickelman, Daniel. 1989. *The Middle East: An Anthropological Approach*. 2nd Edn. Englewood Cliffs, NJ: Prentice Hall.
Erskine, Toni. 2008. *Embedded Cosmopolitanism: Duties to Strangers and Enemies in a World of "Dislocated Communities"*. Oxford: Oxford University Press.
Ezzat, Heba Raouf. 2011. "The Umma: From Global Civil Society to Global Public Sphere". In Denisa Kostovicova and Marlies Glasius (eds), *Bottom-Up Politics: An Agency-Centred Approach to Globalization*. London and New York: Palgrave Macmillan, pp. 40–49.
Foer, Franklin. 2004. *How Soccer Explains the World: An Unlikely Theory of Globalization*. New York: Harper Collins.
Furia, Peter. 2005. "Global Citizenship, Anyone? Cosmopolitanism, Privilege and Public Opinion". *Global Studies* 19(4): 331–359.
Gaertner, Samuel and John Dovidio. 2000. *Reducing Intergroup Bias: The Common Ingroup Identity Model*. Philadelphia, PA: Psychology Press.
Gellner, Ernest. 1991. "Tribalism and the State in the Middle East". In P. Khoury and J. Kostiner (eds), *Tribes and State Formation in the Middle East*. Berkeley, CA: University of California Press, pp. 109–126.
Hanley, Will. 2008. "Grieving Cosmopolitanism in Middle East Studies". *History Compass* 6(5): 1346–1367.

Hazenberg, Haye. 2015. "The Legitimacy of the Global Order". *International Theory* 7(2): 294–329.
Holton, Robert. 2009. *Cosmopolitanisms: New Thinking and New Directions*. London and New York: Palgrave Macmillan.
Huntington, Samuel. 1996. *The Clash of Civilizations and the Remaking of World Order*. New York: Simon & Schuster.
Jabri, Vivienne. 2011. "Cosmopolitan Politics, Security, Political Subjectivity". *European Journal of International Relations* 18(4): 625–644.
Katzarska-Miller, Iva, Stephen Reysen, Shanmukh Kamble, and Nandini Vithoji. 2012. "Cross-National Differences in Global Citizenship: Comparison of Bulgaria, India and the United States". *Journal of Globalization Studies* 3(2): 166–183.
Khoury, Philip and Joseph Kostiner. 1991. "Introduction: Tribes and the Complexities of State Formation in the Middle East". In P. Khoury and J. Kostiner (eds), *Tribes and State Formation in the Middle East*. Berkeley, CA: University of California Press, pp. 1–20.
Kinnvall, Catarina and Paul Nesbitt-Larking. 2011. *The Political Psychology of Globalization: Muslims in the West*. Oxford: Oxford University Press.
Lawrence, Bruce. 2009. "Islam in Afro-Eurasia: A Bridge Civilization". In Peter Katzenstein (ed.), *Civilizations in World Politics: Plural and Pluralist Perspectives*. London and New York: Routledge, pp. 157–175.
Lawson, Fred. 2006. *Constructing International Relations in the Arab World*. Stanford, CA: Stanford University Press.
Lewis, Bernard. 1998. *The Multiple Identities of the Middle East*. New York: Schocken.
McCauley, John. 2014. "The Political Mobilization of Ethnic and Religious Identities in Africa". *American Political Science Review* 108(4): 801–816.
Mirsepassi, Ali and Tadd Graham Fernee. 2014. *Islam, Democracy, and Cosmopolitanism: At Home and in the World*. Cambridge: Cambridge University Press.
Moussalli, Mohammad. 2003. "Impact of Globalization". *Daily Star*. 25 August. Available at: www.dailystar.com.lb/Opinion/Commentary/2003/Aug-25/103861-impact-of-globalization.ashx.
Norris, Pippa and Ronald Inglehart. 2009. *Cosmopolitan Communications: Cultural Diversity in a Globalized World*. Cambridge: Cambridge University Press.
Roy, Olivier. 2004. *Globalized Islam: The Search for a New Umma*. New York: Columbia University Press.
Salvatore, Armando. 2007. "The Exit from a Westphalian Framing of Political Space and the Emergence of a Transnational Islamic Public". *Theory, Culture, and Society* 24(4): 45–52.
Schattle, Hans. 2008. *The Practices of Global Citizenship*. Lanham, MD: Rowman & Littlefield.
Telhami, Shibley. 2008. "Annual Arab Public Opinion Poll". Available at: http://sadat.umd.edu/new per cent20surveys/surveys.htm (accessed 17 October 2015).
Tibi, Bassam. 1991. "The Simultaneity of the Unsimultaneous: Old Tribes and Imposed Nation-States in the Modern Middle East". In P. Khoury and J. Kostiner (eds), *Tribes and State Formation in the Middle East*. Berkeley, CA: University of California Press, pp. 127–152.
Tilly, Charles. 2002. *Stories, Identities, and Political Change*. Lanham, MD: Rowman & Littlefield.

Weber, Linda, and Allison Carter. 2003. *The Social Construction of Trust*. New York: Kluwer Academic/Plenum.
World Values Survey. Available at: www.worldvaluessurvey.org/WVSOnline.jsp; Spss data longitudinal download: www.worldvaluessurvey.org/WVSDocumentationWVL.jsp.
Yunker, James. 2000. *The Grand Convergence: Economic and Political Aspects of Human Progress*. London and New York: Palgrave Macmillan.

15 China and the world

Convergence on global governance, divergence on global citizenship?

Johan Lagerkvist

The slogan of the 2008 Beijing Summer Olympics, "one world, one dream", offered the abstract promise of a global community of peoples, overshadowing their nation state belongings. Yet in the months prior to the Games violent protests in Lhasa evidenced again that, when national Chinese citizenship becomes challenged by ethnic minorities such as Tibetans, the Han Chinese population tends to unite as a whole. Under the leadership of the Chinese Communist Party, China continues to use enormous resources to defend its political system and uphold its firm position on state sovereignty.

Since 2008, Chinese nationalistic and parochial impulses continue to grow stronger in a dynamic where state nationalism and popular nationalism fuel one another. After his ascension to power at the eighteenth National Party Congress in 2012, General Secretary Xi Jinping launched a campaign that he called "the Chinese dream", seeking to install a sense of superpower identity and aspiration amidst further global economic and financial integration. Clearly, this Chinese dream is a domestic "value project". At the same time, rising China has also initiated international value projects. In addition to efforts that aim to increase transnational connections, an attempt to spread Chinese values and norms worldwide has become a surging phenomenon. I argue that it makes a significant difference if these expanding values are of state origin or spring from the people of the People's Republic. The specificity of the values that are incorporated into what has been termed a "contra-flow" of non-Western popular culture and news networks to a Western mainstream audience needs to be identified (Thussu 2006). Contra-flow is best conceptualized as a counterforce to the longstanding Western hegemonic cultural and information order. By offering non-Western perspectives on socioeconomic development, modernization, and the relationship between citizens and the state, countries of the Global South no longer contest the ideas and practices of liberal democracy at home, but also abroad.

In light of these transnational processes, is *global citizenship* a useful concept to understand China's deepening integration with international society? Is the world moving toward a convergence on global citizenship and global governance, or are we about to witness some kind of divergence on these bottom-up and top-down phenomena? Since civil society in China continues to be severely constrained, and the voice of China in international organizations and transnational public sphere(s) is heavily scripted by state media and government organizations, this chapter focuses more on the strategies and international behaviour of the Chinese state – and, therefore, issues of governance – than the Chinese citizenry or civil society organizations. In so doing, and to help answer the above questions, two aspects of global governance, Internet regulation and economic cooperation, two issues of paramount national interest to both authoritarian and democratic states, are employed to illustrate how contra-flow and norm-diffusion work at the international level of politics today.

Despite opening up to the world in 1978 and profiting immensely from globalization, the Chinese Party-state has remained decidedly more ambivalent about the cultural aspects of globalization than the material and scientific diffusion of technology and foreign direct investment. Scepticism still rules within the Party-state regarding cultural globalization, the role of the foreign news media, and academic knowledge produced within social sciences, the art world, and cultural institutions outside China. Thus, China's longstanding position on state sovereignty is employed whenever undesirable flows of thought heave and break on China's real and virtual territories. Even in the early days of the People's Republic in the 1950s, Chinese leaders were aware of the intentions of the United States to undo the young communist regime by "soft" means. Mao Zedong and Bo Yibo closely studied US Secretary of State John Foster Dulles's address in 1953 on peaceful evolution (Zhai 2009). Orthodox Marxists within the party remain very wary of the accelerated erosion of socialist ideology, traditional Chinese values (however defined), and the sovereignty of the People's Republic. With the advent of digital communication channels in the middle of the 1990s, this vigilance has become more acute, with the subsequent setting up of virtual firewalls around and inside China to protect its citizens from accessing "harmful" information. At the same time, a UNESCO study that was published in 2005 showed a strong emergence of the export of Chinese cultural goods (UNESCO 2005). Nonetheless, the Chinese government continues to be insecure about a "cultural balance of power" between countries. For instance, in state-controlled Chinese media, there have always been concerns about the influence of cultural imperialism and, since the beginning of the twenty-first century, about China's "cultural deficit" with other nations. To a large extent, this anxiety stems from the enduring feeling that Chinese society is about to become Westernized, and that Western movies, literature, and Internet culture are a Trojan horse undermining the core values of the Chinese political system. That is why the Communist Party and state officials continue to wage a battle against "universal values", which Chinese journalists and jurists have advocated to spur legal reform. The Party-state equalizes universal values with Western values that carry an inherent challenge to nativist, i.e. Confucian and sinified socialist, ideas on governance and liberties.

Increasingly, this battle against universal values is fought also beyond China's borders in multilateral institutions such as the United Nations system and by producing a non-Western contra-flow in the world of television, talk radio and social media. In this way, the Chinese leaders tell the world that China is well governed and that "Western-style democracy" is not suitable for domestic conditions (Huang 2013).

Issues of global governance: Internet friction and economic cooperation

In her well-known address in Washington, DC on 21 January 2010, former US Secretary of State Hillary Clinton emphasized that an "information curtain" had descended between free and closed nations of the world. Clinton invoked and echoed Winston Churchill's famous words on the Iron Curtain that came to divide Europe for more than fifty years when she said that "an information curtain now separates the free from the unfree" (2010). Two years later, on 14 December 2012, the International Telecommunication Union's (ITU) World Conference on International Communications (WCIT-12) meeting, negotiated a revision to the 1988 international telecommunications regulations. However, the negotiations broke down due to diverging positions on Internet governance in the final resolution. Russia, China, and other authoritarian ruled countries contested Western, and particularly American, hegemony on Internet governance. Subsequently, *The Economist* (2012) magazine ran the headline "A digital cold war?" In today's world, flows of people, capital, and information move differently and in larger volumes than the beginning of the Cold War some seventy years ago – a trend in contemporary globalization that sociologist Zygmunt Bauman (2006) has termed "liquid". This has led to a situation where all nation-states grapple with an arms race in information warfare and new cybersecurity challenges as non-state actors and citizens have become more empowered, making the security branches of governments insecure (Nye 2011).

In recent years China has become more vocal in various multilateral forums, seeking to buttress its domestic information order and its defence internationally of the legitimacy and soundness of maintaining it. This has been advanced primarily through arguments that global Internet governance needs order and control in order to avoid information highway "traffic accidents". These "traffic accidents" are a euphemism for the socio-political challenges posed to authoritarian leaders of sovereign nation-states. At the ITU meeting, China and Russia sought to gain recognition for their position on global Internet governance and "Internet sovereignty". Secretary of State Hillary Clinton's piercing remarks on Internet freedom in January 2010 were primarily directed at China, Iran, and Russia, who continue to strengthen their already firm control over their respective communication systems. Since her address, countries like China and Russia now want more say in global Internet governance to safeguard their control over their domestic information territory. To that end they have stepped up their efforts to influence such issues in various multilateral forums. The most important of these include the United Nations agency the ITU, multi-stakeholder settings such as the Internet Corporation of Assigned Names and Numbers (ICANN), and the Internet Governance Forum (IGF).

The rhetoric on Internet freedom and Internet sovereignty differs substantially between authoritarian and democratic countries. Real-world practices, however, reveal another story (Lagerkvist & Eriksson forthcoming). Although the extent to which states are losing control over citizen communications vary across countries and contexts, the issues of flow security and, increasingly, strategies of cyber security, have become the Achilles' heel of many policy-makers of the Western world, especially after the revelations by Edward Snowden that the US government engages in mass surveillance of states and citizens across the world. In order to relativize Chinese state monitoring of online activity, diplomats at the Foreign Ministry in Beijing have been quick to point out Western hypocrisy on human rights issues such as freedom of speech.[1]

In the field of global economic governance, there is more convergence on the merits of a particular kind of openness: a liberal economic trading order. In recent commentary on global economic governance that seeks to explain the outcome of the huge recession of 2008, arguments abound about the remarkable staying power of American hegemony and the formidable resilience of the liberal international order. This position holds that China and other emerging powers did not actively challenge the existing order because of a lack of resolve or capacity. Daniel Drezner has argued that despite a power diffusion worldwide, i.e. a transfer of economic and political power and influence from the West to the East, China's adherence to, and paradoxically perhaps also its inability to articulate an alternative to the open liberal economic order proved instrumental in upholding it (2013). 2Yet the role of China in global economic governance has probably been underestimated. The structural strength of the dollar and US financial markets, as well as the inertia of the G20 forums, has certainly been important, but it is not all about American power. Rather Sino-Western collaboration within the framework of the international political economy, propelled by the further integration of China into global production networks and institutions of global economic governance, is shifting the balance of economic power and voice in the world. From this transformation, there follows important implications for future development and definition(s) of global citizenship. Within-order Western accommodation of the demands of rising China leading to modification of human rights and democratic values is not a foregone conclusion, as Western elites may be prepared to bargain with authoritarian technocracy, leading to an undermining of the liberal world order of Anglo-American making (Lagerkvist 2015). In fact there is clear evidence that this process has already been set in motion, sometimes for all to see and sometimes behind closed doors. As convincingly shown by Katrin Kinzelbach (2014), the European Union's approach of so-called quiet diplomacy has not helped to improve human rights in the People's Republic.

Global citizenship: diffusion of regime voice or people's voice?

For long it has been taken for granted that the diffusion of norms, values, and ideas are transferred from the Global North to the Global South – and that that particular diffusion has largely been effective in shaping national discourse on, for example, human rights. However, developing countries, their governments, and some elites have tried to constrain and counteract such diffusion. Arguably, it may be easier for emerging powers and economies like China, India, and Brazil to shape new norms in-the-making, i.e. international norms such as the Responsibility to Protect (R2P), cyber security, and Internet freedom, rather than older norms established by Western powers. For these emergent norms, rising powers are afforded the room to chisel out and work new norms in early stages in the norm cycle, beginning at an early stage with *agenda-framing* and intense multilateral debates on how to define the new norm.

In the case of China, conservative factions of the Communist Party worried throughout the 1980s about "peaceful evolution" and the conditioning of Chinese mindsets susceptible to Western philosophical and political notions. Today, with the continued economic rise and increasing global influence of China, it is time to study not only the defensive strategies of constraining norms-shaping at home, but also the efforts at shaping attitudes and norms abroad. In fact, China is trying hard to affect global values and norms through the diffusion of its popular culture and news programs in foreign languages. In China, the Party-state invests in educational programs and institutions such as the Confucius institutes that are located at foreign universities and satellite news channels in new media markets in the Global South. *Thus, cultural globalization is no longer equivalent to the movement of goods and ideas from the West to the rest.*

Given the trend of norm diffusion and competitive contra-flows against the dominant Western flow of news and information, important questions concern China's impact on the formation of global norms. These questions also concern the likelihood of rejecting old – as well as establishing new – values and norms associated with global citizenship and global governance as China and other emerging countries of the Global South rise from regional to global power status. Will there be convergence or friction? The shaping of alternative norms for the global polity and global citizenship has been theorized by Acharya (2011). His concept of norm subsidiarity is useful as it "is outward-looking. Its main focus is on relations between local actors and external powers, in terms of the former's fear of domination by the latter". Thus, it offers a helpful departure for understanding China's fear of becoming dominated by Western agendas on freedom and human rights. The concept acknowledges the agency of "local actors [who] can be norm rejecters and/or norm makers" who may seek to "export or 'universalize' locally constructed norms" (Kirsch 1977). According to Acharya, "This may involve using locally constructed norms to support or amplify existing global norms against the parochial ideas of powerful actors"

(2011, 97). Over time, China has traversed from being a peripheral local actor bent on overt ideological export of locally constructed norms of Maoist ideology in the 1960s to de-ideologized, to becoming a powerful local producer of norms to the international community through the more neutral language of technocracy and defence of state sovereignty. Chinese diplomats and government think-tanks have appropriated the tools of the advertising industry, and a toned-down rhetoric and well-researched arguments to yield effective contra-flow in the global battle of ideas.

In the People's Republic, both state-controlled organizations and private entrepreneurs invest in and produce satellite news channels and export cultural goods such as computer games, documentaries, and feature films. Yet, overwhelmingly this messaging from China is heavily mediated and scripted by government entities in Beijing. A case in point concerns the fear of a rise in anti-Chinese sentiment in other developing countries, e.g. those in Africa, which is often caused by non-transparent operations and badly managed labour relations in Chinese companies. Therefore, China has worked to establish an ambitious media presence in African and Latin American countries. Participating in global media discourse has become more important for China as Chinese state-owned business operations and no-strings-attached aid policy are increasingly scrutinized. Thus, public diplomacy and the expansion of Chinese media are judged by Beijing to be crucial to alter the unfair Western bias of the international information order. To this end, media budgets have increased and more Chinese journalists and communications specialists have been deployed for work abroad. It is obvious that as the Chinese state now actively funds an increasing media presence worldwide, it also embarks upon a quest of framing Chinese economic activity, influencing public opinion, and building a counter-discourse to the often very negative portrayals of China that dominates Western media flows.

In the analysis of cultural dissemination and soft power, there is a need to make distinctions between the information and propaganda clearly originating from the political centres of a country and the role and influence of the centres of commercial creative industries. Since the start of the reform period in 1978, the Chinese film industry and the art and literary worlds have witnessed a contestation between the demands of political propaganda on the one hand and the desires of those who run the creative industries on the other. Despite the fact that independent social critique can – and has been – suppressed by political power, the authoritarian Chinese Party-state has in recent years been very keen on using popular culture as a way to present a more modern and less bureaucratic face to the rest of the world. This strategy worked well for the Koizumi government of democratic Japan, which in the 1990s sought to build a successful content industry to present a "cool Japan" to the world. Following the Japanese example, strategic launches have sought improve the image of China by making use of popular culture. Arguably, the Chinese government maintains double standards on rights and norm diffusion in domestic news and international news production. The Chinese Party-state seeks to convince overseas publics of China's position on many issues through its increasingly sophisticated participation in the global media landscape, although it filters critical foreign news on China from dissemination inside the People's Republic. This double standard originates from the regime's sense of vulnerability, fear of "peaceful evolution", and professed need for domestic stability, as well as the formidable hegemony of Western countries in global communication flows.

Within the research literature on global mass media products, there exist two different schools. The first school, as exemplified by the works of Boyd-Barrett, affirms the thesis of media and cultural imperialism, which emphasizes Western dominance and the hegemony of global media (Boyd-Barrett 1998). The other school of thought, illustrated by Volkmer, focuses on the emergence of a global or transnational public sphere in which a multitude of mass media from different cultural regions seek to increase their geographical reach (Volkmer 2003; Crack 2008). Both perspectives offer important insights on both the difficulties and potential that the existing global information order present to China and other developing countries as they seek to communicate their views of the world, to the world.

Yet, in the time between the UNESCO's studies of 1974 and 2005, it is evident that the cultural production of non-Western nations increased in importance in global media. The global media landscape can no longer be characterized simply as a one-way flow from the West to the rest, as an increasing "contra-flow" is picking up speed. According to Volkmer, this is evidenced both inside the Western mainstream and through the appearance of new non-Western satellite television networks. Future empirical research on the narratives and values that are communicated in the contra-flow could yield more granulated findings on the issue of convergence/divergence around contested concepts such as global citizenship.

Convergence or divergence?

As argued by Richard Falk (1994), the implicit notion of global citizenship is that traditional citizenship is being challenged by social activism and social movements. Many people are believed to identify with a community that is no longer bound by a formal relationship to one's territorial society, as best embodied in the form of a nation-state. From this follows that the concept of citizenship is no longer tied to the emergence of members of a polity with specified privileges and duties. Transferring this concept from the national to global arena is a difficult task, however, as global citizens are not subjected to a global, legal authority they can either oppose or support, from which they can demand rights, or that can bestow duties upon them. Thus, global citizenship is bound to clash with the legal authorities that run the territories where they exist as national citizens. This may be a minor problem in Western countries with freer media systems and advanced digital communication technology flows that easily create and expand transnational and global loyalties and identities. However, notwithstanding the increasingly advanced communications infrastructure in countries with authoritarian or colonialist legacies such as China and India, de-territorialization of citizenship is not on the nation state agenda. This is even less so in China than in India. Therefore, an important question asks: to what extent is discussion on global citizenship a global phenomenon at all? Is it something that further reflects the post-materialist values of a liberal Western agenda, which is energized by non-governmental organizations? In answer to the question "Do rights exist outside the context of state sovereignty?" the Chinese state would most certainly say no – foreign nationals and states have no right to outright criticize China, and Chinese nationals should likewise refrain from condemning the political and social practices of other countries. Yet, influencing overseas public opinion through mass media on the merits of China's domestic social system and model of modernization is definitely not a problem for the propaganda cadres in Beijing.

There is also a need to address the question of whether debates about global governance and global citizenship are really global in scope, and if the existing definitions are adhered to, or even understood by, different peoples across the globe. In fact, large parts of the non-democratic world do not participate in discussions regarding global citizenship because there are limits to the extent they may discuss universal values and issues of citizenship. In many countries, the merits of authoritarian ideas and state sovereignty outweigh the values of democracy, and rather worryingly this is increasingly the case in established democracies too. Thus, these ideas are still very much a part of the contemporary global world. Different aspects of modernity are negotiated by local culture, often to be inserted into a mélange of values and norms. Thus, in the light of the Chinese government's management of the issue of global governance and citizens' rights in the field of global Internet governance, the world is indeed far from having achieved a common understanding of what global citizenship is, or even how it should be performed by citizens still constrained by their national citizenship.

It seems likely that convergence on issues of *global governance* is more likely than fruitful state deliberation on *global citizenship*, conflating these two concepts is problematic as bottom-up citizen influence on global governance remains limited even in liberal democratic settings despite the activity of non-governmental organizations. Differences between political systems, and arguably also social institutions and cultural variation, are yet too wide to bridge the conceptual gaps on citizenship in the global arena. Thus, in the foreseeable future, it would probably be more realistic to foreshadow a convergence on some issues of global governance between China and the West than establishing anything near a consensus on global citizenship rights. Settled arrangements are more likely on issues such as trade and climate change prevention than on thornier issues that concern the rights and responsibilities of citizenries and states. Thus, norms on global governance may be established, and perhaps tweaked by way of effective contra-flow of non-Western countries, in some issue areas across the differences of political systems. Without universal access to unfiltered information, the foundational work of global citizenship across democratic and non-democratic states is a difficult task. If the citizens of the world's largest economy (in purchasing power parity terms) can only participate in forums such as the world economic forum in Davos and the world social forum in Porto Alegre if they subscribe to the political agenda of the Chinese Party-state, one may ask if it is meaningful to speak of global citizenship only as a long-term objective. The world remains far away from a common understanding of what global citizenship is, or even how it should be performed by citizens, who are still constrained by parochial notions of national citizenship. And, of course, the necessity to have a sound working relationship with China dominates contemporary Western thinking and practice. Therefore, it cannot be ruled out that continued accommodation of Chinese positions could lead to a modification of rights in the liberal international order. Such modifications could gradually affect norms and practices in a more illiberal fashion and consequently change practices that weaken the promotion of democratic values, human rights and, in the end, global citizenship.

Note

1 Interview with foreign ministry official, conducted in Beijing, 28 September 2011.

References

Acharya, Amitav. 2011. "Norm Subsidiarity and Regional Orders: Sovereignty, Regionalism, and Rule-Making in the Third World". *International Studies Quarterly* 55: 95–123.
Bauman, Zymunt. 2006. *Liquid Fear*. Cambridge: Polity Press.
Boyd-Barrett, Oliver. 1998. "Media Imperialism Reformulated". In Daya K. Thussu (ed.), *Electronic Empires: Global Media and Local Resistance*. London: Arnold.
Clinton, Hillary. 2010. "Remarks on Internet Freedom". Available at: www.state.gov/secretary/rm/2010/01/135519.htm.
Crack, Angela M. 2008. *Global Communication and Transnational Public Spheres*. New York: Palgrave Macmillan.
Drezner, Daniel. 2013. "The System Worked: Global Economic Governance During the Great Recession". *World Politics* 66(1): 123–164.
Economist. 2012. "Internet Regulation: A Digital Cold War?". 4 December. Available at: www.economist.com/blogs/babbage/2012/12/internet-regulation?fsrc=scn/tw_ec/a_digital_cold_war_.
Economist Intelligence Unit. 2015. *Democracy on the Edge: Populism and Protest*.
Falk, Richard. 1994. "The Making of Global Citizenship". In Bart van Steenbergen (ed.), *The Condition of Citizenship*. London: Sage.
Huang, Cary. 2013. "'Western-Style Reform Not on Agenda', Says CPPCC Chief Yu Zhengsheng". *South China Morning Post*, 12 March. Available at: www.scmp.com/news/china/article/1189149/western-style-reform-not-agenda-says-cppcc-chief-yu-zhengsheng.
Ikenberry, John. 2001. *After Victory: Institutions, Strategic Restraint, and the Rebuilding of Order after Major Wars*. Princeton, NJ: Princeton University Press.

Kinzelbach, Katrin. 2014. *The EU's Human Rights Dialogue with China: Quiet Diplomacy and Its Limits*. London: Routledge.

Kirsch, Thomas A. 1977. "Complexity in the Thai Religious System: An Interpretation". *Journal of Asian Studies* 36(2): 241–266.

Kleinwachter, Wolfgang. 2013. "'Cold Internet War' or 'Peaceful Internet Coexistence'?". 3 January. Available at: www.circleid.com/posts/20130103_internet_governance_outlook_2013 (accessed 15 September 2015).

Lagerkvist, Johan. 2015. "The Ordoliberal Turn? Getting China and Global Economic Governance Right". *Global Affairs* 1(3).

Lagerkvist, Johan and Johan Eriksson. Forthcoming. "Cybersecurity in Sweden and China: Going on the Attack?". In Karsten Friis (ed.), *Conflict in Cyberspace*. London: Routledge.

Nye, Joseph. 2011. *The Future of Power*. New York: Public Affairs.

"Remarks on Internet Freedom". Available at: www.state.gov/secretary/rm/2010/01/135519.htm.

Thussu, Daya. 2006. *Media on the Move: Global Flow and Contra-flow*. London: Routledge.

UNESCO Institute for Statistics and UNESCO Sector for Culture. 2005. *International Flows of Selected Cultural Goods and Services, 1994–2003: Defining and Capturing the Flows of Global Cultural Trade*. Montreal.

Volkmer, Ingrid. 2003. "The Global Network Society and the Global Public Sphere". *Development 46* 1: 9–16.

White Paper on the Internet. 2010. Available at: http://english.gov.cn/2010-06/08/content_1622956.htm (accessed 19 February 2013).

Zhai, Qiang. 2009. "1959: Presenting Peaceful Evolution". *China Heritage Quarterly* 18 (June). Available at: www.chinaheritagequarterly.org/features.php?searchterm=018_1959preventingpeace.inc&issue=018 (accessed 13 October 2015).

16 An assessment of Southeast Asian regional identity

Shaun Narine

Since its inception in 1967, the Association of Southeast Nations (ASEAN) has held the creation of "One Southeast Asia" as one of its long-term goals (Wanandi 2001, 25; Ba 2009, 32). This term reflected an aspiration on the part of ASEAN's leaders for the region to develop some level of economic and political unity, though the parameters of this unity were never defined. At the start of the twenty-first century, ASEAN began a process of significant reform, seeking to create an "ASEAN Community" which consists of three "pillars": the ASEAN Economic Community (AEC), the ASEAN Political Security Community (APSC), and the ASEAN Socio Cultural Community (ASCC). An explicit goal of the new ASEAN Community is to promote a sense of regional identity and citizenship among the peoples of Southeast Asia. The key objectives of this chapter are to assess critically ASEAN's stated goals, examine how questions of identity and citizenship influence the leaders and people of Southeast Asia, and see what the Southeast Asian experience says about the larger question of global citizenship.[1]

This chapter argues that the sense of regional identity in Southeast Asia is very weak. A small coterie of individuals in Southeast Asia feels a larger sense of "belonging" to the region as a whole. These are mostly academics and government officials who have been engaged in constructing the many regional institutions, especially ASEAN. However, these individuals have a limited effect on state behaviour and interests. Some members of the NGO community also have a larger sense of regional and global citizenship. However, their perspectives do not reflect those of most Southeast Asians. The ruling elites of Southeast Asia remain preoccupied with building and maintaining the sovereign authority of their individual states. Most importantly, the general populations of Southeast Asian states often have a weak sense of national identity, let alone regional identity (Ba 2009, 33; Acharya 2012, 105–148). It is true that many people in Southeast Asia have a sense of global consciousness and even citizenship. However, this identity coexists with the far more important local ethnic, religious, and community identities and interests that define the region's people. Indeed, in some cases, the challenge posed by external identities to established local identities has exacerbated the differences among and within ASEAN's member states. This argument is supported by drawing on regional attitudinal surveys and historical and contemporary examples of ethnic and religious conflict in Southeast Asia.

From this perspective, ideas of "cosmopolitan citizenship" and other notions of global belonging sometimes challenge and conflict with the realities of what it means to live in states that are engaged in the state-building process. This process involves the effort to construct national identities out of the many disparate identities that presently define all Southeast Asian states. Given how difficult this process continues to be, the creation of regional or global identities are, at best, distant long-term aspirations.

ASEAN and its role in building regional identity

ASEAN's original members were Indonesia, Malaysia, the Philippines, Singapore, and Thailand. The organization was created in the aftermath of the Konfrontasi (Confrontation) between Indonesia and Malaysia/Singapore (1963–1966). Indonesia considered the creation of Malaysia as a move by Britain to assert a neo-colonial presence in Southeast Asia. The Philippines and Malaysia also had territorial disputes. Konfrontasi ended in 1966, but it left a legacy of antagonism and suspicion between the states of the region. From the start, ASEAN formally expressed a desire to nurture a larger sense of regional identity as well as economic interaction. But its primary focus and purpose were to alleviate political and security tensions among its members. ASEAN emphasized the need for its members to respect each other's sovereign rights. This focus on sovereignty and non-interference in each other's domestic affairs followed directly from the lessons of Konfrontasi and, in practice, worked against the creation of a larger regional identity. The ASEAN states understood ASEAN as an organization that was meant to be limited in scope and which, by its very nature, should never force them to choose between their national interests and ASEAN's institutional interests. As ASEAN evolved, the norms of non-intervention and respect for member state sovereignty became the organization's core principles (Narine 2002, 9–38; Acharya 2012, 159–164). Despite rhetoric to the contrary, this has not changed. Even today, ASEAN remains fundamentally about protecting and respecting the sovereignty of its members.

This tension between what ASEAN is and the rhetoric of its political development has shaped the organization. Many outsiders assumed that ASEAN was the Southeast Asian version of the European Union, or that ASEAN aspired to follow in the EU's footsteps. In reality, ASEAN's leaders never intended for the organization to be a strongly institutionalized, overarching structure (Frost 2008, 11). To them, ASEAN was primarily a mutual promise to stay out of each other's affairs so that each state could concentrate its efforts on defeating communist and ethnic insurgencies and allaying domestic unrest without having to worry about externally sponsored subversion. ASEAN's early aspirations included efforts at regional economic cooperation. However, various efforts to build region-wide industries or encourage regional economic integration failed or made little headway.

ASEAN's most important institutional growth was usually in response to events external to the organization and its members. For example, the first meeting of the member states' leaders occurred in 1976, in response to Vietnam's unification under communist rule. Before then, ASEAN's top-level meetings were between its member states' foreign ministers. ASEAN later organized global opposition to Vietnam's 1978 invasion and subsequent occupation of Cambodia. The occupation lasted through the 1980s, finally ending in the early 1990s. ASEAN's campaign against Vietnam was externally focused and distracted ASEAN from building its internal institutional structures and linkages. Moreover, by the time the conflict ended, ASEAN's unity faltered as different members, with different interpretations of their national security, began to pursue their individual national interests in relation to Vietnam. Nonetheless, most observers still regard ASEAN's efforts against Vietnam as the high point of the organization's unity and international influence (Acharya 2012, 181–201).

In all of these cases, the failures reflected not just a lack of political will, but also a realistic understanding of the obstacles faced by developing world states in the process of creating themselves as states. Most of ASEAN's members were dealing with threats of communist insurgency and ethnic conflict within their own borders. These disputes originated in economic disparity and the struggle for limited resources between ethnic, religious, and other communities. Under these circumstances, no ASEAN state was willing to give up any amount of sovereign control or compromise national interests for the sake of the regional organization. The one exception to this rule may be Indonesia which, for a time, was willing to put aside its own misgivings about ASEAN's approach to Vietnam to maintain ASEAN unity. However, Indonesia did this because it saw ASEAN as a possible instrument of its own regional leadership aspirations. It was still acting out of its own sense of long-term national interest. The process of state-building was and remains a primary concern of all of the ASEAN states (and, indeed, of almost every state in Asia) (Moon and Chun 2003; Narine 2004a).

In terms of humanitarian issues, ASEAN has consistently supported the sovereign rights of its members over other considerations. In 1975 to 1976, ASEAN remained silent when Indonesia invaded and annexed East Timor. ASEAN treated the East Timorese situation, and Indonesia's subsequent use of extreme violence against the people of East Timor over the next 25 years, as part of the domestic politics of Indonesia. In 1999, East Timorese voted overwhelmingly to establish an independent state. In response, the Indonesian military unleashed Indonesian-backed militias against the East Timorese. The violence attracted the condemnation of the United Nations and eventually led to the Australian-led UN interventionary force, the International Force for East Timor (INTERFET). Initially, states outside of Southeast Asia had expected ASEAN to rein in Indonesia's actions. This expectation underlined the extent to which external actors misunderstood ASEAN's operations and its actual priorities. Ironically, when it became clear that international intervention was going to occur, Indonesia appealed to its fellow ASEAN states to lead the intervention. However, ASEAN members were reluctant to become involved under the banner of ASEAN. They did not want to risk the possibility of their militaries coming into conflict with the Indonesian military and were concerned about the implications of such violent clashes on ASEAN unity. Nonetheless, a number of ASEAN states participated in INTERFET. ASEAN's members preferred to operate under the auspices of another international organization rather than set the precedent of ASEAN intervening in a member's domestic affairs (Narine 2004a).

The East Timor situation further undermined ASEAN's international standing as it demonstrated that the organization was incapable of managing a major regional security problem, even when its own members were directly involved. This limitation was not surprising, however: ASEAN had never been equipped to deal with internal conflict and, indeed, had been explicitly forbidden from such activity. Faced with a real regional crisis, ASEAN was unable to act. As we shall see, this tension between the expectations that were created by ASEAN's self-professed role as a centre of regional organization versus the real political and practical restraints on its actions continues, even after considerable institutional reform.

The ASEAN community and the ASEAN Intergovernmental Commission on Human Rights

In 2003, ASEAN initiated a process of becoming an "ASEAN Community" (AC). ASEAN announced its intention of establishing an AC based on three "pillars": the ASEAN Economic Community (AEC), the ASEAN Political and Security Community (APSC), and the ASEAN Socio-Cultural Community (ASCC) (Weatherbee 2005, 107–110). The drive to create an AC seems, on the surface, to reflect ASEAN's intention of creating a political, economic, and social union, perhaps suggesting that it had decided to emulate the European Union after all. However, this impression is misleading. In fact, ASEAN's decision to pursue an AC came together somewhat haphazardly.

ASEAN's initial intention was to create an AEC as a way to counter the rise of China and its attraction as a destination for foreign investment. The AEC was also a response to the fallout from the economic crisis of 1997–1999, which had undermined ASEAN's international standing. The decision to create an ASEAN Security Community ("Political" was added later) was proposed by Indonesia, the chair of the 2003 meeting. Indonesia was concerned about being overshadowed in its own meeting by a focus on regional economics, an area in which it was a weak actor. The idea of a "security community" played to Indonesia's importance as a regional security presence. Critics in other ASEAN states felt that the ASC initiative was pushed on the other states with little consultation, even though it eventually gained unanimous support (Roberts 2012,

120–121). The idea of an "ASEAN Socio-Cultural Community" was even more of an afterthought. It was suggested by the Philippines largely to counter criticism that ASEAN was too focused on governmental priorities and not enough on civil society (Severino 2006, 368–369).

The somewhat random nature of the creation of two of the AC's three pillars speaks to the fragility of the AC enterprise. It is not the result of a carefully considered process or a response to a deep wellspring of elite or public opinion. Even though the AC aspires to create a sense of regional identity and it is implementing measures to further this goal, it is, at best, at a very preliminary stage in its development. This is made doubly clear when one realizes that the ASCC, the least developed and defined of the AC's three "pillars", is the pillar responsible for advancing the mission of identity-building.

There is convincing evidence that Southeast Asia is in a very preliminary stage of community building. In a seminal survey study on "affinity and trust" in the region, done between 2004 and 2007, Roberts demonstrated that extremely high numbers of "communal" (ordinary) Southeast Asians had very little knowledge of or awareness of ASEAN, the organization, and did not have a sense of "region" that extended beyond the immediate neighbouring states. Levels of trust were also not a sufficient basis for a strong community: 37.5 per cent of the communal survey participants said "yes" when asked if they could trust all of the ASEAN countries, but 36.1 per cent were "unsure" and 26.4 per cent said "no" (Roberts 2007, 86–87). Myanmar, Singapore, and Indonesia were the most distrustful – a significant point, given that Singapore and Indonesia are original members of ASEAN and have been key actors in it from the start. Even more telling, Roberts's survey indicated that Southeast Asian elites were even more distrustful of their ASEAN counterparts than ordinary people, with 66.7 per cent of academics answering "no" to the question of whether they could trust other countries in Southeast Asia to be "good neighbours" (ibid., 88). These results could be parsed in different ways; for example, the elites who are most distrustful of other ASEAN states could be those who have the least contact with their foreign counterparts. But the lesson is the same: distrust and a lack of regional identity remain high among the very groups in Southeast Asia who have the greatest influence over state policy. These results underline the reality that "Southeast Asian" identity is very low in the hierarchy of identities and interests that define the behaviour of Southeast Asian states. This does not mean that the ASEAN Community is doomed to fail, but it does mean that it has substantial obstacles that more than 40 years of ASEAN have failed to overcome.

The clash between cosmopolitan values and ASEAN's established priorities is exemplified in the creation of the ASEAN Intergovernmental Commission on Human Rights (AICHR). The AICHR embodies many of the problems and limitations inherent in the ASEAN community-building process. For more than two decades, the ASEAN states had resisted UN calls to establish a regional human rights mechanism and had been careful to respond to such calls by emphasizing the need for any understanding of human rights to include regional conceptions of social responsibility and cultural norms. For several years, LAWASIA, a regional non-governmental organization consisting of lawyers and judges, had established a Working Group (WG) which met regularly with Southeast Asia's foreign ministers. The WG pushed for ASEAN to adopt human rights norms that were in accordance with universal human rights as articulated in international law. ASEAN received and acknowledged the WG's reports, but gave no sign that it was considering a shift in its approach to human rights. In 2003 to 2004, when ASEAN began the process of creating an ASEAN Community, however, some of the language and recommendations of the WG began to appear in ASEAN's statements and declarations. In December 2005, ASEAN issued the Kuala Lumpur Declaration on the Establishment of the ASEAN Charter. ASEAN created an Eminent Persons Group (EPG) to provide recommendations on the proposed Charter. Human rights NGOs in the region lobbied the EPG and its successor, the High Level Task Force (HLTF), to establish a human rights mechanism within the Charter. The EPG accepted this petition and the HLTF agreed, but it could not decide how to insert such a mechanism in the Charter. The decision was left to the ASEAN foreign ministers (Ginbar 2010, 505–510; Narine 2012, 368–370). The political bargaining that followed resulted in an AICHR that lacked enforcement capability.

The ASEAN Charter itself illustrated the considerable tension between ASEAN's established institutional norms, which focus on the importance of state sovereignty and non-intervention, and the norms of universal human rights, which the Charter also acknowledged. The Charter confirmed the importance of democracy and human rights and it encouraged its members to adhere to international norms, values, and standards. However, it also clearly placed priority on the importance of state sovereignty and emphasized the right of individual states to make decisions based upon their particular political and cultural circumstances. The terms of reference for the AICHR reinforced these limitations (Ginbar 2010).

The limitations of the AICHR have become particularly apparent with the situation created by Myanmar's treatment of its Rohingya minority. The Rohingya are a Muslim minority group within Myanmar who are officially regarded by the state government as illegal migrants from Bangladesh (Leider 2014). The Rohingya are subjected to considerable violence and discrimination by the Buddhist majority on the basis of their religion and ethnicity (Fuller 2015a). Discrimination against the Rohingya is so widespread within Myanmar that even Aung Saan Suu Kyii, the country's idolized opposition leader and Nobel Peace Prize recipient, has been criticized by some observers for failing to support the Rohingya's rights, or condemn their mistreatment (Fuller 2015a). Starting in 2012 to 2013, the Rohingya were subjected to a level of abuse from the Buddhist majority that resulted in more than 140,000 Rohingya being forced into government-run concentration camps (Fuller 2015b). The Rohingya were forced out of Myanmar or fled in large numbers, becoming a problem of illegal migration for many of the surrounding ASEAN states. For a time, Indonesia, Thailand, and Malaysia followed policies of pushing the boats carrying the migrants back out to sea, leaving starving and desperate people to the mercy of the elements (Cochrane and Fuller 2015). This cold-hearted response to a human rights and humanitarian catastrophe reflected both the economic concerns of relatively poor states and the ever-present concern for maintaining ethnic and religious balance within Southeast Asian countries. It also underlines the extent to which ethnic and religious divisions continue to motivate domestic politics in the ASEAN states. Even so, the situation with the Rohingya has created tensions within ASEAN. Mohamad Mahathir, the former Prime Minister of Malaysia who was instrumental in getting Myanmar admitted to ASEAN, has now called for Myanmar to be expelled from ASEAN because of its human rights record (Aung 2015).

The AICHR has responded to this ongoing humanitarian crisis by not saying anything at all (Talib 2015). The board of the AICHR consists of representatives from every member state. It is likely that the representative from Myanmar blocked any potential efforts to address the problem. This underlines the lack of independence of the organization and, by extension, the weak commitment that ASEAN has made to "universal values". The AICHR stands as an instructive case. It exists, in large part, because ASEAN and its members wish to be seen as a progressive and respected part of the international community. Universal human rights are important (at least rhetorically) to most of the leading states of the Western world, which set the tone for the international community. These transnational ideas clearly affect how ASEAN understands the requirements of the international community. However, despite paying lip-service to these values, ASEAN is not prepared to enforce the norms of an emerging international society (Narine 2012).

As this overview suggests, there is little reason to believe that cosmopolitan values and the idea of global citizenship have much resonance in the political context of Southeast Asia. However, it is too simplistic to suggest that the limitations and even failures of ASEAN are entirely the result of lack of political will or that they can be solved through a change in attitude. Rather, the importance of sovereignty and the regional ambivalence around issues of human rights reflect real and legitimate considerations that are faced by developing world states.

Sovereignty and identity

The question of how important sovereignty remains to the states of Southeast Asia and its relationship to the creation of a cosmopolitan sense of citizenship is a key concern of this chapter. As noted, ASEAN holds non-intervention and the associated respect for state sovereignty as fundamental norms. There are many reasons for a state to want to protect its sovereignty. One obvious motivation is that state elites wish to protect and preserve their privileges within the state. Sovereignty acts as the shield behind which dominant and often corrupt elites use force and other forms of oppression to maintain their control over their states. There is, undoubtedly, some truth to this criticism in Southeast Asia (and other parts of Asia). However, this criticism also oversimplifies what is a fundamentally important and difficult problem: how to build a functioning state out of many disparate identities. Every Southeast Asian state is a multi-ethnic, multi-religious entity that encompasses communities who, in some instances, have been thrown together against their will. In other cases, the communities have long histories of conflict. Within traditional societies, strong communal bonds have proven essential to the survival and prosperity of people. Most developing world states are faced with the difficult task of creating national identities out of different ethnic, religious, and cultural identities, which means overcoming or at least providing viable alternatives to the traditional identities. The successful modern democracies of the West can provide little guidance on how to achieve this goal. Most Western states have histories of civil war and destructive religious conflict that were part of their pathway towards relative prosperity and stability today. The European colonial settler states of the Americas and Oceania have, in most cases, histories of genocide and slavery. This does not mean that human rights abuse is a necessary part of creating state identities, but it does underline that creating such identities is a hard process that, historically, has usually been extremely violent. The fixation of Southeast Asian elites on creating national identities is, perhaps, an outdated goal in a globalized world. It may reflect their desire to consolidate their own power, but the great majority of the regional states experienced colonialism and were forged in anti-colonial struggles. Maintaining their independence against powerful structures dominated by Western powers is a defining element of their nationalism (Narine 2004b; Acharya 2012, 51–104).

The fact that national ruling elites are trying to construct a sense of nationalism out of disparate identities is one side of the equation. It is precisely because the people of Southeast Asia put their parochial identities ahead of larger, more national senses of identification that this process is necessary. There is nothing mysterious in this parochialism. In Southeast Asia, regional governments find their authority subject to "performance legitimacy" – i.e., the legitimacy of their rule is based on how well they perform in bringing the benefits of economic development to their people (Ciorciari 2010, 139–141). It is probable that the legitimacy of all states is rooted in some variation on this formula. A state cannot function well if its ruling elites cannot demonstrate their right to rule by providing their people with the benefits of economic and social progress. In exchange, the elites gain disproportionately from the wealth of society. This formula certainly applies in the West, though there the gains of the economic elite at the expense of everyone else have begun to fray the social contract (Piketty 2014). In Southeast Asia, the operation of this mechanism has been closer to the surface. An excellent example of this mechanism was the Suharto regime in Indonesia. During Suharto's reign, most of the people of the country saw their personal wealth and standards of living increase exponentially. They were willing to overlook the extraordinary corruption that enabled the Suharto family and its cronies to accrue vast wealth. When the Asian economic crisis hit in 1997, the Indonesian state was rocked to its foundations, more than half the Indonesian population fell below the poverty line, and political instability followed (Ciorciari 2010, 136–146). Suharto was forced to resign and his personal empire fell apart. Significantly, the dissolution of the state was accompanied by enormous violence directed against the ethnic Chinese minority.

Every state in contemporary Southeast Asia contends with political instability as the result of issues related to competing identities. Thailand is dealing with a long-running Muslim insurgency in its south. At the same time, Thailand's political landscape is in upheaval as different socio-economic classes within Thai society struggle over the shape and control of its democracy. Malaysia remains a society sensitive to religious and ethnic differences. Islamic identity, promoted by the state, has become more exclusionary, feeding the pre-existing divisions. Indonesia's democratic government is far more representative of its population than it was during the Suharto years, but the state remains a fragile experiment in representative democracy. Singapore remains an island of stability in Southeast Asia, but it continues to monitor and control relations between its most numerous ethnic groups. The Philippines has made considerable progress in dealing with Muslim insurgency in Mindanao. Nonetheless, tensions persist and the peace is fragile (Narine 2004b; Weatherbee 2005, 139–147).

It is doubtless the case that many people in Southeast Asia see themselves as "global citizens". Precisely what they mean by this is unclear, however. Does this simply mean that people recognize that they are part of an interconnected humanity? Moreover, how important this identity is can only be measured by how far actors are willing to put the interests of one identity ahead of another when they come into conflict. The evidence from Southeast Asia fairly conclusively shows that local ethnic, linguistic, and religious identities take priority over regional identities. Sometimes these local identities and some form of regional identity may intersect and reinforce each other – for example, the identification of Muslims in Malaysia with the Rohingya speaks to a pan-Islamic identity that is politically significant and consequential. However, this kind of identification has the potential to foment divisions along other lines.

Conclusion

Southeast Asia is a cauldron of multiple and competing identities. In that stew of identities, a sense of global citizenship and cosmopolitanism is present, but it is very low in the hierarchy of the multiple identities by which most Southeast Asians define themselves. ASEAN reflects these limitations. Over the years, but especially since 2003, ASEAN has made a concerted effort to create transnational economic, political, and cultural ties between its member states and their peoples. But these efforts have been somewhat half-hearted, often ambiguous, and sometimes almost accidental. ASEAN's core documents make it clear that, while ideals of democracy and human rights are appealing and aspirational, the organization still protects the right of every Southeast Asian state to choose how far down that road they wish to go. Every Southeast Asian state remains concerned about its long-term survival as a state, largely because of internal political and economic instability. So long as this continues, the range for the development of genuine cosmopolitanism is limited.

Note

1 The 1967 membership of ASEAN was: Indonesia, Malaysia, the Philippines, Singapore, and Thailand. ASEAN gradually expanded to include: Brunei, Cambodia, Laos, Myanmar, and Vietnam.

References

Acharya, Amitav. 2012. *The Making of Southeast Asia*. Singapore: ISEAS.

Aung, Nyan Lynn. 2015. "Myanmar Rejects Mahathir's Push for ASEAN Expulsion". *Myanmar Times*. 16 June. Available at: www.mmtimes.com/index.php/national-news/15052-myanmar-rejects-mahathir-s-push-for-asean-expulsion.html.

Ba, Alice. 2009. *(Re)Negotiating East and Southeast Asia*. Stanford, CA: Stanford University Press.

Chun, Chaesung and Chung-In Moon. 2003. "Sovereignty: Dominance of the Westphalian Concept and Implications for Regional Security". In Muthiah Alagappa (ed.), *Asian Security Order*. Stanford, CA: Stanford University Press, pp. 106–137.

Ciorciari, John D. 2010. *The Limits of Alignment: Southeast Asia and the Great Powers since 1975*. Georgetown, WA: Georgetown University Press.

Cochrane, Joe and Thomas Fuller. 2015. "Rohingya Migrants from Myanmar, Shunned by Malaysia, Are Spotted Adrift in the Adaman Sea". *New York Times*. 14 May. Available at: www.nytimes.com/2015/05/15/world/asia/burmese-rohingya-bangladeshi-migrants-andaman-sea.html.

Frost, Ellen L. 2008. *Asia's New Regionalism*. Boulder, CO: Lynne Rienner.

Fuller, Thomas. 2015a. "Dalai Lama Urges Aung San Suu Kyii to Help Myanmar's Rohingya". *New York Times*. 28 May. Available at: www.nytimes.com/2015/05/29/world/asia/dalai-lama-urges-aung-san-suu-kyi-to-help-myanmars-rohingya.html.

Fuller, Thomas. 2015b. "Myanmar to Bar Rohingya from Fleeing, But Won't Address Their Plight". *New York Times*. 12 June. Available at: www.nytimes.com/2015/06/13/world/asia/myanmar-to-bar-rohingya-from-fleeing-but-wont-address-their-plight.html.

Ginbar, Yuval. 2010. "Human Rights in ASEAN – Setting Sail or Treading Water?". *Human Rights Law Review* 10(3): 504–518. Available at: http://search.proquest.com/docview/818808930?accountid=14611.

Leider, Jacques. 2014. "Rohingya. The Name. The Movement. The Quest for Identity". In *Nation Building in Myanmar*. Myanmar Peace Center: 204–255. Available at: www.networkmyanmar.org/images/stories/PDF17/Leider-2014.pdf.

Narine, Shaun. 2002. *Explaining ASEAN: Regionalism in Southeast Asia*. Boulder, CO: Lynne Rienner.

Narine, Shaun. 2004a. "Peacebuilding in Southeast Asia: An Assessment of ASEAN". In Tom Keating and W. Andy Knight (eds), *Building Sustainable Peace*. Edmonton: University of Alberta Press, pp. 213–239.

Narine, Shaun. 2004b. "State Sovereignty, Political Legitimacy and Regional Institutionalism in the Asia Pacific". *Pacific Review* 17(3): 423–450.

Narine, Shaun. 2012. "Human Rights Norms and the Evolution of ASEAN: Moving Without Moving in a Changing Regional Environment". *Contemporary Southeast Asia* 34: 365–388.

Piketty, Thomas. 2014. *Capital in the Twenty-First Century*. Cambridge, MA: Harvard University Press.

Roberts, Christopher. 2007. "Affinity and Trust in Southeast Asia: A Regional Survey". In Hiro Katsumata and See Seng Tan (eds), *People's ASEAN and Governments' ASEAN*. IISS Monograph Number 11. Singapore: S. Rajaratnam School of International Studies, pp. 84–92.

Roberts, Christopher. 2012. *ASEAN Regionalism*. London: Routledge.

Severino, Rodolfo C. 2006. *Southeast Asia in Search of an ASEAN Community*. Singapore: ISEAS.

Talib, Ahmad. 2015. "ASEAN Has Failed the Rohingyas". *New Strait Times*. 14 June. Available at: www.nst.com.my/node/88234.

Wanandi, Jusuf. 2001. "ASEAN's Past and the Challenges Ahead". In Simon S. C. Tay, Jesus P. Estanislao, and Hadi Soesastro (eds), *Reinventing ASEAN*. Singapore: ISEAS, pp. 25–34.

Weatherbee, Donald. 2005. *Southeast Asia: The Struggle for Autonomy*. New York: Rowman & Littlefield.

17 The rhetoric of globalization and global citizenship

Reconstructing active citizenships in post-cold war sub-Saharan Africa

Ali A. Abdi

With the political fall of the Eastern bloc in the late 1980s and with the ushering in of what some have termed the new world order with unipolar realties, sub-Saharan African (hereafter shortened as African) countries suddenly found themselves in global political and economic environments that not only demanded new exigencies and prescriptions for *abetura politica* (political openness), but also some new global citizenship expectations. In studying the continent, this is perhaps one of the most important – if certainly a very complex – historical and political situation to extensively understand and analyse the changes that have taken place since then. The necessity of extensively – or at least situationally – attending to this complexity in scholarly and related senses is not just important for an inclusive, contemporaneously linked ascertaining of the political and economic reforms of the past 25 or so years. It is also, and equally, necessary for critically discerning the locations as well as the fluid nature of current citizenship manifestations that are affecting state–public relations in almost all the countries of the subcontinent. The case is also crucial for a more inclusive and connecting appreciation of the region's current attachments with the increasing debates and possibilities of global citizenship. As things are now, the rising graph of global citizenship and global citizenship education scholarship is presumably as much about Africa as any other place. In effect therefore, the assumption seems to have become by default that Africa, as historically the least developed zone of the world (something that should change in coming decades as the continent's economies have been among the fastest growing in the world), has to benefit from the perceived need for active and horizontally viable citizenship contexts in this part of the world. In reality though, with the fall of the Eastern bloc and the assumed ending of the cold war, the situation of citizenship practice and relationships did not actually improve as rapidly as one expected. There were (are) a number of reasons for the slow or even lack of citizenship changes even when African publics expected otherwise. Before I discuss some of these reasons, let me say a few things about the many political crises that were ushered in by the introduction of a one superpower, unipolar world. Since the late 1980s, these crises have had a significant impact on the African situation which has affected so much that has taken place in the African situation since the late 1980s, into the early 1990s, and beyond.

With the decline and eventual fall of the socialist bloc in Eastern Europe, many African governments that were not in power via any quasi-verifiable democratic structure or through remotely measurable popular support, but more or less, at the behest of superpower opportunism had to deal suddenly with new realities on the ground. Superpower opportunism was one such reality. By superpower opportunism, I mean to say that the United States of America or the Soviet Union would economically support and arm these mostly dictatorial regimes and then sustain them in power as long as they adhered to some pronouncements of certain capitalist or socialist ideologies and accordingly rendered their global political or policy loyalty to one patron superpower over the other. I know this first-hand as I was once a presumably endowed citizen of the grossly misnamed Somali Democratic Republic. As I have discussed elsewhere (Abdi 2008), the Somali case and what happened in that East African country since the emergence of the US as the sole military and relative economic superpower should perhaps illustrate, as much as any other place in the world, the essence and the workings of a superpower opportunism client state where global political interests literally rescinded the citizenship rights of people.

As in most other countries in Africa, Somalia's political independence came in the early 1960s, and as a former Western-colonized country, its immediate post-freedom political connections were with the US and Western Europe. Later though, Somali politicians accepted offers of free weapons consignments and some measure of rudimentary industrialization from the Soviet Union, and that slowly made it an announced socialist state where thin exhortations of collectivization and national resources co-ownership became the prevailing political and economic parlance in the country. I do not need to go too deeply into this as I am only using the Somali case as a convenient and illustrative example for the African context, but to complete my point, Somalia's strategic importance to the Soviet Union included its geographical connection with its western and southern neighbours, i.e., Ethiopia and Kenya, which were then both US client states. As was so happening in few other places in Africa though, those arrangements had to change during the Somalia–Ethiopia war of 1977 which was actually symptomatic of renewed tensions among the two superpowers (Farer 1979). The Soviet Union, which was already slowly supplanting the US in Ethiopia, suddenly decided to fully arm it against Somalia. To make this eventful story as short as possible but without missing its importance, Somalia expelled thousands of Soviet military and civilian experts in November 1977, which expectedly endeared it to the US, making a new American client state. In the following section, I will discuss Africa's recent experiences with globalization, global citizenship, and the need to rearrange things so life contexts get better for people.

Perforce globalizations of Africa: select analysis

In deploying the above observations, one of my objectives is to highlight, as much as possible, some central points and events that have shaped the recent developments of what we might term perverse globalizations of Africa through problematic geopolitics that actually didn't focus that much on the political, economic, and overall citizenship needs of people in Somalia or elsewhere in Africa. That is, a combination of forced globalizations through colonialism basically rescinded the basic citizenship rights of the colonized. This, in turn, was complemented by the normalized clientelization of the African state through superpower opportunism and the lack of policy and programme preparedness after the end of the cold war, all followed by the marginalizing trends of currently prevailing systems of globalization. These systems of globalization heap a high number of demerit points on citizenship realities in most African countries as we move deeper into the twenty-first century. As much as anything, it is these imposed historical conjectures that have shaped current state–public relations. In essence, therefore, from the period of Africa's independence in the 1960s into to the end of the cold war, the situation was largely characterized by suppressed citizenship contexts that did not elevate the political and economic rights of citizens. But things had to change from there and over time, many rulers, most of them in army uniforms who gained power through military coup d'états and used the state as their personal and family fortune (Bayart 1993), were no longer able to retain the security apparatuses that were previously constructed and maintained through foreign support. It became necessary for these rulers to devise new claims to remain in power.

One of those claims was how many rulers who neither understood democracy nor voluntarily wanted it started exhorting their adherence to the principles of democracy. Clearly, though, what was happening was nothing more than an institutionally deceitful, non-democratic "reconstitutionalization" of the old order, which should actually give us an early snapshot of the dwarfed development of viable citizenship situations in most places in the continent in the past two decades. With the reality of a unipolar world, the message from the West was at least linguistically stark: the primary condition for aid was now to be predicated on the articulation of a programme of democratic platforms that were to start as soon as possible. I will say more about the outcome of this as I continue writing, but perhaps I shall make one simple analytical insertion here: irrespective of the local dynamics of African politics, it is important not to miss the role of Western governments and their institutions perforce globalizing a Western-constructed democratic ideal and practice with no contextual consideration or explanations, into contexts where the fit for this kind of political and economic system might not be there. As many students of the case should recall, for the rest, the fall of the Eastern bloc represented and I must say, rather prematurely, a totalizing victory of capitalism and a total political victory of liberal democracy over everything else. The often-referenced work of the conservative American intellectual, Francis Fukuyama (1993), should speak volumes about the ideological fabrication of the ending of history. As Fukuyama saw it, there was to be only one form of political life and attached institutional as well as general life management destination called liberal democracy. Here and suddenly, there was no reason to understand the historico-cultural and social lives of people, or even the contemporary politico-economic needs of post-cold war Africans or others in similar circumstances. It also seemed that there was no need to reread the central tenets of liberal democracy and how those could be applicable to life systems outside the West.

Liberal democracy is a system of governance that emanates from specific historical, social, and economistic thinking that elevates the citizenship rights of the individual above all collective or other attendant communal needs and intentions. It is indeed this basic belief that should entice us to study the economic origins of liberal democracy, as it actually – and perhaps more so than any other ideology – emanates from classical economic thoughts as these were articulated by its main founders and adherents including Adam Smith (2003), David Ricardo (2004), Friedrich Hayek (2011), and Milton Friedman (2002). Indeed, when studied closely the general threads of liberal democracy slowly become clear in that it could be actually described as a political arm of classical economics which in its totality advances how market forces should reign supreme in all policy, monetary, and programme relationships. In prioritizing the rights of the individual over the possible needs of the collective, liberal democracy basically reduces the role of the state as mediating the general competition among individuals to gain life essentialities against everybody else. Here one can also critically discern the connecting points with unfettered capitalism where the survival of the fittest should reign high. The case is also fully attached to the current contexts of neo-liberal globalization where competition among all is extended into all corners of the world. Indeed, the neo-liberal globalization of Africa which gained momentum with the end of the cold war and was spearheaded by what have been the two most important global financial institutions, the World Bank and International Monetary Fund (IMF), has wrought havoc on the lives of more people in Africa than otherwise and certainly elsewhere in the world (Roy 2002; Harvey 2007). Indeed, as Wendy Brown notes in her new book, *Undoing the Demos* (2015), the dominant neo-liberal system, whether local or global, is actually bad for democracy and, by extension, not good for viable citizenship rights that advance the needs of all.

Especially for Africa, this unidirectional project of globalization also applies to the global citizenship impositions to which Africa is currently being subjected to through the presumptive development blueprint of Structural Adjustment Programmes (SAPs), which, as its main principles were explained in the *World Bank Report* of 1994, constricted Africa to an experimental platform to conduct the major objectives of the overall project. These objectives included privatization of public institutions as well as monetary and taxation schemes that were to be responsive to liberalization demands (see World Bank 1994). These demands were not constructed or analysed for their fitness for the African situation. In fact, the SAPs schemes were not detached from the overall rhetoric of democratization which was, as indicated above, emanating from the triumphalist exhortations of the supposed end of history where presumably and quite hastily, all countries were either practicing liberal democracy or were on their way to that platform of governance arrangements. The SAPs project was initially designed in the early 1980s, but gained intensity after the political collapse of the Eastern bloc in the late 1980s. So perhaps one attached question for us should be: how did these programmes fare as developmental mandates for the already marginalized people of Africa? Without any pretence, they simply became another component of the successive forces of colonization, dictatorial post-independence regimes, and problematic post-cold war schemes of rhetorical – but generally irrelevant – democratization assumptions (Ihonvbere 1996). SAPs also became symptomatic of the harsh structures of neo-liberal globalization that forced Africa and other post-colonial spaces to compete economically with everybody else in the world without taking into account all of the conditions that have selectively stunted these countries' social development in the first place (Ake 1996). In addition, even a more practical response to this important question came in the 2003 report of the United Nations Development Programme's highly respected annual document known as the Human Development Report (UNDP 2003), which showed that the majority of African countries were actually in worse economic shape in the early 2000s than they were in 1990. For me, and I am sure for others who study the African context with a permanent attention to the historical and cultural categories of development, complemented when relevant by rereading the problematic citizenship realities that people face, this was not that much of a surprise.

As the Nigerian political theorist and politician Julius Ihonvbere (1996) discussed in his aptly titled and interrogative essay, "On the Threshold of Another False Start?", the ways things moved for the old continent on the globalization, citizenship, and development fronts, fully informed by all the points discussed above, was anything but effectively responsive to the needs of the public. Especially on the citizenship situation which will be the focus for the remainder of this chapter, the story is anything but cheerful. In my reading, for people who have been through successive regimes of rights suppression, malmanagement of resources, externally imposed ideologies of mainly and exclusively marginalizing geopolitical interests, and, ultimately, the foreign-designed, sovereign-damaging projects of neo-liberal globalization, should have been at least given even a semi-prospectus on the nature of the now mainly rhetoricized democratic and citizenship platforms that are being prescribed. No, that did not happen, and even in the primary literature of democratization (Dewey 1926), the simple task of informing people about democracy before you ask them to practise it was widely missed. As Ihonvbere noted in his essay, the nominal democratizations that were masquerading as something good for Africa were actually exactly that: nominal changes with no applications that could be transformative or even reform-intended. In citizenship terms and especially in the case of the now much heralded global citizenship discussions, one could speak about the potential for a fourth or fifth false start in governance and social development possibilities. In Claude Ake's cogent reading (2005), the introduction of democracy as a platform for citizenship rights and responsibilities in Africa should have been at least subjected to some feasibility study where its viability for people who hardly miss the primacy of the collective in their daily lives and aspirations, could have been more pragmatically understood. This does not necessarily mean that what we know today as democracy never existed in Africa. As the late British cultural anthropologist I. M. Lewis narrated in his excellent work *Pastoral Democracy* (1999), some societies in Africa had thick primordial democratic systems that were, in my reading at least, more advanced than the limited claims of democracy in classical Greece where only one segment of the population, out of several, enjoyed any viable citizenship rights. While pastoral democracy in Lewis's research was not perfect and predicated on a gender-biased platform, it at least was missing some of the other problematic exclusions that characterized the Greek experience.

Rhetorics of global citizenship: revoicing global citizenship studies

It was with this complicated but overall liable citizenship and social development backdrop that Africans found themselves in the midst of the current discussions on global citizenship. For starters, while the idea of citizenship is, by and large, about territorially bound rationalizations of one's place of birth, parents' nationality, and via constitutionally explicated processes of naturalization (Isin 2009), the issue of global citizenship should be more complicated as it is transports us to new aspirations, at least at the conceptual and theoretical levels, which are extra-national and even extra-continental whereby through some still unpragamatizable platform, we may be citizens of all countries irrespective of everything else. This certainly and immediately poses a number of rights and responsibilities obstacles that must be considered. As Nigel Dower (2003, 2008) noted, in thinking about global citizenship, and we are still technically at the thinking level, we must realize that we are still dealing with ideals that could only be realizable possibilities, and which must be therefore, qualified at multiple levels and via inter-public–institutional relationships. And to be relatively clear, there is nothing wrong with being aspirational about one's possible citizenship connections with other peoples or countries, but in practical terms, I or someone else is no more a citizen beyond current legally recognized national boundaries. To the contrary, in most other places, such false claims could put the claimant in legal or even in more severe troubles, and as far as I can tell, most people wouldn't attempt to make such futile claims. So once again, and mainly for analytical reinforcements that should help my observations in the coming paragraphs on the complicated relationships Africans have with current exhortations and attached proliferations of the global citizenship perspective, one thing that could be good about the enlarged conceptions of the citizenship prospect should be the noble objective of belonging more to the world. Stated otherwise, there is actually nothing bad about aiming to be an aspirational and ideational global citizen. But it certainly gets more complicated beyond that point. Indeed, to selectively respond to this important concern, Dower's question on who could qualify as a global citizen in the early twenty-first century is important and applies directly to the citizenship and global citizenship locations of Africans, especially in these times of expanding discussions on the topic of global citizenship. Again, with so many books, papers, and conferences emanating from Western institutions and Western as well as non-Western but still Western-based scholars, and with so much of these designed to describe and analyse the lives of people who reside in the so-called developing world, we already have some presumptive global citizens speaking on behalf of potential but otherwise de-voiced global citizens. It seems that Africans, for some de-rational thinking and via problematic as well as unreasonable conclusions, need not be consulted at all about these citizenship assumptions and analyses about their lives.

It is therefore at the epistemic representational level that we need to qualify critically what is now basically a theoretical claim and not much more than that. Indeed, as Dower (2003, 2008) noted, the claim of global citizenship, even from those who have more means to theorize it, has more ethical extensions than real-life practical outcomes. That is, those of us who aspire for global citizenship would adhere to a global ethical commitment where we do what we can in our current locations to advocate the rights of all. That could be – indeed should be – a noble and humanist objective. It is ethically significant to strive for basic citizenship rights for all, to strive for as everyone in our planet deserves a minimum of basic citizenship rights, irrespective of where they reside and regardless of their economic or educational endowments. But even that level of commitment still requires some inclusive analysis as it can also problematically do few things that may not be necessarily good.

First, and to repeat, it disturbs, sometimes very acutely, the needed epistemic pluralism and epistemological inclusiveness that should characterize all knowledge-based relationships that minimally purport to sincerely understand the lives of other people and concretely care about their educational and overall well-being and rights (Andreotti et al. 2012). Second, it assumes, and more unreasonably perpetuates, the problematic power relations that have already done so much damage to marginalized peoples, especially when these relations are sustained via a unitary access to the textualized knowledges that are discursively appointed as the main epistemic life and by extension, relational categories to abide by. As Foucault (1980) and Said (1993), among others, counter-institutionally have noted, the rationalizations of interconnected but situationally dominant power/knowledge and culture/knowledge systems are perforce established, thus normatively and slowly institutionalizing the lives of people which are always so much more complicated than they are system-wise depicted.

Indeed, with the institutional globalization of Africa via the SAPs ideological constructions that somehow assumed what development platforms were fit for the continent and its people, which actually represents a new form of policy recolonizations, the new global citizenship epistemicalizations by +extension represent a new form of knowledge imperialism that refuses to read the historical, cultural, and discursive establishments of lived citizenship realities in Africa and elsewhere in the world. As Gianni Vattimo, in his excellent work, *Addio all Veritá* ("Farewell to Truth") (2008), so cogently discussed, the tragedy of dominant knowledge constructions and their possible practical outcomes suffer from one severe ailment: they associate conceptual and theoretical validities with Western knowledge systems that are presumed to always stand for the truth. The sadder part of this epistemic unilateralism is that it is now infecting an area – global citizenship – that lays claims to analysing and, perhaps eventually aiming, both policy-wise and programmatically, to elevating the citizenship rights of people, and which also purports to espouse an ethic of care about the basic rights of people all over the world. As much as any area in the social sciences, global citizenship studies should minimally exercise an active project of epistemic pluralism that reads and practices citizenship realities from the living contexts of the people whose actualities are being analysed.

Beyond the global ethics perspective that Dower talked about, which is mainly confined to the mental level for now, we must move one step further, and speak about what the Canadian Aboriginal scholar Willie Ermine terms "the ethical space" (Ermine 2007). The ethical space, in its conceptual notations and possible practice, should apply to all things humans interactively engage among themselves and for my purpose here, in relation to our overall ecological realities that go beyond anthropocentricism or the sole focus on humans. Indeed, it should be how we do the ethical space, i.e., how we constructively relate to the subjectivities and experiences of others with whom we share select social, political, economic, and yes, as much as anything, epistemic spaces. For me, therefore, the ethical space actually takes a higher meaning when one factors in differential normative knowledge relations which should be, sans exception, interactive with the power connections thus established.

The use of the term normative here is deliberate as I want to qualify how knowledge platforms are inextricably present and achieved in all societies, but as an endowed trader of epistemic analysis and epistemological criticisms myself, I am fully aware of the quasi-hegemonic normativizations of school-based/university-sanctioned and text-borne forms of knowledge clusters that are accepted as real knowledge at the expense of all other possible epistemic representations that might be resident in other contexts of our world. In selectively deploying the epistemic ethical space in the discussion, I submit that current theorizations of global citizenship education – with their unidirectional and hegemonic institutionalizations of concerned knowledge systems – inhibit the needed revoicing of indigenous readings and informal theorizations of people's citizenships as well as their possible localized responses to the presumptions of ideas and perspectives that claim to know their social platforms and politico-economic and social relations, needs, and expectations. Here, the ongoing danger of this important story is how the centrality of citizenship discussions and practices which are now essential to a world where governance and resources management structures are at the behest of the nation state as the main sociopolitical entity that rules the lives of people, must be seriously studied, understood, and improved on the basis of locally inclusive recommendations that can immediately respond to the needs of the public. So basically, and especially in social development terms, non-inclusive theorizations of contemporary global citizenship studies have the potential to apply not only impractical suggestions for the lives of concerned people, but also, a perhaps unintended epistemic violence that damages future policy directions for citizenship practices which will be de-presentative of the real and immediate needs of concerned populations.

It is on the basis of all those conceptual and learning as well as policy and eventual programmatic implications that should entice us to rethink the situation of current global citizenship scholarship and extensively seek new ways of multi-voicing the constructions of global citizenship and social development. My repetition of the terms "social development" here is not for descriptive convenience; it is actually a deliberate implication of my prospective reading and criticisms of the intentions and potential outcomes of the case. That is, the new and expansive emergence, indeed the proliferation of unidirectional global citizenship scholarship in the past two decades or so, should still have some objective for the social well-being of people. So the centrality of the ethical concern and space (Dower 2003, 2008; Ermine 2007) must be continuously applied. If that social well-being prospect is missed, then we will be facing most of the concerns explicated in this chapter, including theoretical determinisms that function, not for the minimal required ethical concerns and intentions of the local situation, but for conceptualizing and recommending about the lives of others who live elsewhere. This will continue de-voicing the potential global citizenship voices of southern populations. Certainly, that will also expand the current epistemic colonizations of the global citizenship literature as not about the advancement of its research destinations, but retroactively about the professional well-being, even careerism, of northern and north-based scholars in northern universities and colleges.

It is on these bases, that the project of the conceptual, and, it is hoped, revoicing of global citizenship studies must be more than just asking people in Africa, and by rational extension, elsewhere in both physically and epistemically colonized locations, to add additional information to a narrative that has been produced about their lives. At a more radically inclusive and epistemic level, the commitments must be sincere, more humanistic, and more historico-culturally respectful. For newcomers to this type of the horizontal criticalizations of contemporary global citizenship claims who are eager to see immediate deconstructions of the case, the inter-Africa–northern dialogues on both the local and global meaning and possible outcomes of concerned citizenship realities must start at the reading and decoding levels, to recode again, the basic fragmental constructions of knowledge, which has to be located as collectively achieved by all humans in all places throughout human history (Harding 1998, 2008). When we do that and analytically stop associating knowledge, achievement, and social development with only the north, we will do well in starting and perhaps achieving an inclusively viable epistemic justice (Santos 2014) that could untether us from colonialist and prospectively arresting assumptions which we have been socialized to accept as the one truth of the world. From that important knowledge origins agreement, we shall allow Africans and others to start, not with responses to what has been already produced about them in global citizenship analysis, as that already biases their perceptions and subjective views, but to join them in an open space where, as the group whose cognitive life intersections have been deformed, potentially de-patterned, they should be given the first chance to start the conversations upon their understandings of local citizenship, global citizenship, the possible ties between the two, and how their daily lives are affected by these issues and relationships.

I have actually seen this type of fully equiticized (not just equal as equity takes into account historical injustices that may not be currently measurable) co-construction of global citizenship concepts and knowledges, not only via contextual theorizations, but as well, through thick experiential readings that highlighted people's lived realities through local citizenship and in relation to what some of those people termed the rhetorical manifestations of global citizenship which they hear through the literature but hardly discern or see it in practical terms. In an open, multi-voiced seminar discussion on the topic in Nairobi (Kenya) that I organized with university colleagues from Canada with teachers and education personnel from Kenya (see Shultz et al. 2012), we immediately saw what was starkly missing from current global citizenship scholarship as it is produced and mostly consumed in the West. When we asked our Kenyan colleagues, who mostly haven't done any text-based analysis of global citizenship, to share with us (before we shared ours, by the way) their perspectives on citizenship and learning for citizenship, we immediately marvelled at how much primary knowledge about citizenship we could learn from them. This approach brought up so many multidirectional rich observations and analyses that achieved for all involved a measure of both cognitive and epistemic justice (Santos 2007, 2014). The presumably and previously privileged scholars from the north not only learned so much in that educational encounter, but they also got brilliant and at times platform-shattering responses on their far-away readings of the Kenyan and African world. For me at least, the outcomes of such knowledge co-construction and dialogue expansively advanced my own analytical conjectures including the point I shared above on epistemic respectability. After that learning session, I now see that our work should actually be moved to a new and more humanized intersubjective space, that of not just respecting but fully accepting the valid multi-locational realities of knowledge, learning perspectives, and inductive epistemic possibilities that can endow us all in our global citizenship scholarships and relations with others in Africa and across the globe. Indeed, such ways of doing global citizenship scholarship should allow us to disembark from the high horse of epistemic arrogance which can, when not globally bridled, expound problematic clusters that normalize the continuing knowledge colonization that perpetuates what Santos (2007, 2014) terms the slow epistemicide of southern epistemologies. Such epistemicide deprives us of so much useful knowledge and related social justice possibilities that we desperately need to live good and inclusively humanized local and global lives. For those who are actually the victims of this, it is even so much worse: the organized epistemic violence which has been – and is being – perforce imposed upon them has the potential to ontologically deform their being, thus de-patterning their epistemological points of reference and decommissioning their potential for social development. Needless to add that doing counter-that would awaken us to the immediate, indeed urgent need to multi-voice and by extension, de-rhetoricize current and future global citizenship theorizations, scholarship, and potential practices.

Conclusion

The intention of this chapter was to provide a wide observational platform that describes and selectively analyses the recent evolutions of politics, globalization, and global citizenship as these have been placed by mostly external actors on the African continent and its people. Early in the chapter, I used the case of Somalia and its problematic location in the era of superpower opportunism. Extending from realities of superpower opportunism and with the ending of the cold war, the discussions in the chapter moved to the wider African context, thus critically analysing the continent's relationship with the impositions of democratization and neo-liberal globalization which presented a number of social development liabilities that did not respond to the immediate needs of people. With those understandings relatively in place, I have discussed the current stylizations of the growing scholarship of global citizenship, which, mainly due to its conceptual and theoretical unidirectionality, happens to be less practical in advancing the citizenship rights of the public in Africa and potentially elsewhere. In all, the contents of the chapter should entice some of us to rethink the dominant constructions of these and related citizenship categories that are more rhetorical in their mono-epistemic realities. We, therefore, need new and inclusive multi-historicizations, multiculturalizations, and certainly multi-epistemicalizations of the situation. When those ethically inclusive platforms are established, then we may talk about new possibilities of globalization and global citizenship that could aid social development and advance overall human emancipation in Africa and elsewhere.

References

Abdi, Ali A. 2008. "From 'Education for All to Education for None': Somalia in the Careless Global Village". In Ali A. Abdi and Shibao Guo (eds), *Education and Social Development: Global Issues and Analyses*. Rotterdam: Sense Publishers, pp. 181–194.
Ake, Claude. 1996. *Democracy and Development in Africa*. Washington, DC: Brookings Institution.
Ake, Claude. 2005. *The Feasibility of Democracy in Africa*. Dakar: CODESRIA.
Andreotti, Vanessa and Lynn Mario de Souza. (eds) 2012. *Postcolonial Perspectives on Global Citizenship Education*. New York: Routledge.
Bayart, Jean-François. 1993. *The State in Africa: The Politics of the Belly*. London: Longman.
Brown, Wendy. 2015. *Undoing the Demos: Neoliberalism's Stealth Revolution*. Cambridge, MA: Zone.
Dewey, John. 1926. *Democracy and Education*. New York: Collier.
Dower, Nigel. 2003. *An Introduction to Global Citizenship*. Edinburgh: Edinburgh University Press.
Dower, Nigel. 2008. "Are We All Global Citizens or Are Only Some of Us Global Citizens? The Relevance of this Question to Education". In Ali A. Abdi and Lynette Shultz (eds), *Educating for Human Rights and Global Citizenship*. Albany, NY: SUNY Press, pp. 39–54.
Ermine, Willie. 2007. "The Ethical Space of Engagement". *Indigenous Law Journal* 6: 193–203.
Farer, Tom. 1979. *War Clouds on the Horn of Africa: A Crisis for Détente*. Washington, DC: Carnegie Endowment for International Peace.
Foucault, Michel. 1980. *Power/Knowledge: Selected Interviews and Other Writings, 1972–1977*. New York: Vintage.
Friedman, Milton. 2002. *Capitalism and Freedom*. Chicago, IL: University of Chicago Press.
Fukuyama, Francis. 1993. *The End of History and the Last Man*. New York: Free Press.
Harding, Sandra. 1998. *Is Science Multicultural? Postcolonialisms, Feminisms and Epistemologies*. Bloomington, IN: Indian University Press.
Harding, Sandra. 2008. *Science from Below: Feminisms, Postcolonialities and Modernities*. Durham, NC: Duke University Press.
Harvey, David. 2007. *A Brief History of Neoliberalism*. Oxford: Oxford University Press.
Hayek, Friedrich. 2011. *The Constitution of Liberty*. Chicago, IL: University of Chicago Press.
Ihonvbere, Julius. 1996. "On the Threshold of Another False Start? A Critical Evaluation of Prodemocracy Movements in Africa". *Journal of Asian and African Studies* 31: 125–142.
Isin, Engin. 2009. *Acts of Citizenship*. London: Zed Books.
Lewis, Ioan. 1999. *A Pastoral Democracy: A Study of Pastoralism and Politics Among the Northern Somali of the Horn of Africa*. London: James Currey.

Ricardo, David. 2004. *The Principles of Political Economy and Taxation*. London: Dover.
Roy, Arundhati. 2002. *The Algebra of Infinite Justice*. New York: Flamingo.
Said, Edward. 1993. *Culture and Imperialism*. New York: Vintage.
Santos, Boaventura. 2007. *Cognitive Justice in a Globalized World: Prudent Knowledges for a Decent Life*. Lanham, MD: Lexington Books.
Santos, Boaventura. 2014. *Epistemologies of the South: Justice against Epistemicide*. Boulder, CO: Paradigm.
Shultz, Lynette, Ali A. Abdi, and Musembi Nungu. 2012. *Field Notes: Education Policy and Citizenship Education*. Nairobi.
Smith, Adam. 2003. *The Wealth of Nations*. London: Bantam Press.
United Nations Development Programme. 2003. *Human Development Report*. New York: Oxford University Press.
Vattimo, Gianni. 2008. *Addio a la Veritá*. Rome: Meltemi Editore.
World Bank. 1994. *World Bank Report*. Washington, DC: World Bank.

Index

#bringbackourgirls 178
9/11 112, 146, 169, 217

Abdi, Ali A. 69, 78–9, 244
Acharya, Amitav 226, 232–4, 239
Adams, J. Michael 58
Addams, Jane 159
Afghanistan 158, 165, 169
Africa 19, 110, 132, 134–6, 227; African Union 135, 189; colonialism 72; connectivity 61; global citizenship rhetoric 243–54; notion of ubuntu 87, 89–91
Agbaria, Ayman K. 76–7
age: and surveys as global citizens 185–7, 193–207; technology 62–3, 66; *see also* youth
Ake, Claude 247–8
Al Qaeda 217, 219
Alavi, Seema 216
Allport, Gordon 218
Alvarez, Walter 138
America *see* United States
Anderson, Benedict 70, 73, 134
Andreotti, Vanessa 249; and global citizenship education 57, 77–8, 81–2, 87, 89, 116–17, 125; and post-colonialism 69–71, 79–80
Annan, Kofi 110, 151
anthropology 130, 145
Appadurai, Arjun 88, 181
Appiah, Kwame Anthony: cosmopolitan views of 40, 89, 156–7, 168, 184; and obligations toward others 29, 93, 95
Aquinas, Thomas 18
Arab Spring 60, 166, 181
Aristotle 31, 144
Armstrong, Jeannette 88, 94–5
Armstrong, Karen 216

Asher, Nina 76
Association of Southeast Nations, ASEAN 189, 232–241
Austin, John 103, 113
Australia 80, 118, 135, 137, 182, 234

Baha'i, Bahai 15, 17
Baker, Peter 135, 165
Ban Ki-moon 82, 122
Banks, James A. 56–7, 77–8
Barber, Benjamin 177–8, 181, 184, 211
Barnes, Christine 122
Bauman, Zygmunt 224
Ben-Nun Bloom, Pazit 218
Bérubé, Michael 41
Biden, Joe 122
Big History 137–9
Boler, Megan 60
Boocock, Kate 117–20, 122, 125
Bosnia 109
Boyd-Barrett, Oliver 228
Bramlett, Brittany 46
Britain 21, 91, 109, 111, 197, 215, 233; *see also* United Kingdom
Brown, Wendy 246
Buddhism 14–17, 237
Burns, K. 72
Bush, George W. 162

Calhoun, Craig 38, 40, 52, 185–6, 191
Cameron, David 111
Camicia, Steven P. 70
Canada 80–1, 92, 110, 125, 252
Carens, Joseph 25, 27, 31–2
Carfagna, Angelo 58
Carson, Rachel 150
Carter, April 22, 30–2, 34–5
Castles, Stephen 32, 78

Index 257

China 19–20, 107, 112, 222–30; and Association of Southeast Asian Nations 235; Internet access 63; religion and philosophy 15, 17; surveys of confidence in UN, world citizenship 181, 183–4, 190
Chouliaraki, Lilie 123, 125
Christian, David 137–8
Christianity 15–19, 22, 73, 89–90, 105
Cicero 18
citizenship: and Africa 243–54; and China 222–3, 229–30; critical 39, 45–6; definitions of 14; democratic 60; dimensions of 25, 194; and education 56–7, 75–6; and European Union 35, 112; historical development 73–4, 104, 107, 109; and identity 31–2; and the Middle East 213–15; national 129, 134, 228–9; rights and obligations 27–30; multiple levels 21, 26, 31, 35, 57, 178, 189; surveys of 178, 195, 201–2; and technology 62–5, 224–5; *see also* global citizen and world citizen
climate change 13, 101–2, 108, 111, 147, 229
Clinton, Hillary 224
coalitional psychology 145, 147, 149–50
cold war 108, 214, 224–5
Confucius, Confucianism 15, 223, 226
Connectivity Declaration 64
Cormier, Harvey 162, 164
corporations 26, 34, 124–5, 143, 151, 161; corporate background 64; as sponsors 121; *see also* transnational corporations
cosmopolitan democracy 35, 184
cosmopolitanism: Appiah, Kwame Anthony 156–7; cultural 41, 48; definition of 3, 39, 40, 49, 52, 72, 156; and Dewey, John 57; discursive field 80–1; and the Enlightenment 20; and the Middle East 166, 209–18; in the nineteenth and twentieth centuries 21; and Obama, Barack 162–3; surveys of 177–81, 184–9, 190–1, 199; and patriotism 31; political 178, 180; and pragmatism 159; and the Renaissance 18; Southeast Asia 240–1; thin 178; traditional 40, 43–4; and United States 168; *see also* critical cosmopolitanism
crimes against humanity 14, 19, 30, 108, 110
critical cosmopolitanism 38, 40–8, 52, 72–3
Cruce, Emeric de 19

Crutzen, Paul J. 129
Curtis, Richard 122

Daesh 65; *see also* ISIS, ISIL, Islamic State
Dagger, Richard 31–2
Daoism 15
Davies, Ian 77
Davies, Lynn 77–8
Delanty, Gerard 41, 49, 73
Democracy, democratic 21, 165–6, 168–70, 177, 184; in Africa 244–8, 253; antidemocratic movement 32; and China 222–6, 229–30; citizenship and technology 60; and education 59, 75, 78; and global citizenship education 80, 82; and globalization 26; Japan 227; local 35; in the Middle East 217–19; in South Africa 90; in Southeast Asia 237, 239–41; surveys of 188; and Western civilization 88; *see also* cosmopolitan democracy
Derrida, Jacques 48
Dewey, John 57, 159, 165, 169, 247
Diderot 20
digital divide 63
Diogenes 156, 177
Donnelly, Jack 27–8
Dovidio, John 217–18
Dower, Nigel 29, 199, 248–51
Drezner, Daniel 225
drones 167–9
Du Bois, W.E.B. 159
Durand, E. Sybil 76

Earth Charter 139
East Timor 109, 234–5
Egypt: ancient 130; and Arab Spring 165–6; surveys of world citizenship 181, 183, 212–13; and Islamic culture 17; nationalism 209, 215
Eickelman, Daniel 215
English School 111
Enlightenment 19–21, 23, 31, 73–4, 79, 81
Environment: conferences, negotiations 112, 139; and cosmopolitanism, global citizenship 51, 57, 125; and globalization 1, 3, 13, 59; movements, activism 14, 135, 143, 146, 149–52; organizations, surveys of confidence in 188–9; threats to 29, 112, 130, 138, 195; US policy response 143–152
Erasmus of Rotterdam 19

Ermine, Willie 250–1
Erskine, Toni 218
Ethiopia 135, 244
European Union, EU 19, 21, 34–5, 112, 178–9, 189, 225; comparison to ASEAN 233, 235
Evans, Hugh 118, 121

Falk, Richard 32, 194, 228
feminist movement 22
Fernee, Tadd Graham 216–18
Flanagan, Constance A. 197, 200
Foer, Franklin 211
Foucault, Michel 249
Franklin, Barry M. 70
Freedom House 184
Friedman, Milton 246
Friedman, Thomas 26, 57, 59–60
Fukuyama, Francis 246
Furia, Peter 32, 181, 185–6, 199, 202, 211

Gaertner, Samuel 217–18
Galtung, Johan 34
Gandhi, Mahatma 22, 87, 92–3
Gates, Bill 137, 187
Gates, Bill and Melinda 64
Gellner, Ernst 134, 215–16
gender 57, 63, 132, 200, 219, 248; group identification 31, 74; traditional cosmopolitanism 40
Geneva Conventions 19
genocide 30, 110, 157, 239
Gentili 18
Geopolitics 245, 247; and global citizenship 129–39; and global citizenship education 70, 78, 82; influence in defining citizenship 72; traditional, national 129, 133
Gills, Barry K. 28–9
Global Citizen Festival 118–19, 121–4
global citizen/citizenship 1, 3, 93–5, 228; and Africa 243, 246, 248–53; and age 195–206; Appiah, Kwame Anthony 156–7; challenges 28, 152; and China 222, 225–6, 230; definition of 3–4, 13–14, 87; and democracy 166; discourse 69, 70–2, 81, 91–2; and education 58–9, 63, 71; formation of 137; and global geopolitics 129–30, 136, 139; and global governance 33, 229–30; and Global Poverty Project 115–25; and globalization 26–32, 157; in higher education 46, 91; historical origins 14–23, 104; identification 31–2; 193–4; and the Middle East 209–10, 212–13; and multiple citizenships 31–2, 35, 46; Obama, Barack 162–5, 167; and pragmatism 156, 159–61; relationship to cosmopolitanism 39–40; Singer, Peter 157; and states 107–8, 111; and Southeast Asia 232, 238, 240; surveys of 31–2, 177–88, 212–13; and technology 61–3; and United Nations 82; and United States 157–8, 168; *see also* world citizen
global citizenship education, GCE: critical 39, 57, 60, 77–8, 116–17, 124; definition 125; as a discursive field 70, 73, 77, 81; and global citizenship 94–5, 194–5; initiatives 93, 115; learning outcomes 116; post-/decolonial 69–70, 75, 79–81; programmes 122; scholarship 78, 81–2, 243, 251; "soft" approaches 80, 87, 116–17; and technology 60–1, 66; Western/non-Western incorporations 87–9
Global Goals, Global Goals for Sustainable Development 64, 115, 119, 122, 125
global governance 2, 26, 33–5, 75, 222–4, 226, 229; and health 34
global identity: 136, 214; and global citizenship 130, 139; and leftist political ideology 202; and youth 193–4, 198–203, 205–6
global issues 2, 33, 73, 115, 144; and education 70–1, 76, 78–80; and Global Poverty Project 118, 122
global learning: 38–9, 89; and critical cosmopolitanism 43, 44–6, 49–50, 52; frameworks 40
Global North 4, 116, 120, 181, 195, 226; education in 41–3, 78, 82
Global Poverty Project, the Project, GPP 115–125
Global South 92, 181, 185, 187, 222, 226
global warming 77, 138, 147–8, 151; *see also* climate change
globalism 1, 32, 143, 149, 152
globalization: and Africa 244–7, 250, 253; and Appiah's cosmopolitan framework 156–7; and China 223, 224, 226; cultural 3, 63, 88, 223, 226; definitions of 1–2; economic 2–3, 26, 28, 59; and education 63, 75–8, 80–1; "from below" 194; and global citizenship 3–4, 13, 25–6, 31–2, 70–3,

129; and global health 33–4; history 60, 136; and identity in the Middle East 209–10, 214, 216; impact on World Values Survey 177; objects of 117; political 2; and pragmatism 159, 162; and states 26, 30, 33, 109, 111; and youth 193–5
glocalization 2, 88
Goldberg, David Theo 74
Goodman, Mike 122
Gore, Al 138
Greece, Greek classical 13, 16–20, 105, 131, 159, 248
Grotius, Hugo 18–19, 30, 106
Guantánamo Bay 112, 164

Haidt, J. 146, 149
Hanley, Will 210–11
Hardin, Garrett 144
Harvey, Peter 15
Haste, Helen 197, 199, 206
Hayek, Friedrich 246
Hazenberg, Haye 218
Heater, Derek 19, 26
Held, David 3, 34–5, 112
Hensby, Alexander 123
Herder, J.G. 177–8
Hickman, Larry 160, 165
higher education 38, 40, 46, 52, 59
Hinduism 14–16
Hitler, Adolf 132
Hogan, Amy 197, 199, 206
Holsti, Kalevi 129
Holton, Robert J. 3, 211
human rights: appeals to 23; and ASEAN 235–9, 241; and China 225–6, 230; and citizenship 35, 46; and connectivity 64; discourse 90–1, 94; education 57–8; and EU 112; and global citizenship 25; and globalization 3–4, 28, 32, 59, 194; history of 13–14, 27–30, 104, 107–9, 111; surveys of 188
humanism 18–19, 79, 91
humanitarian law 18–19, 22, 30
humanitarianism 87, 91, 94, 115, 125
Hume, David 21
Huntington, Samuel 3, 181, 210, 216

idealist, idealism 102, 193
Ihonvbere, Julius 247
immigration 65, 134, 218; surveys of 194–5, 200, 203–5

imperialism: cultural 23, 88, 209, 211, 223, 228; and Dewey, John 169; and DuBois, W.E.B. 159; eighteenth century 20–1; and geopolitics 130; and global citizenship 1, 158; and Obama, Barack 163–4; and globalization 32; knowledge 250; Western 25, 27, 40, 43–4, 112, 181, 214
India 19, 216, 226, 229; access to technology 63; globalization 26; surveys of confidence in UN 182, 184; religion 14, 16
Indonesia 34, 233–36, 238–40
information/communications technology 33; and global citizenship education 56–66; and globalization 2, 25–6, 29; influence on global identity 31–2, 210; political uses of technology 31–3; Western flows of 228
Inglehart, Ronald 218
interdependence 2, 29, 77, 90–1, 125, 199–200
interdisciplinary approach 4, 6
intergovernmental organizations, IGOs 5, 25–7, 33–4
Intergovernmental Panel on Climate Change, IPCC 147–8
International Court of Justice, ICJ 19, 108–9, 112
International Criminal Court, ICC 19, 30, 110, 112
international law 2, 14, 23, 26–7, 74; and ASEAN 237; in civic education 58; and the ICC 30; and philosophy of Grotius 18–9; state sovereignty 103, 107–9, 111
International Monetary Fund, IMF 26, 125, 246
international relations 5, 104, 111, 161, 163, 167
international society 104, 109; and ASEAN 238; and China 222; Grotius's definition 19; the "English school" 111
Internet: digital divide 61, 63–4; global Internet governance and China 223–6, 229; and globalization 71; as a learning tool 57–9, 66, 115, 119; and "netizens", activism 32, 123; politics 63–6; and social networking 59–62, 65–6; source of terrorist recruitment 30; structure and corporate interests

64–5; surveys of usage and cosmopolitan attitudes 185
Iran 17, 60, 164, 212–13, 215, 224
Iraq 17, 158, 165, 169, 180–1, 183, 212–3
ISIL 30, 65; *see also* Daesh, ISIS, Islamic State
Isin, Engin F. 74, 248
ISIS 30, 65, 219; *see also* Daesh, ISIL, Islamic State
Islam, Islamic: 16–17, 19–20, 22, 215, 240; civilization 210; pan-Islam and ummah 105, 209, 215–6, 240; relationship to cosmopolitan identity 214, 216
Islamic State 30, 217–18; *see also* Daesh, ISIS, ISIL
Israel 130, 164, 181
Israeli-Palestinian conflict 181
Iyall Smith, Keri E. 1

Jabri, Vivienne 211
Jackman, Hugh 119
Jainism 14–15
James, William 159, 160, 162
Japan 19, 63, 179, 227
Jefferess, David 42, 50, 87, 88, 93, 117, 120
Jew(s), Jewish 15–17, 164, 215–16, 218
justice: 28–9, 104–5, 107–8, 111–12, 158, 197, 200; cosmopolitan 105; distributive 112; ecological 92, 94; epistemic 252; global 29, 88, 107; and global citizenship education 76, 78–9, 81, 89, 91–2, 94; social 39, 57, 253; transnational 39

Kant, Immanuel 21, 23, 32, 177, 218
Kenya 62, 244, 252
Keohane, Robert 1
Khoury, Philip 214
King, Martin Luther, Jr. 16
Kinnvall, Catarina 211, 216, 219
Kinzelbach, Katrin 225
Klees, Steven 124
Kohlberg, L. 146
KONY 2012 178
Koopman, Colin 161
Kosovo 109
Kostiner, Joseph 214
Krahmann, Elke 22
Kratochwil, Friedrich 193–4, 199
Kyoto Convention 112

Langran, Irene 4, 143
law: natural 14, 18, 105–7; Roman 14, 18 *see also* humanitarian law, international law
Lawrence, Bruce 216
Lawson, Fred 215
League of Nations 14, 22
Lewis, Bernard 210, 215, 219
Lewis, I.M. 248
liberalism, liberal: and cosmopolitanism 184, 211; democratic 222, 245–7; framework 40, 77; and human rights 91, 230; international relations 162–4; political ideology 198; Western/Anglo American 75, 225, 229
Libya 110–11, 165, 183
Lipsius 18
Live Below the Line, LBTL 118–21, 126–7
localism 40, 45, 216–17; reflected in World Values Survey 177–80, 187–90
Locke, Alain 159, 162–3
Lorrance, Arleen 92

MacMullan, Terrance 162
Make Poverty History campaign 118
Mannion, Greg 70
Marcus Aurelius 20
Marshall, T. H. 74
Martin, Chris 119
Massey, Doreen 50
media: and activism 118–19, 121; and China 223, 226–9; freedom 218; and identity, community 32, 210; interactive 59–60; literacy 65–6
meliorism 161–4
Melville, Herman 146
Middle East: 17; and global or cosmopolitan identity 209–19; Obama, Barack foreign 164–5
Mignolo, Walter 41, 43, 72–4, 78–9
migration 31, 134–6, 215, 238
Mirsepassi, Ali 216–8
Molina, M. J. 151
Montaigne, Michel de 18
Montesquieu 20–1
Montreal Protocol 151
Morsi, Muhammad 166
Morton, Brian 92
Moss, Simon 118
Muslim(s): historical influence on global citizenship 15–17, 105; in the Middle East 166, 209, 213–18; and opinion

Index 261

surveys 190; in Southeast Asia 237–40; *see also* Islam
Myers, John P. 197–8, 206

Naim, Moises 26, 30
Nash, Kate 118
national identity 90, 112, 134, 136, 202, 215, 232
nationalism, nationalists: 131, 133–4; in China 222; economic 2; ethno-nationalism 215; in the Middle East 210–11, 213, 215; in Southeast Asia 239; *see also* supra-nationalism
neo-liberal globalization 246–7, 253
neo-liberalism, neo-liberal policies 26, 28, 32, 41, 78–9, 90
neo-Stoic attitudes 18
Nesbitt-Larking, Paul 211, 216, 219
netizen 32, 60
nongovernmental organizations, NGOs: 1, 92, 118, 189, 229; 237; in ASEAN 232; and education 87, 116; influence on global governance 25–7, 33–4
non-intervention norm 30, 104, 107, 110; in ASEAN 233, 237–8
non-state actors 2, 4, 33, 111–12, 139, 161, 224
Norris, Pippa 189, 218
North America 21, 89, 160, 189
Nussbaum, Martha 31–2, 49, 52, 59, 77
Nye, Joseph 1, 224

O'Byrne, Darren 123
Obama, Barack 5, 65, 122, 135; as pragmatist 156, 161–5, 167–8
Osborne, Ken 75
otherness 43–4, 47–8, 77, 94
Oxfam 28–9

Paine, Thomas 21, 157–8
Pakistan 164, 168, 182–3
Palestine 130, 164, 215
Papini, Giovanni 160
patriotism: patriotism-cosmopolitanism debate 21, 31, 156, 184; supranational 211; surveys of 177–80, 187–90
peace movement 21–2
Peirce, C.S. 159
Penn, William 19
Pew Research Center 158, 167; Internet and American Life Project 65
Pike, Graham 70, 77–8, 82
Pinker, Steven 143, 149
Pinochet, Augusto 109

post-colonial, postcolonialism: 28, 247; influence on global citizenship education 69, 71, 78–82; notions of resistance 89; cosmopolitanism 181
post-Westphalian 26–7, 33
Praeg, Leonhard 90–1
Pragmatism 156, 159–70
Progressive Movement 150
Protestantism 16, 18–19, 22
Pufendorf 106

Qargha, Omar 124
Quakers 17 *see also* Penn, William

Rabinow, Paul 41–2
racism 77, 79, 159, 169
Ralston, Shane 159, 161–3, 166
rationalism 17, 20, 217
Rawls, John 107
Reagan, Ronald 143
realism, realist 33, 102, 111, 156, 163–4, 167
refugees 27, 30, 60–1, 108
Reisman, Michael 111
Reisman, Michael W. 111
religion: historical influences on global citizenship 13–23; and identity 31, 56, 72, 132, 146, 157; in the Middle East 209–16, 218; in Southeast Asia 232–40; in surveys 188, 201, 203–5
Responsibility to Protect, R2P 30, 110, 226
Ricardo, David 246
rights: and Africa 244–50, 253; and ASEAN 233, 235; and China 227–30; for colonized peoples 22, 105; and cosmopolitanism 218; and education 60, 66, 70, 74, 77, 79; and equality 32; and EU 112; and states 25, 29, 74, 104; social 194; and the US 150, 157; Western views 23; *see also* human rights
Rizvi, Fazal 72
Robbins, Bruce 41, 43, 52
Roberts, Christopher 235–6
Robertson, Geoffrey 107
Rochester, J. Martin 28
Rodrik, Dani 2
Rogers, Richard A. 88–9
Rome, classical views of cosmopolitanism 13–14, 18–20, 105
Romano, Carlin 162
Roosevelt, Franklin 150
Roosevelt, Teddy 150
Rorty, Richard 158
Rosenau, James N. 1

Ross, Alec 66
Rowland, F. S. 151
Russia 19, 63, 112, 135, 181, 183, 224
Rwanda 110, 181–2, 190

Sagan, Carl 136–8
Said, Edward 20, 71, 74, 88–9, 249
Santos, Boaventura 252–3
Sassen, Saskia 27
Sayer, Andrew 41
Schattle, Hans 196, 200, 206, 211
Schwittay, Anke 117–20, 122, 125
Sen, Amartya 15, 17, 88
Seneca 18, 20
Shiva, Vandana 26
Shorter, John 193–4, 199
Simon, Roger 42, 121
Singer, Peter 149, 157, 168
slave trade, slavery 14, 20–2, 239; ISIS and sexual slavery 30
Smith, Adam 246
social media 66, 119, 123, 224
social movements 21–2, 33, 115, 150–2, 228
social sciences 70, 75, 131, 198, 200, 233, 250
socialist movement 22
Somalia 109, 244–5, 253
South Africa 89–91, 108, 179, 182, 190
South African Truth and Reconciliation Commission, TRC 89–90
South America 19, 133, 135
Southeast Asia 232–41
Souza, Lynn Mario de 69, 71, 79–80, 82
sovereignty 30, 103–4, 107–8, 111–12, 164, 211; and Southeast Asia 232–4, 237–8; and China 222–4, 227, 229; historical influences 18–19, 105–6; impact of globalization 4, 25–7, 33, 58, 247; International Commission on Intervention and State Sovereignty 110; Internet sovereignty 224–5; and realists 33; "viral sovereignty" 34; and world federalists 33; *see also* non-intervention norm
Soviet Union 108, 244
Spivak 89
Stoermer, Eugene F. 129
Stoic philosophy 14, 18, 20, 105
Strand, Torill 72–3
Structural Adjustment Programmes, SAPs 246–7, 250
Suarez, Francisco 18, 105–6
Sunstein, Cass 162

supranationalism 74, 109, 178, 189, 211, 217
Sustainable Development Goals, SDGs 115–6, 121–5; *see also* Global Goals
Syria 17, 30, 61, 111, 113

Tainter, Joseph 147–8
Taylor, Lisa 121, 125
terrorism 146, 167
Thucydides 104
Tikly, Leon 76, 79
Tilly, Charles 217
tragedy of the commons 144
transnational corporations, TNCs 3, 25–7, 33, 136, 139; *see also* corporations
transnational: communities 32, 46–7; education 115, 118; justice 39; identities in Middle East 209, 214, 216; movements 21–2 , 194
Tully, James 70, 74–5
Turner, Bryan 41, 193–4, 199
Tutu, Desmond 90

ubuntu 87–92, 94
UNESCO 57, 82, 223, 228
Unitarianism 17
United Kingdom 91, 184; *see also* Britain
United Nations 34, 61, 74, 82, 112, 223–4; human rights 107–8, 111, 236; intervention 104, 109–10, 234; Millennium Development Goals 118, 200, 203–4; surveys of confidence in 178 89; and world peace 14, 21; *see also* Earth Charter, Global Goals, Global Poverty Project
United Nations Development Programme, UNDP 28, 31, 57, 247
United States, America: and Africa 244; and China 223–5; and connectivity within and foreign aid for 63–4; and cosmopolitanism 21, 184–5, 217; foreign policy 156–62, 168–70, 112; environmental issues 143–52; and global citizenship education 78, 80; groups in 40, 56, 185, 187, 225; hegemony 224–5; and human rights 28, 112; Obama, Barack and pragmatism 162–8; political identity 133–4, 137; surveys of 179, 181, 183, 197, 213; technology and elections 60, 65; and trade 28; youth 60, 196
universalism 19–20, 40, 81
utilitarian perspective, strategy 148–9

Vattel, Emerich de 103–4
Vattimo, Gianni 250
Velvet Revolution 166
Vietnam 234, 241; war with US 150
Volkmer, Ingrid 228
Voltaire 20
von Wolff, Christian 7

West, Darrell M. 63–4
West, Western: colonialism/post-colonialism 72–4; corporations 125; cosmopolitanism, global citizenship 40, 43, 91, 209–11, 214, 239, 252; culture 222–3; democratic ideal 245–6; and education 38, 75–80, 87–89, 94, 249–50; individual rights 23; human rights 27–8, 108, 112, 238; imperialism 20–1, 23, 25, 112, 181, 214, 217–18; and Live Beneath the Line 119–20; relations with China 224–30; religious traditions 13; surveys of status and cosmopolitanism 181, 187
Westernization, Westernizing 2, 3, 216
Willinsky, John 42, 69, 71, 76
Wilson, Edward O. 131
Wood, Patricia K. 74
World Bank 26, 125, 246–7
world citizen 14, 16, 20–1, 58, 159; surveys of 31, 177–91, 193, 198, 212; *see also* global citizen
world federalism 33
world government 33, 103, 180, 211
World Health Organization 34
World Values Survey, WVS 31, 177–91, 196, 198–207, 209, 212; tables 182, 186–8, 202–5, 212–3
Wrigley, Terry 75

Xi Jinping 222

Yemen 168, 183
youth, young people: activism 92–3; as critical cosmopolitans 46; global citizenship education 70, 77, 87, 117; political socialization 193; surveys of 186, 196–207; and technology 62, 65; *see also* age
Yugoslavia 110
Yunker, James 211, 216

Zeno 18, 20
Zogby International 209, 212–14
Zogby, John 196
Zuckerman, Ethan 57, 59, 64–7

eBooks
from Taylor & Francis
Helping you to choose the right eBooks for your Library

Add to your library's digital collection today with Taylor & Francis eBooks. We have over 50,000 eBooks in the Humanities, Social Sciences, Behavioural Sciences, Built Environment and Law, from leading imprints, including Routledge, Focal Press and Psychology Press.

Choose from a range of subject packages or create your own!

Benefits for you
- Free MARC records
- COUNTER-compliant usage statistics
- Flexible purchase and pricing options
- 70% approx of our eBooks are now DRM-free.

Benefits for your user
- Off-site, anytime access via Athens or referring URL
- Print or copy pages or chapters
- Full content search
- Bookmark, highlight and annotate text
- Access to thousands of pages of quality research at the click of a button.

Free Trials Available

We offer free trials to qualifying academic, corporate and government customers.

eCollections
Choose from 20 different subject eCollections, including:

- Asian Studies
- Economics
- Health Studies
- Law
- Middle East Studies

eFocus
We have 16 cutting-edge interdisciplinary collections, including:

- Development Studies
- The Environment
- Islam
- Korea
- Urban Studies

For more information, pricing enquiries or to order a free trial, please contact your local sales team:
UK/Rest of World: **online.sales@tandf.co.uk**
USA/Canada/Latin America: **e-reference@taylorandfrancis.com**
East/Southeast Asia: **martin.jack@tandf.com.sg**
India: **journalsales@tandfindia.com**

www.tandfebooks.com